T0212124

Lecture Notes in Computer Science   12048

More information about this series at http://www.springer.com/series/7411

Anna Sperotto · Alberto Dainotti ·
Burkhard Stiller (Eds.)

Passive and Active Measurement

21st International Conference, PAM 2020
Eugene, Oregon, USA, March 30–31, 2020
Proceedings

 Springer

Editors
Anna Sperotto
University of Twente
Enschede, The Netherlands

Alberto Dainotti
University of California
San Diego, CA, USA

Burkhard Stiller
University of Zürich
Zürich, Switzerland

ISSN 0302-9743   ISSN 1611-3349   (electronic)
Lecture Notes in Computer Science
ISBN 978-3-030-44080-0   ISBN 978-3-030-44081-7   (eBook)
https://doi.org/10.1007/978-3-030-44081-7

LNCS Sublibrary: SL5 – Computer Communication Networks and Telecommunications

This Springer imprint is published by the registered company Springer Nature Switzerland AG
The registered company address is: Gewerbestrasse 11, 6330 Cham, Switzerland

Preface

It is our pleasure to present you with the proceedings of the 21st International Conference on Passive and Active Measurements (PAM 2020)! PAM 2020 took place during March 30–31, 2020, in Eugene, Oregon, USA, and was hosted by the University of Oregon.

This year's technical program was comprised of 19 papers, carefully selected among a pool of 65 submissions from more than 200 authors from 100 institutions and more than 20 countries. The technical program covered a variety of topics in networking, ranging from routing and alias resolution, to Web-related measurements, DNS, security, active measurements, and best practices. The work of selecting such a competitive program would have not been possible without the hard work of the 44 members of the Technical Program Committee (TCP). The TPC provided critical but constructive and substantiated reviews to the assigned papers. Each submission was assigned to at least four reviewers, with the exception of some submissions, where we felt additional reviewers were needed. All but 6 papers received the assigned reviews, while the remaining 6 were evaluated based on 3 reviews, but had a clear consensus. After the review phase, the TPC engaged in a lively online discussion phase, during which all submitted papers were discussed by the respective reviewers until a consensus was reached. Finally, all 19 accepted papers were assigned to shepherds that had the task of supporting the authors in addressing the review comments in the final version. In this preface, we want to extend a warm thank you to the TPC members for the dedication demonstrated to the PAM conference via the high-quality reviews, during the discussion phase, and in the shepherding process!

Due to the global outbreak of COVID-19 and in order to protect the health and safety of PAM participants as well as the local host community, the PAM 2020 conference has been organized as a virtual meeting with attendees only participating remotely.

We also want to thank the members of the Organization Committee as usually the focus of a conference remains on the technical content, however without the help and efforts of all the people involved in the organization, PAM 2020 would not have been possible. Special thanks therefore go to the general chairs, Ramakrishnan Durairajan and Reza Rejaie, who took care of the local arrangements, Pedro Casas who manned his well-oiled publicity machine, Burkhard Stiller who handled communications with LNCS, and finally Soheil Jamshidi who kept the website continously up to date. Last, we would like to thank PAM 2020 authors and participants, and we hope that these two days of novel research and interesting discussions were of use to your future work.

February 2020

Anna Sperotto
Alberto Dainotti

Organization

General Chairs

Ramakrishnan Durairajan   University of Oregon, USA
Reza Rejaie   University of Oregon, USA

Technical Program Committee Co-chairs

Anna Sperotto   University of Twente, The Netherlands
Alberto Dainotti   CAIDA, UC San Diego, USA

Publicity Chair

Pedro Casas   AIT, Austria

Publications Chair

Burkhard Stiller   University of Zürich, Switzerland

Local Chair

Soheil Jamshidi   University of Oregon, USA

Steering Committee

Anja Feldmann   MPI Informatik, Germany
Fabian E. Bustamante   Northwestern University, USA
Georg Carle   TU München, Germany
David Choffnes   Northeastern University, USA
Rocky Chang   The Hong Kong Polytechnic University, Hong Kong
Mohamed Ali (Dali) Kaafar   Data61, CSIRO, Australia
Xenofontas Dimitropoulos   University of Crete, FORTH, Greece
Georgios Smaragdakis   TU Berlin, Germany
Javier Bustos   University de Chile, Chile
Johanna Amann   University of California, Berkeley, USA
Marinho P. Barcellos   University of Waikato, New Zealand
Michalis Faloutsos   University of California, Riverside, USA
Jelena Mirkovic   University of Southern California, USA
Nevil Brownlee   The University of Auckland, New Zealand
Robert Beverly   Naval Postgraduate School, USA
Steve Uhlig   Queen Mary University of London, UK
Yong Liu   New York University, USA

Technical Program Committee

Aaron Schulman	UC San Diego, USA
Amogh Dhamdhere	Amazon, USA
Anja Feldmann	MPI Informatik, Germany
Balakrishnan Chandrasekaran	Max Planck Institute for Informatics, Germany
Brian Trammell	Google, Switzerland
Casey Deccio	Brigham Young University, USA
Cristian Hesselman	University of Twente, SIDNLabs, The Netherlands
Dario Rossi	Huwaei, France
Dave Levin	University of Maryland, USA
David Choffnes	Northeastern University, USA
Fabian E. Bustamante	Northwestern University, USA
Georgios Smaragdakis	MIT, USA, and TU Berlin, Germany
Giovane Moura	Delft University, SIDNLabs, The Netherlands
Idilio Drago	Politecnico di Torino, Italy
Ignacio Castro	Queen Mary University of London, UK
Italo Cunha	Federal University of Minas Gerais, Brazil
Jeroen van der Ham	University of Twente, National Cyber Security Center, The Netherlands
Johanna Amann	ICSI, USA
John Heideman	USC, ISI, USA
Kensuke Fukuda	National Institute of Informatics, Japan
Luca Vassio	Politecnico di Torino, Italy
Maciej Korczynski	Grenoble Institute of Technology, France
Marinho Barcellos	Federal University of Rio Grande do Sul, Brazil
Mark Allman	ICSI, USA
Matthew Luckie	University of Waikato, New Zealand
Mirja Kühlewind	Ericsson, Switzerland
Oliver Hohlfeld	Brandenburg University of Technology, Germany
Philipp Richter	MIT, USA
Ralph Holz	The University of Sydney, Australia
Ramakrishna Padmanabhan	CAIDA, UC San Diego, USA
Ramakrishnan Durairajan	University of Oregon, USA
Ramin Sadre	KU Louvain, Belgium
Renata Cruz Teixeira	Inria Paris, France
Ricardo de Oliveira Schmidt	University of Passo Fundo, Brazil
Ricky Mok	CAIDA, UC San Diego, USA
Robert Beverly	Naval Postgraduate School, USA
Romain Fontugne	Internet Initiative Japan, Japan
Roland van Rijswijk-Deij	University of Twente, NLNetLabs, The Netherlands
Stephen Strowes	RIPE NCC, The Netherlands
Steve Uhlig	Queen Mary University of London, UK
Taejoong Chung	RIT, USA
Thomas Karagiannakis	MSR, UK

Vaibhav Bajpai   TU München, Germany
Xenofontas Dimitropoulos   University of Crete, FORTH, Greece

Additional Reviewers

Detailed reviews for papers submitted to PAM 2020 were performed by the Technical Program Committee, as stated above, and additionally by the following reviewer: Hang Guo, University of Southern California, USA.

Contents

Domain Names

Topology and Routing

Topology: Alias Resolution

Web

Active Measurement

Discovering the IPv6 Network Periphery

Erik C. Rye$^{(\boxtimes)}$ ⓘ and Robert Beverly ⓘ

Naval Postgraduate School, Monterey, CA, USA
`rye@cmand.org, rbeverly@nps.edu`

Abstract. We consider the problem of discovering the IPv6 network periphery, i.e., the last hop router connecting endhosts in the IPv6 Internet. Finding the IPv6 periphery using active probing is challenging due to the IPv6 address space size, wide variety of provider addressing and subnetting schemes, and incomplete topology traces. As such, existing topology mapping systems can miss the large footprint of the IPv6 periphery, disadvantaging applications ranging from IPv6 census studies to geolocation and network resilience. We introduce "edgy," an approach to explicitly discover the IPv6 network periphery, and use it to find >64M IPv6 periphery router addresses and >87M links to these last hops – several orders of magnitude more than in currently available IPv6 topologies. Further, only 0.2% of edgy's discovered addresses are known to existing IPv6 hitlists.

Keywords: IPv6 · Topology · Discovery · Reconnaissance · Security

1 Introduction

Among the unique properties inherent to IPv6's large address space size are ephemeral and dynamic addressing, allocation sparsity and diversity, and a lack of address translation. These well-known properties complicate efforts to map the infrastructure topology of the IPv6 Internet. While previous research has tackled problems of target selection, speed, and response rate-limiting in active IPv6 topology probing [7], the IPv6 *periphery* – last hop routed infrastructure connecting end hosts – is challenging to discover, and difficult to discern.

Discovery of the IPv6 periphery is important not only to the completeness of network topology mapping, but provides a crucial supporting basis for many applications. For instance, IPv6 adoption [12,27,34], census [26], and reliability and outage studies [21] all depend in part on a complete and accurate map of the IPv6 topology inclusive of the periphery, while understanding provider address allocation policies and utilization also requires completeness [15,29]. Similarly, work on IPv4 to IPv6 network congruence [13,20] and IPv6 geolocation [5] can utilize IPv6 topologies. Further, our work illuminates potential security and privacy vulnerabilities inherent in the way today's IPv6 periphery is deployed [11,31].

We present "edgy," a new technique to explicitly discover the IPv6 periphery. In contrast to IPv6 scanning [17,23], passive collection [26], or hitlists [14,16],

A. Sperotto et al. (Eds.): PAM 2020, LNCS 12048, pp. 3–18, 2020.
https://doi.org/10.1007/978-3-030-44081-7_1

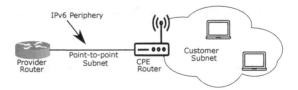

Fig. 1. Common IPv6 architecture: an IPv6 subnet is assigned to the link between the provider and last hop CPE routers. There is no NAT or private addressing; a separate distinct routed IPv6 subnet is assigned to devices attached to the last hop CPE.

which, by construction, target endhosts, edgy is specifically designed to find last hop routers and subnetworks in the IPv6 Internet. Our contributions include:

1. Edgy, an algorithm to discover, identify, and enumerate the IPv6 periphery.
2. Active measurement using edgy to find 64.8M last hop router addresses and 87.1M edges to these last hops from a single vantage.
3. Discovery of periphery addresses that are 99.8% disjoint from current IPv6 hitlists [16] and orders of magnitude larger than existing IPv6 topology snapshots [8], suggesting that edgy is complementary to these prior approaches.
4. Discovery of 16M EUI-64 last hop addresses, suggesting a potential vulnerability to security and privacy.

2   Background and Related Work

In this work, we define the "periphery" not to be servers or clients, but rather the last hop router connecting network endhosts. Whereas significant prior work has developed techniques for IPv6 endhost discovery [16,17,23], comparatively little work has explored the IPv6 periphery.

The large address space in IPv6 removes the need for address translation; thus, while many IPv4 hosts are connected via NATs [32], the IPv6 periphery typically extends into customer premises. Indeed, in IPv6, the Customer Premises Equipment (CPE) is a router, implying that in conjunction with the rapid increase in IPv6 adoption [12,34], the IPv6 periphery is considerably larger than in IPv4, especially for residential networks.

Figure 1 shows an example of the IPv6 periphery we attempt to discover. Here, the point-to-point subnet between the provider and the CPE is assigned a public IPv6 prefix; the subnet on the other side of the CPE (e.g., in the customer's home) is also a publicly-routed prefix. While this example shows a common residential IPv6 architecture, similar designs exist in the enterprise.

Consider an IPv6 traceroute to a random address within a provider's globally advertised BGP prefix, such as is routinely performed by existing production topology mapping systems [18]. The traceroute (Fig. 2): (i) is unlikely to hit the prefix allocated to a customer CPE or her network; (ii) is even less likely to reach a host within the customer's network; and (iii) does not illuminate the scope, characteristics, or breadth of subnets within the prefix. When a traceroute does

```
traceroute to 2a03:4980:2b6:9624:8643:b70f:adae:4f40
      . . .
 5   2001:7f8:1::a502:4904:1   16.862 ms
 6   2a03:4980::6:0:2   25.948 ms
 7   2a03:4980::b:0:5   39.560 ms
 8   *
 9   *
```

Fig. 2. Randomly chosen trace targets are unlikely to discover subnets within a prefix, or to elicit a response. It is thus ambiguous whether hop 7 is a periphery address in this example, even though the trace reaches into the destination's /32.

not reach its target destination it is ambiguous: does the last responsive hop belong to the core of the network, or the periphery?

Passive techniques suffer similar problems in revealing the network periphery. For instance, BGP, by design aggregates routes such that the aggregate visible in a looking glass does not reveal the subnets within. And, while there has been significant prior work in characterizing the IPv6 address space, these primarily focus on endhosts. For example, Plonka and Berger examine and analyze the addresses and behaviors of IPv6 clients connecting to a large CDN [26]. However, this passive collection of client requests alone does not reveal the network periphery on the path to those clients.

3   Methodology

Our work seeks to perform active probing in a way that elicits responses from the last hop IPv6 periphery, rather than network core infrastructure, servers or other endhosts. Enumerating last hop router addresses, e.g., CPE, and inferring networks beyond the last hops are the principal goals of edgy.

Edgy is divided into an initialization stage, followed by active probing that proceeds in rounds. Results from one round of probing are used to guide probing in subsequent rounds. This section describes edgy; the complete algorithm is given in Appendix A.

3.1   Edgy

Because of the massive size of the IPv6 address space, edgy relies on an input set of "seed traces" to focus and guide its discovery. Thus, the ability of edgy to discover the network periphery depends strongly on the input seed traces it uses. In Sect. 3.2 we describe two specific realistic seed traces we utilize: (i) BGP-informed; and (ii) hitlist-informed.

Algorithm 1 describes edgy's initialization stage. Edgy iterates through the input seed and examines the last responsive hop in each trace, regardless of whether a sequence of same last IP responses or loops occur. It maintains the set of targets that, when used as the traceroute destination, had a given last hop. Edgy then finds *unique* last hops – those that were only discovered by probing destinations that reside within a single /48 prefix. The intuition is to find candidate /48 prefixes that are likely to be subnetted, and hence contain periphery routers. By contrast, if there are two or more probes to targets in different /48s that elicit the same last hop, those /48s are less likely to be subnetted, or traces to targets in these /48s are unresponsive beyond the middle of the network. In either case, edgy terminates exploration of these target /48s rather than continuing to probe them.

These candidate target /48 prefixes are fed to Algorithm 2 which probes targets within the input prefixes at progressively finer granularities until a stopping condition (a discovery threshold η) is reached. A random Interface IDentifier (IID) (the 64 least significant bits in an IPv6 address) for each target subnet is used as the trace destination. Figure 3 depicts an illustration of edgy's first round behavior targeting an example /48 belonging to Cox Communications.

The first subnet discovery round probes different /56 prefixes and serves as a coarse filter to determine which candidate /48s exhibit an appreciable amount of subnetting and merit further probing. /56s are used initially as [28] recommends this as a potential subnet size for residential customers; therefore, if a /48 is allocated entirely to residential customers with /56s, the initial probing round should discover all of the /56 allocations. We note, however, that these prefix delegation boundaries are not mandatory, that it is impossible to know *a priori* what prefix delegation strategy a provider has chosen, and that networks can be subdivided in a non-uniform manner for allocations to customers. If the number of distinct last hops found during a probing round exceeds the threshold η, we further subdivide responsive prefixes for additional probing in the next round. The choice and sensitivity of η are discussed in [30].

It has been shown that aliased networks are common in the IPv6 Internet, where every address within a prefix is responsive despite no actual host being present. We remove last hops equal to the probe target, as well as networks and addresses present in the publicly curated list of aliases from Gasser et al. [16]. In addition, we remove replies from non-routable prefixes – we observe site- and link-local addresses that fall into this category – as well as IPv4-in-IPv6 addresses and replies that appear to be spoofed.

After removing aliases and bogus replies, target /48s that generate $>\eta$ unique last hop addresses proceed to the second round of probing. In the second round, edgy sends probes to addresses within each /60 of the target /48. Figure 4 depicts an illustration of edgy's second round behavior, again for the same Cox Communications /48. Target /48 networks that generate $>\eta$ unique last hop addresses (exclusive of aliases) move to the next round. The third probing round sends probes to a random IPv6 address in each /62 of the target networks. Finally, target /48s that exhibit subnetting beyond the /60 level (as evidenced by four unique last hops for each /62 within any /60), are probed at /64 granularity.

Note that, during testing, we initially explored other periphery discovery mechanisms. For instance, intuitively, a binary-tree discovery process that bisects prefixes and probes each half would programmatically explore subnets. Unfortu-

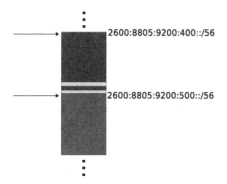

Fig. 3. A portion of a target /48 (2600:8805:9200::/48) is shown; colors correspond to the true delegated customer subnet sizes that edgy discovers. Green represents /64, yellow /60, and red /56. In the first probing round, edgy sends probes to each /56 in a target /48 (represented by arrows). (Color figure online)

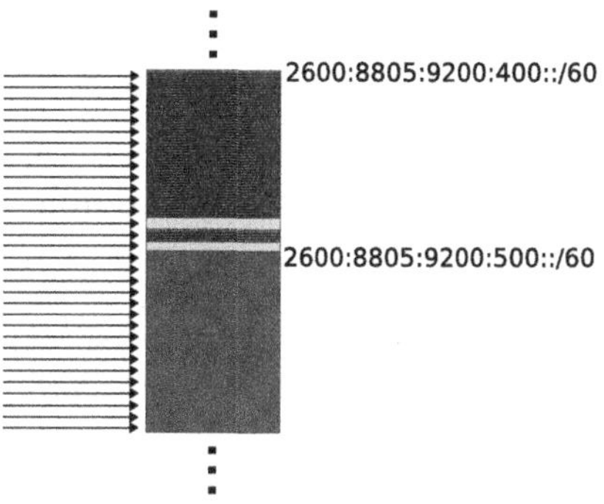

Fig. 4. In the second round, probes are sent to each /60 in the target /48. New addresses are discovered in the upper half of this portion of the target address space where subnet allocation is finer-grained, but not in the lower half. Many operators mix allocation sizes within the same /48.

nately, such an efficient approach performs poorly as providers do not allocate subnets uniformly. In this case, a core router can falsely appear as the common last hop for destinations in a common prefix, even when significant subnetting is present. Additionally, the third round of probing was added to limit time spent probing target networks at the /64 granularity to those proven to subnet within the final nybble of the network prefix.

3.2 Edgy Input

Edgy takes as input a seed set of traces. These seed traces are created from running traceroutes to corresponding seed targets. We consider two realistic potential seed target lists: BGP-informed and hitlist-informed. The BGP-informed targets assume no prior knowledge other than global BGP advertisements. Since BGP routes are readily available from looking glasses, this scenario is easily replicated by anyone and models what CAIDA uses to inform their probing. In our experiments, we utilize publicly available BGP-informed seed traces collected as part of an August 2018 effort to uniformly probe every /48 in the IPv6 Internet [9,29]. Herein, we term this trace seed data as the *BGP-informed* seed.

Second, we consider a target set informed by prior knowledge in the form of passive traces, server logs, or hitlists. In our experiments, we utilize a publicly available IPv6 hitlist [16] that was used to generate a seed set of hitlist-informed traces [7]. Herein, we term this trace seed the *hitlist-informed seed*.

3.3   Limitations

There are several potential complications that edgy may encounter, and corresponding limitations of our approach and evaluation. First, during probing, we depend on receiving a response from the penultimate traceroute hop along the data path to a destination. However, the last responsive hop may instead be a different router due to filtering, loss, or rate-limiting, i.e., if the last hop remains anonymous. This case does not cause false inferences of periphery addresses, but instead causes edgy to terminate probing of a prefix prematurely.

Second, we do not have ground-truth in order to determine whether the periphery we discover is indeed the last hop before a destination endhost. While various, and at times conflicting, guidance exists regarding the size of delegated prefixes [10,19,25] discovery of unique /64s is strongly indicative of discovering the periphery. Additionally, the periphery addresses we find are frequently formed using EUI-64 addresses where we can infer the device type based on the encoded MAC address (see Sect. 4.5). These MAC addresses specifically point to CPE. Further, we examine several metrics of "edginess" to better understand the results in Sect. 4.3. In particular, we determine whether traces enter their target network and, if so, quantify how far inside the target network they reach. We also analyze the last hop addresses edgy discovers in order to understand how many also appear as intermediate hops to different targets. As intermediate hops, such addresses are unlikely to exist in the IPv6 periphery.

3.4   Probing

Probing consists of sending hop-limited ICMPv6 packets; we used the high-speed randomized yarrp topology prober [6] due to the large number of traces required during edgy's exploration, as well as to minimize the potential for ICMPv6 rate limiting (which is mandated and common in IPv6 [7]).

We use ICMPv6 probes as these packets are designed for diagnostics and therefore are less intrusive than UDP probes. Further, we send at a conservative rate while yarrp, by design, randomizes its probing in order to minimize network impact. Last, we follow best established practices for performing active topology probing: we coordinated with the network administrators of the vantage point prior to our experiments and hosted an informative web page on the vantage point itself describing the experiment and providing opt-out instructions. We received no opt-out requests during this work.

4   Results

From Sept. to Oct. 2019 we ran edgy from a well-connected server in Lausanne, Switzerland. Edgy used yarrp at less than 10 kpps with the neighborhood TTL setting to reduce load on routers within five hops of the vantage point.

Table 1. BGP and hitlist-informed routable address discovery by round

Round	BGP-informed				Hitlist-informed			
	Prefixes probed	Unique last hops	Unique last hop /48s	Cum. unique last hops	Prefixes probed	Unique last hops	Unique last hop /48s	Cum. unique last hops
1 (/56)	130,447	4,619,692	33,831	4,619,692	111,670	9,217,137	89,268	9,217,137
2 (/60)	34,520	12,228,916	26,082	13,410,601	67,107	11,021,329	74,302	11,365,910
3 (/62)	12,014	14,770,061	11,675	24,832,391	4,462	5,428,992	19,942	15,569,221
4 (/64)	2,641	15,326,298	7,833	37,169,357	1,531	15,340,591	32,718	29,248,703

4.1 BGP-Informed Seed Results

Initializing edgy with the BGP-informed seed data yielded 130,447 candidate /48 prefixes. Following Algorithm 2, edgy traced to a random IID in each of the 256 constituent /56 subnets in each /48s (a total of 33,394,432 distinct traces).

This first round of probing 33.4M targets discovered 4.6M unique, non-aliased last hop IPv6 addresses residing in 33,831 distinct /48 prefixes (Table 1). Often, the last hop address is not contained within the target /48 prefix but in a different /48 prefix belonging to the same Autonomous System (AS). Further, probing different target /48 prefixes in round one resulted in last hops within the same /48 (but different than the target /48). This phenomenon of a many-to-one relationship between the target prefix and the last hop prefix persists across rounds as the probing granularity increases.

The density of discovered last hop addresses across target prefixes is non-uniform: nearly 75% of the targeted /48 prefixes produce 16 or fewer distinct last hops. The prefixes in which the last hops reside is also highly non-uniform. Of the 33,831 /48s in which last hop addresses reside, 11,064 were responsible for only a single last hop address. This is likely indicative of a /48 allocation to an end site. On the other end of the spectrum, a single /48 (2001:1970:4000::/48) contained over 200,000 unique last hop addresses. 2001:1970:4000::/48 was the last hop prefix in traces to 1,008 distinct /48 target prefixes, the most extreme example of many target /48s mapping to a single last hop prefix.

Because a /48 prefix entirely subnetted into /52s should exhibit 16 distinct last hops, we choose $\eta = 16$ empirically as a baseline indication of more granular subnetting. The choice and sensitivity of η are discussed in detail in [30].

34,520 of the input 130,447 /48 target prefixes passed the η threshold in round one. Each of these /48 prefixes were then probed at a /60 granularity (4,096 probes to each /48). Edgy discovers significantly more unique non-aliased last hop addresses in this round, ~12.2M, as the probing is focused on known address-producing target subnetworks identified in the first round.

To select target /48s for round three, we use $\eta = 256$ as an indicator of subnetting at a granularity finer than /56. 12,014 /48s meet this criteria, and were used as targets for probing at the /62 granularity (~196.8M traces).

Round three, while probing <10% of the input target seed prefixes, is focused on those with fine-grained subnetting and helps to expose subnetting strategies.

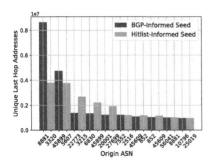

Fig. 5. Top 10 last hop ASN

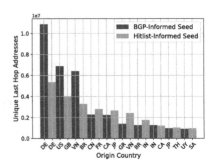

Fig. 6. Top 10 last hop country

As the IETF now discourages, but does not forbid, /64 or more-specific subnetting [25], we are interested in the prevalence of fine-grained subnetting, but must balance inferring this delegation behavior with probing load. Because subnetting generally occurs on nybble boundaries [25], by probing /62s, we are able to detect when target prefixes are subnetted beyond /60s, which is an indication that perhaps the operator is allocating /64 subnets. The /62 probing round produced ~14.7M unique last hop addresses.

The final round is designed to enumerate last hop addresses for /64 subnets. Edgy selects any prefix with $\eta = 4$ prefix-unique last hops within a /60 (because we probe each /62, each /60 contains four targets). We surmise that four prefix-unique last hops is an indication that either the operator subnets at the /62 level, or is assigning /64 networks to their customers. The final /64 probing round discovered 15.3M distinct IPv6 addresses through exhaustive probing of 2,641 /48 target prefixes that met the η threshold to be in round four.

Cumulatively, edgy discovers more than 37M distinct IPv6 last hop addresses using the BGP-informed seed. Table 1 quantifies discovery across probing rounds. 3,989 ASes are represented in the last hop addresses, corresponding to 143 countries, as reported by Team Cymru's IP to ASN service [33]. Figures 5 and 6 summarize the ASes and countries that produced the largest number of periphery last hop addresses.

4.2   Hitlist-Informed Seed Results

We replicate the experiment described in Sect. 4.1 seeded with the hitlist-informed seed traces (from [7]). Table 1 shows the per-round results for both the BGP-informed and hitlist-informed seeds. Algorithm 1 on this input seed yielded 111,670 target /48 prefixes, about 20k fewer than the BGP-informed seed. However, the initial /56 probing round discovered nearly twice as many unique last hop addresses. The hitlist-informed seed led to almost double the number of target prefixes in the /60 round as compared to the BGP-informed seed, but discovered nearly 1M fewer last hops. As a result, only 4,462 /48 target prefixes were probed in the /62 probing round, discovering 5.4M last hops from 19,942 /48 prefixes. 1,531 target /48s were exhaustively probed at the /64 granularity in the fourth round, about 1% of the input hitlist seed prefixes. The /64 probing round discovered over 15M unique last hops, indicating that the 1,500 target /48s each contributed about 10,000 unique addresses on average. We attribute the differences between the BGP-informed and hitlist-informed seed data results to differences in how the original source data was collected. For example, the BGP-informed seed data was derived from a uniform sweep of the advertised IPv6 space, while the hitlist-informed seed data derived from a measurement campaign aimed at networks known to be dense in customers.

In total, periphery on the hitlist-informed seed discovers over 29M unique last hop router addresses. Nearly half of those addresses are found in the /64 probing round, during which edgy exhaustively probes all of the /64s in 1,531 /48 target prefixes. This suggests that a small number of prefixes have fine-grained subnetting, and that substantial periphery topology can be gained by probing a carefully selected set of target prefixes. Figures 5 and 6 display the top ten ASes and countries from which we obtain last hops; for the hitlist-informed seed, 141 countries and 3,578 ASNs contribute to the total.

4.3   Edginess Metrics

To better understand the extent to which edgy discovers IPv6 periphery infrastructure, we introduce three metrics of "edginess." The first coarse metric is simply the fraction of traces with a last hop within the same AS as the probe destination. Clearly, this condition does not imply that the last hop is truly an interface of the periphery router. However, it provides a rudimentary measure of whether traces are reaching the target network's AS. In contrast, a trace to a non-existent network will be dropped at an earlier hop in a default-free network.

We compare edgy's results against a day's worth of CAIDA's IPv6 Ark traceroute results from 105 different vantage points on Oct 1, 2019 [8]. Across nearly 17M traceroutes performed on that day, 1.7M (10%) produced a response from the target destination. However, of those 1.7M traceroutes that reached the destination, 86.2% were from probing the ::1 address, while 13.3% came from destinations known to be aliased, i.e., a fake reply. Unsurprisingly, fewer than 0.5% of the probes to random targets reached the destination.

40.2% of the CAIDA traces elicit a response from a last hop address that belongs to a BGP prefix originated by the same AS as the destination. In contrast, 87.1% of edgy's traces reach the target AS. While these results cannot be directly compared – edgy performs two orders of magnitude more traces than CAIDA; see Sect. 4.7 – it does demonstrate that the probing performed by edgy is in fact largely reaching the target network, if not the periphery.

Our second edginess metric is a more granular measure of how deep into the target network, and hence how close to the periphery, traces traverse. For each trace, we find the number of most significant bits (MSBs) that match between the target and the last hop response, i.e., the netmask of the most specific IPv6 prefix that encompasses the target and last hop. As before, this metric does not provide a definitive measure of reaching the periphery. Indeed, we empirically observe many networks that use very different IPv6 prefixes for the last hop

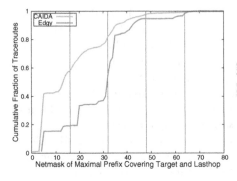

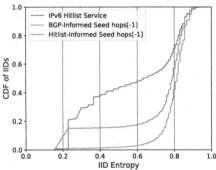

Fig. 7. Size of prefix encompassing both target and last hop IPv6 addresses

Fig. 8. IID entropies by data source

point-to-point subnetwork as compared to the customer's prefix. However, the basis of this metric is that hierarchical routing implies more matching MSBs the closer the trace gets to the target.

Figure 7 shows the distribution of matching bits across the traceroutes from both CAIDA and edgy. Whereas the median size of the matching prefix is a /13 for CAIDA, it is nearly a /32 for edgy. The target and last hop share the same /48 for more than 5% of the edgy traces, but just 2% of the CAIDA traces. Thus, again, we see edgy's probing reaching more of the network periphery.

Finally, we quantify how many of our last hop addresses appear *only* as periphery addresses in our traces, and therefore do not appear as an intermediate hop in traceroutes to other target addresses. In the BGP-informed seed's first round, 0.9% of discovered last hop addresses to a target appear as an intermediate hop to another target. In the second round, the same is true of 21% of last hops, 23% in the third round, and 4% in the fourth probing round. However, closer examination indicates that these numbers, particularly in the second and third round, are skewed by providers that frequently cycle periphery prefixes. For example, in the second round, 1.6M of the 2.5M addresses seen both as a last and an intermediate hop are located in ASN8881, which we observe cycling customer prefixes on a daily basis [30]. This often causes traces to appear to "bounce" between two (or more) different addresses toward the end of a trace. Sorting by the time the response was received shows that a single IPv6 address was responsible for high hop count responses until after a distinct point at which a second address becomes responsive. This erroneously causes the address that was not responsible for the highest hop count response to appear as if it were an intermediate hop for the target.

We also observe a second class of IPv6 address that appears both as a last hop and an intermediate hop to other targets. These addresses appear as the last hop for a large number of target networks that are most likely unallocated by the provider; these addresses typically have low entropy IID (e.g., ::1 or ::2) and are likely provider infrastructure. These last hop addresses also appear on the path to addresses that appear to be CPE, based on the high entropy or EUI-64 last hop returned when they are an intermediate hop.

4.4 Consolidated Results and Seed Data Comparison

Although both probing campaigns began with approximately the same number of target /48 prefixes in the first probing round (130,447 and 111,670 in the BGP and hitlist-informed seeds, respectively), only 9,684 /48s are common between the two data sets. The number of target prefixes in common decreases at each round, reaching 177 in /64 probing round. Only ~1.6M (2.5%) last hop IPv6 addresses are present in both data sets. These results demonstrate edgy's sensitivity to seed input, and suggest that additional seed sources may aid discovery.

Of the top ten ASNs, only four are common between the two data sets – ASNs 852, 8881, 45899, and 45609. Of the top ten countries, however, six are common: Germany, Vietnam, Canada, Brazil, India, and Japan, with Germany ranking first in both. While the US is the second-leading producer of last hop addresses in the BGP-informed seed data with ~6.9M unique last hops, it is fourteenth in the hitlist-informed data with only 357,877 addresses. Finally, we consider the last hop provider type using CAIDA's AS type classification [3]. By this classification, edgy's results come overwhelmingly from transit/access networks (99.9%) rather than content or enterprise ASes. This matches our intent for edgy to focus on IPv6 periphery discovery.

4.5 EUI-64 Addresses

Previous studies, e.g., [7,16] identified the presence of many EUI-64 addresses in IPv6 traceroutes, where the host identifier in the IPv6 address is a deterministic function of the interface's Media Access Control (MAC) address. Our study similarly found a significant fraction of EUI-64 addresses, despite the introduction of privacy extensions for Stateless Address Autoconfiguration (SLAAC) addresses in 2007 [24]. We discover slightly more than 16M EUI-64 last hop addresses, identifiable from the `ff:fe` at byte positions 4 and 5 in an IID, using the BGP-informed seed data, or approximately 42% of the total last hops. However, only 5.4M (34%) of the MAC addresses in these 16M last hops are unique.

The discrepancy between unique EUI-64last hop addresses and MAC addresses appears to have two root causes. The first is delegated prefix rotation. Although 3.5M of the 5.4M unique MAC addresses observed appear in only one last hop address, 1.9M appear multiple times. Of these, the vast majority appear in only several addresses in the same /48, suggesting that the provider periodically rotates the remaining 16 bits of the network address portion [1,30,31]. We observe some providers rotating the prefix delegated to their customers on a daily basis, and further examination of forced prefix cycling is a topic of future work. The second cause behind the disparity between number of MAC addresses and EUI-64 last hop addresses is due to what we believe is MAC address reuse.

For instance, the MAC address 58:02:03:04:05:06 occurs in more than 266k BGP-informed seed last hop addresses in 76 /48s allocated to providers throughout Asia and Africa. Because our probing took place over a period of several weeks, we believe it is unlikely that a combination of provider prefix rotation and mobility substantially contributed to these; its simple incremental pattern in bytes 2 through 6 further suggest it is likely a hard-coded MAC address assigned to every model of a certain device. Support forums indicate that some models of Huawei LTE router [2,4] use 58:02:03:04:05 as an arbitrary MAC address for their LTE WAN interface.

4.6 Comparison to the IPv6 Hitlist Service

We compare our results to an open-source, frequently updated hitlist [16]. In mid-October 2019, the hitlist provides approximately 3.2M addresses responsive to ICMPv6, and TCP and UDP probes on ports 80 and 443.

Both the structure and magnitude of the addresses we discover differentiate our work from [16], which is unsurprising given our focus on finding addresses at the network periphery. Unlike our results, the addresses in the hitlist are less likely to be EUI-64 addresses. Only ∼441,000 EUI-64 addresses (with ∼338,000 unique MAC addresses) appear in the hitlist, representing approximately 14% of the total responsive addresses. Figure 8 plots the normalized Shannon entropies of the IIDs of addresses in our datasets compared with addresses in the IPv6 hitlist service. We see that the IPv6 hitlist contains a far greater proportion of low-entropy IIDs addresses than the last hop addresses edgy discovers. As periphery devices, particularly CPE in residential ISPs, are unlikely to be statically assigned a small constant IID and instead generate a high-entropy address via SLAAC, this reinforces edgy's discovery of a different portion of the IPv6 Internet than prior work. Further emphasizing the complementary nature of edgy's probing, only 0.2% of the addresses we discover appear in this hitlist, indicating that edgy discovers different topology. Finally, while the last hops edgy discovers overwhelmingly (99.9%) reside in access networks (Sect. 4.4), CAIDA's AS-type classifier categorizes 1.8M of the hitlist's IPv6 addresses as residing in access/transit networks, 1.2M in content networks, and 48k in enterprise networks.

4.7 Comparison with CAIDA IPv6 Topology Mapping

We again examine a day's worth of CAIDA's IPv6 Ark traceroute results from 105 different vantage points on Oct 1, 2019 [8], to understand edgy's complementary value. Because edgy sends nearly two orders of magnitude more probes (544M vs 8.5M), these are not directly comparable; however, we note that edgy discovers 64.8M non-aliased, routable last hop addresses that CAIDA does not. CAIDA finds 163,952 unique, non-aliased, routable last hop addresses. However, despite focusing on only target networks that are dense in last hops, edgy still discovers ∼25% of the last hop addresses that CAIDA does. Edgy similarly finds 87.1M links to the last hop address that CAIDA does not, but discovers 54,024 of the 365,822 edges that contain only routable addresses from CAIDA's probing. Edgy's discovery of ~37M unique periphery last hops from ~544M targets probed in the BGP-informed seed yields 0.068 unique last hops per target, while the Ark traceroutes discover 0.019 unique last hops per target.

4.8 Comparison with Seed Data Source

Edgy, by design, extends topology discovery methodologies and is complementary to existing topology mapping campaigns. However, because we believe edgy provides increased address discovery over existing mapping systems, we compare the results obtained with edgy to the trace seeds used as input to edgy.

The BGP-informed seed source consists of traces conducted in August, 2018 to every /48 in the routed IPv6 Internet conducted from CAIDA's Archipelago [9]. These traces to ~711M unique targets produce ~5.8M unique last edges and ~5.4M unique last hops after removing non-routable addresses. By contrast, edgy discovers ~59.5M unique final edges and ~37.1M unique IPv6 last hops by probing to ~545M targets when seeded with the BGP-informed data. Thus, edgy significantly expands the discovered topology of an input seed.

Likewise, edgy discovers significantly more last hop addresses and edges than the hitlist-informed seed. The hitlist-informed seed discovers 434,560 unique last hops and 656,849 unique final edges, while edgy, informed by this data, discovers ~29.2M unique last hops and ~32.0M final edges.

5 Conclusions and Future Work

We introduce edgy, an algorithm to discover previously unknown portions of the IPv6 Internet, namely, the IPv6 periphery. Edgy extends and augments existing IPv6 discovery mapping systems, and the last hop periphery addresses that it discovers are nearly entirely disjoint from previous topology mapping campaigns. Because of privacy concerns involved with EUI-64 addresses and the ephemeral nature of many addresses, we are not releasing the periphery addresses edgy discovers at this time; however, we expect our results to be reproducible.

Several topics are planned for future work. First, we observe service providers that cycle their customers' periphery prefix periodically. This rotation leads to high levels of address discovery for these providers, but, based on examining IID reuse, over counts the number of actual device interfaces present. We plan to: (i) discover which networks implement high-frequency prefix rotation; (ii) quantify the rates at which new prefixes are issued; and (iii) determine whether the prefix issuing mechanism is deterministic and predictable. Second, we discover large numbers of EUI-64 IPv6 addresses more than a decade after the introduction of SLAAC privacy extensions [24]. Because edgy discovers periphery devices like CPE, quantifying device types present in networks may be possible by cross-referencing the models providers issue to customers, and through correlation with protocols that leak model information [22]. Third, we wish to obtain more ground truth information on the IPv6 periphery as well as explicit validation of our results and algorithm. Fourth, we plan to improve edgy's efficiency by training it with historical data and leveraging multiple vantage points. For instance, periphery networks that exhibit frequent customer prefix cycling may need to be probed on a regular basis, while those with stable last hops may be re-probed infrequently. Finally, because of the ephemeral nature of some of the addresses we discover, we intend to couple other measurements tightly with address discovery. For example, to further elucidate these addresses' value, we will send ICMPv6 Echo Requests and capture service banners immediately after receiving probe responses.

Acknowledgments. We thank Jeremy Martin, Thomas Krenc, and Ricky Mok for early feedback, John Heidemann for shepherding, Mike Monahan and Will van Gulik for measurement infrastructure, and the anonymous reviewers for insightful critique. This work supported in part by NSF grant CNS-1855614. Views and conclusions are those of the authors and should not be interpreted as representing the official policies or position of the U.S. government or the NSF.

Appendix A: Algorithm Details

Algorithm 1. Discover_Init($seed\_traces$)

$density = []$
$targets = []$
for $(hops, dst) \in seed\_traces$ **do**
    $dst48 \leftarrow dst \mathrel{\&} (2^{48} - 1 \gg 80)$
    $LH \leftarrow hops[-1]$
    $density[LH] \leftarrow density[LH] \cup dst48$
for $LH \in density$ **do**
    if $|LH| = 1$ **then**
        $targets \leftarrow density[LH]$
for $prefix \in targets$ **do**
    Discover($prefix$)

Algorithm 2. Discover($prefix$)

$masks = \{56, 60, 62, 64\}$
$LH \leftarrow \{\}$
$t \leftarrow rand(0, 2^{64})$
for $n \in masks$ **do**
    for $i \leftarrow \{0 \ldots 2^{n-48} - 1\}$ **do**
        $hops \leftarrow$ yarrp($prefix + (i \ll (128 - n)) + t$)
        $LH \leftarrow hops[-1]$
    if $|LH| \leq \eta$ or $n = 64$ **then**
        $break$

References

1. Zwangstrennung (forced IP address change) (2018). https://de.wikipedia.org/wiki/Zwangstrennung
2. Huawei LTE CPE B315 (MTS 8212FT) - discussion (2019). http://4pda.ru/forum/index.php?showtopic=700481&st=3580
3. The CAIDA UCSD AS Classification Dataset (2019). http://www.caida.org/data/as-classification
4. Speedport II LTE router status (2020). https://telekomhilft.telekom.de/riokc95758/attachments/riokc95758/552/327892/1/routerstatus.pdf
5. Berger, A., Weaver, N., Beverly, R., Campbell, L.: Internet nameserver IPv4 and IPv6 address relationships. In: Proceedings of ACM Internet Measurement Conference (IMC) (2013)
6. Beverly, R.: Yarrp'ing the Internet: randomized high-speed active topology discovery. In: Proceedings of ACM Internet Measurement Conference (IMC), November 2016
7. Beverly, R., Durairajan, R., Plonka, D., Rohrer, J.P.: In the IP of the beholder: strategies for active IPv6 topology discovery. In: Proceedings of ACM Internet Measurement Conference (IMC), November 2018
8. CAIDA: The CAIDA UCSD IPv6 Topology Dataset (2018). http://www.caida.org/data/active/ipv6_allpref_topology_dataset.xml
9. CAIDA: The CAIDA UCSD IPv6 Routed /48 Topology Dataset (2019). https://www.caida.org/data/active/ipv6_routed_48_topology_dataset.xml
10. Chittimaneni, K., Chown, T., Howard, L., Kuarsingh, V., Pouffary, Y., Vyncke, E.: Enterprise IPv6 Deployment Guidelines. RFC 7381 (Informational), October 2014. https://www.rfc-editor.org/rfc/rfc7381.txt
11. Czyz, J., Luckie, M., Allman, M., Bailey, M.: Don't forget to lock the back door! A characterization of IPv6 network security policy. In: Network and Distributed Systems Security (NDSS) (2016)
12. Czyz, J., Allman, M., Zhang, J., Iekel-Johnson, S., Osterweil, E., Bailey, M.: Measuring IPv6 adoption. SIGCOMM Comput. Commun. Rev. **44**(4), 1–32 (2014)
13. Dhamdhere, A., Luckie, M., Huffaker, B., Claffy, K., Elmokashfi, A., Aben, E.: Measuring the deployment of IPv6: topology, routing and performance. In: Proceedings of ACM Internet Measurement Conference (IMC) (2012)
14. Fan, X., Heidemann, J.: Selecting representative IP addresses for internet topology studies. In: Proceedings of ACM Internet Measurement Conference (IMC) (2010)
15. Foremski, P., Plonka, D., Berger, A.: Entropy/IP: uncovering structure in IPv6 addresses. In: Proceedings of ACM Internet Measurement Conference (IMC) (2016)
16. Gasser, O., et al.: Clusters in the expanse: understanding and unbiasing IPv6 hitlists. In: Proceedings of ACM Internet Measurement Conference (IMC) (2018)
17. Gont, F., Chown, T.: Network reconnaissance in IPv6 networks. RFC 7707 (Informational), March 2016. http://www.ietf.org/rfc/rfc7707.txt
18. Hyun, Y., Claffy, K.: Archipelago measurement infrastructure (2018). http://www.caida.org/projects/ark/
19. IAB, IESG: Recommendations on IPv6 Address Allocations to Sites. RFC 3177 (Informational), September 2001. http://www.ietf.org/rfc/rfc3177.txt
20. Livadariu, I., Ferlin, S., Alay, Ö., Dreibholz, T., Dhamdhere, A., Elmokashfi, A.: Leveraging the IPv4/IPv6 identity duality by using multi-path transport. In: 2015 IEEE Conference on Computer Communications Workshops (2015)

21. Luckie, M., Beverly, R.: The impact of router outages on the AS-level Internet. In: Proceedings of ACM SIGCOMM (2017)
22. Martin, J., Rye, E.C., Beverly, R.: Decomposition of MAC address structure for granular device inference. In: Proceedings of the Annual Computer Security Applications Conference (ACSAC), December 2016
23. Murdock, A., Li, F., Bramsen, P., Durumeric, Z., Paxson, V.: Target generation for Internet-wide IPv6 scanning. In: Proceedings of ACM Internet Measurement Conference (IMC) (2017)
24. Narten, T., Draves, R., Krishnan, S.: Privacy extensions for stateless address autoconfiguration in IPv6. RFC 4941, September 2007. http://www.ietf.org/rfc/rfc4941.txt
25. Narten, T., Huston, G., Roberts, L.: IPv6 address assignment to end sites. RFC 6177 (Best Current Practice), March 2011. http://www.ietf.org/rfc/rfc6177.txt
26. Plonka, D., Berger, A.: Temporal and spatial classification of active IPv6 addresses. In: Proceedings of ACM Internet Measurement Conference (IMC) (2015)
27. Pujol, E., Richter, P., Feldmann, A.: Understanding the share of IPv6 traffic in a dual-stack ISP. In: Passive and Active Measurement (PAM) (2017)
28. RIPE: Best current operational practice for operators: IPv6 prefix assignment for end-users - persistent vs non-persistent, and what size to choose (2017). https://www.ripe.net/publications/docs/ripe-690
29. Rohrer, J.P., LaFever, B., Beverly, R.: Empirical study of router IPv6 interface address distributions. IEEE Internet Comput. **20**, 36–45 (2016)
30. Rye, E.C., Beverly, R.: Discovering the IPv6 network periphery (2020). https://arxiv.org/abs/2001.08684
31. Rye, E.C., Martin, J., Beverly, R.: EUI-64 considered harmful (2019). https://arxiv.org/pdf/1902.08968.pdf
32. Srisuresh, P., Holdrege, M.: IP Network Address Translator (NAT) terminology and considerations. RFC 2663 (Informational), August 1999. http://www.ietf.org/rfc/rfc2663.txt
33. Team Cymru: IP to ASN mapping (2019). https://www.team-cymru.org/IP-ASN-mapping.html
34. Zander, S., Wang, X.: Are we there yet? IPv6 in Australia and China. ACM Trans. Internet Technol. **18**(3), 1–20 (2018)

Improving Coverage of Internet Outage Detection in Sparse Blocks

Guillermo Baltra[1,2]([✉]) and John Heidemann[1,2]

[1] University of Southern California, Los Angeles, CA 90089, USA
[2] Information Sciences Institute, Marina del Rey, CA 90292, USA
{baltra,johnh}@isi.edu

Abstract. There is a growing interest in carefully observing the reliability of the Internet's edge. Outage information can inform our understanding of Internet reliability and planning, and it can help guide operations. Active outage detection methods provide results for more than
3M blocks, and passive methods more than 2M, but both are challenged
by *sparse blocks* where few addresses respond or send traffic. We propose
a new *Full Block Scanning* (FBS) algorithm to improve coverage for
active scanning by providing reliable results for sparse blocks by gathering more information before making a decision. FBS identifies sparse
blocks and takes additional time before making decisions about their
outages, thereby addressing previous concerns about false outages while
preserving strict limits on probe rates. We show that FBS can improve
coverage by correcting 1.2M blocks that would otherwise be too sparse to
correctly report, and potentially adding 1.7M additional blocks. FBS can
be applied retroactively to existing datasets to improve prior coverage
and accuracy.

1 Introduction

Internet reliability is of concern to all Internet users, and improving reliability is
the goal of industry and governments. Yet government intervention, operational
misconfiguration, natural disasters, and even regular weather all cause network
outages that affect many. The challenge of measuring outages has prompted a
number of approaches, including active measurements of weather-related behavior [15], passive observation of government interference [4], active measurement of
most of the IPv4 Internet [12], passive observation from distributed probes [16],
analysis of CDN traffic [14], and statistical modeling of background radiation [6].

Broad coverage is an important goal of outage detection systems. Since outages are rare, it is important to look everywhere. Active detection systems report
coverage for more than 3M /24 blocks [12], and passive systems using CDN
data report coverage for more than 2M blocks [14]. More specialized systems
focus coverage on areas with bad weather (ThunderPing [15]), or provide broad,
country-level or regional coverage, but perhaps without /24-level granularity
inside the regions (CAIDA darknet outage analysis [4] and Chocolatine [6]).
Although each of the systems provide broad coverage, each recognizes there are

© Springer Nature Switzerland AG 2020
A. Sperotto et al. (Eds.): PAM 2020, LNCS 12048, pp. 19–36, 2020.
https://doi.org/10.1007/978-3-030-44081-7_2

Table 1. Coverage comparison in /24 blocks of different measuring approaches.

	Approach	Coverage
UCSD-NT	Darknet	3.2M observed [3]
Akamai	Passive/CDN	5.1M observed/2.3M trackable [14]
ThunderPing	Active/addrs	10.8M US IP addresses [11]
Disco	TCP disconnections	10.5k [16]
Trinocular	Active/blocks	5.9M responsive/3.4M trackable [12]

portions of the Internet that it cannot measure because the signal it measures is not strong enough. Systems typically detect and ignore areas where they have insufficient signal (in Trinocular, blocks with fewer than 15 addresses; in ThunderPing, events with fewer than 100 addresses in its region; the Akamai/MIT system, blocks fewer than 40 active addresses; in Chocolatine, blocks with fewer than 20 active IPs). Setting thresholds too high reduces coverage, yet setting them too low risks false outages from misinterpreting a weak signal.

The first contribution of our paper is two new algorithms: *Full Block Scanning* (FBS), to improve coverage in outage detection with active probing, while retaining accuracy and limits on probing rates (Sect. 3.1), and *Lone-Address-Block Recovery* (LABR), to increase coverage by providing partial results blocks with very few active addresses (Sect. 3.2). Our insight is to recognize that *sparse blocks* signal outages more weakly than other blocks, and so they require more information to make a decision. We chose to delay decisions until all block addresses (the full block) have been observed, thus gathering more information while maintaining limits on the probing rate. (An alternative we decline is to probe more aggressively.) We evaluate FBS as an extension to Trinocular Sect. 4.2, but the concept may apply to other outage detection systems.

Our second contribution is to show that FBS can *increase coverage* in two ways (Sect. 4.5). First, it correctly handles 1.2M blocks that would otherwise be too sparse to correctly report. Second, it allows addition of 1.7M sparse blocks that were previously excluded as unmeasurable. Together, coverage for 2017q4 can be 5.7M blocks. Moreover, FBS *improves accuracy* by reducing the number of false outage events seen in sparse blocks (Sect. 4.1). We confirm that it addresses most previously reported false outage events (Sect. 4.3).

The cost of FBS is reduced temporal precision, since it takes more time to gather more information (assuming we hold the probe rate fixed). We show that this cost is limited (Sect. 4.4): FBS is required for about one-fifth of blocks (only sparse blocks, about 22% of all blocks). Timing for non-sparse majority of blocks is unaffected, and 74% of recovered uptime for sparse blocks is within 22 min. About 40% of accepted outages in sparse blocks are reported within 33 min, and nearly all within 3.3 h. (Reanalysis of old data shows the same results for non-sparse and recovered uptime, but requires twice the time for accepted outages.) Finally, we examine false uptime by testing against a series of known outages that affected Iraq in February 2017.

All of the datasets used in this paper that we created are available at no cost [17]. Our work was IRB reviewed and identified as non-human subjects research (USC IRB IIR00001648).

2 Challenges to Broad Coverage

Our goal is to detect Internet outages with broad coverage. Table 1 shows coverage of several methods that have been published, showing that active probing methods like Trinocular provide results for about 3.4M /24 blocks [12] and CDN-based passive methods provide good but somewhat less coverage (2.3M blocks for the Akamai/MIT system [14]). Passive methods with network telescopes provide very broad coverage (3.2M blocks [3]), but less spatial precision (for example, for entire countries, but not individual blocks in that country). Combinations of methods will provide better coverage: Trinocular and the Akamai/MIT system have a 1.6M blocks overlap, and unique contributions, each providing 1.9M unique 0.7M, from [14]. However, Akamai/MIT data is not publicly available.

Here we examine how to *improve coverage of active probing systems like Trinocular.* Trinocular gets results for 3.4M blocks, and another 2.5M blocks have some response but are not considered "trackable" since they have too few reliably responding addresses.

Our goal in this paper is to expand coverage by making these previously untrackable blocks trackable. We face two problems: sparse blocks and lone addresses, each described below. In the next section we describe two new algorithms to make these blocks trackable: *Full Block Scanning (FBS)*, which retains spatial precision and limited probing rates, but loses some temporal precision; and Lone Address Block Recovery (LABR), an approach that allows confirmation that lone-address blocks are up, although it cannot definitively identify when they are down.

Other active probing systems that follow the Trinocular algorithms (such as the active part of IODA [1]) might benefit from solutions to these problems. We seek algorithms that can reevaluate existing years of Trinocular data, so we follow Trinocular's use of IPv4 /24-prefix blocks and 11-min rounds.

2.1 Problem: Sparse Blocks

Sparse blocks limit coverage: active scanning requires responses, so we decline to measure blocks with long-term sparsity, and we see a large number of *false outages* in blocks that are not sparse long-term, but often are temporarily sparse.

Sparse blocks challenge accuracy because of a tension between the amount of probing and likelihood of getting a response. To constrain traffic to each block, and to track millions of blocks, Trinocular limits each block to 15 probes per round. Limited probing can cause false outages in two ways: First, it may fail to reach a definitive belief and mark the block as *unknown*. Alternatively, if the block is usually responsive, a few non-responses may produce a down belief.

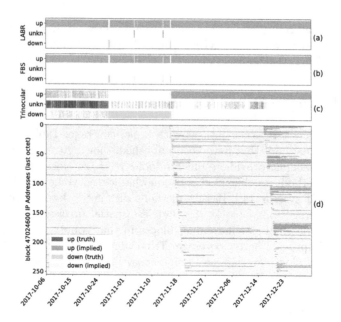

Fig. 1. A sample block over time (columns). The bottom (d) shows individual address as rows, with colored dots when the address responds to Trinocular. Bar (c) shows Trinocular status (up, unknown, and down), bar (b) is Full Block Scanning, and the top bar (a), Lone Address Block Recovery. (Color figure online)

As an example, Fig. 1 shows four different levels of sparsity, (each starting 2017-10-06, 2017-10-27, 2017-11-14 and 2017-12-16) as (d) individual address responses to Trinocular probes, and (c) Trinocular state inferences. As the block gets denser, Trinocular improves its inference correctness.

Furthermore, every address in this block has responded in the past. But for the first three periods, only a few *are actually* used, making the block *temporarily sparse*. For precision, we use definitions from [12]: $E(b)$ are the addresses in block b that have *ever* responded, and $A(E(b))$ is the long-term probability that these addresses will respond. We also consider a short-term estimate, $\hat{A}(E(b))$. Thus problematic blocks have low $A(E(b))$ or $\hat{A}(E(b))$. We provide further block examples in Appendix A.

Prior systems sought to filter out these sparse blocks, both before and after measurement. Trinocular marks very sparse blocks as *untrackable* (when $A(E(b)) < 0.10$ or $|E(b)| < 15$). It also marked blocks as untrackable when observed A doesn't match predicted A [12], and later used an adaptive estimate for A [13]. Trinocular notes that its unmeasurability test is not strict enough: indeterminate belief can occur when the $A(E(b)) < 0.3$ and $|E(b)| \geq 15$. Accordingly, Richter's use of Trinocular data dropped all blocks with 5 or more outages in 3 months [14], based on our recommendation.

We consider blocks sparse when it is less than a threshold ($\hat{A}_s(E(b)) < T_{sparse}$), where $\hat{A}_s(E(b)$ is a short-term estimate of the *current* availability of the block, and T_{sparse} is a threshold, currently 0.2. Blocks have frequent outages (like Fig. 1) when they are sparse. We find that 80% of blocks with 10 or more down events are sparse, and yet sparse blocks represent only 22% of all blocks (see CDFs in Appendix B).

2.2 Problem: Lone Addresses

The second challenge to coverage are blocks where only one or two addresses are active—we call this problem *lone address blocks*. When a single address is active, then lack of a response may be a network outage, but it may also be a reboot of a single specific computer or other causes—the implication of non-response from a single address is ambiguous. Trinocular has avoided blocks with few addresses as untrackable (when $|E(b)| < 15$). ThunderPing [15] tracks individual addresses, but recognizing the risk of decisions on single addresses, they typically probe multiple targets per weather event [11].

An example block with a lone-address is in Fig. 1. Of the four phases of use, the second phase, starting 2017-10-27, and for 18 days, only the .85 address replies. Our goal is to handle this block correctly in both of its active states, with many addresses and with a lone address.

3 Improving Outage Detection

3.1 Full Block Scanning for Sparse Blocks

The challenge of evaluating sparse blocks is that Trinocular makes decisions on too little information, forcing a decision after 15 probes, each *Trinocular Round* (*TR*, 11 min), even without reaching a definitive belief. We address this problem with *more* information: we consider a *Full Round* (*FR*), combining multiple TRs until all active addresses (all of $E(b)$) have been scanned. This *Full Block Scanning* algorithm makes decisions only on complete information, while retaining the promise of limiting scanning rate.

Formally, a Full Round ends at time t when the minimum N TRs before t that cover all $E(b)$ ever-active addresses of the block: $\sum_{i=t-N}^{t}(|TR_i|) \geq |E(b)|$.

Trinocular probes all addresses in $E(b)$ in a pseudo-random sequence that is fixed once per quarter, so we can guarantee each address is probed when we count enough addresses across sequential TRs. (Versions of Trinocular prior to 2020q1 reverse direction at end of sequence, reanalysis of data before this time must sense $2|E(b)|$ addresses to guarantee observing each. We call this retrospective version the 2FR version of FBS, and will use 1FR FBS for new data. They differ in temporal precision, see Sect. 4.4.)

Full Block Scanning (FBS) layers over Trinocular outage detection, re-evaluating outages it reports and reverting some decisions. If the block is currently sparse ($\hat{A}_s < T_{sparse}$) and the most recent Full Round included a positive response, then we override the outage. That is, if there are any positive responses in the last Full Round FR_t, we convert any outages to up if $\forall TR_i$ where $i \in [t - N, t]$.

The cost of FBS is that combining multiple TRs loses temporal precision, so we use FBS only when it is required: for blocks that are currently sparse. A block is currently sparse if the short-term running average of the response rate for the block $\hat{A}_s^{3FR}$, computed over the last three FRs, is below the sparse threshold ($\hat{A}_s^{3FR} < T_{sparse}$). (We choose three FRs to smooth $\hat{A}$ from multiple estimates.)

The reduction in temporal precision depends on how many addresses are scanned in each TR and the size of FR (that is, $E(b)$). When FBS verifies an outage, we know the block was up at the last positive response, and we know it is down after the full round of non-responses, so an outage could have begun any time in between. We therefore select a start time as the time of the last confirmed down event (the first known lit address, now down). That time has uncertainty of the difference between the earliest possible start time and the confirmed start time. Theoretically, if all 256 addresses in a block are in use and 15 addresses are scanned each TR, a FR lasts 187 min. In practice, timing is often better; we show empirical results in Sect. 4.4.

3.2 Lone-Address-Block Recovery

The FBS algorithm repairs any block with at least one responsive address in the last FR, allowing us to extend coverage to many sparse blocks. However, when a block has only a single active address, a non-reply may indicate an outage of the network *or* a problem with that single host.

To avoid false down events resulting from non-outage problems with a lone address, we define *Lone-Address-Block Recovery* (LABR). We accept up events, but because outages are rare (much rarer than packet loss), we convert down events to "unknown" for blocks with very few recently active addresses. We define "few" as one or two active addresses, and recently as the last three Full Rounds, so we use LABR when $|\hat{E}^{3FR}| < 3$. We require at least three addresses to avoid making decisions on one or two addresses where packet loss could change results.

This algorithm gives an asymmetric outcome: we can confirm blocks are up, but not that they are down. We believe that outcome is preferable to the alternatives: completely ignoring the block, or tolerating false outages. However, we identify LABR blocks to allow researchers wanting an estimator that can be both up and down to omit them.

4   Evaluation

4.1   Full Block Scanning Reduces Noise

Case Study of One Block. Figure 1 shows one block in CenturyLink (AS209, a U.S. ISP) with outage analysis as a case study.

This block has initially only 8 addresses responding. On 2017-10-27, there is a usage change that causes a down event with no address response for ~13 h. This event is matched in other blocks for the same AS. Then, we see a lone address

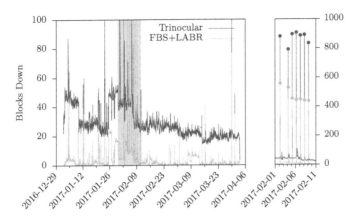

Fig. 2. Iraqi Government mandated outages Feb 2–9, 2017. Whole quarter (left), and exam week (right). Dataset A27. FBS processed using 2FR. (Color figure online)

responding for 18 days. On 2017-11-14, the block starts receiving new users, and once again starting 2017-12-17. On 2017-11-16, it shows a partial outage that is observed only from our Los Angeles site, not from other Trinocular sites.

Trinocular results ((b), third bar) show frequent unknown states that result in false down events, particularly when block usage is sparse in October and early November.

By contrast, Full Block Scanning ((b), the second graph), resolves this uncertainty. FBS' more information confirms the block is usually up, while recognizing the usage change and the partial outage. However, in between, there are two down events inferred by a lone address which are changed to unknown by LABR ((a), the top graph).

False Outages: Does FBS Remove Noise? From this single block example, we next consider a country's Internet. Our goal is to see if FBS reduces noise by examining false down events (blocks correctly recovered by FBS because they were observation noise).

We study series of known outages that affected Iraq in February 2017. That country had seven government-mandated Internet outages (the local mornings on February 2, and also the 4th through 9th) with the goal of preventing cheating during academic placement exams [5]. This is a particularly challenging scenario to FBS, as closely spaced short outages test the algorithm's accuracy and precision. Furthermore, the fraction of sparse blocks is high in this country. We identified 1176 Iraqi blocks using Maxmind's city-level database [9]; 666 of these are sparse.

Figure 2 shows Iraqi outages in 2017q1, grouped in 660 s timebins. We show outages without Full Block Scanning (the purple, top line) and with it (the green line). The Iraqi exam week is highlighted in gray on the left, and we plot that week with a larger scale on the right.

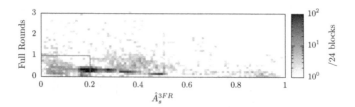

Fig. 3. Outage events during the 7 Iraqi outages, measured of their $\hat{A}_s^{3FR}$ and full round values. Single site W. Dataset: A27 (2017q1) subsetted to the 7 outage periods.

Table 2. Confusion matrix of 5200 Trinocular detected down events in 50 random blocks. Dataset A30, 2017q4.

FBS	True condition (manually observed)	
	UP (Trinocular false down events)	DOWN (Trinocular true down events)
UP	4133 (79%, FBS fixes)	0
DOWN	621 (12%, FBS misses)	446 (9%, FBS confirms)

In each of the seven large peaks during exam week, most Iraqi blocks (nearly 900, or 76%) are out—our true outages. Outside the peaks, a few blocks (the 20 to 40 purple line, without FBS) are often down, likely false outages.

FBS suppresses most of the background outages (85% of outage area), from a median of 26 to a median of 1; these differences can be seen comparing the higher purple line to the lower green line. We confirm this reduction was due to noise by examining blocks that FBS recovers in 10 randomly-selected time periods with 34 down events. Nearly all down events (33 events, 97% of purple) were in sparse blocks that resemble Fig. 1; the other block was diurnal. This study confirms that FBS recovers false outages due to sparseness.

True Outages: Does FBS Remove Legitimate Outages? We next look at how Full Block Scanning interacts with known outage events. Its goal is to remove noise and false outages, but if FBS is too aggressive it may accidentally remove legitimate outages (a "true down event") (Fig. 3).

We treat the seven nationwide outages corresponding with Iraqi exams as true down events and compare this ground truth, with and without FBS.

The seven peaks in Fig. 2 (right) show known Iraqi outages, with purple dots at "peak outage" without FBS, and lower, green dots with FBS. FBS removes somewhat less than half of the down events, with peaks around 440 to 560 instead of 790 to 910 blocks.

To understand this reduction we looked at the duration of the Iraqi events. FBS affects only the 35% of events in the red box in the lower left corner. (Examination of just sparse blocks confirms that they are the source of attenuation.)

It is important to note that these are *worst case* for FBS—many blocks are sparse, and the events are just shorter than one full round. If the event was

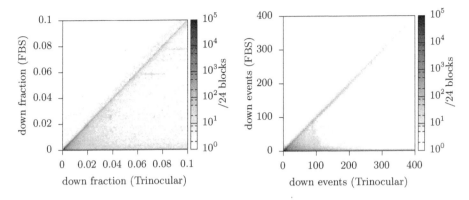

Fig. 4. Comparison of per-block down time (left) and number of down events (right) between 2FR-FBS and Trinocular during 2017q4 as seen from six sites. Dataset A30.

longer or more blocks were not sparse, there would be no attenuation. A lower FBS threshold ($\hat{A}^{3FR}$) of 0.15 trims only 15% of events. However, we choose to leave FBS threshold at 0.2 to avoid overfitting our parameters to Iraq.

Random Sampling of Outage Events. Finally, we confirm our results with a random sample of events. We select 50 random blocks that show some outage from the Trinocular 2017q4 dataset, then a best-estimate ground truth through manual examination. Table 2 shows the confusion matrix after applying FBS. Of the total 5200 down events detected by Trinocular, FBS fixes 4133 (79% are false outages), misses 621 down events (12% are not fixed, but should have been), and confirms 446 true down events (9% are not changed). The FBS Error Rate is 0.12 (621 false outages of 5200 events), so it is fairly successful at removing noise. Many of the false outages are due to moderately sparse blocks ($0.2 < A(E(b)) < 0.4$) where FBS does not trigger.

4.2   How Often Does FBS and LABR Change Outages?

We next evaluate how FBS and LABR change the overall down event duration and the number of down events. We expect FBS to repair false down events, so it should show less downtime and fewer down events.

We evaluate merged results from six Trinocular sites as measured during 2017q4 (dataset A30) and compute fraction of time and number of occurrences across the whole quarter each block was observed down. We repeat the procedure with data processed with FBS.

We compare outages for 2017q4 (dataset A30), processing and merging results from six sites with and without FBS. We found similar results when we repeated this study on a different quarter (2017q2, dataset A28).

FBS and Down Time: Figure 4 (left) compares the fraction of total down time (0.0130) with FBS (0.0027). First, the vast majority of blocks (91%) have both

Table 3. Trinocular-detected disruptions in CDN logs. Dataset A28, 2017q2.

	Trinocular		Filtered trinocular		FBS	
# disruptions	380k		132k		119k	
Confirmed	103k	27%	98k	74%	92k	77%
Reduced activity	49k	13%	~13k	10%	16k	14%
No change	228k	60%	~21k	16%	11k	9%

values less than 0.02—they have little or no down time. (see Appendix C). Many of the remaining blocks are on the diagonal, with prior and new values within 0.005. We also see most of the changed blocks (9% of all blocks) appear below the diagonal, showing that FBS usually decreases downtime.

Surprisingly, 0.5% of blocks show *more* downtime after FBS. We examined a sample of these blocks and found that some sparse blocks did not transition from up-to-down in one round when 15 negative results did not fully change belief. FBS gathers more information and retrospectively marks the block down earlier. We believe this result better reflects truth.

FBS and Down Events: We can also evaluate how FBS affects the number of down *events* in addition to down *time* in Fig. 4 (right). FBS reduces the number of down events by 6% of blocks, often considerably (see the large number of blocks near the x-axis). In these cases FBS is repairing false outages. Again, we see a small number of blocks (0.1%) where FBS shows more down events than without. Examination of these cases shows that FBS sometimes breaks longer down events into several shorter ones, interspersed with an up event. We believe these results better reflect the true state of the block.

LABR: In 2017q4, LABR affects only a few blocks (250k, 6% of trackable), where it resets 4M down events to unknown. LABR affects only a few blocks, but it allows them to be reported up much of the time, increasing coverage.

4.3   Comparing FBS Active and Passive Outages

Prior CDN-based results showed the large number of false outages that come from a few blocks [14]. To match their system, they compare the subset of 1.6M blocks from 2017q2 that are trackable in both Trinocular and their system and that are at least 1 h or longer in Trinocular. We next review that result and show that FBS solves the problem they identified.

Table 3 shows this comparison of CDN events to Trinocular with both filtering (discarding blocks with more than 5 events, a short-term fix proposed for their paper at the time) and FBS. To recap prior results: The CDN-based results summarized in confirm that 27% of outage events found by Trinocular without FBS also appear in the CDN-based passive analysis. The remaining outages are either false outages in Trinocular (likely, since 60% show *no* change in the

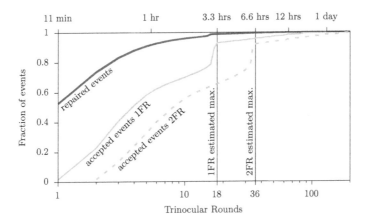

Fig. 5. FBS temporal precision analysis measured in repaired down events (false outages) and accepted events minimum (true outages) duration considering 1FR and 2FRs during 2017q4 as seen from Los Angeles. Dataset A30. (Color figure online)

CDN) or false uptimes from the CDN. Given sparse blocks produce many events, discarding blocks with 5 or more events (the "filtered Trinocular" column) should avoid most false outages, although it may cause false uptime. As expected, most events (74%) that remain after this filter are confirmed by the CDN.

While CDN-data is proprietary and is not available, we thank Philipp Richter for redoing this comparison with a similar subset of our data updated, but now with FBS. The FBS column of Table 3 shows analysis of Trinocular with FBS compared to the same CDN results, now filtered only by the CDN requirements (1 h events, and reported in the CDN system). FBS brings an even larger fraction of disruptions in-line with the CDN, with 77% of events being confirmed. Moreover, FBS is much more sensitive than the 5-event filter, applying only to the 22% of blocks that are sparse blocks. FBS therefore preserves Trinocular's 11-min timing for the majority of blocks, reducing temporal precision only where necessary while providing generally good accuracy for outage detection across all blocks.

This result suggests that FBS addresses the majority of false outages, and confirms that most false outages are due to a small set of sparse blocks. (Addressing false outages due to ISP renumbering is ongoing work [2].)

Finally, we note that FBS provides much larger coverage: 5.7M blocks compared to 2.3M trackable blocks in the CDN-system. We discuss coverage in detail in Sect. 4.5.

4.4 FBS Effects on Temporal Precision

We first examine how FBS affects temporal precision of outages. In sparse blocks, FBS will repair down events that are shorter than a Full Round. But the exact

Table 4. IPv4 address space coverage of Trinocular and FBS. (a), (b) and (c) different methods for filtering sparse blocks. (d) blocks fixed by FBS.

	Threshold	Blocks (in M)			%Tri
		Reject	Accept	%resp	
IPv4 responsive	$|E(b)| \geq 1$	8.6	5.9	100	
Trinocular trackable	$|E(b)| \geq 15 \wedge A \geq 0.1$	1.9	4.0	67	100
(a) mostly up blocks	up time > 0.8	0.2	3.8	64	95
(b) infrequently down blocks	# down events < 5	0.3	3.7	63	93
(c) non-sparse blocks	$A \geq 0.2$	0.9	3.1	53	78
(d) FBS considered	$\hat{A}^{3FR} < 0.2$	2.8	1.2	–	30
overlap with (c)		0.6	0.8	–	–
FBS trackable	$|E(b)| \geq 3$	0.2	5.7	96	142

duration of a FR depends how many addresses are considered in the block ($E(b)$) and how active they are ($\hat{A}(E(b))$).

To analyze FBS changes to temporal precision, we consider *repaired events*, false down events corrected by FBS, and *accepted events*, true down events that pass through FBS unchanged. LABR does not affect temporal precision.

We study FBS effects by examining the 2017q4 outage dataset (A30) from one site (Los Angeles). Most blocks (2.8M blocks, 70%) are never affected by FBS because they are not sparse or do not have an outage. For the remaining 1.2M blocks that are at some point sparse ($\hat{A}^{3FR} < 0.2$) and for which Trinocular reports an outage, we examine each outage event.

We first examine the 308M events that FBS repairs (the top left, red line in Fig. 5, 1.2M blocks). We see that for about half the cases (53% of the events), FBS repairs a single-round of outage in 11 min. Almost all the remaining events are recovered in 15 or fewer rounds, as expected. Only a tiny fraction (0.5%) require longer than 18 rounds, for the few times when Trinocular is slow to detect large changes in $\hat{A}$ because it thinks the block may be down.

The light green solid line in the middle Fig. 5 shows how long full rounds last for outages that pass FBS. Of 5.1M events, we see that 60% are approved in less than one hour (five or fewer TRs). About 8% of events take longer than our expected maximum of 18 TRs. We examined these cases and determined these are cases where Trinocular has such confidence the block should be up it does not probe all 15 tries. We confirm this result examining 50 random blocks within the tail.

Use of FBS on old Trinocular data requires the 2FR variant of FBS, with more TRs per FR (see Sect. 3.1). Dashed lines in Fig. 5 show 2FR analysis. We see almost no change in temporal precision of repaired events (nearly all the range of the solid and dashed red lines overlap). Accepted outages take roughly twice as long as with 1FR FBS, and the number drops to roughly one half (3.1M accepted down events); fortunately only 0.13% of all 4M blocks require 2FR and have actual outages in 2017q4.

We currently use FBS in batch processing, and we plan to implement it in our near-realtime (NRT) outage pipeline soon. For NRT processing one can either delay results while FBS is considered, or report preliminary results and then change them if FBS corrects.

4.5   Increasing Coverage

Sparse blocks limit coverage. If historical information suggests they are sparse, they may be discarded from probing as untrackable. Blocks that become sparse during measurement can create false outages and are discarded during post-processing. We next show how FBS and LABR allow us to increase coverage by correctly handling sparse blocks.

Correctly Tracking Sparse Blocks. We first look at how the accuracy improvements with our algorithms increase coverage. Three thresholds have been used to identify (and discard) sparse blocks: a low response probability ($A < 0.2$, quarter average, from [12]), low up time (up time < 0.8, from [13]), and high number of down events (5 or more down events, from [14]).

We use these three thresholds over one quarter of Trinocular data (2017q4-A30W), reporting on coverage with each filter in Table 4. With 5.9M responsible blocks, but only 4M of those (67%) are considered trackable by Trinocular. Filtering removes another 0.2M to 0.9M blocks, leaving an average of 53 to 64%.

Trinocular with FBS gets larger coverage than other methods of filtering or detection. FBS repairs 1.2M blocks, most sparse: of 0.9M sparse blocks, we find that FBS fixes 0.8M. The remaining 100k correspond to either good blocks that went dark due to usage change and therefore pushing the quarterly average of A down, or sparse blocks with few active addresses (for example, $|E(b)| < 100$) where Trinocular can make a better job inferring the correct state.

Can FBS+LABR Expand Baseline Coverage? Finally, we examine the number of blocks discarded as untrackable from historical data, and are not tracked for outages. For instance, Trinocular looks at the last 16 surveys [7], and filter all blocks with $|E(b)| < 15$ and $A < 0.1$, left with its baseline of 4M blocks.

In a similar approach, we use the 2017-04-27 survey as our upper bound of the responsive Internet [8]. As Table 4 shows, we find 5.9M responsive blocks, of which 5.7M had at least three active addresses during the measured period. That is 1.7M (43%) more blocks than the baseline become trackable. When adding 1.7M with the number of FBS-repaired blocks (1.2M), our effective coverage increment adds to 2.9M blocks.

5   Related Work

Several groups have methods to detect outages at the Internet's edge: ThunderPing first used active measurements to track weather-related outages on the

Internet [11,15]. Dainotti et al. use passive observations at network telescope to detect disasters and government censorship [4], providing the first view into firewalled networks. Chocolatine provides the first published algorithm using passive network telescope data [6], with a 5 min detection delay, but it requires AS or country level granularity, much more data than /24s. Trinocular uses active probes to study about 4M, /24-block level outages [12] every 11 min, the largest active coverage. Disco observes connectivity from devices at home [16], providing strong ground truth, but limited coverage. Richter et al. detect outages that last at least one hour with CDN-traffic, confirming with software at the edge [14]. They define disruptions, showing renumbering and frequent disagreements in a few blocks are false down events in prior work. Finally, recent work has looked at dynamic addressing, one source of sparsity [10]. Our work builds on prior active probing systems and the Trinocular data and algorithms, and addresses problems identified by Richter, ultimately due to sparsity and dynamics.

6   Conclusions

This paper defines two algorithms: Full Block Scanning (FBS), to address false outages seen in active measurements of sparse blocks, and Lone Address Block Recovery (LABR), to handle blocks with one or two responsive addresses. We show that these algorithms increase coverage, from a nominal 67% (and as low as 53% after filtering) of responsive blocks before to 5.7M blocks, 96% of responsive blocks. We showed these algorithms work well using multiple datasets and natural experiments; they can improve existing and future outage datasets.

Acknowledgments. We thank Yuri Pradkin for his input on the algorithms and paper.

We thank Philipp Richter and Arthur Berger for discussions about their work, and Philipp for re-running his comparison with CDN data.

The work is supported in part by the National Science Foundation, CISE Directorate, award CNS-1806785; by the Department of Homeland Security (DHS) Science and Technology Directorate, Cyber Security Division (DHS S&T/CSD) via contract number 70RSAT18CB0000014; and by Air Force Research Laboratory under agreement number FA8750-18-2-0280. The U.S. Government is authorized to reproduce and distribute reprints for Governmental purposes notwithstanding any copyright notation thereon.

A   Other Block Examples

Section 2.1 described the problem of sparse blocks and why FBS is needed. Here we provide examples of other blocks where sparsity changes to illustrate when FBS is required.

The block in the left part of Fig. 6 has no activity for three weeks, then sparse use for a week, then moderate use, and back to sparse use for the last two weeks. Reverse DNS suggests this block uses DHCP, and gradual changes in use suggest the ISP is migrating users. The block was provably reachable after

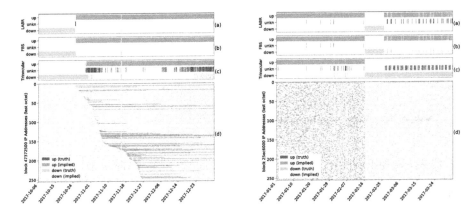

Fig. 6. Sample blocks over time (columns). The bottom (d) shows individual address as rows, with colored dots when the address responds to Trinocular. Bar (c) shows Trinocular status (up, unknown, and down), bar (b) is Full Block Scanning, and the top bar (a), Lone Address Block Recovery. (Color figure online)

the first three weeks. Before then it may have been reachable but unused, a false outage because the block is inactive.

The third bar from the top (c) of the left of Fig. 6 we show that Trinocular often marks the block unknown (in red) for the week starting 2017-10-30, and again for weeks after 2017-12-12. Every address in this block has responded in the past. But for these two periods, only a few *are actually* used, making the block *temporarily sparse*. Figure 6 (left, bar b) shows how FBS is able to accurately fix Trinocular's pitfalls in such a DHCP scenario.

Figure 6 (right) shows a block example with a lone address. This block has three phases of use: before 2017-02-16, many addresses are in use; then for about 9 days, *nothing* replies; then, starting on 2017-02-25 only the .1 address replies. During the last phase, Trinocular (Fig. 6 (right, bar c)) completely ignores that there is one address responding, while FBS (Fig. 6 (right, bar b)) sets block status depending on responses of this lone-address. However, LABR (Fig. 6 (right, bar a)) changes all the FBS detected down events to unknown, as there is not information to claim a down event, in contrast to what the end of phase one shows.

B   Block Usage Change

As mentioned in Sect. 2.1, when blocks become temporarily sparse (showing a small $A(E(b))$), the number of false outages increases. On the other hand, denser blocks offer higher inference correctness.

Our prior work dynamically estimated A [13], but Richter et al. showed that block usage changes dramatically, so blocks can *become* overly sparse even with tracking [14].

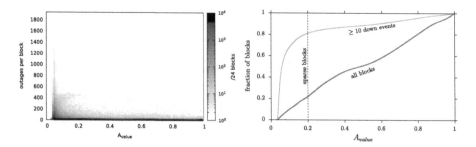

Fig. 7. Blocks distributed according to the number of outages versus their $A(E(b))$ (left), and cumulative distribution function of the A value per block (right) as collected during 2017q4 for the whole responsive IPv4 address scope. Dataset A30. (Color figure online)

We first show that sparse blocks cause the majority of outage events. In Fig. 7 (left) we compare the number of outages in all 4M responsive blocks with their measured $A(E(b))$ value during 2017q4. Blocks with a higher number of outages tend to have a lower $A(E(b))$ value. In particular those closer to the lower bound. Trinocular does not track blocks with long term $A(E(B)) < 0.1$, however as blocks sparseness changes, this value does change during measure time.

The correlation between sparse blocks and frequent outage events is clearer when we look at a cumulative distribution. Figure 7 (right) shows the cumulative distribution of A for all 4M responsive blocks (light green, the lower line), and for blocks with 10 or more down events (the red, upper line) as measured during 2017q4. These lines are after merging observations obtained from six Trinocular vantage points. We find that 80% of blocks with 10 or more down events have an $A < 0.2$, at around the knee of the curve, and yet these sparse blocks represent only 22% of all blocks. The figure suggests a correlation between high number of down events and low $A(E(b))$ per block due to the faster convergence of the line representing blocks with multiple down events. (It confirms the heuristic of "more than 5 events" that was used to filter sparse Trinocular blocks in the 2017 CDN comparison [14].)

Although we observe from multiple locations, merging results from different vantage points is not sufficient to deal with sparse blocks, because these multiple sites all face the same problem of sparseness leading to inconsistent results. Addressing this problem is a goal of FBS, and it also allows us to grow coverage.

C   Comparing Trinocular and FBS

In Sect. 4.2 we discuss how often FBS changes outages when compared to Trinocular. We examine two different metrics: total block down time and number of down events. Here we provide further information distribution about the distribution of these metrics.

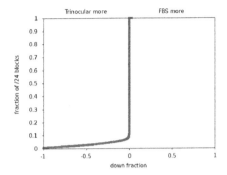
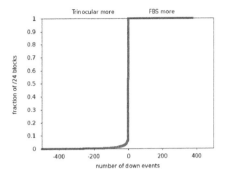

Fig. 8. Cumulative distribution of down fraction difference (left) and number of down events difference (right) between Trinocular and FBS for 2017q4. Dataset A30.

In Fig. 8 (left) we show block distribution of Trinocular and FBS down time fraction difference. The majority of blocks (91%) have little or no change. Blocks on the left side of the figure representing 9% of the total, have a higher down time fraction when processed only with Trinocular than when processed with FBS. For example, a -1 shows a block that was down for Trinocular during the whole quarter, while FBS was able to completely recover it. This outcome occurs when a historically high $|E(b)|$ block has temporarily dropped to just a few stable addresses.

We also see a small percentage (0.5%) where FBS has a higher down fraction than Trinocular. This increase in outages fraction happens when Trinocular erroneously marks a block as UP. With more information, FBS is able to correctly change block state and more accurately reflect truth.

In Fig. 8 (right) we look to the distribution of blocks when compared by the number of down events observed in FBS and Trinocular. Similarly, the number of down events remains mostly unchanged for the majority of blocks (94%). Trinocular has more down events for 6% of blocks, and FBS shows more events for 0.1%. FBS can increase the absolute number of events in a block when breaking long events into shorter pieces.

References

1. IODA: Internet outage detection & analysis. https://ioda.caida.org
2. Baltra, G., Heidemann, J.: Improving the optics of active outage detection (extended). Technical report ISI-TR-733, May 2019. https://www.isi.edu/%7ejohnh/PAPERS/Baltra19a.html
3. Dainotti, A., et al.: Lost in space: improving inference of IPv4 address space utilization. IEEE J. Sel. Areas Commun. (JSAC) **34**(6), 1862–1876 (2016)
4. Dainotti, A., et al.: Analysis of country-wide Internet outages caused by censorship. In: Proceedings of the ACM Internet Measurement Conference, Berlin, Germany, pp. 1–18. ACM, November 2011. https://doi.org/10.1145/2068816.2068818
5. Madory, D.: Iraq downs internet to combat cheating...again! (2017). https://dyn.com/blog/iraq-downs-internet-to-combat-cheating-again/. Accessed 01 Aug 2019

6. Guillot, A., et al.: Chocolatine: outage detection for internet background radiation. In: Proceedings of the IFIP International Workshop on Traffic Monitoring and Analysis. IFIP, Paris, France, June 2019. https://clarinet.u-strasbg.fr/~pelsser/publications/Guillot-chocolatine-TMA2019.pdf

7. Heidemann, J., Pradkin, Y., Govindan, R., Papadopoulos, C., Bartlett, G., Bannister, J.: Census and survey of the visible Internet. In: Proceedings of the ACM Internet Measurement Conference, Vouliagmeni, Greece, pp. 169–182. ACM, October 2008. https://doi.org/10.1145/1452520.1452542

8. Internet Addresses Survey dataset, PREDICT ID: USC-LANDER/internet-address-survey-reprobing-it75w-20170427

9. MaxMind: GeoIP Geolocation Products (2017). http://www.maxmind.com/en/city

10. Padmanabhan, R., Dhamdhere, A., Aben, E., Claffy, K.C., Spring, N.: Reasons dynamic addresses change. In: Proceedings of the ACM Internet Measurement Conference, Santa Monica, CA, USA. ACM, November 2016. https://doi.org/10.1145/2987443.2987461

11. Padmanabhan, R., Schulman, A., Levin, D., Spring, N.: Residential links under the weather. In: Proceedings of the ACM Special Interest Group on Data Communication, pp. 145–158. ACM (2019)

12. Quan, L., Heidemann, J., Pradkin, Y.: Trinocular: understanding Internet reliability through adaptive probing. In: Proceedings of the ACM SIGCOMM Conference, Hong Kong, China, pp. 255–266. ACM, August 2013. https://doi.org/10.1145/2486001.2486017

13. Quan, L., Heidemann, J., Pradkin, Y.: When the Internet sleeps: correlating diurnal networks with external factors. In: Proceedings of the ACM Internet Measurement Conference, Vancouver, BC, Canada, pp. 87–100. ACM, November 2014. https://doi.org/10.1145/2663716.2663721

14. Richter, P., Padmanabhan, R., Spring, N., Berger, A., Clark, D.: Advancing the art of Internet edge outage detection. In: Proceedings of the ACM Internet Measurement Conference, Boston, Massachusetts, USA. ACM, October 2018. https://doi.org/10.1145/3278532.3278563

15. Schulman, A., Spring, N.: Pingin' in the rain. In: Proceedings of the ACM Internet Measurement Conference, pp. 19–25. Berlin, Germany. ACM, November 2011. https://doi.org/10.1145/2068816.2068819

16. Shah, A., Fontugne, R., Aben, E., Pelsser, C., Bush, R.: Disco: fast, good, and cheap outage detection. In: Proceedings of the IEEE International Conference on Traffic Monitoring and Analysis, Dublin, Ireland, pp. 1–9. IEEE, June 2017. https://doi.org/10.23919/TMA.2017.8002902

17. USC/ISI ANT Project. https://ant.isi.edu/datasets/outage/index.html

FLOWTRACE: A Framework for Active Bandwidth Measurements Using In-band Packet Trains

Adnan Ahmed[1(✉)], Ricky Mok[2], and Zubair Shafiq[1]

[1] The University of Iowa, Iowa City, USA
{adnan-ahmed,zubair-shafiq}@uiowa.edu
[2] CAIDA/UC San Diego, San Diego, USA
cskpmok@caida.org

Abstract. Active measurement tools are important to understand and diagnose performance bottlenecks on the Internet. However, their overhead is a concern because a high number of additional measurement packets can congest the network they try to measure. To address this issue, prior work has proposed in-band approaches that piggyback application traffic for active measurements. However, prior approaches are hard to deploy because they require either specialized hardware or modifications in the Linux kernel. In this paper, we propose FLOWTRACE–a readily deployable user-space active measurement framework that leverages application TCP flows to carry out in-band network measurements. Our implementation of PATHNECK using FLOWTRACE creates recursive packet trains to locate bandwidth bottlenecks. The experimental evaluation on a testbed shows that FLOWTRACE is able to locate bandwidth bottlenecks as accurately as PATHNECK with significantly less overhead.

1 Introduction

Background. Internet performance measurement plays an important role in diagnosing network paths, improving web application performance, and inferring quality of experience (QoE). A notable example is the use of available bandwidth measurement in adaptive video streaming [15,20]. ISPs and content providers are motivated to build web-based measurement tests (e.g., M-Lab NDT [19], Ookla speed test, and Netflix fast.com [8]) to provide throughput measurement services for end-users. These platforms estimate access link capacity by flooding the network with one or more concurrent TCP flows [2], which result in very high overhead [9]. Note that while such tools can be used by the end-users to measure network performance, large scale deployment (e.g. by CDNs) to conduct Internet-wide network measurements poses scalability concerns due to high overheads.

Limitations of Prior Work. Over the last decade, many light-weight end-to-end active network measurement methods have been proposed to accurately measure network path metrics, including latency [17], packet loss rate [26], available bandwidth [13,25,28], and capacity [3,5,14]. These tools inject crafted probe

© Springer Nature Switzerland AG 2020
A. Sperotto et al. (Eds.): PAM 2020, LNCS 12048, pp. 37–51, 2020.
https://doi.org/10.1007/978-3-030-44081-7_3

packets into the network with a specific packet sending pattern, and analyze the timing or events of responses to compute the network metrics. However, these tools are not widely adopted for measuring web service performance for two main reasons.

(1) *Out-of-band.* The measurement probes often used different flow tuples (types of packets, source/destination ports) to user traffic [21]. The network path traversed by the measurement flow could be different from the user traffic, and thus the results may not be representative. In addition, some measurement tools (e.g., PATHLOAD [13], PATHCHIRP [25]) typically generate a significant amount of traffic—carrying no useful data—to interact with and measure the network.

(2) *Prior solutions are hard to deploy.* Various solutions such as MGRP [24] and MINPROBE [29] have been proposed to mitigate the impact of these measurement tools on the network, by leveraging application traffic to conduct measurements. Ideally, such tools can be deployed at the server-side to leverage ongoing downstream traffic to conduct end-to-end measurements to the client-side. However, these solutions are limited in terms of feasibility of deployment. For instance, MGRP requires modifications in the Linux kernel, making it OS-specific, while MINPROBE requires dedicated FPGA-based SoNIC hardware.

Proposed Approach. In this paper, we propose FLOWTRACE, a user-space measurement framework to deploy in-band network measurement systems. FLOWTRACE overcomes the limitations of prior work as follows. First, it conducts in-band measurements by intercepting and rescheduling application data packets. Second, it only uses commodity Linux utilities such as `iptables` and `NFQUEUE`, thereby avoiding the need to patch the kernel or additional hardware, making it feasible to deploy across large scale infrastructures such as Content Delivery Networks or measurement platforms such as M-Lab. Overall, FLOW-TRACE intercepts packets from the application flows and shapes them so as to implement different measurement algorithms.

Evaluation. We have implemented a prototype of FLOWTRACE and evaluated it using Emulab. Specifically, we demonstrate the effectiveness of FLOWTRACE by implementing a well-known measurement tool PATHNECK [10] over FLOW-TRACE, and comparing the measurements done using both implementations. Note that PATHNECK uses recursive packet trains (RPTs) to locate the bottleneck by analyzing the packet dispersion of the ICMP TTL exceeded messages returned by the intermediate hops. We show in our evaluation that measurements done using PATHNECK implemented on FLOWTRACE closely follow the measurements done using PATHNECK. Lastly, we show that using FLOWTRACE only increases the application-perceived latency by at most 1.44 ms.

We remark that FLOWTRACE can be used by various measurement platforms to efficiently implement a vast array of measurement algorithms, that would otherwise be infeasible to deploy at large scale.

2   Background

There is a long line of research on active network measurements to measure different network performance metrics such as round-trip-time (RTT), packet loss rate, and bandwidth [10–13, 18, 25, 28]. These active measurement tools provide useful insights for network performance diagnosis, management, and even protocol design. For instance, `ping` [16] is a simple yet effective tool to measure RTT and packet loss between two hosts by constructing specially-crafted ICMP messages that, when received by a receiver, are echoed back to the sender. iPerf [6] is commonly used to measure bandwidth between two hosts by measuring the time it takes to complete a bulk transfer between the two hosts. These tools and their variants are used to conduct Internet-scale measurements using dedicated measurement platforms such as M-Lab [18].

Prior work has proposed more sophisticated active measurement tools such as PATHLOAD [12] and PATHCHIRP [25] to measure available bandwidth as well as PATHNECK [10] to localize the bandwidth bottleneck between two hosts. Instead of relying on bulk data transfers, these tools probe the network and measure the timing information of the responses to estimate the bandwidth characteristics. More specifically, these tools craft *probe packets* that traverses the end-to-end path between a source and a destination host and interacts with the underlying network along the path. As a result, the underlying network modulates the probe traffic (such as packet transmission rates at the links) and generates a "response" (such as inter-packet gaps) as the *probe packets* move forward through the links along the path. The tools then analyze this timing information to estimate the bandwidth characteristics of the underlying network.

Even though these more sophisticated bandwidth measurement tools generate relatively less traffic as compared to iPerf, they still introduce non-trivial probe traffic that can cause congestion in the very network they are trying to measure. For instance, PATHNECK identifies the location of the bottleneck along the path by constructing recursive packet trains (RPTs), consisting of large payload packets wrapped around with small probe packets. Note that even though the probe packets in the RPTs are negligible in size, payload packets are typically much larger and carry dummy payload that can congest the network. Such non-trivial overheads make it infeasible to deploy these bandwidth measurement tools on a large-scale.

To address this issue, prior work has proposed methods that allow these measurement tools to piggyback *useful* application traffic onto the measurement traffic [24, 29]. More specifically, MGRP [24] was designed to mitigate the overheads of measurement tools such as PATHLOAD and PATHCHIRP by piggybacking payload data from all application flows destined to the remote host—to which the measurement is to be done—into probe packets. These probe packets are received and demultiplexed into the constituent application flows by the remote host, while the measurement is done by observing the arrival times of the MGRP probes. In the same vein, MINPROBE was proposed to leverage application traffic in a middlebox environment for Gigabit-speed networks. Specifically, MINPROBE [29] intercepts application flows destined to the target host at middleboxes and modulates (and measures) the transmission (and arrival) times of these packets with nanosecond precision to allow for high-speed network measurements.

While existing methods such as MGRP [24] and MINPROBE [29] do mini-mize measurement overheads by leveraging application traffic for probing, their deployment requires specialized hardware or kernel-level modifications at the hosts. MINPROBE requires specialized hardware such as FPGA pluggable boards and Software-defined Network Interface Cards (SoNIC) making it infeasible for Internet-scale deployment. MGRP requires changes to the Linux Kernel, making it OS- and Kernel-specific and severely limiting its deployability as acknowledged by [24].

3   FLOWTRACE

In this section, we first discuss some design goals of FLOWTRACE (Sect. 3.1), and then describe the technical challenges we tackled in implementing FLOWTRACE (Sect. 3.2).

3.1   Overview

The design of FLOWTRACE revolves around two main goals. First, FLOWTRACE leverages ongoing TCP flows to conduct *in-band* network measurement. By embedding measurement probes into the flows nwe make sure that the measure-ment traffic follows the same path as the application traffic, thereby enabling measurements along the paths undertaken by the application traffic. In addition, leveraging application traffic to conduct measurements can significantly reduce the measurement overheads. Second, FLOWTRACE can be feasibly deployed by various server-end entities such as content-providers and measurement platforms (such as M-lab) to measure the application of web services and conduct Internet-wide measurements, without requiring significant changes to the Linux Kernel and additional hardware respectively.

We use FLOWTRACE to perform PATHNECK-like measurements to locate net-work bottlenecks. Identifying under-provisioned links is useful for load-balancing traffic and improving the service quality. FLOWTRACE is implemented as an in-band, user-space tool that leverages ongoing TCP flows for measurement.

FLOWTRACE monitors traffic to identify new TCP flows and decides which flows to be measurement flows, and then intercepts packets from measurement flows to construct RPTs, which comprise of large *payload packets* wrapped around with TTL-limited *probe packets*. The routers on the path subsequently drop the first and the last *probe packets* and generate TTL-exceeded ICMP response mes-sages [10]. FLOWTRACE captures these response messages to infer the location of the bottleneck. To this end, FLOWTRACE treats data packets in the flow as *pay-load packets*, and inserts leading and trailing *probe packets*—called head packets and tail packets, respectively. FLOWTRACE conducts bottleneck identification and localization by analyzing the arrival time of the response packets triggered by the dropped hand and tail packets. FLOWTRACE does not manipulate the

TTL of data packets, allowing them to be received by the remote host without any disruptions. Note that a large amount of data in the constructed RPT is the original *payload packets* carrying useful application data, with FLOWTRACE inserting only a number of small *probe packets* to conduct measurement.

3.2   Technical Challenges

While the basic concept behind FLOWTRACE is intuitive, as we discuss below, it presents a unique set of technical challenges.

Lack of Kernel-Level Visibility. The first and foremost challenge in leveraging ongoing application traffic to deploy active measurement techniques in user-space is the lack of kernel-space visibility and packet-level control. Specifically, when an application generates data that is to be sent to a remote host, it passes the data down to the kernel where it is fragmented and formed into TCP/IP packets after filling all the corresponding packet header fields, and is finally sent over the wire. Prior approaches such as MGRP implemented an in-kernel solution to intercept and piggyback application layer packets in probe packets to implement various active measurement techniques. However, as mentioned before, MGRP requires changes in Linux kernel, and is OS-specific, which makes it difficult to deploy at a large scale.

On the contrary, we use commodity Linux-based utilities such as firewalls and basic user-space libraries to implement FLOWTRACE. More specifically, FLOWTRACE relies on utilities such as iptables and NFQUEUE to obtain fine-grained per-packet control *in user-space*. In this manner, FLOWTRACE intercepts packets from application traffic, modifies (or modulates) packet transmission times, and inserts *probe packets* to create RPTs. All in all, these commodity Linux-based utilities provide relatively fine-grained control and visibility over application layer traffic without compromising on the feasibility for large-scale deployment.

Interception vs. "Respawning". In addition to fine-grained control over application traffic, active measurement techniques require control over the transmission rate of the measurement traffic. Specifically, PATHNECK transmits a "well-packed" RPTs at line rate from the source host to effectively locate bottlenecks along the path. However, since FLOWTRACE leverages application layer traffic to construct RPTs and conduct measurement, it is limited by the traffic characteristics of the application. For instance, if the application generates payload data at a rate slower than the line rate, FLOWTRACE will be unable to construct "well-packed" RPTs, resulting in inaccurate network measurements.

To enable FLOWTRACE to send RPTs at line rate, we can *buffer* application packets in the kernel using NFQUEUE, and transmit a "well-packed" RPT when FLOWTRACE has received enough packets from the application layer. However, a limitation of using NFQUEUE is that FLOWTRACE only has visibility at the *head* of the queue, with no information about the number of packets in the queue. To solve this, FLOWTRACE "respawns" the application layer traffic in the user space.

FLOWTRACE retrieves and copies available packets in NFQUEUE, and notifies the kernel to discard the original packet by returning NF_DROP. Lastly, upon receiving the specified number of application layer packets, FLOWTRACE constructs a "well-packed" RPT using the buffered data packets, and (re-)transmits them using pcap at line rate.

Minimizing the Impact of Packet Buffering. Lastly, FLOWTRACE largely depends on the traffic generation behavior of the application conduct measurements. Note that traffic generation patterns and volume of traffic can vary significantly across applications, ranging from small short-lived flows generated by web browsing to long-lived flows for video streaming services. As a result, FLOW-TRACE may not be able to receive and intercept sufficient data packets to generate measurement traffic according to the specified measurement configuration. To this end, we can increase the time FLOWTRACE waits for the next packet to accumulate more data packets. However, application packets may perceive excessive buffering period before they are sent, thereby hurting the throughput and responsiveness of the application.

To reduce the impact on the application performance, FLOWTRACE employs an opportunistic approach to conduct measurement. FLOWTRACE continuously monitors the inter-arrival delays of the new data packets. Whenever the inter-arrival delay exceeds a certain time threshold, t_{ipa}, FLOWTRACE gives up on that round of measurement, and immediately sends out all the buffered packets over the wire using pcap, thereby resuming the flow. After resuming the flow, FLOW-TRACE waits for the next chance to conduct the required measurement using subsequent application packets. Note that the value of t_{ipa} governs the tradeoff between the capability of FLOWTRACE to consistently conduct measurements and application layer performance.

Another alternative approach to minimize the impact of buffering is to introduce additional dummy data packets when the number of data packets from the application is not enough. However, this approach introduces additional congestion to the network which is against the design goal for FLOWTRACE. Therefore, in this paper, we use t_{ipa} to configure the wait time and resume application flows when FLOWTRACE receives insufficient data packets.

3.3 Implementation

FLOWTRACE employs NFQUEUE [22], which is a user-space library to intercept an ongoing network flow from the system. FLOWTRACE identifies a flow of interest based on the IP address provided by the operator, and sets up iptables to intercept the application flow. Specifically, FLOWTRACE sets up iptables rules inside the Linux kernel with NFQUEUE as the target, effectively redirecting packets from the flow of interest to NFQUEUE. Consequently, whenever a packet satisfies an iptables rule with an NFQUEUE target, the firewall enqueues the packet and its metadata (a Linux kernel skb) into a packet queue such that the decision regarding the corresponding packets can be delegated to a user-space

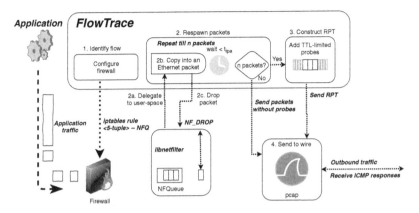

Fig. 1. High level work flow of FLOWTRACE. FLOWTRACE first identifies an application flow based on the 5-tuple. It then configures `iptables` rules such that the packets from the application flow are directed towards the NFQUEUE target. NFQUEUE delegates the decision of each packet to a user-space program spawned by FLOWTRACE, which buffers the payload from each packet in user-space and directs NFQUEUE to drop the packets. When FLOWTRACE receives enough application packets, it creates a "well-packed" RPT out of the buffered application packets and transmits them on the wire via `pcap`. Otherwise, FLOWTRACE transmits the buffered application packets without any additional probe packets.

program. To this end, the kernel then executes a callback registered by the user-space program, and sends the enqueued packet with the metadata using *nfnetlink* protocol. The user-space program then parses the packet information and payload, and can decide a verdict on dropping (NF_DROP) or releasing (NF_ACCEPT) the packet. At a high-level, FLOWTRACE intercepts the packets from the flow of interest, then handles these packets in the user-space and modulates traffic accordingly to implement the measurement algorithm specified by the user. We implemented a prototype of FLOWTRACE using GO programming language, that supports lightweight concurrency using `goroutine`. As a result, we can conduct measurement to multiple concurrent flows with small overheads.

Implementing Pathneck. Based on the high-level idea described above, we now describe how FLOWTRACE can be used to implement PATHNECK, as illustrated in Fig. 1.

1. *Identifying the flow of interest.* To avoid process all incoming/outgoing packets, the operator provides the IP address and port information of the flows, directed towards the clients that we are interested in measuring (such as port 80 and 443 for web servers). Consequently, FLOWTRACE can initialize `iptables` rules and `pcap` filters to reduce workload. All the flows matched the specified IP and ports consider as the flow of interest.
2. *Intercepting flows.* Once the initialization completed, FLOWTRACE creates a map of flows using the 5-tuple (source IP, destination IP, source port,

destination port, protocol), and starts to handle packets using NFQUEUE and record the state of the flows. We do not perform any measurement in the beginning of the flows, because the TCP congestion window during the slow-start phase is too small for us to receive sufficient data packets to construct measurement probes. In our implementation, we do not manipulate the first 10 packets of the flows.

3. *Constructing measurement probes.* We use the flows that transferred more than 10 data packets to conduct measurements. FLOWTRACE waits for n load packets from the TCP flow to construct a "well-packed" RPT. Figure 2 depicts the construction of one RPT. As the application data arrives, FLOW-TRACE first buffers the load packets and drops the original packets (using NF_DROP) (Sect. 3.2). When FLOWTRACE has n payload packets from the application flow in the buffer, it first sends m TTL-limited zero-size measurement packets, followed by the n load packets, and m tail packets. This way, FLOWTRACE injects a "well-packed" RPT constructed from the application traffic, into the network.

4. *Capturing and analyzing response packets.* The final step is to monitor the incoming traffic using pcap for the ICMP messages triggered by the RPT. Based on the ICMP response messages from each hop, FLOWTRACE computes the per-hop packet train dispersion and determine the network bottleneck.

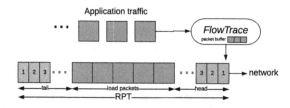

Fig. 2. Details of RPT generation. Light blue squares are data packets from the application, and green rectangles are probe packets. The number inside the green rectangles are the TTL values of the packet.

Minimizing the Impact of Packet Buffering. In step 3, the flow is effectively stopped while we wait to receive n flow packets. Because the amount of application data is unpredictable, it is possible that FLOWTRACE intercepts less than n packets and keeps waiting for the next data packet to arrive. This can seriously affect the throughput, RTT, and congestion control mechanisms of the application. Therefore, we choose a small inter-packet-arrival timeout, $t_{ipa} = 1,000\mu s$, to ensure that FLOWTRACE does not wait and hold the flow packets for too long while constructing RPTs. When FLOWTRACE receives a flow packet in user-space, it sets up a timer of t_{ipa} for receiving the next flow packet. Upon the arrival of the next packet, FLOWTRACE resets the timer.

In the event that timer expired, FLOWTRACE decides to not generate the RPT and instead just reconstructs and sends the intercepted flow packets to recover

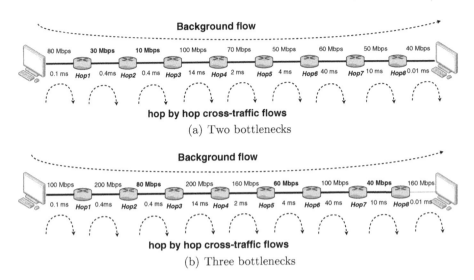

Fig. 3. Emulab topology configurations for our evaluation of the performance of both PATHNECK and FLOWTRACE. The bottleneck hops in both Fig. 3(a) and (b) are highlighted. (Color figure online)

the flow. This way FLOWTRACE ensures that the flow RTT and congestion control mechanisms are not significantly affected as we will demonstrate in Sect. 4.3.

4 Evaluation

We now evaluate the implementation of PATHNECK on FLOWTRACE in a controlled testbed environment for different network conditions. Specifically, we want to see how closely the measurements done using PATHNECK implemented on FLOWTRACE agree with the measurements done using PATHNECK. Emulab [23] allows us to test and compare the measurements of the two against known traffic workloads in a controlled testbed environment.

To this end, we create a linear network topology in Emulab as shown in Fig. 3 similar to that studied in [10]. Our network consists of a sender and a receiver machine, connected to each other via a series of intermediate routers. In our evaluation, we evaluate the performance of both PATHNECK and FLOWTRACE in "two-bottlenecks scenario" and "three-bottlenecks scenario" as shown in Fig. 3(a) and (b) respectively.

In addition to the routers along the path from the sender to the receiver machine, we generate background traffic as well, across the network as shown in Fig. 3. The background traffic comprises of two kinds of flows, (1) the background flow from the source machine to the destination machine, and (2) the hop-by-hop cross-traffic flows that traverse the links between the intermediate routers. In our setup, we use iPerf to set up bandwidth-constrained TCP flows as the hop-by-hop cross-traffic flows. On the other hand, we set up a large file transfer

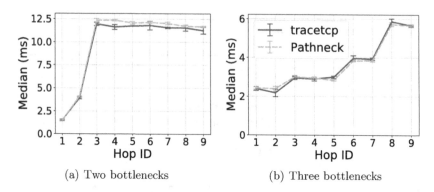

(a) Two bottlenecks   (b) Three bottlenecks

Fig. 4. Comparison of gap values reported by PATHNECK and FLOWTRACE across and end-to-end network without cross traffic in a controlled emulab testbed.

between a web server at the sender machine and a `wget` client at the receiver machine as the background flow. Note that since FLOWTRACE leverages ongoing traffic to construct RPTs and conduct measurement, we configure it to leverage the background flow from source machine to the destination machine in our experiments. In particular, each RPT constructed by FLOWTRACE is composed of $n = 10$ *payload packets*, intercepted from the background flow, and $n = 15$ TTL-limited *probe packets*. Lastly, we configure the link characteristics such as link delays and link bandwidths, along the path, using commodity Linux utilities such as `tc` and `netem` to create the aforementioned testbed scenarios.

4.1 Minimal Cross Traffic

We first consider the "bare-bones" scenario where there is minimal cross traffic along the links in the network and the choke points and bottlenecks are primarily dictated by the change in link capacities along the end-to-end path. This scenario is ideal for PATHNECK, as the RPTs are affected only by the capacity of the links along the path without any interference from the cross traffic, making it easier to identify choke points and locate bottleneck. To this end, we configure the hop-by-hop cross traffic across all the links in Fig. 3 to be only 0.01 Mbps.

Figure 4 plots the median gap values along with the standard deviation (for 15 runs each), across the hops in the end-to-end path reported by both PATHNECK and FLOWTRACE for both "two-bottlenecks" and "three-bottlenecks" scenarios. We note that both PATHNECK and FLOWTRACE report similar gap values across the hops for both scenarios. For instance, FLOWTRACE exhibits a gap value increase of 2.41 ms and 8.05 ms, whereas PATHNECK exhibits a gap value increase of 2.59 ms and 8.27 ms in gap values at hops 2 and 3, where the link capacities decrease by 50 Mbps and 20 Mbps respectively, in Fig. 4(a). On the other hand, FLOWTRACE exhibits a gap value increase of 0.77 ms, 0.97 ms, and 1.95 ms, whereas PATHNECK exhibits a gap value increase of 0.62 ms, 1.0 ms, and 1.88 ms in gap values at hops 3, 6, and 8, where the link capacities decrease from 100

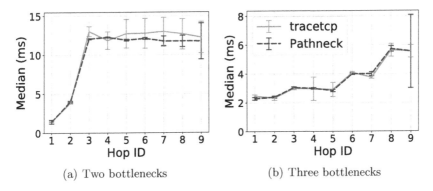

(a) Two bottlenecks   (b) Three bottlenecks

Fig. 5. Comparison of gap values reported by PATHNECK and FLOWTRACE across and end-to-end network with cross traffic in a controlled emulab testbed.

Mbps to 80 Mbps, 60 Mbps, and 40 Mbps respectively, in Fig. 4(a). All in all, our results show that both PATHNECK and FLOWTRACE largely agree with one another in terms of reported gap values for various network configurations given that cross-traffic is minimal—which has been shown to be largely the case across the Internet in prior literature [10].

4.2   With Cross-Traffic

We now evaluate the impact of cross-traffic along the links in the end-to-end path, on the gap values reported by both PATHNECK and FLOWTRACE. To this end, we consider the impact of forward (upstream) cross-traffic—the downstream links do not experience any cross-traffic[1]. Note that ideally, in this scenario, the returning ICMP messages from each hop should be received by the sender machine without experiencing any interference from cross-traffic. In this case, we configure the hop-by-hop iPerf clients to generate cross-traffic equal to 5% of the corresponding link capacities.

Figure 5 plots the median gap values along with the standard deviation (for 15 runs each), across each hop in the end-to-end path as reported by both PATH-NECK and FLOWTRACE for both "two-bottlenecks" and "three-bottlenecks" scenario. We again note that both PATHNECK and FLOWTRACE report similar gap values across the hops in the end-to-end path. For instance, FLOWTRACE exhibits a gap value increase of 2.38 ms and 9.16 ms, whereas PATHNECK exhibits a gap value increase of 2.55 ms and 8.04 ms in gap values at hops 2 and 3, where the link capacities decrease by 50 Mbps and 20 Mbps respectively, in Fig. 5(a). We observe similar pattern for the "three-bottlenecks" scenario in Fig. 5(b). We

---

[1] Hu et al. [10] reported that reverse path effects may impact the performance of PATHNECK as they may perturb the gaps between the ICMP response messages on the way back. Our goal is that FLOWTRACE performs well *when* PATHNECK performs well. Therefore, we do not evaluate the impact of reverse path effects on the performance of FLOWTRACE in this work for brevity.

do note that the forward cross-traffic results in significantly higher variance as compared to the scenarios without cross-traffic, especially for the hops farther away from the sender machine in both scenarios in Fig. 5. For instance, the standard deviation for FLOWTRACE increased from 0.05 ms at hop 1 to 2.01 ms at the last hop, whereas the standard deviation for PATHNECK increased from 0.23 ms at hop 1 to 2.31 ms at the last hop in Fig. 5(a). This is because the error in gap values *accumulates* as the packets traverse the network.

4.3   Latency Overhead

Since FLOWTRACE leverages application flows to construct RPTs and conduct measurement, we evaluate the
impact of FLOWTRACE on the latency
experienced by the application flows.
Specifically, since FLOWTRACE buffers
and "respawns" the application packets in the user-space, we report the
additional latency each application
packet experienced by the application
flow for different values of the inter-
arrival delay threshold, t_{ipa}, in Fig. 6.
As expected, we observe a piece-wise

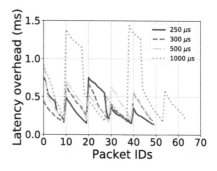

Fig. 6. Latency overheads involved in FLOWTRACE perceived by the application.

linear pattern in Fig. 6. This is because the first packet generated by the appli-
cation, when intercepted by FLOWTRACE, has to be buffered all the while FLOW-
TRACE waits for more application packets. On the other hand, as soon as FLOW-
TRACE received enough application packets, it creates a RPT and transmits it on
the wire, thereby adding minimal latency for the last application packet in the
RPT.

Note that this overhead is primarily dictated by t_{ipa} and traffic characteristics
of the application as discussed in Sect. 3.2—the higher the value of t_{ipa}, the longer
the packets can potentially be buffered and therefore, the higher the overheads
in Fig. 6. This may result in FLOWTRACE affecting the latency characteristics—
such as RTT and jitter—perceived by the application. In our evaluation, from
Fig. 6, we observe that an application flow may experience an inflation of at
most 1.44 ms increase in application perceived latency, for $t_{ipa} = 1$ ms, when
leveraged by FLOWTRACE to conduct measurements. This overhead decreases
to 0.75 ms for $t_{ipa} = 0.25$ ms, because FLOWTRACE waits for a shorter period
of time for application packets before releasing the buffered packets without
constructing the RPT. To summarize, these latency overheads are dictated by
the traffic patterns of the underlying application—burst of packets generated by
the application may result in FLOWTRACE having to wait for a lesser amount
of time as compared to spaced out traffic patterns.

5   Related Work

Prior literature has proposed various tools and techniques to measure path performance in terms of metrics such as available bandwidth [4,11,13,25,28], bottleneck location [1,10], and loss rates [26]. However, most of these tools can only perform measurement out-of-band.

Few existing works adopted in-band measurement paradigm. Prior research has proposed different approaches such as paratrace [7], Service traceroute [21], and TCP Sidecar [27] to map Internet paths more effectively. These techniques rely on embedding TTL-limited measurement probes alongside the nonmeasurement application traffic, evading firewalls and NATs, and increasing the coverage of measurement systems across the Internet. Papageorge et al. proposed MGRP [24]—an in-kernel service that allows users to write measurement algorithms which are subsequently implemented by piggybacking application data inside probe traffic to minimize overheads and lower the impact of conducting measurements on competing application traffic. However, MGRP requires changes to the kernel at both the client- and the server-side machines, making it difficult to deploy at a large scale. In the similar vein, Wang et al. proposed MINPROBE [29]—a middlebox architecture that used application network traffic as probe traffic to conduct measurements such as available bandwidth by modulating packet transmissions with high fidelity. However MINPROBE requires specialized hardware and physical access to both end-points, which is often hard to deploy.

QDASH [20] integrates PATHLOAD [13] into adaptive streaming flows. It reshapes video data packets into different sending rates to detect the highest video bitrate the network can support. However, QDASH can only obtain end-to-end available bandwidth information. It cannot locate the bottleneck on the path. In this paper, we leverage application traffic to deploy PATHNECK, locating choke points along the path and facilitate the measurements of bandwidth characteristics of the network at a large scale.

6   Conclusion

We presented FLOWTRACE, an active measurement framework that conducts in-band network measurements by piggybacking application data. We showed that FLOWTRACE can transparently create recursive packet trains to locate bandwidth bottlenecks with minimal impact on application performance. FLOWTRACE not only significantly reduces the overhead of active measurements but can also be readily deployed in user-space without needing kernel modifications or specialized hardware. The experimental evaluation showed that PATHNECK's implementation of using FLOWTRACE as well as the original PATHNECK implementation can both accurately locate bandwidth bottlenecks. As part of our future work, we are interested in extending FLOWTRACE to implement other active bandwidth measurement techniques. Furthermore, we aim to study the impact of FLOWTRACE on the performance of different types of applications, such as realtime video and web. We are also interested in large-scale deployment of FLOWTRACE to conduct Internet measurements in the wild.

Acknowledgement. We thank the anonymous reviewers and our shepherd, Mirja Kühlewind, for helpful suggestions that improved the paper. We also thank Amogh Dhamdhere for his input in the early stage of this work. This work is supported in part by the National Science Foundation under grant numbers CNS-1617288, CNS-1750175, and CNS-1414177.

References

1. Baranasuriya, N., Navda, V., Padmanabhan, V.N., Gilbert, S.: QProbe: locating the bottleneck in cellular communication. In: CoNEXT (2015)
2. Bauer, S., Clark, D., Lehr, W.: Understanding broadband speed measurements. In: TPRC (2010)
3. Chan, E., Chen, A., Luo, X., Mok, R., Li, W., Chang, R.: TRIO: measuring asymmetric capacity with three minimum round-trip times. In: ACM CoNEXT (2011)
4. Croce, D., Mellia, M., Leonardi, E.: The quest for bandwidth estimation techniques for large-scale distributed systems. In: ACM SIGMETRICS (2009)
5. Dovrolis, C., Ramanathan, P., Moore, D.: Packet dispersion techniques and a capacity-estimation methodology. IEEE/ACM Trans. Netw. **12**(6), 963–977 (2004)
6. Dugan, J., Elliott, S., Mah, B.A., Poskanzer, J., Prabhu, K.: iPerf.fr. https://iperf.fr
7. Erich: Paratrace (2018). http://www.adeptus-mechanicus.com/codex/paratrc/paratrc.php
8. Fast.com: Internet speed test. https://fast.com
9. Goga, O., Teixeira, R.: Speed measurements of residential internet access. In: Taft, N., Ricciato, F. (eds.) PAM 2012. LNCS, vol. 7192, pp. 168–178. Springer, Heidelberg (2012). https://doi.org/10.1007/978-3-642-28537-0_17
10. Hu, N., Li, L.E., Mao, Z.M., Steenkiste, P., Wang, J.: Locating internet bottlenecks: algorithms, measurements, and implications. In: Proceedings of the ACM SIGCOMM (2004)
11. Hu, N., Steenkiste, P.: Evaluation and characterization of available bandwidth probing techniques. IEEE JSAC **21**, 879–894 (2003)
12. Jain, M., Dovrolis, C.: Pathload: a measurement tool for end-to-end available bandwidth. In: PAM (2002)
13. Jain, M., Dovrolis, C.: End-to-end available bandwidth: measurement methodology, dynamics, and relation with TCP throughput. Trans. Netw. **11**, 537–549 (2003)
14. Kapoor, R., Chen, L.-J., Lao, L., Gerla, M., Sanadidi, M.Y.: CapProbe: a simple and accurate capacity estimation technique. In: ACM SIGCOMM (2004)
15. Li, Z., et al.: Probe and adapt: rate adaptation for HTTP video streaming at scale. IEEE JSAC **32**(4), 719–733 (2014)
16. Linux: Ping. https://linux.die.net/man/8/ping
17. Luo, X., Chan, E., Chang, R.: Design and implementation of TCP data probes for reliable and metric-rich network path monitoring. In: USENIX ATC (2009)
18. M-Lab: Internet measurement tests. https://www.measurementlab.net/tests/
19. M-Lab: NDT (network diagnostic tool) (2017). https://www.measurementlab.net/tests/ndt/

20. Mok, R., Luo, X., Chan, E., Chang, R.: QDASH: a QoE-aware DASH system. In: Proceedings of ACM MMSys (2012)
21. Morandi, I., Bronzino, F., Teixeira, R., Sundaresan, S.: Service traceroute: tracing paths of application flows. In: PAM (2019)
22. netfiler: The netfilter.org "libnetfilter_queue" project. https://netfilter.org/projects/libnetfilter_queue/
23. The University of Utah: emulab. https://www.emulab.net/
24. Papageorge, P., McCann, J., Hicks, M.: Passive aggressive measurement with MGRP. In: SIGCOMM (2009)
25. Ribeiro, V., Riedi, R., Baraniuk, R., Navratil, J., Cottrell, L.: pathChirp: efficient available bandwidth estimation for network paths. In: Passive and Active Measurement Workshop (2003)
26. Savage, S.: Sting: a TCP-based network measurement tool. In: Proceedings of the USENIX Symposium on Internet Technologies and Systems (1999)
27. Sherwood, R., Spring, N.: Touring the internet in a TCP sidecar. In: IMC (2006)
28. Strauss, J., Katabi, D., Kaashoek, F.: A measurement study of available bandwidth estimation tools. In: IMC (2003)
29. Wang, H., Lee, K.S., Li, E., Lim, C.L., Tang, A., Weatherspoon, H.: Timing is everything: accurate, minimum overhead, available bandwidth estimation in high-speed wired networks. In: IMC (2014)

Security

Leopard: Understanding the Threat of Blockchain Domain Name Based Malware

Zhangrong Huang[1,2], Ji Huang[1,2], and Tianning Zang[2(✉)]

[1] School of Cyber Security, University of Chinese Academy of Sciences, Beijing, China
[2] Institute of Information Engineering, Chinese Academy of Sciences, Beijing, China
{huangzhangrong,huangji,zangtianning}@iie.ac.cn

Abstract. Recently, as various detection approaches of malicious domains and malware are proposed, the malware which connects to its command and control (C&C) server using techniques like domain flux can be identified effectively. Therefore, cybercriminals seek new alternative methods and discover that DNS based on blockchains can be used to connect C&C servers. Because of the distributed ledger technology, domain names resolved by blockchain DNS, called blockchain domain names (BDNs), are of inherent anonymity and censorship-resistance. We analyzed the work mechanism of this new type of malware. In order to detect malicious BDNs, we propose a prototype system, named Leopard, which analyzes DNS traffic patterns and resource records of BDNs. To our best knowledge, we are the first to propose the automatic detection of malicious BDNs. In Leopard, we extracted 17 features from collected traffic and distinguished between malicious BDNs and domains operated by generic and country-code top-level domains registries from the Alexa top 5000 using a random forest model. In our experiments, we evaluate Leopard on a nine-day real-world dataset. The experimental results show that Leopard can effectively detect malicious BDNs with an AUC of 0.9980 and discover 286 unknown malicious BDNs from the dataset.

Keywords: BDN-based malware · Malicious domain · Random forest

1 Introduction

Modern botnets adopt IP flux or domain flux techniques to connect to their command and control (C&C) servers [2,3]. Recently, cybercriminals rely on a new type of domain names which have special top-level domains (TLDs) beyond the namespace of the root zone authorized by Internet Corporation for Assigned Names and Numbers (ICANN) and the domain names can not be resolved by standard DNS servers. We named them blockchain domain names (BDNs). BDNs leverage a new decentralized domain name system (DNS) to map domain names to IP addresses. The new decentralized DNS stores resource records on

© Springer Nature Switzerland AG 2020
A. Sperotto et al. (Eds.): PAM 2020, LNCS 12048, pp. 55–70, 2020.
https://doi.org/10.1007/978-3-030-44081-7_4

the blockchains instead of zone files, and we call it blockchain DNS (BDNS). Because of the distributed ledger technology of blockchains, BDNs are of the inherent anonymity and censorship-resistance.

The abuse of inconspicuous BDNs is increasingly popular. Over 106,000 BDNs in total had been registered until 2013 [6] and now the number has exceeded 140,000 [26]. BDN-based malware issue queries about BDN using DNS protocol, to DNS servers which provide BDNs resolution service. However, only a few DNS servers are providing BDNs resolution service[1], so IP addresses or domain names of the DNS servers usually are hard-coded in BDN-based malware. At present, some cybercriminals have already adopted BDNs. For instance, security researchers of FireEye shared the analysis of a Neutrino sample which uses a BDN to host the C&C server. More miscreants add the feature of supporting BDNs into their malware [5]. Therefore, BDN-based malware is becoming a real threat to Internet users.

In this paper, we propose a novel system, called Leopard, which distinguishes between malicious BDNs and domains operated by generic and country-code TLDs registries from the Alexa top 5000. Leopard uses the supervised learning algorithm, specifically the random forest, and automatically detects BDNs of C&C servers in a real-world network environment based on the extracted 17 features. We implemented a prototype system and evaluated it on the large volume of DNS traffic obtained from an Internet service provider (ISP). Leopard can identify known and unknown malicious BDNs.

This paper makes the following contributions:

- To our best knowledge, we present the first prototype of the automatic detection of malicious BDNs, named Leopard, which analyzes the large volume of DNS traffic in a real-world network environment.
- Leopard has a great performance on the real-world datasets, reaching a mean AUC of 0.9945 in the cross-validation phase and reaching an AUC of 0.9980 on the testing dataset. Also, Leopard discovered 286 unknown malicious BDNs.
- We published two datasets[2]: (1) The set of malicious BDNs that are identified by Leopard or labeled manually by us; (2) The list of DNS servers providing BDNs resolution service. It is the first time to collect and publish information about BDN-supported infrastructures.

The remainder of the paper is organized as follows. In Sect. 2 we introduce the background related to BDNS and BDNs. We elaborate on an overview of Leopard, the properties of datasets and the features we selected in Sect. 3. Section 4 presents the results of experimental evaluations. Then, we discuss the limitations of Leopard in Sect. 5 while the related works are illustrated in Sect. 6. We conclude this paper in Sect. 7.

---

[1] In the remainder of the paper, DNS servers we discuss refer to the servers which provide BDNs resolution service.

[2] The link of the public datasets is https://drive.google.com/open?id=1YzVB7cZi MspnTAERBATyvqWKGj0CqGT.

2   Background

In this section, we briefly introduce the background of BDNS. Then, the work mechanism of BDNS will be presented. At last, we show a real-world case that a BDN hosts the C&C server of a malware sample.

Blockchain DNS. In recent years, some cryptocurrency companies apply the blockchain technology to domain resolution and build the public and decentralized BDNS. It is different from the standard DNS that we daily use. The standard DNS resolves domains ending with TLDs authorized by ICANN and users can obtain the ownership of the domain through the whois service. However, BDNS has the special TLD namespaces (shown in Table 1) and there is no information about the ownership of a BDN and hence no whois service you can query. The query process of the standard DNS includes the recursive query and the iterative query. The resolution process of a domain is hierarchical. However, the resolution process of a BDN is quite different, which we discuss later. Besides, the blockchain technology ensures that no one can tamper with resource records except the domain owner. Hence, BDN is of some inherent properties: anonymity, privacy, and censorship-resistance [1,6] and BDN provides cybercriminals with a reliable method to host malicious content.

Table 1. A part of organizations which has the BDN-related services.

Organizations	TLDs	DNS servers
Namecoin [17]	.bit	–
Emercoin [18]	.coin .emc .lib .bazar	seed1.emercoin.com
		seed1.emercoin.com
OpenNIC	.bbs .chan .cyb .dyn	ns1.any.dns.opennic.glue
	.geek .gopher .indy	ns3.any.dns.opennic.glue
	.libre .neo .null .o	ns1.ca.dns.opennic.glue
	.oss .oz .parody .pirate	...
BitName	–	dns1.bitname.ru
		dns2.bitname.ru
DNSPod	–	a.dnspod.com
		b.dnspod.com
		c.dnspod.com

BDNS Resolution Process. Here we discuss BDN resolution. The ways of BDN resolution can be divided into Local BDNS and Third-party BDNS. (1) Local BDNS: This method requires command-line usage and downloading blockchain data in advance. In other words, the blockchain data is a large version of the 'hosts' file. If a client queries A records of *example.bit* using the command lines, it will look up the local data without generating DNS traffic. (2) Third-party BDNS: This method leverages third-party DNS servers that provide BDN resolution service and it can be implemented in three ways, web proxy, browser plugin, and public DNS. The first two ways use the configured proxy server and the special plugins to forward DNS queries to the specific DNS servers. The third way means setting the third-party DNS servers as the default DNS resolver. Because of the flexibility and practicality of malware, BDN-based malware usually directly issue queries to the third-party DNS servers.

Real-World Case. In this case, we obtained a sample of AZORult family from Abuse.ch [7]. The sample ran in the ThreatBook Cloud Sandbox [8]. We analyzed the DNS traffic of the sample and found that the IP addresses of the DNS servers queried by the malware and the BDN of the C&C server were hard-coded. In Fig. 1, the malware failed to resolve *voda.bit* at 151.80.147.153, and then sent DNS queries to 91.217.137.44 where the domain was successfully resolved. We manually validated the records of *voda.bit* with DiG [9] and discovered that BitName [10] was an organization providing BDNs resolution service.

192.168.122.210	91.217.137.44	DNS	68 Standard query 0xa8f5 A voda.bit
91.217.137.44	192.168.122.210	DNS	128 Standard query response 0xa8f5 A voda.bit A 217.23.12.211 NS dns.bitname.ru A 91.217.137.44

```
; <<>> DiG 9.10.6 <<>> @91.217.137.44 voda.bit    ;; QUESTION SECTION:
; (1 server found)                                ;voda.bit.              IN    A
;; global options: +cmd                           ;; ANSWER SECTION:
;; Got answer:                                     voda.bit.     1800 IN   A    217.23.12.211
;; ->>HEADER<<- opcode: QUERY, status: NOERROR, id: 35601    ;; AUTHORITY SECTION:
;; flags: qr aa rd; QUERY: 1, ANSWER: 1, AUTHORITY: 1,       voda.bit.     1800 IN   NS   dns.bitname.ru.
ADDITIONAL: 1                                     ;; ADDITIONAL SECTION:
;; WARNING: recursion requested but not available  dns.bitname.ru.  1800 IN   A    91.217.137.44
```

Fig. 1. One sample of AZORult family issues DNS queries (*voda.bit*) to the third-party DNS server (*dns.bitname.ru*).

3   Automatic Detection

In this section, we first provide a high-level overview of the malicious BDNs detection system Leopard and then elaborate on the datasets used in the experiments. At last, we describe the features used to distinguish malicious BDNs and benign ordinary domain names (ODNs) which refer to domains operated by generic TLDs and country-code TLDs registries.

3.1   Overview

In Fig. 2, Leopard consists of three main modules: the *Data Collection* module, the *Data Processing* module, and the *Malicious BDNs Discovery* module. We discuss the functions of these modules and how they collaborate.

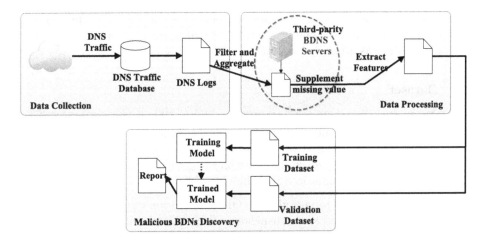

Fig. 2. The workflow of Leopard.

Data Collection. We collected and analyzed the traffic generated by BDN-based malware[3] using ThreatBook Cloud Sandbox. We noted that the malware iteratively queried the hard-coded DNS servers. Unfortunately, most of BDNs in the collected traffic cannot be resolved correctly, because they might be blocked by DNS servers like OpenNIC or abandoned by cybercriminals. We want to capture DNS traffic generated by the active BDN-based malware in a real-world network environment. First, we collected 169 BDNs from 400 captured traffic files of the BDN-based malware. Then, we gathered NS records of the 169 BDNs with DiG. Finally, combined the DNS servers in the captured traffic with the NS records, we built a name server list (NS-list), including 152 servers. We captured DNS packets which matched the IPs in the NS-list assisted by the ISP and dumped the packets as DNS logs.

Data Processing. Most of the servers in the NS-list provide both BDNs and ODNs resolution services. We filtered out the ODNs which were after the top 5000 in the Alexa [15], so as to eliminate the influence of suspicious ODNs such as algorithmically generated domains. The rest of DNS logs in the epoch E (e.g. 1 day) are aggregated in the designed format. Furthermore, we found that about 60.02% of BDNS requests are routed to the servers of OpenNIC and the servers of OpenNIC are owned by volunteers [14]. We had successfully set up a server of OpenNIC and stayed online for a week. Therefore, these servers are unstable and they probably resulted in the failure of BDNs resolution. We had to look up the original data of the BDNs that failed in resolution. Finally, we extracted the features for the downstream training and classification tasks.

Malicious BDNs Discovery. In this module, we trained different classifiers based on different techniques, the support vector machine, the random forest, the

---

[3] The samples of BDN-based malware are obtained from Abuse.ch.

neural network, and the logistic regression. After comparing the performances of four classifiers, the best one was tested on real-world datasets. At last, the detection result was given by Leopard.

3.2   Dataset

The DNS traffic was provided by the ISP located in China. We collected 9-day traffic (from July 29 to August 6, 2019) and observed a total of 13035 IPs. The raw packets were represented by the necessary fields like time, IP, port, etc. Take the D_1[4] as an example, we elaborate on the details of data processing. The processed results are summarized in Tables 2 and 3.

Filter. Because the DNS servers also ran ODNs resolution service, we considered that DNS traffic included some suspicious ODNs. Meanwhile, compared with ODNs, it is difficult to verify whether a BDN is benign. Hence, to build benign samples, we removed ODNs which ranked after the top 5000 in the Alexa list [15]. It reduced about 68.44%–78.75% volume of daily traffic.

Aggregation. We designed an aggregation format of DNS logs. The final aggregated result is formatted as follow:

$$(domain\_name, requested\_IP) : src\_list, rdata\_set$$
$$src\_list = [(IP1, port1, time1), (IP2, port2, time2), \dots)]$$
$$rdata\_set = \{(record1, ttl1), (record2, ttl2), \dots\}$$

and where $requested\_IP$ is the destination IP of the DNS queries, $(IPi, porti, timei)$ are respectively the source IP, the source port, and the timestamp of the DNS queries, $(recordi, ttli)$ are respectively the resource records and the corresponding time-to-live (TTL) values of the DNS responses. All the packets which are related to the specific domain name and server, are formatted into one record. The schema provides a server-side view to observe the behavior of clients who have queried the domain name.

Label. We assumed the ODNs which ranked in the top 5000 in the Alexa list were benign. As for malicious BDNs, a BDN is regarded as the malicious if it satisfied any of the following conditions: (1) The domain is in the blacklist. We built up a BDN blacklist, including 169 BDNs, grounded upon the traffic of the BDN-based malware; (2) The domain is blocked by the DNS servers. We noted that some malicious BDNs were blocked by a part of DNS servers like OpenNIC[5]; (3) VirusTotal (VT) [16] has detected the domain. In a total of 13458 BDNs, 306 BDNs are blocked by the servers and 6028 BDNs are detected by VT. Unfortunately, some BDNs are still unlabeled, due to non-existent domain (NXDomain), server-failure responses and not be detected by VT.

---

[4] We named July 29 dataset as D_1, July 30 dataset as D_2, and so on.

[5] If BDNs are blocked by OpenNIC, the servers responded the A records of the special IPs such as 192.168.0.1, 0.0.0.0, 127.0.0.1, and 192.0.2.1.

Table 2. The summary of the daily datasets.

Dataset	# Packets	# Remaining Packets	# Blockchain Domains Packets	# Aggregated Records
D_1	38,258,120	10,431,757	215,095	104,132
D_2	32,269,248	9,235,243	818,722	191,564
D_3	29,418,020	8,486,445	413,467	139,957
D_4	33,177,324	8,938,011	398,898	136,488
D_5	33,195,292	10,477,746	390,216	102,825
D_6	26,940,188	7,770,275	383,729	132,534
D_7	25,767,291	6,010,492	388,978	118,139
D_8	25,370,998	6,227,078	390,026	124,657
D_9	30,977,692	6,582,441	316,279	134,590

Table 3. The datasets for training and testing.

Dataset	# Benign Records	# Malicious Records	# Aggregated Records
D_{train_val}	329,850	709	330,559
D_{test}	147,879	160	148,039
$D_{unknown}$	–	–	403

Data Supplement. Blockchain explorer[6] is a type of software which lets users browse the information of blocks using browsers like Chrome, Firefox, etc. Leveraging blockchain explorers, we found out the latest resource records of NXDomains, blocked domains and domains getting server-failure responses. Then, we updated the $rdata\_set$ of these BDNs.

In practice, we excluded the domains which were queried only once in epoch E and removed the ODNs which lacked the resource records. Then, we combined the data from the first day to the sixth day as D_{train_val}, and merged the rest of them as D_{test}. Moreover, all the unlabeled records were organized as $D_{unknown}$.

3.3 Features

After analyzing the datasets, some notable characteristics were extracted to distinguish the malicious BDNs from the benign traffic. The features can be divided into three categories: the time sequence features, the source IPs features, and the resource records features (shown in Table 4).

Time Sequence Features. When BDN-based malware do not receive commands, they only issue DNS queries in low frequency to keep in touch with C&C

---

[6] The explorer of Namecoin is https://namecha.in and the explorer of Emercoin is https://explorer.emercoin.com/nvs.

Table 4. Feature selection

Category	Feature	Feature domain	Novelty
Time Sequence	TimeDiffMin (f1)	Real	New
	TimeDiffMax (f2)	Real	New
	TimeDiffMedian (f3)	Real	New
	TimeDiffStd (f4)	Real	New
	PktNumPerMinMin (f5)	Real	New
	PktNumPerMinMax (f6)	Real	New
	PktNumPerMinMedian (f7)	Real	New
	PktNumPerMinStd (f8)	Real	New
Source IP	SrcIPNum (f9)	Integer	[27]
	ASNNum (f10)	Integer	[22]
	CountryNum (f11)	Integer	[27]
Resource Records	ARecordNum (f12)	Integer	New
	NSRecordNum (f13)	Integer	New
	TTLMin (f14)	Integer	New
	TTLMax (f15)	Integer	New
	TTLMedian(f16)	Integer	New
	TTLStd(f17)	Real	[27]

servers. In comparison, the access of benign ODNs is more consistent. To vectorize this information, we calculated the statistics of the time difference between the adjacency packets (f1–f4). Also, BDN-based malware always act simultaneously. When the BDN-based malware locate their C&C servers, the frequency of accessing malicious BDNs increases rapidly. Thus, the features (f5–f8) were considered to quantify the information.

Source IP Features. Compared with a benign ODN query, a malicious BDN query has fewer unique source IPs, and the geographical distribution of the source IPs of the malicious BDNs is limited. As such, we counted the number of the unique source IPs for each record (f9), the number of the deduplicated autonomous system numbers (ASNs) which IPs belong to (f10), and the number of the countries where IPs are located (f11).

Resource Records Features. We noted that there were some differences in resource records between common ODNs and malicious BDNs. The number of resource records of a benign ODN is usually more than the number of malicious BDN's(f12, f13). Besides, as for common ODNs, TTL values usually are set to relatively small values, because of flexibly updating business. Conversely, miscreants prefer to set longer TTLs for resource records, so malicious BDNs can cause a long time effect (f14–f17). However, the dataset is biased. TTL values of popular domains are relatively short (as later discussed in Sect. 5).

4   Evaluation

4.1   Cross-Validation on D_{train_val}

We used the scikit-learn library [19] to implement four popular classifiers including the support vector machine (SVM) with a linear kernel, the random forest, the neural network, and the L2-regularized logistic regression. Then we trained four classifiers on D_{train_val} using 5-fold cross-validation. In order to keep the dataset balanced, we randomly sampled 5000 records from benign records and mixed them with all malicious records. In each round, we randomly selected one fifth of the mixed data for validation and used the rest of them to train the models.

The metric used to evaluate the model is the area under ROC curve[7] (AUC). The x-axis of the ROC curve is the false positive rate (FPR) and the y-axis is the true positive rate (TPR). The TPR and the FPR are separately defined as $TPR = \frac{TP}{TP+FN}$, $FPR = \frac{FP}{FP+TN}$.

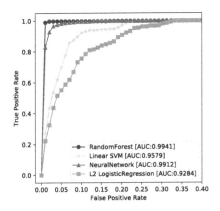

Fig. 3. ROC curves of the different classifiers based on 5-fold cross-validation.

As Fig. 3 shows, the random forest classifier outperforms the other classifiers. We noticed that the non-linear models (the random forest and the neural network) are more suitable for this problem. Meanwhile, the malicious samples account for about 12% in each round, which suggests that the random forest is good at handling the unbalanced dataset [20]. In the experiment, the number of trees used in the random forest is 370 and the maximum iterations of other classifiers are 10000. The rest of the parameters are the default configurations. In each round, the random forest reaches a TPR of 98% and the FPR is always less than 1.5%. Thus, we selected the random forest as the detection model.

---

[7] ROC curve is the receiver operating characteristic curve.

4.2 Feature Analysis

We assessed the importance of each feature through the mean decrease impurity [21] which is defined as follows:

$$MDI(X_m) = \frac{1}{N_T} \sum_{T} \sum_{t \in T : v(s_t) = X_m} p(t) \Delta f(s_t, t) \tag{1}$$

and where X_m is a feature, N_T is the number of trees, $p(t)$ is the proportion of samples reaching node t, $v(s_t)$ is the variable which is used to split s_t, and $f(s_t, t)$ is the impurity decrease measure (Gini index in our experiment). The MDIs of our features are presented in Table 5. The result proves that the selected features are effective. Also, it is worth to mention that the feature set of resource records are most important (f12–f17), accounting for six in the top seven.

Moreover, we assessed the contribution of the different feature sets which are shown in Table 4 to the TPR. We compared the performances of the random forest classifier which used different combinations of the feature sets. The baseline classifier used all the features. In Table 6, the classifier using the feature set of resource records reaches an AUC of 0.9935 and exceeds the classifiers using only the feature set of source IP and of time sequence. It also illustrates that the feature set of resource records are the most important among the three independent feature sets.

Because the classifier using the feature set of source IP performs poorly, we inspected the nine-day dataset and found that the numbers of unique source IPs in ODNs records ($\mathcal{N}_{ODN}$) vary from 1 to 339, but the proportion of the numbers which are less than 10 ($\mathcal{P}_{ODN}$) is 95.64% and the mean value of the numbers ($\mathcal{M}_{ODN}$) is 1.994. For malicious BDNs, the $\mathcal{N}_{BDN}$ range from 1 to 188, the $\mathcal{P}_{BDN}$ is 93.51% and the $\mathcal{M}_{BDN}$ is 2.185. It is obvious that unpopular ODNs accounts for a large part. Hence, the feature set of source IP is not so suitable to distinguish between malicious BDNs and benign ODNs.

Table 5. MDIs of the features.

Rank	Feature	Score	Rank	Feature	Score	Rank	Feature	Score
1	f16	0.23220529	7	f13	0.02745297	13	f7	0.01823298
2	f15	0.21952513	8	f9	0.02673914	14	f1	0.01623537
3	f14	0.21214118	9	f8	0.02664864	15	f3	0.01490099
4	f12	0.05541738	10	f11	0.02521994	16	f10	0.01249088
5	f17	0.03356060	11	f6	0.02384570	17	f5	0.00369699
6	f2	0.02831889	12	f4	0.02336793			

As for the combined feature sets, the results of the three groups are extremely close and also close to the baseline. A probability is the size of D_{train_val} is small and most of the noises have been filtered out by data processing.

Table 6. AUCs of the classifiers using the different combinations of the feature sets.

Combinations	AUC
All Features	0.9945
Time Sequence	0.8850
Source IP	0.7920
Resource Records	0.9935
Resource Records + Source IP	0.9944
Resource Records + Time Sequence	0.9944
Time Sequence + Source IP	0.9944

4.3   Evaluation on D_{test}

We evaluated Leopard on the D_{test} which simulates the real-world situation. Leopard predicted the labels of all records in the D_{test} using the trained classifier. In Fig. 4, Leopard reaches an AUC of 0.9980. When the detection rate reaches 98.125%, the FPR is 1.010%. Thus, Leopard can accurately detect malicious BDNs in the real-world network.

4.4   Evaluation on $D_{unknown}$

Some BDNs are unlabeled due to several reasons: (1) The BDN has already expired and results in the NXDomain response. (2) The server does not provide the BDNs resolution service anymore. (3) The malicious BDN is still active but has not been discovered by vendors like VT.

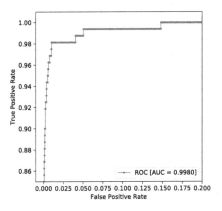

Fig. 4. The AUC of Leopard on D_{test}.

In order to identify unknown malicious BDNs, we trained the classifier on the whole nine-day dataset. The trained classifier predicted the labels of the records in $D_{unknown}$ and reported 309 malicious records out of 403.

To verify the results, we considered a series of rules: (1) Any of the historical IPs of the BDN is malicious. (2) Any of the client IPs of the BDN is compromised. (3) Any threat intelligence related to the BDN exists. If a BDN satisfies one of them, we deemed it is malicious. We manually verified the IPs leveraging VT and searched the threat intelligence using Google. All the reported records were verified as malicious and the 309 records included 286 unique BDNs and 23 server IPs. However, it is strange that 271 BDNs which come from 87.98.175.85 are meaningless and look like randomly generated. The rest 15 BDNs are readable (presented in Table 7). Besides, all the BDNs from 87.98.175.85 are the NXDomains, even not existed on the blockchains. We believe that cybercriminals may try to combine the domain generation algorithm (DGA) technique with BDNs. Leveraging DGArchive [29], we confirmed that BDNs from 87.98.175.85 were generated by Necurs [30]. It suggests that Necurs is the known DGA family that combines DGA technique with BDNs.

Table 7. Examples of the malicious BDNs.

BDNs from 87.98.175.85	BDNs from the other IPs
bafometh.bit	goshan.bit
nenhqlbxxiewmflyckqa.bit	thereis.null
gkgyrwtocxrkrixcxou.bit	log.null
jjffpcvbsyayrluwidxo.bit	ali2.null
lcqpwfvim.bit	systemblink.bit

Besides, we found that most of the server IPs were located in Internet Data Centers (IDC) (22 out of 23), which implied that most of the DNS servers were virtual private servers (VPS). There are eight servers belong to AS37963 which is operated by CNNICALIBABA-CN-NET-AP Hangzhou Alibaba Advertising Co., Ltd., CN. It illustrates that virtual private servers of companies like Alibaba are becoming vital infrastructures of botnets.

5   Discussion

Although Leopard has great performances in the experiments, the limitations of the system still exist.

Leopard is designed for BDN-based malware. If the malware adopts other techniques more than BDNs (e.g., the combination of BDNs and DGA), Leopard may fail the detection. However, this upgrade of malware will increase the attacker's development cost. In response, we adopt the existing methods [2,4], to complement the shortage of Leopard. Besides, an attacker who knows the features we used to detect malicious BDNs, changes the strategies like sending DNS queries in batches or spreading malware to a wider range of IP addresses, to bypass the system. However, it will increase the operational difficulty of BDN-based malware. Furthermore, adding the resource records of malicious BDNs is a low-cost way to evade the detection of Leopard. For instance, an attacker adds the A record pointing to the backup C&C server or the NS record pointing to other DNS servers, and the corresponding TTLs are set to short values. Although Leopard might fail to detect it, meanwhile, it risks their backup C&C servers and the innocent accomplices. In short, evading detection requires the meticulous adjustment to simulate the behavior of benign ODNs, while the side-effects are inevitable.

Also, the dataset we used is biased. We just randomly sampled 5000 records from benign records corresponding to domains listed in Alexa top 5000. TTL values of popular domains (Alexa top 5000) are short but in general the TTLs in use range from as short as 5 min to one or two days for common domains [28]. The data processing and experiments need to be improved in the future.

Besides, lacking valid methods to label benign BDNs, we failed to collect benign BDNs which should be very important samples and did not know how many benign BDNs were active. Thus, it is unwise to filter out all domains using TLDs that are not ICANN approved or filter all DNS packets that were sent to the local resolver. Next, it is significant to collect benign BDNs to comprehensively observe the current situation of BDN.

Leopard does not consider the features of domain name strings, merely depending on the behavior of DNS traffic and the information of resource records. If the features of other types of malicious domains are similar to the features of BDNs, they may be detected by Leopard as well.

Unfortunately, the performance of Leopard mainly depends on the training data, but the high-quality DNS traffic of BDNs is in shortage, which may weaken the ability of Leopard. It is still a challenge that collecting the large volume of the BDN traffic over the world. According to the NS-list, the DNS servers are scattered and most of them are the virtual private servers of the different companies. We deem that the survey on the passive DNS resources (e.g., Farsight PDNS sharing program) of the different organizations is worth try.

6 Related Work

A wealth of researches has been conducted on detecting malware and malicious domains. Some works focus on the error information (e.g., NXDomain and HTTP errors) generated by malware [2,12,24], and others concentrate on DNS traffic analysis [13,22,23]. Gu et al. detected botnets based on the clustering analysis of network traffic of the bots [11] and Prasse et al. detected the HTTPS traffic of malware communication [25]. However, there are few prior works related to BDNs. Patsakis et al. discussed the threats of BDNS and mentioned that BDNS provided botnets with a more stealthy way of C&C communication [31], but did not propose a specific method to detect them. Then, the approaches that are similar to Leopard will be discussed.

Pleiades, FANCI. Antonakakis et al. [2] noted that most of the DGA-generated domains would result in NXDomain responses and designed a DGA detection system named *Pleiades*. *Pleiades* can detect known and unknown DGAs. Compared with *Pleiades*, *FANCI* does not require tracking of DNS responses for feature extraction and more efficient than *Pleiades*. In addition, *FANCI* was evaluated on the malicious data generated by 59 DGAs.

Error-Sensor. *Error-Sensor* exploits the error intelligence of HTTP when malware fails to communicate with C&C servers. It can detect both compromised servers and malicious servers, with a high detection rate (99.79%) and a low false positive (0.005%) on the real-world enterprise network.

HTTPS-Based Method, BotMiner. Prasse et al. [25] proposed a detection method of malware based on the analysis of HTTPS traffic. Leveraging the features of domain names and packet heads, the system achieved a great result on the collected dataset. However, this method is limited to the specific protocol. *BotMiner* [11] can detect botnets on the campus network and it is a protocol- and structure- independent detection. Compared with the HTTPS-based method, *BotMiner* has greater generalizability.

7 Conclusion

In this paper, we analyze the working mechanism of the BDN-based malware and are the first to propose an automatic detection of malicious BDNs. Leopard identifies malicious BDNs based on the features of DNS traffic and resource records using the random forest. It distinguishes between malicious BDNs and domains from the Alexa top 5000. In the experiments, we compared the performances of the different classifiers and accessed the importance of the features. Moreover, Leopard has been evaluated on the real-world dataset. The experimental results showed that Leopard can effectively detect malicious BDNs and discover unknown malicious BDNs. Last but not least, we published two datasets: (1) The malicious BDNs which manually labeled by us or identified by Leopard. (2) The list of DNS servers which provide the BDNs resolution service.

Acknowledgments. We would like to thank the anonymous reviewers for their insightful comments and suggestions on this paper. We are grateful for Roman Huessy from Abuse.ch sharing the malware samples. This work is supported by the National Key Research and Development Program of China under Grant No. 2016QY05X1002 and No. 2018YFB0804702.

References

1. Namecoin Homepage. https://namecoin.org/dot-bit/. Accessed 23 Oct 2019
2. Antonakakis, M., et al.: From throw-away traffic to bots: detecting the rise of DGA-based malware. In: Proceedings of the 21st USENIX Conference on Security Symposium (2012)

3. Plohmann, D., Yakdan, K., Klatt, M., Bader, J.: A comprehensive measurement study of domain generating malware. In: Proceedings of the 25th USENIX Conference on Security Symposium (2016)
4. Anderson, H.S., Woodbridge, J., Filar, B.: DeepDGA: adversarially-tuned domain generation and detection. (2016). http://arxiv.org/abs/1610.01969
5. How the Rise of Cryptocurrencies Is Shaping the Cyber Crime Landscape: Blockchain Infrastructure Use. https://www.fireeye.com/blog/threat-research/2018/04/cryptocurrencies-cyber-crime-blockchain-infrastructure-use.html. Accessed 23 Oct 2019
6. Bitcoin Domains. https://www.trendmicro.de/cloud-content/us/pdfs/security-intelligence/white-papers/wp-bitcoin-domains.pdf. Accessed 23 Oct 2019
7. Abuse.ch Homepage. https://abuse.ch/. Accessed 23 Oct 2019
8. ThreatBook Cloud Sandbox Homepage. https://s.threatbook.cn. Accessed 23 Oct 2019
9. Dig Homepage. https://linux.die.net/man/1/dig. Accessed 23 Oct 2019
10. BitName Homepage. https://bitname.ru/index.php?lang=en. Accessed 23 Oct 2019
11. Gu, G., Perdisci, R., Zhang, J., Lee W.: BotMiner: clustering analysis of network traffic for protocol- and structure-independent botnet detection. In: Proceedings of the 15th Annual Network and Distributed System Security Symposium (2008)
12. Zhang, J., Jang, J., Gu, G., Stoecklin, M.P., Hu, X.: Error-sensor: mining information from HTTP error traffic for malware intelligence. In: Bailey, M., Holz, T., Stamatogiannakis, M., Ioannidis, S. (eds.) RAID 2018. LNCS, vol. 11050, pp. 467–489. Springer, Cham (2018). https://doi.org/10.1007/978-3-030-00470-5_22
13. Wang, T.S., Lin, H.T., Cheng, W.T., Chen, C.Y.: DBod: clustering and detecting DGA-based botnets using DNS traffic analysis. Comput. Secur. **64**, 1–15 (2017)
14. .Bit-The Next Generation of Bulletproof Hosting. https://abuse.ch/blog/dot-bit-the-next-generation-of-bulletproof-hosting/. Accessed 23 Oct 2019
15. Alexa Top Sites Homepage. https://www.alexa.com/topsites. Accessed 23 Oct 2019
16. VirusTotal Homepage. https://www.virustotal.com/. Accessed 23 Oct 2019
17. Namecoin Homepage. https://www.namecoin.org. Accessed 23 Oct 2019
18. Emercoin Homepage. https://emercoin.com/en. Accessed 23 Oct 2019
19. Scikit-Learn Homepage. https://scikit-learn.org/stable/. Accessed 23 Oct 2019
20. Random Forests. https://www.stat.berkeley.edu/~breiman/RandomForests/cc_home.htm. Accessed 23 Oct 2019
21. Breiman, L., Friedman, J., Stone, C.J., Olshen, R.A.: Classification and Regression Trees. CRC Press, Boca Raton (1984)
22. Antonakakis, M., Perdisci, R., Dagon, D., Lee, W., Feamster, N.: Building a dynamic reputation system for DNS. In: Proceedings of the 19th USENIX Conference on Security (2010)
23. Antonakakis, M., Perdisci, R., Lee, W., Vasiloglou, N., Dagon, D.: Detecting malware domains at the upper DNS hierarchy. In: Proceedings of the 19th USENIX Conference on Security (2011)
24. Schüppen, S., Teubert, D., Herrmann, P., Meyer, U.: FANCI: feature-based automated NXDomain classification and intelligence. In: Proceedings of the 27th USENIX Security Symposium (2018)
25. Prasse, P., Machlica, L., Pevny, T., Havelka, J., Scheffer, T.: Malware detection by analysing network traffic with neural networks. In: Proceedings of IEEE Security and Privacy Workshops (2017)

26. The Explorer Page of Blockchain-DNS.info. https://blockchain-dns.info/explorer/. Accessed 28 Oct 2019
27. Bilge, L., Kirda, E., Kruegel, C., Balduzzi M.: EXPOSURE: finding malicious domains using passive DNS analysis. In: Proceedings of the 18th Annual Network and Distributed System Security Symposium (2011)
28. Moura, G.C.M., Heidemann, J.S., Schmidt, R.O., Hardaker W.: Cache me if you can: effects of DNS time-to-live. In: Proceedings of Internet Measurement Conference (2019)
29. DGArchive. https://dgarchive.caad.fkie.fraunhofer.de/site/. Accessed 25 Jan 2020
30. Necurs botnet. https://en.wikipedia.org/wiki/Necurs_botnet. Last accessed 24 Jan 2020
31. Patsakis, C., Casino, F., Lykousas, N., Katos, V.: Unravelling Ariadne's thread: exploring the threats of decentalised DNS. arXiv:1912.03552v1 (2019)

To Filter or Not to Filter: Measuring the Benefits of Registering in the RPKI Today

Cecilia Testart[1]([✉]), Philipp Richter[1], Alistair King[2], Alberto Dainotti[2], and David Clark[1]

[1] MIT, Cambridge, USA
{ctestart,richterp,ddc}@csail.mit.edu
[2] CAIDA, UC San Diego, San Diego, USA
{alistair,alberto}@caida.org

Abstract. Securing the Internet's inter-domain routing system against illicit prefix advertisements by third-party networks remains a great concern for the research, standardization, and operator communities. After many unsuccessful attempts to deploy additional security mechanisms for BGP, we now witness increasing adoption of the RPKI (Resource Public Key Infrastructure). Backed by strong cryptography, the RPKI allows network operators to register their BGP prefixes together with the legitimate Autonomous System (AS) number that may originate them via BGP. Recent research shows an encouraging trend: an increasing number of networks around the globe start to register their prefixes in the RPKI. While encouraging, the actual *benefit* of registering prefixes in the RPKI eventually depends on whether transit providers in the Internet enforce the RPKI's content, *i.e.,* configure their routers to validate prefix announcements and *filter* invalid BGP announcements. In this work, we present a broad empirical study tackling the question: To what degree does registration in the RPKI protect a network from illicit announcements of their prefixes, such as prefix hijacks? To this end, we first present a longitudinal study of filtering behavior of transit providers in the Internet, and second we carry out a detailed study of the visibility of legitimate and illegitimate prefix announcements in the global routing table, contrasting prefixes registered in the RPKI with those not registered. We find that an increasing number of transit and access providers indeed do enforce RPKI filtering, which translates to a direct benefit for the networks using the RPKI in the case of illicit announcements of their address space. Our findings bode well for further RPKI adoption and for increasing routing security in the Internet.

Keywords: Internet security · Routing · RPKI · BGP

1 Introduction

The inter-domain routing system of the Internet continues to suffer from major routing incidents, including accidental route leaks causing widespread

© Springer Nature Switzerland AG 2020
A. Sperotto et al. (Eds.): PAM 2020, LNCS 12048, pp. 71–87, 2020.
https://doi.org/10.1007/978-3-030-44081-7_5

disruptions [28], and intentional prefix hijacks for malicious purposes [8,14,29]. At the heart of the problem lies BGP's lack of mechanisms for route authentication: a network that receives a route advertisement from a neighbor has no easy means to validate its correctness. The RPKI [20] represents one of the most recent attempts to increase BGP security, providing networks in the Internet with a trustworthy database that maps BGP prefixes to the Autonomous System (AS) number that is authorized to originate them. The RPKI is backed by strong cryptography, with the Regional Internet Registries (RIRs) serving as trust anchors. Networks can leverage this data to validate that incoming BGP announcements point to the correct origin AS. Recent research shows an encouraging trend of both increasing global registration of prefixes in the RPKI (17% of routed prefixes are registered in the RPKI as of September 2019), as well as increasing data quality of actual RPKI records [11]. The RPKI has thus the potential to finally provide a universally trusted route origins database, a major building block to greatly improve routing security.

While encouraging, we point out that increasing registration of prefixes in the RPKI only represents a first step towards securing BGP. The eventual benefit of RPKI registration depends on whether the networks of the Internet enforce the RPKI's contents, *i.e.,* drop invalid announcements and hence do not propagate them to their neighbors. Recently, AT&T, a major transit ISP, publicly announced that they started filtering BGP announcements that are invalid as per the RPKI [2], suggesting increasing acceptance and trust by major transit providers in the RPKI. However, besides such anecdotal evidence, we know little about current levels of RPKI *enforcement* in the Internet and, as of today, have no way to assess the resulting benefits of RPKI registration.

To tackle these questions, we empirically study to what degree networks in the Internet filter BGP announcements based on RPKI validation and show to what extent registration in the RPKI benefits networks in situations in which RPKI is needed the most: instances of conflicting prefix announcements in the global routing table, such as those caused by misconfiguration and prefix hijacking. Our key contributions are as follows:

- Leveraging historical snapshots of the global routing table and validated RPKI records, we develop a passive method to detect filtering of RPKI invalid prefixes for IPv4 and IPv6 and study filtering deployment over time. While RPKI filtering was virtually nonexistent just two years ago, RPKI enforcement has increased substantially: we found that—as of January 2020—approximately 10% of the networks we considered, including major transit providers, filter invalid announcements.
- We study the effect of RPKI filtering on global prefix reachability in the case of conflicting announcements: Multiple-Origin AS (MOAS) conflicts, and sub-prefix announcements, contrasting our findings with a baseline of non-RPKI-registered prefixes. We find that, already as of today, RPKI filtering starts to show effect in real-world cases: in all considered scenarios, registration of prefixes in the RPKI results in limited reachability of conflicting and invalid (potentially illicit) prefix announcements in the global routing table.

Our findings are encouraging for the research, standardization, and operator communities. Increasing RPKI *enforcement* starts to translate to a direct benefit for a network registering its prefixes. Our results bode well for increasing routing security in the Internet, and our metrics allow for easy assessment of current levels of filtering and the resulting benefit in conflicting-announcement scenarios. Our study is entirely based on publicly available datasets, allowing both for reproducibility, and for continuous monitoring.

2   Background and Datasets

2.1   Related Work

The IETF has devoted substantial efforts to develop, and document in detail, the RPKI over the last years [9,15–17,19–21,24]. Recently, the research community started to measure RPKI deployment in the Internet. Chung *et al.* provide both an accessible overview of today's RPKI deployment and an extensive study of RPKI registration and usage patterns. They find increasing registration of prefixes and networks in the RPKI, and overall higher data quality of RPKI records, resulting in lower numbers of RPKI-invalid prefixes caused by misconfiguration by the respective operators [11]. Iamartino *et al.* had previously measured problems with RPKI registered ROAs and the potential impact that validation and filtering of RPKI-invalid announcements could have in production [18].

To the best of our knowledge, only two previous academic studies, using two different methods, touched upon the adoption of RPKI-invalid filtering, finding only negligible RPKI filtering in 2016 and 2017. Gilad *et al.* analyze a month of BGP RIB dumps from 44 ASes [13]. Their passive approach uses all the ASes but the last hop in the AS path of RPKI-valid and -invalid announcements to identify ASes filtering invalid announcements. They find that, in July 2016, only 3 of the top 100 ASes (by customer cone size) were enforcing RPKI-invalid filtering. Reuter *et al.* instead, actively advertise RPKI-valid and -invalid prefixes of address space under their control [26]. They infer which ASes filter RPKI-invalid announcements based on the propagation path of their announcements, finding only 3 ASes filtering in 2017. Measuring RPKI filtering also caught attention from the operator community: Cartwright-Cox uses active measurements to infer filtering based on presence or absence of ICMP responses from probed IP addresses in RPKI-valid and -invalid prefixes [10].

Our study complements and extends prior work: our passive method to detect filtering of RPKI-invalid announcement focuses on networks that provide a direct and full feed to BGP collectors, which allows for definitive and detailed assessment of RPKI filtering of these networks. Our study is longitudinal, revealing a strong uptake in RPKI filtering deployment in recent years. Most importantly, however, we present a first-of-its-kind assessment of RPKI enforcement and its actual impact and benefit in situations in which the RPKI is needed the most: instances of conflicting prefix announcements in the global routing table.

2.2   RPKI and BGP Datasets

To study the visibility of RPKI-valid and RPKI-invalid announcements in the global routing table, we leverage the following datasets.

Longitudinal BGP Dataset: To study long-term trends of RPKI filtering behavior, we download and process—using CAIDA BGPStream [25]—snapshots of the routing tables (RIB dumps) of all RouteViews and RIPE RIS collectors on the first day of each month[1] from April 1, 2017 until January 22, 2020.

Fine-Grained BGP Dataset: To assess the visibility of RPKI-invalid announcements in detail, we process all the BGP updates generated over the month of September 2019 by RouteViews and RIPE RIS collector peers' and we compute 5-min snapshots of their routing tables using CAIDA BGPStream [25].

RPKI Data: We take daily snapshots of validated Route Origin Authorizations (ROAs) for every day in September 2019, made available through the RIPE NCC RPKI validator [5]. For longitudinal analysis, we instead leverage the historical dataset of validated ROAs made publicly available by Chung *et al.* [11], selecting snapshots that align with our BGP dataset. A validated ROA consists of a prefix and the AS number authorized to originate that prefix in BGP according to cryptographically signed records in the RPKI. ROAs may include a *maxLen* attribute specifying up to which prefix length the de-aggregation of the ROA prefix is to be considered valid.

2.3   Preprocessing

From BGP Snapshots to Prefix-Origin Pairs: As a first step, we remove *bogon* prefixes from our BGP dataset, these include IETF reserved address space, and portions of address space not allocated by IANA to RIRs [3]. We further remove any IPv4 prefixes more specific than /24 or less specific than /8 (more specific than /64 or less specific than /8 for IPv6). Then we extract, for each BGP snapshot (both RIB dumps and those we derive from updates), all visible prefixes together with the advertised origin AS, obtaining *prefix-origin pairs.*[2] For each prefix-origin pair, we save the set of *feeders*—that is, ASes that directly peer with any of the RouteViews and RIPE RIS route collectors—that have a route to the given prefix-origin in their routing table. In the following, we will leverage the set of feeders to assess filtering and to estimate visibility of prefix-origin pairs in the global routing table.

Tagging Prefix-Origin Pairs: We next tag each individual prefix-origin pair in our dataset with its corresponding RPKI state. For each prefix-origin pair, we find the closest snapshot available of validated ROAs and tag the prefix-origin pair with one of the following states: *(i) unknown*: the prefix is not covered by

---

[1] Or the closest day for which validated historical RPKI data is available.

[2] Note that a prefix can have multiple origins in the global routing table, in this case we extract multiple prefix-origin pairs.

any prefix of validated ROAs in the RPKI; *(ii) valid:* the prefix is covered by a validated ROA, the AS number in BGP matches the one in the ROA, and the prefix length in BGP is at most the maxLen attribute of the ROA; *(iii) invalid ASN:* the prefix is covered by a validated ROA, but the origin AS in BGP does not match the origin AS in any ROA covering the prefix; *(iv) invalid length:* the prefix is covered by a validated ROA, the origin AS in BGP matches the origin AS in the ROA, but the prefix length in BGP is longer than the maxLen attribute, *i.e.,* the prefix is more specific than what is allowed as per the ROA.

3   To Filter or Not to Filter: Longitudinal Study

In this section, we provide a macroscopic perspective on RPKI filtering deployment in today's Internet. In particular, we study to which extent some of the transit networks in the Internet do filter BGP announcements with invalid RPKI state and how this filtering behavior evolved over time.

3.1   Detecting Filtering

While there is no practical way to comprehensively study filtering behavior of all networks, we introduce a method to infer RPKI filtering with high confidence for a small but relevant set of ASes. At a high-level, our method is made of two steps: *(i)* we select *full-feeder* ASes, *i.e.,* ASes that share with BGP collectors a number of routes (and thus prefix-origin pairs) comparable to what is globally visible in BGP—in other words, they tend to share the vast majority of, if not all, their preferred routes; *(ii)* we leverage our set of RPKI-invalid prefix-origin pairs to look for significant presence/absence of them in what full-feeders share.

The essence of this approach is to look for statistically significant absence of RPKI-invalid prefix-origin pairs: *e.g.,* the absence of a single invalid pair in the routes shared by a full-feeder is not a strong indication of RPKI-based filtering; similarly, the absence of a large number of invalid pairs in a shared routing table that is already missing many other valid routes (*i.e.,* from a *partial-feeder*) is not a strong indication of RPKI-based filtering either. The combination of the two factors instead, provides a high degree of confidence. In Sect. 3.3, we validate our method for a few ASes that have publicly stated when they started applying RPKI-based filtering. In detail, we operate as follows.

(i) **Selecting full-feeders:** We consider a collector's peer a *full-feeder* if the number of prefix-origin pairs shared by that AS is at least 75% of the maximum prefix-origin pair count sent by all feeders. We perform our analysis for IPv4 and IPv6 independently. In Fig. 1a, the orange line shows this threshold for IPv4 in September 2019: out of 578 ASes peering with the collectors, we consider 276 to be full-feeders for IPv4 (232 for IPv6, see the Appendix). We chose 75%, since it separates recent and historical snapshots well.

(ii) **Detecting filtering of RPKI-invalid announcements:** From the set of full-feeder ASes, we infer an AS to be filtering RPKI-invalid announcements if the number of RPKI-invalid prefix-origin pairs received from that AS is less than 20% of the maximum number of invalid records sent by all full-feeders. Here, we leave some leeway, since previous research [26] has shown that, even if ASes are filtering *most* RPKI-invalid announcements, they usually never filter *all* invalid announcements due to churn in RPKI records and selective filtering (*cf.* Sect. 3.3). The green dashed line in Fig. 1a, shows this threshold for IPv4, we infer 21 ASes were filtering RPKI-invalids announcements in September 2019.

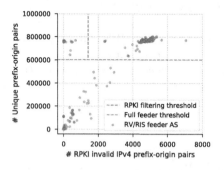 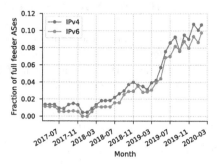

(a) Count of RPKI-invalid prefix-origin pairs and total count of prefix-origin pairs by feeder AS to BGP collectors on Sept. 1st, 2019. We infer the group on the upper left corner is filtering RPKI-invalid announcements.

(b) Fraction of RouteViews and RIPE RIS collector full-feeder ASes filtering RPKI-invalid announcements over time. A major increase happens between April and August 2019.

Fig. 1. Full-feeder ASes filtering of RPKI-invalid announcements.

The representativeness of our approach is limited by the comparably small number of full-feeder ASes: 290 ASes for IPv4 and 246 ASes for IPv6 in January 2020. However, we find that these networks include many global transit providers and mid-sized networks: 187 transit and access ASes (of which 12 are Tier-1 ASes), 36 content providers, and 47 educational/non-profit networks, according to PeeringDB [4]. In total there are 36 ASes in the top 100 CAIDA AS rank and 93 in the top 1,000. This set of ASes thus provides a reasonable approximation to study macroscopic filtering trends of major networks in the Internet.

3.2 Filtering Networks: Longitudinal Trends and Current Status

With our method in hand, we now present a longitudinal analysis of RPKI-invalid filtering behavior. Figure 1b shows the evolution of the fraction of full-feeder ASes that filter RPKI-invalid announcements for IPv4 and IPv6. Both protocols follow a similar trend, with slightly fewer ASes filtering RPKI-invalid IPv6 announcements compared to IPv4. We detect that in April 2017, less than

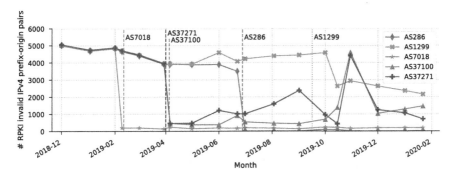

Fig. 2. RPKI-invalid IPv4 prefix-origin pairs from networks that publicly announced RPKI filtering deployment, vertical lines show the announcement date of deployment completion (dashed) or beginning of deployment (dotted).

2% full-feeders were filtering RPKI invalid announcements: 3 out of 219 full-feeder ASes for IPv4 and 2 out of 176 for IPv6. We witness overall low levels of RPKI filtering until April 2018, when a few full-feeder ASes start to filter each month, reaching about 3% one year later in March 2019. From April until August 2019, we see a 3-fold increase in the rate of RPKI filtering adoption. In late January 2020, 11% of full-feeder ASes filter RPKI-invalid announcements in IPv4 and 10% in IPv6, 30 out of 290 and 23 out of 246 respectively.

The bulk of the networks filtering RPKI-invalid announcements are either transit or access network providers (17 ASes, 9% of such networks) or educational-research/non-profit networks (9 ASes, 19% of such networks). We find lower levels of filtering deployment in larger networks: only 2 of the 36 full-feeder ASes in the top 100 CAIDA AS Rank do filter invalid prefix-origins and 10 out of the 93 ASes in the top 1,000 CAIDA AS Rank filter. We only find one out of 36 content providers filtering invalid prefix-origins. RIPE, ARIN and APNIC are the regions with most full-feeder ASes, and we find 22, 5, 1 filtering ASes, representing 13%, 8% and 3% of full-feeders ASes from these regions respectively.

3.3 A Closer Look at Filtering Networks

Comparison with Public Announcements of RPKI Filtering: Five transit ISPs that provide direct and full BGP feeds to one of our considered collectors have publicly stated that they have deployed or are currently deploying RPKI-invalid filtering: AT&T (AS7018), KPN (AS286), Seacom (AS37100), Workonline Communications (AS37271) and Telia (AS1299) [1,2,6,7]. Figure 2 shows the count of invalid prefix-origin pairs propagated by these five ASes during 2019, annotated with their public announcement date of filtering implementation.

In our data, we see over 4,000 invalid prefix-origins from all networks in early 2019. In mid February 2019, AT&T publicly stated that they started filtering

RPKI-invalid route announcements and afterwards we only detect a few hundred invalid prefix-origins sent to collectors by AT&T. In early April 2019, two major African ISPs, Workonline Communication and Seacom, announced completion of deployment of RPKI filtering, after which we observe only several hundred invalid prefix-origins from these two networks. However, these ASes have encountered operational issues when deploying RPKI filtering and have (partially) stopped filtering for some periods of time, see intermittent upticks [22].

In late June 2019, KPN announced completion of deployment of RPKI-filtering and has only propagated a few dozen invalid prefix-origins to collectors since. Finally, in mid September 2019, Telia announced that it began to deploy RPKI filtering. Shortly after their announcement, we detect a continual decline in the number of invalid prefix-origins forwarded by Telia. However, since RPKI enforcement deployment is not finished at the time of this writing, we still see over 2,000 invalid prefix-origins from Telia in early 2020, hence not meeting our detection thresholds yet. Our method detected RPKI-invalid filtering after all announcements of completion of full deployment of RPKI filtering.

Partial RPKI Filtering: In our longitudinal study, no full-feeder network ever filters *all* RPKI-invalid announcements. Besides some expected short-term churn, *e.g.*, caused by delays when updating filtering rules, we identified 3 main reasons for persistent partial RPKI filtering: *(i)* selective RPKI Trust Anchor (TA) filtering: we find 6 networks not validating ROAs from the ARIN TA, resulting in a higher share of propagated invalid prefix-origins. Indeed, legal barriers limiting availability of ARIN ROAs have been reported [30]. *(ii)* Selective filtering depending on AS relationships: several network operators announced to implement filtering only for routes received from peers, but not customer networks [2]. *(iii)* Operational deployment issues: network operators reported compatibility issues with RPKI validator implementations and router software, prompting them to deploy RPKI-filtering in a subset of their border routers [22].

4   RPKI to the Rescue: Conflicting Announcements

Our findings of increasing deployment of RPKI filtering in the recent years motivate us to study the effect of filtering in more detail. We first introduce how we process our dataset to allow for analysis of visibility of individual routing events and study the overall visibility of valid/invalid prefixes. Next, we showcase several relevant real-world case studies of conflicting, and hence potentially malicious, prefix announcements. Visibility of a prefix in the global routing table translates directly into its *reachability*, and thus serves as a proxy to study the benefit of RPKI filtering in the wild. In this section, we present our findings for IPv4. Our findings for IPv6 are similar and can be found in the Appendix.

4.1   Tracking Visibility in the Global Routing Table

Aggregating Prefix-Origin Snapshots into *Timelines*: To study the visibility of RPKI-registered prefixes, we leverage our fine-grained BGP dataset,

Table 1. Properties of our IPv4 prefix-origin timelines and their respective RPKI validity states (September 2019).

Prefix-origin timelines	Count	%
IPv4 total	883,400	100%
RPKI covered	147,870	16.7%
RPKI-valid	139,537	15.8%
RPKI-invalid ASN	4,203	0.47%
RPKI-invalid length	4,130	0.46%

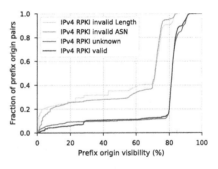

Fig. 3. CDF of IPv4 prefix-origin pairs by visibility during September 2019 for different RPKI states. (Color figure online)

consisting of per-feeder snapshots of all prefix-origin pairs every 5 min in September 2019 (*cf.* Sect. 2.2). As a first step, we aggregate adjacent prefix-origin pairs into continuous *timelines*. We require *(i)* that the maximum deviation in visibility within each timeline is less than 10%, otherwise we terminate the timeline and start a new one. We express visibility of a prefix-origin pair timeline as the fraction of active feeder ASes that propagate a route to given prefix and origin AS. Secondly, *(ii)* we require consistent RPKI state (valid/invalid ASN/invalid length/unknown) for each prefix-origin timeline.[3] The resulting timelines consist of a tuple of a prefix, an origin AS, a visibility level, its RPKI state, and timestamps. We filter prefix-origin timelines with a private AS number or AS-Set as origin, and prefix-origin timelines with very low visibility, *i.e.,* seen by 3 or fewer peers, since such very low visibility prefixes are unlikely to represent actual events in the global routing table. Table 1 shows the properties of our resulting dataset.

Overall Prefix-Origin Visibility by RPKI State: Figure 3 shows CDFs of the visibility of prefix-origin timelines, expressed as percentage of active feeder ASes seeing a prefix-origin. Overall, we find that RPKI-valid as well as RPKI-unknown prefix-origins (*i.e.,* prefixes not covered by validated ROAs) show similar visibility levels, with 80% of all prefix-origins seen by 80% or more of feeder ASes (see green and blue lines). RPKI invalid prefix-origins, however, show vastly different visibility: some 20% of these prefix-origins are very localized announcements (seen by less than 5% of feeder ASes, see orange and red lines), and we speculate that these cases are instances of misconfigurations, whether in BGP or RPKI records, which happen to also show up as RPKI-invalid artifacts. More importantly, we find that even invalid prefix-origins with higher visibility show distinctively lower visibility when compared to valid prefix-origins (see concentration of RPKI-invalid at around 70%, compared to over 80% for RPKI-valid).

---

[3] For 0.37% IPv4 prefix-origin timelines, the RPKI state changed due to churn in the RPKI database caused by changes of RPKI entries during our measurement window. We remove these instances.

This difference in prefix-origin propagation is the direct result of filtering of RPKI-invalid announcements.

4.2 Conflicting Prefix Announcement Scenarios

Next, we study *RPKI in action, i.e.,* we want to understand if registration in the RPKI benefits networks in cases of conflicting announcements. In particular, we cover 3 scenarios: *(i)* Multiple Origin AS (MOAS) announcements: instances where two equal prefixes are announced with two different origins, often caused by intentional or unintentional prefix hijacks; *(ii)* subMOAS announcements: instances where an announcement of a more specific prefix points to a different origin AS, also a potential prefix hijack scenario; *(iii)* same-origin subprefixes, instances where a more specific prefix is visible, points to the same origin AS as its parent, but fails RPKI validation due to max length restrictions. This scenario is what we would expect to see in the case of a path hijack, the most advanced form of prefix hijacks [27]. We note that in this work, we do not attempt to classify instances of conflicting prefix announcements into malicious activity vs. misconfigurations. Instead, we base our notion of illicit announcements on the RPKI state of the involved prefixes: if two prefix announcements are in conflict, and only one of them passes RPKI validation, in our analysis we treat the invalid one as if it is an illicit announcement (while it might also be due to incorrect/unissued ROAs). Our argument here is that, irrespective of the root cause of these conflicts, we can study the effectiveness of RPKI filtering under the same conditions that would also hold when a malicious actor injects BGP prefixes to hijack address space.

4.3 Visibility of Multiple Origin as (MOAS) Prefixes

To study the visibility of prefixes that are concurrently originated by multiple origin ASes, we first isolate our prefix-origin timelines that show *(i)* two origin ASes for the same prefix and *(ii)* one of these prefix-origins is registered in the RPKI and valid. In total, we find about 90,000 instances of MOAS prefix-origin pairs in September 2019 for IPv4, of which some 10% are cases in which at least one prefix-origin is RPKI-valid, while others are not. Of these cases, about 20% (N = 1898) are cases of exactly 2 MOAS prefix-origin pairs one valid and the other invalid according to RPKI records.

Figure 4 shows the distribution of the maximum visibility of prefix-origin timelines during MOAS conflicts of two prefix-origin pairs, where we partition RPKI-valid and -invalid state, see positive y-dimension in Fig. 4. We see a stark difference: RPKI-valid prefixes clearly dominate visibility, with more than 70% of valid prefixes having visibility greater than 70%, and we only see few instances of RPKI-valid prefixes with low visibility (only 12% of instances with less than 30% visibility). Their invalid counterparts, on the other hand, show distinctively lower visibility: some 60% have a visibility level lower than 30%. Some invalid prefixes do reach substantial visibility levels, but we do point out that even those higher-visibility invalid prefixes cluster at around ≈65%, that is, significantly lower when compared to valid prefixes, which cluster at around ≈80%. These results are consistent with our expectations: the RPKI benefit should be significant in instances of exact MOAS conflicts, since two prefixes compete for reachability in the global routing table, and even when RPKI filtering is not enforced, some routers still give preference to RPKI-valid announcements over RPKI-invalid announcements as part of the route selection process (discarding an invalid route only if a valid one is available) [12].

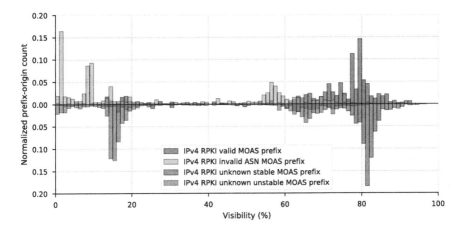

Fig. 4. Visibility of prefix-origin pairs during MOAS conflicts: RPKI-valid and invalid ASN MOAS prefix pairs in the positive y-dimension, RPKI-unknown MOAS prefix pairs in the negative y-dimension, partitioned as stable/unstable according to total advertisement time during September 2019.

To assess the potential benefit of registering a prefix in the RPKI vs. not registering it, we next compare the above studied instances of MOAS conflicts in which the concerning prefix is registered in the RPKI against vanilla cases of MOAS, in which the concerning prefix is not registered, and hence both prefix-origins are of type RPKI-unknown. Here, in the absence of RPKI information, we face the difficult problem of determining which of the conflicting announcements represents the legitimate announcement vs. the illicit one. Taking a pragmatic approach, we leverage stability of announcements as a proxy: In the case of a MOAS conflict where neither prefix-origin is registered in the RPKI, we tag the prefix-origin that was visible for a longer period of time as *stable*, and the conflicting prefix-origin that was visible for a shorter period of time as *unstable*. We pick only MOAS cases where the stable prefix-origin is announced for a period at least 3 times longer[4] than the unstable prefix-origin counterpart ($N = 6{,}374$ MOAS events for IPv4). We acknowledge that this heuristic is not a hard-and-fast rule, since there are many potential root causes for unstable announcements

---

[4] We tested different thresholds, finding that the modes of the distribution do not change much.

(*e.g.*, rewiring, address space transfers, etc.) but it allows us to present a one-to-one comparison of RPKI vs. non-RPKI scenarios.

We plot the distribution of prefix-origin visibility of RPKI-unknown prefixes in the negative y-dimension in Fig. 4. We find that, overall, stable prefixes show much greater visibility when a MOAS conflict happens, when compared to their conflicting unstable counterparts. However, contrasting the vanilla case (no RPKI registration, negative y-dimension) against the case in which the prefix is registered in the RPKI (positive y-dimension), we see a difference: unstable RPKI-unknown prefixes generally reach higher levels of visibility when compared to RPKI-invalid prefixes. This difference manifests both for very low visibility cases, where RPKI-unknown cluster at around ≈15% visibility, higher than their RPKI-invalid counterparts which cluster at ≈8%, as well as for cases of higher visibility: unstable RPKI-unknown prefixes reach visibility levels of some 70%, while RPKI-invalid cluster below 60%. Indeed, less than 14% of RPKI-invalid MOAS instances reach a visibility over 60% compared to 37% for unstable RPKI-unknown MOAS instances. RPKI registration shows a clear effect on prefix visibility when MOAS conflicts happen.

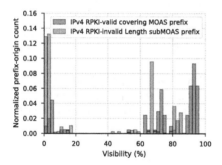 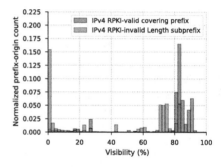

(a) Visibility of RPKI-covered prefix-origins during subMOAS conflicts.

(b) Visibility of RPKI-covered prefix-origins during subprefix conflicts.

Fig. 5. Impact of RPKI registration in subMOAS and subprefix conflicts.

4.4   Visibility of Subprefix Announcements

We next study instances of subprefix announcements, which instead do not compete with the covering prefix for visibility, since routers use longest-prefix matching, preferring more-specific routes for packet forwarding. For this reason, subprefix announcements can be a powerful and dangerous tool to, *e.g.*, hijack address space and redirect traffic, and their effect has been also evidenced in large-scale routing incidents, including route leaks [23,28].

To study the impact of RPKI registration on subprefix announcements, we first isolate all incidents of subprefix announcements in our dataset, *i.e.*, we observe a covering (that is, less specific) prefix, covered by a validated ROA in the RPKI, and concurrently a more specific prefix announcement that does not pass RPKI validation—either because of an invalid ASN (subMOAS) or invalid prefix length (subprefix). In total, we find 10,450 instances of RPKI-invalid subprefix and subMOAS announcements in IPv4, conflicting with 2,291 RPKI-valid covering prefixes. Figure 5a shows the distribution of prefix visibility in the case of subMOAS: if a more-specific prefix announcement fails RPKI validation because it has a different origin AS (N = 5,401 subMOAS prefixes, N = 966 covering prefixes). While the RPKI-valid covering prefixes show high visibility, their invalid counterpart, subMOAS prefixes, show two modes of visibility: some 35% of invalid subMOAS show very low visibility, *i.e.*, lower than 10%. More importantly, however, is the finding that none of the subMOAS prefixes reach the same visibility level as their valid parent: while subMOAS prefixes barely exceed 75% visibility, their valid covering prefixes typically reach some 85%–90% visibility and 75% reach at least 80% visibility. These observations are consistent with our earlier findings of increasing RPKI filtering, and highlight that RPKI registration also benefits registrants in the case of difficult-to-combat subMOAS situations.

Figure 5b shows the visibility for invalid-length subprefix announcements having the same origin AS as their covering RPKI-valid counterpart (N = 5,049 subprefix, N = 1,325 covering prefixes). Recall that the RPKI permits to specify a maxLength attribute, limiting the prefix length of any prefix matching the RPKI record, irrespective of the origin AS. Besides cases of misconfiguration, this scenario also applies in the case of *path hijacks*: instances where an attacker injects a subprefix that allegedly points to the same origin AS as its valid covering prefix, but in fact the attacker redirects traffic to its network. Such attacks can, *e.g.*, be carried out by prepending the valid origin AS at the end of the path after the hijacker's AS number. Such path hijacks present advanced forms of prefix hijacks and are difficult to detect using today's methods [27]. In Fig. 5b, we see similarly lowered levels of visibility for RPKI-invalid subprefix announcements, even if they point to the registered origin AS. Invalid announcements reach some 70% of visibility, substantially lower when compared to their valid covering prefix. These results show that RPKI registration can benefit networks even in this most advanced case of illicit announcements: subprefix path hijacks.

5 Discussion and Conclusion

Recent research has shown increasing registration in the RPKI by networks around the globe. Our work complements these observations, adding an important dimension: RPKI enforcement. We find that a substantial, and growing, number of ISPs in the Internet begin to filter invalid RPKI announcements, including major players such as AT&T. Increasing RPKI enforcement starts to bring direct value to networks, since registration in the RPKI benefits them in real-world scenarios, such as prefix hijacks. Our findings show that already as of today, registration in the RPKI limits the propagation of illicit announcements, in MOAS conflicts as well as in instances of subMOAS and subprefix announcements. Evidence of direct value for networks could incentivize even more transit providers to deploy RPKI filtering to benefit their customers. While the RPKI protects its registrants in the case of such illicit announcements, we can also expect that increasing RPKI enforcement provides further incentives for networks to keep their RPKI records up-to-date, since stale records and other misconfigurations will have a direct impact on reachability of the respective address blocks. Our method provides a simple way to track current levels of RPKI filtering and to study its impact on illicit prefix announcements. Continuous monitoring of deployment of filtering allows for more transparency in the process, and empirical evidence of benefits of registration provides further incentives for network operators to join the growing group of networks that protect their prefixes by registering them in the RPKI.

Acknowledgments. We thank the anonymous reviewers for their thoughtful feedback. This work was partially supported by the MIT Internet Policy Research Initiative, William and Flora Hewlett Foundation grant 2014-1601. We acknowledge funding support from the NSF Grants CNS 1705024 and OAC 1724853. This material is based on research sponsored by Air Force Research Laboratory under agreement number FA8750-18-2-0049. The U.S. Government is authorized to reproduce and distribute reprints for Governmental purposes notwithstanding any copyright notation thereon. The views and conclusions in this paper are those of the authors and do not necessarily reflect the opinions of a sponsor, Air Force Research Laboratory or the U.S. Government.

Appendix: IPv6 Results

Detecting RPKI-Filtering in IPv6: We apply the method described in Sect. 3.1, setting equivalent thresholds to those used for IPv4. In September 2019, out of 402 ASes peering with collectors for IPv6, we consider 232 to be full-feeders, and of those 232 we infer 18 are filtering RPKI-invalid announcements (Fig. 6).

Tracking Visibility in the Global IPv6 Routing Table: Using the methodology described in Sect. 4.1, we build prefix-origin timelines for IPv6 prefixes[5]. Table 2 shows the properties of our resulting dataset.

Overall IPv6 Prefix-Origin Visibility by RPKI State: Figure 7 shows CDFs of the visibility of prefix-origin timelines, which show very similar behavior to the ones described in Sect. 4.1 for IPv4. In IPv6, there are even fewer RPKI-valid prefix-origins with low visibility compared to IPv4: less than 10% IPv6 prefix-origins have less than 80% visibility compared to 20% for IPv4.

---

[5] 0.13% of IPv6 prefix-origin timelines whose RPKI state changed during our measurement window were removed.

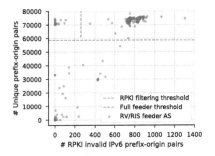

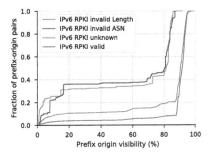

Fig. 6. Count of RPKI-invalid IPv6 prefix-origin pairs and total count of prefix-origin pairs by feeder AS to BGP collectors on Sept. 1st, 2019.

Fig. 7. CDF of IPv6 prefix-origin pairs by visibility during September 2019 for different RPKI states.

Table 2. Properties of our IPv6 prefix-origin timelines and their respective RPKI validity state.

Prefix-origin timelines	Count	%
IPv6 Total	91,313	100%
RPKI covered	19,173	20.1%
RPKI-valid	17,656	19.3%
RPKI-invalid ASN	362	0.40%
RPKI-invalid length	1155	1.26%

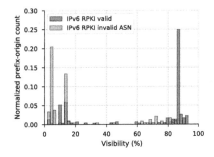

Fig. 8. Visibility of RPKI covered IPv6 prefix-origin pairs during MOAS conflicts.

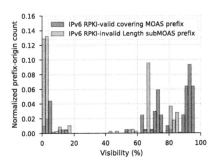

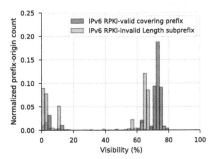

(a) Visibility of RPKI-covered IPv6 prefix-origins during subMOAS conflicts.

(b) Visibility of RPKI-covered IPv6 prefix-origins during subprefix conflicts.

Fig. 9. Impact of RPKI registration in subMOAS and subprefix conflicts.

Visibility of Multiple Origin AS (MOAS) IPv6 Prefixes: In total, we find about 41,000 instances of MOAS prefix-origin pairs in September 2019 for IPv6, of which some 133 are cases in which at least one prefix-origin is RPKI-valid while others are not. Figure 8 shows the distribution of the maximum visibility of prefix-origin timelines during MOAS conflicts.

Visibility of IPv6 Subprefix Announcements: We find 575 subMOAS prefix conflicting with 102 covering prefixes (Fig. 9a) and 1,903 subprefixes conflicting with 235 covering prefixes (Fig. 9b).

Issuing RPKI records for IPv6 prefixes also benefit networks in the case of conflicting (and potentially malicious) announcements.

References

1. AS286 Routing Policy. https://as286.net/AS286-routing-policy.html
2. AT&T/as7018 now drops invalid prefixes from peers. https://mailman.nanog.org/pipermail/nanog/2019-February/099501.html
3. Cymru BGP Bogon Refence. http://www.team-cymru.org/bogon-reference-bgp.html
4. PeeringDB. https://www.peeringdb.com
5. RIPE NCC RPKI Validator. https://rpki-validator.ripe.net/
6. RPKI Route Origin Validation - Africa. https://mailman.nanog.org/pipermail/nanog/2019-April/100445.html
7. Telia Carrier Takes Major Step to Improve the Integrity of the Internet Core. https://www.teliacarrier.com/Press-room/Press-releases/Telia-Carrier-Takes-Major-Step-to-Improve-the-Integrity-of-the-Internet-Core-.html
8. The hunt for 3ve: taking down a major ad fraud operation through industry collaboration. Technical report, November 2018. https://services.google.com/fh/files/blogs/3ve_google_whiteops_whitepaper_final_nov_2018.pdf?_hstc=&__hssc=&hsCtaTracking=c7b87c5c-1676-4d53-99fb-927a07720b17%7C9d63bf77-0926-4d08-b5ec-46b1a06846bc
9. Bush, R., Austein, R.: The Resource Public Key Infrastructure (RPKI) to Router Protocol. RFC 6810 (Proposed Standard), January 2013. https://www.rfc-editor.org/rfc/rfc6810.txt (updated by RFC 8210)
10. Cartwright-Cox, B.: The year of RPKI on the control plane, September 2019. https://blog.benjojo.co.uk/post/the-year-of-rpki-on-the-control-plane
11. Chung, T., et al.: RPKI is coming of age: a longitudinal study of RPKI deployment and invalid route origins. In: Proceedings of the Internet Measurement Conference (IMC 2019), pp. 406–419. Association for Computing Machinery, Amsterdam, Netherlands, October 2019. https://doi.org/10.1145/3355369.3355596
12. Cisco: IP Routing: BGP Configuration Guide, Cisco IOS XE Release 3S. https://www.cisco.com/c/en/us/td/docs/ios-xml/ios/iproute_bgp/configuration/xe-3s/irg-xe-3s-book/bgp-origin-as-validation.html
13. Gilad, Y., Cohen, A., Herzberg, A., Schapira, M., Shulman, H.: Are we there yet? On RPKI's deployment and security. In: Proceedings 2017 Network and Distributed System Security Symposium. Internet Society, San Diego (2017)
14. Goodin, D.: Suspicious event hijacks Amazon traffic for 2 hours, steals cryptocurrency, April 2018. https://arstechnica.com/information-technology/2018/04/suspicious-event-hijacks-amazon-traffic-for-2-hours-steals-cryptocurrency/

15. Huston, G., Michaelson, G., Loomans, R.: A Profile for X.509 PKIX Resource Certificates. RFC 6487 (Proposed Standard), February 2012. https://www.rfc-editor.org/rfc/rfc6487.txt (updated by RFCs 7318, 8209)
16. Huston, G., Michaelson, G., Martinez, C., Bruijnzeels, T., Newton, A., Shaw, D.: Resource Public Key Infrastructure (RPKI) Validation Reconsidered. RFC 8360 (Proposed Standard), April 2018. https://www.rfc-editor.org/rfc/rfc8360.txt
17. Huston, G., Michaelson, G.: RFC 6483: Validation of Route Origination Using the Resource Certificate Public Key Infrastructure (PKI) and Route Origin Authorizations (ROAs), February 2012. https://tools.ietf.org/html/rfc6483
18. Iamartino, D., Pelsser, C., Bush, R.: Measuring BGP route origin registration and validation. In: Mirkovic, J., Liu, Y. (eds.) PAM 2015. LNCS, vol. 8995, pp. 28–40. Springer, Cham (2015). https://doi.org/10.1007/978-3-319-15509-8_3
19. Kent, S., Kong, D., Seo, K., Watro, R.: Certificate Policy (CP) for the Resource Public Key Infrastructure (RPKI). RFC 6484 (Best Current Practice), February 2012. https://www.rfc-editor.org/rfc/rfc6484.txt
20. Lepinski, M., Kent, S.: An Infrastructure to Support Secure Internet Routing. RFC 6480 (Informational), February 2012. https://www.rfc-editor.org/rfc/rfc6480.txt
21. Lepinski, M., Kent, S., Kong, D.: A Profile for Route Origin Authorizations (ROAs). RFC 6482 (Proposed Standard), February 2012. https://www.rfc-editor.org/rfc/rfc6482.txt
22. Maddison, B.: RIPE Forum - Routing Working Group - RPKI Route Origin Validation - Africa, April 2019. https://www.ripe.net/participate/mail/forum/routing-wg/PDZlMzAzMzhhLWVhOTAtNzIxOC1lMzI0LTBjZjMyYOGl1Y2NkkM0BzZWFjb20ubXU+
23. Newman, L.H.: Why Google Internet Traffic Rerouted Through China and Russia. Wired, November 2018. https://www.wired.com/story/google-internet-traffic-china-russia-rerouted/
24. Newton, A., Huston, G.: Policy Qualifiers in Resource Public Key Infrastructure (RPKI) Certificates. RFC 7318 (Proposed Standard), July 2014. https://www.rfc-editor.org/rfc/rfc7318.txt
25. Orsini, C., King, A., Giordano, D., Giotsas, V., Dainotti, A.: BGPStream: a software framework for live and historical BGP data analysis. In: Proceedings of the 2016 Internet Measurement Conference (IMC 2016), pp. 429–444. Association for Computing Machinery, Santa Monica, November 2016. https://doi.org/10.1145/2987443.2987482
26. Reuter, A., Bush, R., Cunha, I., Katz-Bassett, E., Schmidt, T.C., Waehlisch, M.: Towards a rigorous methodology for measuring adoption of RPKI route validation and filtering. ACM SIGCOMM Comput. Commun. Rev. **48**(1), 9 (2018)
27. Sermpezis, P., et al.: ARTEMIS: Neutralizing BGP Hijacking within a Minute. arXiv:1801.01085 [cs], January 2018. http://arxiv.org/abs/1801.01085
28. Strickx, T.: How Verizon and a BGP Optimizer Knocked Large Parts of the Internet Offline Today, June 2019. https://blog.cloudflare.com/how-verizon-and-a-bgp-optimizer-knocked-large-parts-of-the-internet-offline-today/
29. Testart, C., Richter, P., King, A., Dainotti, A., Clark, D.: Profiling BGP serial hijackers: capturing persistent misbehavior in the global routing table. In: Proceedings of the Internet Measurement Conference (IMC 2019), pp. 420–434. ACM Press, Amsterdam (2019). https://doi.org/10.1145/3355369.3355581
30. Yoo, C., Wishnick, D.: Lowering legal barriers to RPKI adoption. Faculty Scholarship at Penn Law, January 2019. https://scholarship.law.upenn.edu/faculty_scholarship/2035

A First Look at the Misuse and Abuse
of the IPv4 Transfer Market

Vasileios Giotsas[1]($\boxtimes$), Ioana Livadariu[2], and Petros Gigis[3,4]

[1] Lancaster University, Lancaster, UK
v.giotsas@lancaster.ac.uk
[2] Simula Metropolitan, Oslo, Norway
[3] University College London, London, UK
[4] Foundation for Research and Technology-Hellas (FORTH-ICS), Patras, Greece

Abstract. The depletion of the unallocated IPv4 addresses and the slow pace of IPv6 deployment have given rise to the IPv4 transfer market, the trading of allocated IPv4 prefixes between organizations. Despite the policies established by RIRs to regulate the IPv4 transfer market, IPv4 transfers pose an opportunity for malicious networks, such as spammers and bulletproof ASes, to bypass reputational penalties by obtaining "clean" IPv4 address space or by offloading blacklisted addresses. Additionally, IP transfers create a window of uncertainty about the legitimate ownership of prefixes, which leads to inconsistencies in WHOIS records and routing advertisements. In this paper we provide the first detailed study of how transferred IPv4 prefixes are misused in the wild, by synthesizing an array of longitudinal IP blacklists, honeypot data, and AS reputation lists. Our findings yield evidence that transferred IPv4 address blocks are used by malicious networks to address botnets and fraudulent sites in much higher rates compared to non-transferred addresses, while the timing of the attacks indicate efforts to evade filtering mechanisms.

Keywords: IPv4 transfers · Routing · BGP · Blacklists

1 Introduction

The depletion of the unallocated IPv4 addresses combined with the slow transition to IPv6 has led to the emergence of a secondary market for ownership transfers of IPv4 addresses. However, the IPv4 market has been poorly regulated due to the lack of widely adopted IP prefix ownership authentication mechanisms, inconsistent contractual requirements between legacy and allocated address space [44], and policy incongruences among Regional Internet Registries (RIRs). As a result, IPv4 transfers have become target of fraud and abuse by malefactors who try to bypass the legal IP ownership processes [19]. RIRs have responded to the emergence of the IPv4 market by establishing policy frameworks that aim to safeguard the hygiene of the accuracy of registered IP blocks and provide oversight and transparency on how organizations trade IPv4 address

© Springer Nature Switzerland AG 2020
A. Sperotto et al. (Eds.): PAM 2020, LNCS 12048, pp. 88–103, 2020.
https://doi.org/10.1007/978-3-030-44081-7_6

blocks [19,38]. However, the effectiveness of these policies in preventing abuse of the IPv4 market remains unclear. Additionally, these policies focus only ownership and utilization issues, and they do not have provisions for malicious usage of the transferred space, for instance by bulletproof hosters who seek clean address space to address botnets and fraudulent sites. Exchanges between operators in mailing lists and messaging boards show that the operational community is worried about these dangers but still face significant difficulties when purchasing or selling address space [32,43].

In this paper we aim to shed light on the misuse and abuse of the IP transfer market. To this end, we combine a large collection of longitudinal control-plane and data-plane data to analyze and verify the information reported by RIRs on IP transfers. We find that the reported transfer dates and recipient organizations do not reflect the state of WHOIS registries and BGP routing for more than 65% of the transferred prefixes. Additionally, 6% of the prefixes covered with ROAs have an inconsistent origin ASN. We then compile and analyze a large-scale dataset of malicious activities that covers a period of more than a decade, derived from IP traffic traces and control-plane paths, including IP blacklists, honeypots, prefix hijacking detection and AS reputation mechanisms. Our findings reveal that the transferred IP space is between 4x to 25x more likely to be blacklisted depending on the type of malicious activity, while the majority of the transferred IPs are blacklisted after the transfer date, even when the transferred address space was deployed and visible to IP scans at least a month before the transfer. The disproportionate representation of transferred prefixes in blacklists persists even when we filter-out the address space used by well-known legitimate networks, such as cloud platforms (*e.g.* Amazon Web Services, Google Cloud) whose Infrastructure-as-a-Serive (IaaS) is often abused to host malware in short-lived Virtual Machines (VMs). Finally, we provide evidence that ASes detected to be serial BGP hijackers or bulletproof hosters are over-represented in the IPv4 market and exhibit suspicious patterns of transactions both as buyers and sellers. These results offer new insights on agile blacklist evasion techniques that can inform the development of more timely and accurate blacklisting mechanisms. Additionally, our work can inform debates on developing and evaluating RIR policies on IP transfers to improve the hygiene of the ecosystem.

2   Background and Related Work

2.1   IP Transfer Market

Today, the available IPv4 address space of all Regional Internet Registries (RIRs) except AFRINIC has been depleted [21]. Despite increasing pressure on network operators to enable IPv6, less than 30% of the ASes are currently originating IPv6 prefixes [22]. Since RIRs are unable to allocate additional IPv4 addresses, many network operators try to prolong the lifespan of IPv4 by buying address space allocated to other networks, which has led to the emergence of a secondary IP market. This market has been characterized as murky [44], due to the lack of transparency and mechanisms to authenticate the ownership of IP space.

In an effort to prevent abuse of this secondary IP market, all RIRs have devised intra-registry transfer policies, starting with RIPE in 2008 [3,6,9,29,51, 51]. All RIRs, except RIPE, have imposed restrictions on IP transactions, that require a minimum size of transferred address space and adequate justification of need from the side of buyers. Inter-regional transfers have been approved by ARIN, APNIC and RIPE. Organizations involved in such transactions have to comply with the inter-RIR transfer policies of their local registry [10,52]. ARIN and APNIC follow the same need-based policy for intra-RIR and inter-RIR transactions. RIPE, in contrast to its intra-RIR policy, requires inter-RIR buyers to document the utilization of at least 50% of the transferred address space for five years. However, these regulations do not apply in the case of transfers that occur due to mergers and acquisitions. Under these policies, the first intra-RIR and inter-RIR transfers occurred October 2009 and October 2012, respectively. The IPv4 transfer market size has significantly increased over the years, from 17, 408 to 40, 463, 872 IPs for intra-RIR transfers, and from 1, 792 to 1, 885, 440 IPs for inter-RIR transfers, with the highest activity occurring within RIPE and ARIN. Moreover, 96% of the IPv4 addresses are exchanged within the same registry and most of these IP transactions occur within the North America region, while 85% of the inter-RIR transfers originate from ARIN. Despite the increasing prominence of the IPv4 market, there are only a few studies of its ecosystem. Periodically, RIRs and IPv4 address brokers report on the trends and evolution of the IP transactions [1,8,47–50,58], but also a portion of buyers have reported their experiences [7,19,37]. Early academic studies [17,30] discussed the possible implications of market-based mechanisms for reallocating IPv4 addresses. Mueller *et al.* [34,35] used the list of published transfers to analyze the emerging IPv4 transfer market by quantifying the amount of legacy allocations exchanged on the markets and the impact of the need-based policies on the utilization of the transferred blocks. Livadariu *et al.* [23] provided a comprehensive study on the IPv4 transfer market evolution, the exchanged IPv4 blocks, and the impact on the routing table and IPv6 adoption. The authors also proposed a method for inferring IP transfers from publicly available data, i.e., routing advertisements, DNS names, RIR allocation and assignment data. To the best of our knowledge, no prior work has studied the IPv4 transfer market from the perspective of fraudulent behavior and misuse.

2.2   Malicious Internet Activities

An *IP blacklist* is an access control mechanism that aims to block traffic from IP addresses which have been detected to originate fraudulent activities, such as spamming, denial of service, malware or phishing. Such blacklists are compiled using spamming sinkholes, honeypots, logs from firewalls, Intrusion Detection Systems (IDS), and anti-virus tools distributed across the Internet. Several works have studied malicious Internet activities based on IP blacklists [4,65]. Ramachandran *et al.* [39] provided one of the first studies, by analyzing over 10 million messages received by a spam sinkhole over a period of 18 months, and by correlating them with lookups to 8 blacklists. Their results showed that

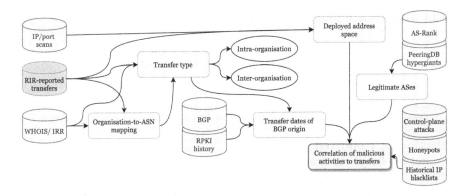

Fig. 1. Overview of datasets and measurement methodology.

combined use of blacklists detects 80% of the spamming hosts. Moreover, the network behavior of serial spammers has distinctive characteristics which can be exploited to develop behavioral and predictive blacklisting [40]. Shina *et al.* [56] evaluated the accuracy of four spamming blacklists, and found that blacklists have a very low False-Positive Rate, with 2 of the blacklists having less than 1% FPR, but high false-negative rate (above 36%) when used individually. A similar study by Kührer *et al.* [28] evaluated the effectiveness of 18 blacklists, 15 public and 3 by AntiVirus (AV) vendors. The authors found that blacklists derived from AntiVirus vendors are able to detect at least 70% of the malicious domains for 13 types of malware, and at least 90% for 7 of these types, outperforming significantly public blacklists. Zhao *et al.* [64] compiled an extensive historical blacklist dataset to analyze the trends and evolution of malicious activity over the span of a decade.

In addition to detecting malicious activity through monitoring data-plane traffic, an array of studies developed techniques to detect attacks through control-plane data. Shue *et al.* [55] studied the connectivity of ASes that are over-represented in 10 popular blacklists. They found that a small number of ASes with a disproportionate fraction of blacklisted address space are more likely to have dense peering connectivity and exhibit higher frequency of peering changes. Konte *et al.* proposed ASwatch [27], a system that aims to identify bulletproof hosting ASes by inferring irregularities in the routing and connectivity patterns. Testart *et al.* [60] profiled serial prefix hijackers by developing a supervised machine learning model, based on which they analyzed 5 years of BGP data to infer 934 ASes that exhibit persistent misbehavior.

We utilize insights and data from the above works to conduct a comprehensive analysis of malicious activity involving transferred IP prefixes and organizations that participate in the transfer market. We combine both data-plane and control-plane data to compile an extensive dataset of attacks. Our blacklist dataset combines a large number of blacklists compiled by AV vendors, which was found to be the best approach to maximize coverage and minimize false-positives.

3   Datasets and Methodology

In this section we present the data and methods that we employ to analyze malicious activities and misuse of transferred IP address space. Figure 1 shows how we synthesize and process an array of chosen datasets.

3.1   Processing of IPv4 Transfers

Collection of Reported IP Transfers. As a first step of our methodology we collect the list of reported intra-RIR and inter-RIR IP transfers, as published by the RIRs. For each transferred resource, we extract the IPv4 address block, the transfer date, and the names of the seller and buyer organizations. Note that none of the RIRs provides the AS Number (ASN) of the organizations involved in the transfer. In the case of inter-RIR IP transactions we also retrieve the RIR for both the seller and the buyer organizations. For intra-RIR IP transfers, ARIN and RIPE also indicate the transfer type, namely if a transfer occurred due to changes within an organization (merger and acquisitions), or as a sale of address space between distinct organizations. However, this information is not available for inter-RIR transfers and for transfers within the APNIC and LACNIC regions. Overall, we collected 30, 335 transfers involving 28, 974 prefixes between 2009-10-12 and 2019-08-24. Of these transfers, 9, 564 (31.5%) are labeled as Mergers/Acquisitions, 17, 934 (59.1%) as IP sales, while the rest 2, 837 (9.4%) are not labeled.

Mapping of Organization Names to ASNs. We aim next to find the ASes that map to the organizations active on the IP transfer markets. To this end, we collect historical WHOIS records every 3 months throughout the IP transfers collection period, i.e., from October 2009 to August 2019. For each allocated ASN we extract the AS name and the corresponding organization name, and we try to match the organization names in the RIR transfer lists against the extracted WHOIS fields. We were able to map 8, 413 out of the 15, 666 organizations involved in the transfer market, 54% of the buyers and 57% of the sellers. Overall, for 48% of the transfers we managed to map both the seller and the buyer, for 68% only the seller, and for 64% of the transfer only the buyers. Organizations may not be mapped to an ASN for multiple reasons: an organization may not have an ASN and instead advertise the transferred address space through its upstream providers, some Local Internet Registries (LIRs) may have operate no ASNs, while other organizations may operate ASNs under different names [54].

Inference of Transfer Types. For the 9.4% of the transfers without reported transfer type (*merger/acquisition*, or *IP prefix sale*), we try to infer if the transfer occurred between siblings. For organizations which we successfully mapped to ASNs, we use CAIDA's AS-to-Organization inference [14] closest to the date of the transfer. Additionally, for inter-RIR transfers and for organizations not

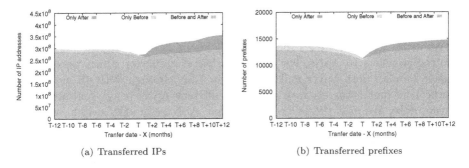

(a) Transferred IPs   (b) Transferred prefixes

Fig. 2. The visibility of transferred address space in BGP advertisments.

mapped to an ASN, we compare the organization names using the string comparison algorithm introduced by Myers [36]. The algorithm returns a value between 0 and 1, where 1 indicates identical strings. For values above 0.8 we consider the organizations as siblings. To improve the accuracy of string comparison, we filter-out from the organization names stop words, and the 100 most common words across all names (*e.g.* Ltd, corporation, limited). Based on the above process we infer 841 (29.6%) of the unlabeled transfers to be between sibling ASes (Fig. 3).

Correlation of Transfers to BGP Activity. We use daily routing tables from all the Routeviews [62] and RIPE RIS [46] collectors, to investigate how the transferred IP address space is advertised across time. For each transfer for which we mapped the organizations to ASNs, we check whether the transferred IP blocks are routed within one year before and one year after their reported transferred date. As shown in Fig. 2, 97.05% of the IPs and 64% of the prefixes are advertised consistently

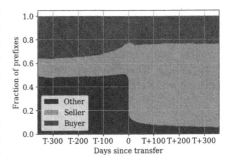

Fig. 3. Shift of origin AS in relation to transfer date

across the entire period. ≈10% of the prefixes are only advertised after the transfer, while about ≈5% are advertised only before the transfer, a practice that may indicate speculative "hoarding" of IP addresses to resell at a higher price, which has been a concern with removing needs-based address allocation [5]. However, the reported transfer date does not correlate with a change in prefix origin for 65% of the transferred prefixes. In 15% of the cases the buyer advertises the prefix one year before the transfer, while in 22% of the cases the seller continues to advertise the prefix one year after the transfer. These disparities can be explained if the buyer organization uses the seller AS as its single-homed transit provider and does not use its ASN to advertise the prefix. Additionally, it is possible that a transfer may unofficially occur before it is reported to the RIR.

We utilize BGP dynamics to expand the mapping of organization names in reported transfers to ASNs. For each transferred prefix for which we did not manage to map both buyer and seller to an ASN through WHOIS, we check whether the prefix was originated by two different ASNs before and after the transfer date. We map the seller to the origin ASN before the switch, and the seller to the origin ASN after the switch if the following three conditions are true: *(i)* the time difference between the switch in the BGP origin and the transfer date is less than two months, *(ii)* the prefix advertisements are visible by at least 10% of the BGP collector peers, and *(iii)* the origin ASNs advertise the prefix consecutively for at least one month. We require condition *(i)* to ensure that the routing shifts correlate with the transfer, and conditions *(ii)* and *(iii)* to filter-out transient misconfigurations or hijacking incidents. Through this process we are able to map the buyer and seller ASNs for an additional 23% of the transfers (70% of the transfers in total).

Measuring the Deployed Transferred IP Space. The behavior of BGP paths will help us interpret more accurately the observed malicious activities, nonetheless routed address space is not necessarily deployed and used in practice [16,45]. To study the malicious behavior of the deployed transferred address space we collect Internet-wide IP scans every 3 months between 2012-01-02 and 2019-09-01. We first collect the ICMP ECHO REQUEST scans from the USC/ISC project LANDER [18], which sweeps the IANA allocated IP ranges, and records all the IPs that respond with an ICMP ECHO REPLY message. We complement these data with Internet-wide UDP and TCP scans collected by RAPID7's project Sonar [41,42], which records the IPs that respond to ZMAP probes against popular UDP and TCP services.

3.2   Detection of Malicious IPs and ASes

After we compile and process the IP transfers, we construct an extensive dataset of cyber-attack sources to analyze the hygiene of the transferred address blocks and the players within the IPv4 market.

Real-time BlackLists (RBLs) provide one of the most popular techniques to detect networks responsible for attacks. Unfortunately, most blacklist providers do not offer historical snapshots, but typically they only publish the blacklist at a certain web location that is refreshed periodically – daily or even hourly – so that firewalls can automatically update their rules. However, we were able to find two large-scale historical blacklist datasets compiled and archived by third-parties.

FinalBlacklist. Zhao *et al.* [64] compiled the FinalBlacklist dataset that contains over 51 million blacklisting reports for 662K IPs between January 2007 and June 2017, as part of a decade-long analysis of malicious Internet activity. To construct the `FinalBlacklist`, the authors collected historical blacklist snapshots through the Wayback Machine [24], which they extended using VirusTotal [63], an API that aggregates periodic data from more than 70 Anti-Virus and blacklist data feeds. 7.6 million (15%) of the blacklisting reports is labeled by the original source with the type of the malicious activity, which the authors abstract into six classes: Exploits, Malware, Fraudulent Services (FS), Spammers, Phishing, and Potentially Unwanted Programs (PUP). Based on the labeled subset they employed a random forest classifier to predict the class of the remaining 44M blacklisted activities with 92.4% accuracy. 90.9% of the blacklisted IPs correspond to malware, while only (0.01%) correspond to Spammers.

RIPE Stat Abuse API. To augment the `FinalBlacklist` dataset with IPs involved in the distribution of Spamming, we rely on data published by RIPE NCC who is archiving daily snapshots since 2009-06-22 of the `UCE-Protect` Network [61] blacklist[1] [57], one of the most prominent anti-spamming blacklists. RIPE NCC provides public access to these data through the RIPE Stat REST API [53], which allows querying the blacklisting reports for a specific IP prefix (no bulk querying). If an IP range within the queried prefix is blacklisted, the API returns the blacklisting period (start and end date), allowing us to collect historical blacklisting reports.

The `UCE-Protect` blacklist uses three different levels of blacklisting policies, according to the severity and persistence of the observed malicious activity. *Level-1* blacklists only single IP addresses detected to deliver e-mails to spam traps, conduct port scans or attack the `UCE-Protect` servers. Level-1 records expire automatically after 7 days if there are no further attacks. *Level-2* aims to stop escalating attacks by blacklisting IP prefixes with multiple IPs that emanate spam repeatedly for a week, implying lack of appropriate security measures or intentional misbehaviour. *Level-3* blacklists all IPs within an ASN if more than 100 IPs, but also a minimum of 0.2% of all IPs allocated to this ASN, are Level-1 blacklisted within 7 days. This aggressive policy assumes that legitimate networks are unlikely to have a sustained high volume of blacklisted IPs. Additionally, a prefix/ASN can get Level-2/3 blacklisted if a network employs evasion techniques against blacklists, such as rotating the IPs of abusers within a prefix, or blocking IP addresses of blacklist providers.

Detection of Persistent C&C Hosters. The activity of botnets is typically coordinated by Command and Control (C&C) servers. C&C servers may only orchestrate and not participate in attacks themselves, therefore their detection is primarily based on honeypots. Shutting down of C&C servers is critical in defending against botnets, an effort that may even involve security agencies such as the FBI [33], therefore legitimate network operators tend to respond quickly in

---

[1] RIPE Stat also provides access to Spamhaus DROP snapshots which we do not use because it covers only directly allocated address space.

Table 1. Analysis of blacklisted IPs. Transferred IP prefixes are disproportionately represented in all the blacklists by a rate between 4x for Malware IPs, to 43x for Fraudulent services.

Blacklist type	Blacklisted IPs part of transfers		Trans Prefixes w/ blacklisted IPs		Non-trans Prefixes w/ blacklisted IPs
	All	Filtered	All	Routed	Routed
Unwanted Programs	55%	43%	3.6%	5.5%	0.95%
Exploits	30%	30%	4.7%	7.2%	0.92%
Malware	36%	29%	16.6%	25.3%	6.2%
Phising	36%	25%	7.5%	11.6%	2%
Fraudulent Services	23%	27%	3.8%	9.6%	0.22%
Spammers	12%	12%	0.6%	0.9%	0.1%

requests for C&C take-downs in contrast to bulletproof hosters. We use data from two distributed honeypots operated by BadPackets [11] and BinaryEdge [12] to detect ASes that host C&C servers for over two weeks, despite notices by the honeypot operators. We were able to detect 28 ASes that are persistent and serial C&C hosters between February 2018 and June 2019.

As Reputation Lists Based on BGP Misbehavior. We complement the set of malicious ASes compiled through the honeypot data with AS reputation lists which are developed by monitoring the BGP routing system to detect ASes with consistent patterns of malicious routing, such as traffic misdirection. We use the list produced by Testart *et al.* [60], which we further extend with examples of bulletproof hosters and hijackers reported by [15,27] resulting in a list of 922 malicious ASes.

4   Analysis and Results

Blacklisted Address Space. We first compare the malicious activity emanating from transferred and non-transferred prefixes as reflected by our IP blacklist reports. Table 1 summarizes the blacklist records per type of malicious activity, for transferred and non-transferred IPs and prefixes. Transferred IPs are disproportionately represented in the blacklist for every type of malicious activity except spamming. In particular, the transferred address space represents only 16% of the total address space, but covers 61% of the blacklisted IPs. The fraction of transferred prefixes with at least one blacklisted IP is 4x to 25x larger than the fraction of non-transferred prefixes for every blacklist type, with spam being the category with the smallest fraction of blacklisting reports per prefix.

As shown in Fig. 4, 40% of the routed transferred prefixes appear at least once in our RBLs, compared to only 6% of the non-transferred routed prefixes. However, the blacklisting activity does not originate uniformly across the address space. When we break down all prefixes to their covered/24 sub-prefixes we find that the blacklisted IPs are concentrated in 6% of the transferred/24s, and in only 1% of the non-transferred/24s (Fig. 4b). This happens because some of the less specific transferred prefixes are owned by large-scale legitimate networks, such as Tier-1 providers, that proportionally originate a very small fraction of blacklisting reports. For example, the prefix 50.128.0.0/9 which was transferred by an acquisition from Comcast includes 32,768/24 sub-prefixes (more than all transferred prefixes), but has only 289 blacklisting reports. Still, transferred/24 sub-prefixes are 6x more likely to be blacklisted, than the non-transferred ones.

Blacklisted ASNs. We analyze the blacklisting reports per ASN, to understand how the detected malicious activity is distributed across the participants of the IP transfer market. Almost 50% of all the ASNs that participate in the transfer market appear at least once in the blacklist, compared to only 16% of the ASNs that do not participate in the transfer market and appear in the BGP table to originate prefixes (Fig. 5a). Moreover, ASes in the transfer market tend to have a larger fraction of their address space blacklisted, with a median of 0.06% compared to 0.03% for ASes not involved in any transfer, which is an indication of more consistent malicious behaviour. This trend is even more pronounced for ASes that are both sellers and buyers of IP prefixes, which for some ASes appear to be a strategy to recycle blacklisted prefixes. To study whether the higher blacklisting rate of ASNs involved in transfers may be explained by a bias in the composition of ASNs that exchange IP space, we compare their user population according to APNIC's estimates [20], and we also compare their self-reported business type in PeeringDB [2]. For both datasets the composition of ASNs is very similar, with ASNs absent from transfers exhibiting slightly higher median user population.

While the blacklisted prefixes are distributed across half of the ASNs involved in transfers, there are 26 ASes with more than 10K blacklisted IPs, including prominent cloud providers (*e.g.* Amazon, Microsoft, Google, OVH) and Tier-1 providers (*e.g.* GTT, CenturyLink, Seabone). Attackers often utilize cloud platforms as a cost-effective way to host malicious software in short-lived Virtual

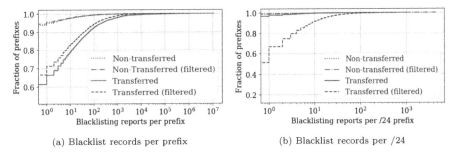

(a) Blacklist records per prefix   (b) Blacklist records per /24

Fig. 4. Distribution of the volume of blacklisting reports for transferred and non-transferred prefixes.

Machines and avoid detection [59], while large providers operate a global network that covers a massive user population. These ASes account for only 0.5% of the blacklisted prefixes, but cover 55% of all the blacklisted IPs, which explains the long tail of the distributions in Fig. 4a. Since our goal is to investigate whether the transfer market is targeted by ASes with potentially malicious business models, we attempt to filter out ASes that are apparently legitimate but may have a large number of blacklisted IPs. These are notably ASes with very large user population (such as big eyeball ISPs and Tier-1 networks) and cloud providers which can be exploited by attackers who lease temporary computing instances for malicious purposes. To this end, we follow a filtering approach similar to the one proposed by Testart et al. [60], and we consider as non-suspicious the 1,000 ASes with the largest customer cones according to AS-Rank [31]. However, cloud providers, CDNs and large-scale eyeballs have relatively small customer cones. Therefore, we complement the filtered ASes with: (i) the 30 ASes with the largest amount of traffic (hypergiants) based on the methodology by Böttger et al. [13], and the 1,000 ASes with the largest user population according to APNIC. The filtered ASNs are involved in 9% of the transfers. As shown in the

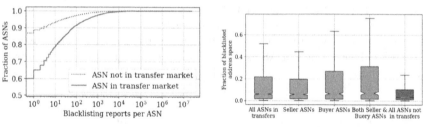

(a) Distribution of blacklisting reports per ASNs (b) Fraction of blacklisted address space per ASN

Fig. 5. Comparison of the blacklisted activity of the ASNs in the transfer market, compared to the rest of the ASNs that originate BGP-routed prefixes.

column "Filtered" of Table 1, even when filtering out these ASes, the fraction of blacklisted transferred IPs is between 2x – 3x higher than the total fraction of transferred IPs, while the fraction of blacklisted prefixes is virtually identical between the filtered and the non-filtered datasets. This is an indication the "non-suspicious" ASes have a proportional fraction of blacklisted transferred and non-transferred prefixes. In contrast, a large number of ASes in the transfer market exhibit higher affinity for malicious activity which is not explained by their business model network footprint. This observation is more apparent when studying how blacklisted prefixes are distributed across the IPv4 address space. Filtered transferred/24 prefixes exhibit a much higher fraction of blacklisted records compared to non-filtered transferred and non-transferred prefixes (Fig. 4b).

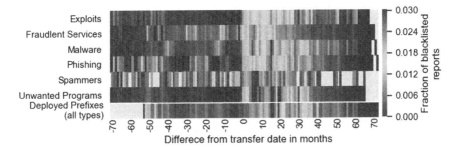

Fig. 6. Blacklist reports per type of malicious activity for transferred IPs, compared to the transfer date. The last row shows the blacklisting activity for deployed prefixes based on the Internet-wide IP and port scans.

Blacklisting Timing. To explore the dynamics between malicious activity and the IP transfers, we compare the timing of the blacklisting reports to the transfer date. We use the effective transfer date, as observed by BGP routing changes (see Sect. 3.1), and the reported transfer time only when the origin AS does not change at all. As shown in Fig. 6, the number of blacklisted IPs peaks within a year of the transfer date for all types of malicious activity. Such blacklisting activity shortly after the transfer date may happen because the transferred addresses were unused before the transfer.

To illuminate this possibility, in the last row of Fig. 6 we plot the blacklisting reports only for prefixes with IPs visible in our IP/port scans at least one month before the transfer date. For deployed prefixes the peak in malicious activity also peaks after the transfer date, but after one year. This finding indicates that recipients of IP addresses are more prone to abuse of the IP space, which agrees with the difference in blacklisting magnitude between buyers and sellers as shown in Fig. 5b.

Per-Region and Per-Transfer Type Differences. We then investigate whether the malicious activity differs between regions and transfer types. Figure 7a compares the fraction of blacklisted transferred address space between prefixes exchanged as Merge & Acquisitions and as IP sales for each region with blacklisted IPs, and for inter-region transfers. Prefixes exchanged within the RIPE region as sales originate have the highest fraction of blacklisted IPs, which is statistically significant. In contrast, ARIN exhibits higher malicious activity from prefixes transferred between siblings, although the spread of values makes it difficult to generalize this observation. For APNIC and inter-RIR transfers we observe only non-sibling blacklisted transactions, while for AFRINIC and LACNIC we do not have any blacklisted transferred IPs (after the AS filtering step).

Participation of Low-Reputation ASes in IPv4 Transfers. The final part of our analysis is to check the participation rate of low-reputation ASes (hijack-

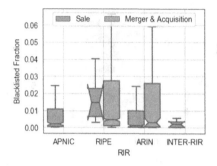 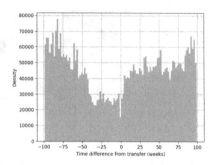

(a) IP sales in the RIPE region exhibit a higher fraction of blacklisting compared to transfers between siblings, and transfers in other RIRss.

(b) The density of blacklisted IPs for low-reputation ASes that participate both as buyers and sellers in the IPv4 market

Fig. 7. Analysis of transferred blacklisted IPs per region, transfer type, and for low-reputation ASes.

ers, C&C and bulletproof hosters) in IP transfers. Although 85% of the ASes visible in the BGP routing table are not involved in IP transfers, 47% of the low-reputation ASes have been either buyers (48%) or sellers (52%). Surprisingly, 32% of these ASes participate both as buyers and sellers. This practice may signal an attempt to recycle "tainted" address space in order to evade blacklist filters, since blacklist providers may remove listed IPs and prefixes when there is a shift in ownership [25,26]. Figure 7b shows that indeed the density of blacklisted IPs for the low-reputation buyer/seller ASes dips at the transfer date and increases shortly thereafter.

5   Conclusion

In this paper we present a first comprehensive measurement study of malicious activities within the transferred IPv4 address space and the networks that are involved in the IPv4 market. We first combine a wide range of control-plane and data-plane data to process the details of the reported IP transfer reports and verify the ownership of the exchanged prefixes based on BGP paths and historical WHOIS data. We find that for more than 65% of the IP transfers, the origin ASes and the transaction dates are inconsistent with the transfer reports. Our results reveal at best poor practices of resource management that can facilitate malicious activities, such as hijacking attacks, and even lead to connectivity issues due to the increasing deployment of IRR-based filtering mechanisms.

We then analyze the exchanged IPv4 address blocks against an extensive dataset of malicious activities that span a decade, which includes IP blacklists, honeypot data, and non-legitimate ASes based on the detection of control-plane misbehavior. Our findings show that the ASes involved in the transfer market exhibit consistently higher malicious behavior compared to the rest of the ASes, even when we account for factors such as business models and network span.

Our findings are likely to be a lower bound of malicious activity from within transferred IP addresses since a number of transactions may occur without being reported to the RIRs [23,44]. As part of our future work we aim to extend our analysis to non-reported IPv4 transfers and develop predictive techniques for blacklisting based on the monitoring of the IPv4 transfer market.

We believe that these insights can inform the debates and development of RIR policies regarding the regulation of IPv4 markets, and help operators and brokers conduct better-informed due diligence to avoid misuse of the transferred address space or unintentionally support malicious actors. Moreover, our results can provide valuable input to blacklist providers, security professionals and researchers who can improve their cyber-threat monitoring and detection approaches, and tackle evasion techniques that exploit IPv4 transfers. We will make available the data of our study at: https://github.com/vgiotsas/ip-transfers-observatory.

Acknowledgments. We thank our shepherd Taejoong Chung, the anonymous reviewers and Carlos Friaça for their constructive feedback. We also thank Randy Bush, and Jim Reid for their replies in our RIPE policy enquiries. Research supported, in part by, Security Lancaster, H2020 EC CONCORDIA GA #830927, Norwegian Research Council grant # 288744 GAIA, and the RIPE NCC Community Projects Fund.

References

1. IPv4 Market Group. https://ipv4marketgroup.com/broker-services/buy
2. PeeringDB. https://www.peeringdb.com
3. AFRINIC: IPv4 Resources transfer within the AFRINIC Region. http://bit.ly/2sFjUZu
4. Alieyan, K., ALmomani, A., Manasrah, A., Kadhum, M.M.: A survey of botnet detection based on DNS. Neural Comput. Appl. **28**(7), 1541–1558 (2017)
5. Anderson, T., Hutty, M.: Post depletion adjustment of procedures to match policy objectives, and clean-up of obsolete policy text. RIPE policy proposal, November 2013
6. APNIC: APNIC transfer, merger, acquisition, and takeover policy (2010). https://www.apnic.net/policy/transfer-policy_obsolete
7. APNIC blog, Huberman, D.: Seven steps to successful IPv4 transfers (2017)
8. APNIC blog, Huston, G.: IPv4 Address Exhaustion in APNIC (2015). https://blog.apnic.net/2015/08/07/ipv4-address-exhaustion-in-apnic
9. ARIN: ARIN Number Resource Policy Manual (Version 2010.1) (2009). https://www.arin.net/policy/nrpm.html
10. ARIN: ARIN Number Resource Policy Manual (Version 2012.3) (2012). https://www.arin.net/policy/nrpm.html
11. BadPackets: Cyber-Threat Intelligence: Botnet C2 Detections (2019). https://badpackets.net/botnet-c2-detections
12. BinaryEdge: HoneyPots/Sensors (2019). https://www.binaryedge.io/data.html
13. Böttger, T., Cuadrado, F., Uhlig, S.: Looking for hypergiants in peeringDB. ACM SIGCOMM Comput. Commun. Rev. **48**(3), 13–19 (2018)
14. CAIDA: Inferred AS to Organization Mapping Dataset. http://www.caida.org/data/as_organizations.xml

15. Cho, S., Fontugne, R., Cho, K., Dainotti, A., Gill, P.: BGP hijacking classification. In: 2019 TMA, pp. 25–32. IEEE (2019)
16. Dainotti, A., et al.: Estimating internet address space usage through passive measurements. SIGCOMM Comput. Commun. Rev. **44**(1), 42–49 (2013)
17. Edelman, B.: Running out of numbers: scarcity of IP addresses and what to do about it. In: Das, S., Ostrovsky, M., Pennock, D., Szymanksi, B. (eds.) AMMA 2009. LNICST, vol. 14, pp. 95–106. Springer, Heidelberg (2009). https://doi.org/10.1007/978-3-642-03821-1_16
18. Heidemann, J., Pradkin, Y., Govindan, R., Papadopoulos, C., Bartlett, G., Bannister, J.: Census and survey of the visible internet. In: Proceedings of the ACM Internet Measurement Conference, pp. 169–182. ACM, October 2008
19. Huberman, D.: Smarter purchasing of IPv4 addresses in the market. NANOG 68, October 2016. http://bit.ly/36H7LkJ
20. Huston, G.: How Big is that Network? October 2014. http://bit.ly/367t6DD
21. Huston, G.: IPv4 Address Report, October 2019. https://ipv4.potaroo.net
22. Huston, G.: IPv6/IPv4 Comparative Statistics, October 2019. http://bit.ly/36G7sGN
23. Livadariu, I., Elmokashfi, A., Dhamdhere, A.: On IPv4 transfer markets: analyzing reported transfers and inferring transfers in the wild. Comput. Commun. **111**, 105–119 (2017)
24. Internet Archive: Wayback Machine (2001). https://archive.org/web
25. IPv4 Brokers: IPv4 blacklist removal service. https://ipv4brokers.net/ipv4-sales
26. IPv4 Market Group: IPv4 blacklist removal service. http://bit.ly/37dfDM3
27. Konte, M., Perdisci, R., Feamster, N.: ASwatch: an as reputation system to expose bulletproof hosting ASes. ACM SIGCOMM CCR **45**(4), 625–638 (2015)
28. Kührer, M., Rossow, C., Holz, T.: Paint it black: evaluating the effectiveness of malware blacklists. In: Stavrou, A., Bos, H., Portokalidis, G. (eds.) RAID 2014. LNCS, vol. 8688, pp. 1–21. Springer, Cham (2014). https://doi.org/10.1007/978-3-319-11379-1_1
29. LACNIC: One-way interregional transfers to LACNIC (2017). http://bit.ly/369F5kd
30. Lehr, W., Vest, T., Lear, E.: Running on empty: the challenge of managing internet addresses. In: TPRC (2008)
31. Luckie, M., Huffaker, B., Dhamdhere, A., Giotsas, V., et al.: AS relationships, customer cones, and validation. In: Proceedings of the 2013 ACM IMC (2013)
32. Torres, M.: Purchasing IPv4 space - due diligence homework. NANOG mailing list, March 2018. http://bit.ly/36L5Trg
33. McMillen, D.: The inside story on botnets. IBM X-Force Research, September 2016
34. Mueller, M., Kuerbis, B.: Buying numbers: an empirical analysis of the IPv4 number market. In: Proceedings of iConference (2013)
35. Mueller, M., Kuerbis, B., Asghari, H.: Dimensioning the elephant: an empirical analysis of the IPv4 number market. In: GigaNet: Global Internet Governance Academic Network, Annual Symposium (2012)
36. Myers, E.W.: An O(ND) difference algorithm and its variations. Algorithmica **1**(1–4), 251–266 (1986)
37. NANOG 68, Potter, A.: How to Navigate Getting IPv4 Space in a Post-Run-Out World (2017)
38. Nobile, L.: Who is accuracy. ARIN 39, April 2017
39. Ramachandran, A., Feamster, N.: Understanding the network-level behavior of spammers. In: ACM SIGCOMM CCR, vol. 36, pp. 291–302. ACM (2006)

40. Ramachandran, A., Feamster, N., Vempala, S.: Filtering spam with behavioral blacklisting. In: Proceedings of the 14th ACM conference CCS. ACM (2007)
41. RAPID7: Project Sonar TCP Scans. RAPID7 Open Data (2019). https://opendata.rapid7.com/sonar.tcp
42. RAPID7: Project Sonar UDP Scans. RAPID7 Open Data (2019). https://opendata.rapid7.com/sonar.udp
43. Reddit Networking: What are your experiences with the IPv4 secondary market? March 2018. https://tinyurl.com/yyumhax5
44. Richter, P., Allman, M., Bush, R., Paxson, V.: A primer on IPv4 scarcity. SIG-COMM Comput. Commun. Rev. **45**(2), 21–31 (2015). http://bit.ly/3b2878Q
45. Richter, P., Smaragdakis, G., Plonka, D., Berger, A.: Beyond counting: new perspectives on the active IPv4 address space. In: Proceedings of the 2016 ACM IMC (2016)
46. RIPE: Routing Information Service (RIS). http://www.ripe.net/ris
47. RIPE Labs, Wilhem, R.: Developments in IPv4 Transfers (2016). https://labs.ripe.net/Members/wilhelm/developments-in-ipv4-transfers
48. RIPE Labs, Wilhem, R.: Impact of IPv4 Transfers on Routing Table Fragmentation (2016). http://bit.ly/30NCBHj
49. RIPE Labs, Wilhem, R.: Trends in RIPE NCC Service Region IPv4 Transfers (2017). https://labs.ripe.net/Members/wilhelm/trends-in-ipv4-transfers
50. RIPE Labs, Wilhem, R.: A Shrinking Pie? The IPv4 Transfer Market in 2017 (2018). http://bit.ly/2topCQ1
51. RIPE NCC: Intra-RIR Transfer Policy Proposal (2012). https://www.ripe.net/participate/policies/proposals/2012-03
52. RIPE NCC: Inter-RIR Transfers (2015). http://bit.ly/2v8kShV
53. RIPE NCC: RIPE Stat Data API: Blacklists (2019). http://bit.ly/2SafbId
54. RIPE NCC Address Policy Working Group: ASNs of organizations in reported IPv4 transfers. https://bit.ly/2v8Krzp
55. Shue, C.A., Kalafut, A.J., Gupta, M.: Abnormally malicious autonomous systems and their internet connectivity. IEEE/ACM TON **20**(1), 220–230 (2012)
56. Sinha, S., Bailey, M., Jahanian, F.: Shades of grey: on the effectiveness of reputation-based "blacklists". In: 3rd International Conference on Malicious and Unwanted Software (MALWARE), pp. 57–64. IEEE (2008)
57. Spamhaus: Don't Route Or Peer List (DROP). https://www.spamhaus.org/drop
58. Streambank, H.: IPv4 Auctions. https://auctions.ipv4.global
59. WatchGuard Technologies: Internet Security Report: Q2 2019, September 2019
60. Testart, C., Richter, P., King, A., Dainotti, A., Clark, D.: Profiling BGP serial hijackers: capturing persistent misbehavior in the global routing table. In: Proceedings of the Internet Measurement Conference, pp. 420–434. ACM (2019)
61. UCEPROTECT: Network Project. http://www.uceprotect.net/en
62. University of Oregon: The Route Views Project. http://www.routeviews.org
63. VirusTotal: Online Virus Malware and URL scanner. https://www.virustotal.com
64. Zhao, B.Z.H., Ikram, M., Asghar, H.J., Kaafar, M.A., Chaabane, A., Thilakarathna, K.: A decade of mal-activity reporting: a retrospective analysis of internet malicious activity blacklists. In: ASIACCS, pp. 193–205. ACM (2019)
65. Zhauniarovich, Y., Khalil, I., Yu, T., Dacier, M.: A survey on malicious domains detection through DNS data analysis. ACM Comput. Surv. **51**(4), 67 (2018)

Best Practices and Conformance

Don't Forget to Lock the Front Door! Inferring the Deployment of Source Address Validation of Inbound Traffic

Maciej Korczyński[1]($\boxtimes$), Yevheniya Nosyk[1], Qasim Lone[2], Marcin Skwarek[1], Baptiste Jonglez[1], and Andrzej Duda[1]

[1] Univ. Grenoble Alpes, CNRS, Grenoble INP, LIG, 38000 Grenoble, France
`maciej.korczynski@univ-grenoble-alpes.fr`
[2] Delft University of Technology, Delft, The Netherlands

Abstract. This paper concerns the problem of the absence of ingress filtering at the network edge, one of the main causes of important network security issues. Numerous network operators do not deploy the best current practice—Source Address Validation (SAV) that aims at mitigating these issues. We perform the first Internet-wide active measurement study to enumerate networks not filtering *incoming packets* by their source address. The measurement method consists of identifying closed and open DNS resolvers handling requests coming from the outside of the network with the source address from the range assigned inside the network under the test. The proposed method provides the most complete picture of the *inbound* SAV deployment state at network providers. We reveal that 32 673 Autonomous Systems (ASes) and 197 641 Border Gateway Protocol (BGP) prefixes are vulnerable to spoofing of inbound traffic. Finally, using the data from the Spoofer project and performing an open resolver scan, we compare the filtering policies in both directions.

Keywords: IP spoofing · Source Address Validation · DNS resolvers

1 Introduction

The Internet relies on IP packets to enable communication between hosts with the destination and source addresses specified in packet headers. However, there is no packet-level authentication mechanism to ensure that the source addresses have not been altered [2]. The modification of a source IP address is referred to as "IP spoofing". It results in the anonymity of the sender and prevents a packet from being traced to its origin. This vulnerability has been leveraged to launch Distributed Denial-of-Service (DDoS) attacks, in particular, the reflection attacks [3]. Due to the absence of a method to block packet header modification, the efforts have been undertaken to prevent spoofed packets from reaching potential victims. This goal can be achieved with packet filtering at the network edge, formalized in RFC 2827 and called *Source Address Validation* (SAV) [25].

© Springer Nature Switzerland AG 2020
A. Sperotto et al. (Eds.): PAM 2020, LNCS 12048, pp. 107–121, 2020.
https://doi.org/10.1007/978-3-030-44081-7_7

The role of IP spoofing in cyberattacks drives the need to estimate the level of SAV deployment by network providers. There exist projects aimed at enumerating networks without packet filtering, for example, the Spoofer [4]. However, a great majority of the existing work concentrates on *outbound* SAV, the root of DDoS attacks [15]. While less obvious, the lack of *inbound* filtering enables an attacker to appear as an internal host of a network and may reveal valuable information about the network infrastructure, not seen from the outside. Inbound IP spoofing may serve as a vector for cache poisoning attacks [10] even if the Domain Name System (DNS) server is correctly configured as a closed resolver.

In this work, we report on the preliminary results of the Closed Resolver Project [5]. We propose a new method to identify networks not filtering inbound traffic by source IP addresses. We perform an Internet-wide scan of BGP prefixes maintained by RouteViews [23] for the IPv4 address space to identify closed and open DNS resolvers in each routable network. We achieve this goal by sending DNS A requests with spoofed source IP addresses for which the destination is every host of every routing prefix and the source is the next host from the same network. If there is no filtering in transit networks and at the network edge, such a packet is received by a server that resolves the DNS A request for a host that seems to be on the same network. As our scanner spoofs the source IP address, the response from the local resolver is directly sent to the spoofed client IP address, preventing us from analyzing it. However, we control the authoritative name server for the queried domains and observe from which networks it receives the requests. This method identifies networks not performing filtering of *incoming packets* without the need for a vantage point inside the network itself.

The above method when applied alone shows the absence of inbound SAV at the network edge. In parallel, we send subsequent unspoofed DNS A record requests to identify open resolvers at the scale of the Internet. If open resolvers reply to the unspoofed requests but not to the spoofed ones, we infer the presence of SAV for incoming traffic either at the network edge or in transit networks. By doing this, we detect both the absence and the presence of inbound packet filtering.

We analyze the geographical distribution of networks vulnerable to inbound spoofing and identify the countries that do not comply with the SAV standard, which is the first step in mitigating the issue by contacting Computer Security Incident Response Teams (CSIRTs).

We also retrieve the Spoofer data and deploy a method proposed by Mauch [20] to infer the absence and the presence of *outbound* SAV. In this way, we study the policies of the SAV deployment per provider in both directions. Previous work demonstrated the difficulty in incentivizing providers to deploy filtering for outbound traffic due to misaligned economic incentives: implementing SAV for outbound traffic benefits other networks and not the network of the deployment [19]. This work shows how the deployment of SAV for inbound traffic protects the provider's own network.

2   Background

Source address validation was proposed in 2000 in RFC 2827 as a result of a growing number of DDoS attacks. The RFC defined the notion of ingress filtering—discarding any packets with source addresses not following filtering rules. This operation is the most effective when applied at the network edge [25]. RFC 3704 proposed different ways to implement SAV including static access control lists (ACLs) and reverse path forwarding [1]. Packet filtering can be applied in two directions: inbound to a customer (coming from the outside to the customer network) and outbound from a customer (coming from inside the customer network to the outside). The lack of SAV in any of these directions may result in different security threats.

Attackers benefit from the absence of outbound SAV to launch DDoS attacks, in particular, amplification attacks. Adversaries make use of public services prone to amplification [22] to which they send requests on behalf of their victims by spoofing their source IP addresses. The victim is then overloaded with the traffic coming from the services rather than from the attacker. In this scenario, the origin of the attack is not traceable. One of the most successful attacks against GitHub resulted in traffic of 1.35 Tbps: attackers redirected Memcached responses by spoofing their source addresses [12]. In such scenarios, spoofed source addresses are usually random globally routable IPs. In some cases, to impersonate an internal host, a spoofed IP address may be from the inside target network, which reveals the absence of inbound SAV [1].

Pretending to be an internal host reveals information about the inner network structure, such as the presence of closed DNS resolvers that resolve only on behalf of clients within the same network. Attackers can further exploit closed resolvers, for instance, for leveraging misconfigurations of the Sender Policy Framework (SPF) [24]. In case of not correctly deployed SPF, attackers can trigger closed DNS resolvers to perform an unlimited number of requests thus introducing a potential DoS attack vector. The possibility of impersonating another host on the victim network can also assist in the zone poisoning attack [11]. A master DNS server, authoritative for a given domain, may be configured to accept DNS dynamic updates from a DHCP server on the same network [27]. Thus, sending a spoofed update from the outside with an IP address of that DHCP server will modify the content of the zone file [11]. The attack may lead to domain hijacking. Another way to target closed resolvers is to perform DNS cache poisoning [10]. An attacker can send a spoofed DNS A request for a specific domain to a closed resolver, followed by forged replies before the arrival of the response from the genuine authoritative server. In this case, the users who query the same domain will be redirected to where the attacker specified until the forged DNS entry reaches its Time To Live (TTL).

Despite the knowledge of the above-mentioned attack scenarios and the costs of the damage they may incur, it has been shown that SAV is not yet widely deployed. Lichtblau et al. surveyed 84 network operators to learn whether they deploy SAV and what challenges they face [16]. The reasons for not performing packet filtering include incidentally filtering out legitimate traffic, equipment limitations, and lack of a direct economic benefit. The last aspect assumes outbound

Table 1. Methods to infer deployment of Source Address Validation.

Method	Direction	Presence/Absence	Remote	Relies on mis-configurations
Spoofer [3,4]	Both	Both	No	No
Forwarders-based [15,20]	Outbound	Absence	Yes	Yes
Traceroute loops [18]	Outbound	Absence	Yes	Yes
Passive detection [16,21]	Outbound	Both	No	No
Our method [5]	Inbound	Both	Yes	No

SAV when the deployed network can become an attack source but cannot be attacked itself. Performing inbound SAV protects networks from, for example, the threats described above, which is beneficial from the economic perspective.

3   Related Work

Table 1 summarizes several methods proposed to infer SAV deployment. They differ in terms of the filtering direction (inbound/outbound), whether they infer the presence or absence of SAV, whether measurements can be done remotely or on a vantage point inside the tested network, and if the method relies on existing network misconfigurations.

The Spoofer project deploys a client-server infrastructure mainly based on volunteers (and "crowdworkers" hired for one study trough five crowdsourcing platforms [17]) that run the client software from inside a network. The active probing client sends both unspoofed and spoofed packets to the Spoofer server either periodically or when it detects a new network. The server inspects received packets (if any) and analyzes whether spoofing is allowed and to what extent [2]. For every client running the software, its/24 IPv4 address block and the autonomous system number (ASN) are identified and measurement results are made publicly available[1]. This approach identifies both the absence and the presence of SAV in both directions. The results obtained by the Spoofer project provide the most confident picture of the deployment of outbound SAV and have covered tests from 7 353 ASes since 2015. However, those that are not aware of this issue or do not deploy SAV are less likely to run Spoofer on their networks.

A more practical approach is to perform such measurements remotely. Kührer et al. [15] scanned for open DNS resolvers, as proposed by Mauch [20], to detect the absence of outbound SAV. They leveraged the misconfiguration of forwarding resolvers. The misbehaving resolver forwards a request to a recursive resolver with either not changing the packet source address to its address or by sending back the response to the client with the source IP of the recursive resolver. They fingerprinted those forwarders and found out that they are mostly embedded devices and routers. Misconfigured forwarders originated from 2 692 autonomous systems. We refer to this technique as *forwarders-based*.

---

[1] https://spoofer.caida.org/summary.php.

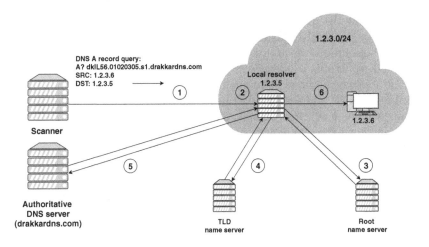

Fig. 1. Inbound spoofing scan setup.

Lone et al. [18] proposed another method that does not require a vantage point inside a tested network. When packets are sent to a customer network with an address that is routable but not allocated, this packet is sent back to the provider router without changing its source IP address. The packet, having the source IP address of the machine that sent it, should be dropped by the router because the source IP does not belong to the customer network. The method detected 703 autonomous systems not deploying outbound SAV.

While the above-mentioned methods rely on actively generated (whether spoofed or not) packets, Lichtblau et al. [16] passively observed and analyzed inter-domain traffic exchanged between more than 700 networks at a large IXP. They classified observed traffic into bogon, unrouted, invalid, and valid based on the source IP addresses and AS paths. The most conservative estimation identified 393 networks where the invalid traffic originated from.

We are the first to propose a method to detect the absence of inbound SAV that is remote and does not rely on existing misconfigurations. Instead, we use local DNS resolvers (both open and closed) to infer the absence of packet filtering and the presence of SAV either at transit networks or at the edge. We are aware of a similar method by Deccio, but his work is in progress and not yet publicly available [6].

4 Methodology

4.1 Spoofing Scan

Figure 1 illustrates the idea of the proposed method. We have developed an efficient scanner that sends hand-crafted DNS A record request packets. We run the scanner on a machine inside a network that does not deploy outbound SAV so that we can send packets with spoofed IP addresses[2]. We set up a DNS server

---

[2] After our initial scan, we learned that one of the three upstream providers deploys SAV, so we temporarily disabled it to perform our measurements.

authoritative for the `drakkardns.com` domain to capture the traffic related to our scans. When a resolver inside a network vulnerable to inbound spoofing performs query resolution, we observe it on our authoritative DNS server. To prevent caching and to be able to identify the true originator in case of forwarding, we query the following unique subdomain every time: a random string, the hex-encoded resolver IP address (the destination of our query), a scan identifier, and the domain name itself, for example, `qGPDBe.02ae52c7.s1.drakkardns.com`.

Figure 1 shows the scanning setup for the `1.2.3.0/24` network. In step 1, the scanner sends one spoofed packet to each host of this network, thus packets to 254 destinations in total. The spoofed source IP address is always the next one after the destination. When the spoofed DNS packet arrives at the destination network edge (therefore it has not been filtered anywhere in transit), there are three possible cases:

- **Packet filtering in place.** The packet filter inspects the packet source address and detects that such a packet cannot arrive from the outside because the address block is allocated inside the network. Thus, the filter drops the packet.
- **No packet filtering in place and nothing prevents the packet from entering the network.** If the packet destination is `1.2.3.5`, the address of the local resolver (step 2), it receives a DNS A record request from what looks to be another host on the same network and performs query resolution. If the destination is not the local resolver, it will drop the packet. However, the scanner will eventually reach all the hosts on the network and the local resolver if there is one. In some cases, the closed DNS resolver may be configured to refuse queries coming from its local area network (for example, if the whole separate network is dedicated to the infrastructure).
- **Other cases.** Regardless of the presence or absence of filtering, packets may be dropped due to reasons not related to IP spoofing such as network congestion [2].

In this study, we distinguish between two types of local resolvers: forwarders (or proxies) that forward queries to other recursive resolvers and non-forwarders (non-proxies) that recursively resolve queries they receive. Therefore, the non-forwarding local resolver (`1.2.3.5`) inspects the query that looks as if it was sent from `1.2.3.6` and performs the resolution by iteratively querying the root (step 3) and the top-level domain name (step 4) servers until it reaches our authoritative DNS server in step 5. Alternatively, it forwards the query to another recursive resolver that repeats the same procedure as described above for non-forwarders. In step 6, the DNS A query response is sent to the spoofed source (`1.2.3.6`).

We aim at scanning the whole IPv4 address space, yet taking into account only globally routable and allocated address ranges. We use the data maintained by the RouteViews Project to get all the IP blocks currently present in the BGP routing table and send spoofed DNS A requests to all the hosts of the prefixes.

4.2 Open Resolver Scan

In parallel, we perform an open resolver scan by sending DNS A requests with the genuine source IP address of the scanner. To avoid temporal changes, we send a non-spoofed query just after the spoofed one to the same host. The format of a non-spoofed query is almost identical to the spoofed one. The only difference is the scan identifier: `qGPDBe.02ae52c7.n1.drakkardns.com`. If we receive a request on our authoritative DNS server, it means that we have reached an open resolver. Moreover, if this open resolver did not resolve a spoofed query, we infer the presence of inbound SAV either in transit or at the tested network edge.

We also analyze traffic on the machine on which we run the scanner to deploy the forwarders-based method, as explained in Sect. 3. We distinguish between two cases: the source of the DNS response is the same as the original destination and the source is different [15,20]. The latter implies that either the source IP address of the original query was not rewritten when the query was forwarded to another recursive resolver or the source IP address of the recursive resolver was not changed on the way back. In either case, such a packet should not be able to leave its network if there is the outbound SAV in place. In Sect. 5.5, we analyze the results from the forwarders-based method and compare the policies of SAV deployment in both directions.

4.3 Ethical Considerations

To make sure that our study follows the ethical rules of network scanning, yet providing complete results, we adopt the recommended best practices [8,9]. We aggregate the BGP routing table to eliminate overlapping prefixes. In this way, we are sure to send no more than two DNS A request packets (spoofed and non-spoofed) to every tested host. Due to packet losses, we potentially miss some results, but we go with this limitation in order not to disrupt the normal operation of tested networks. In addition, we randomize our input list for the scanner so that we do not send consecutive requests to the same network (apart from two consecutive spoofed and non-spoofed packets). Our scanning activities are spread over 10 days.

We set up a homepage for this study on **drakkardns.com** and all queried subdomains with a description of our scan and provide the contact information if someone wants to exclude her networks from testing. We received 9 requests from operators and excluded 29 360 925 IP addresses from our future scans. We also exclude those addresses from our analysis. We do not publicly reveal the source address validation policies of individual networks and AS operators. We also plan a notification campaign through CSIRTs and by directly informing the operators of affected networks.

5 Results

5.1 Filtering Levels

When evaluating the SAV deployment, we aim at finding the unit of analysis that will show the most consistent results. Each received request reveals the

Table 2. Spoofing scan results

Metric	Number	Proportion (%)
DNS forwarders	6 530 799	94.01
Open resolvers	2 317 607	35.49
Closed resolvers	4 213 192	64.51
DNS non-forwarders	415 983	5.99
Open resolvers	39 924	9.6
Closed resolvers	376 059	90.4
Vulnerable to spoofing/24 IPv4 networks	959 666	8.62
Vulnerable to spoofing longest matching prefixes	197 641	23.61
Vulnerable to spoofing autonomous systems	32 673	49.34

IP address of the original target of the query. We map this IP address to the corresponding/24 address block, the longest matching BGP prefix, and its ASN. This granularity allows us to evaluate the SAV practices at different levels:

- Autonomous systems: while based on a few received queries, we cannot by any means conclude on the filtering policies of the whole AS—they reveal SAV compliance for a part of it [3,4,18,19].
- Longest matching BGP prefixes: as the provider ASes may sub-allocate their address space to their customers by prefix delegation [13], the analysis of the SAV deployment at the longest matching prefix is another commonly used unit of analysis [3,19].
- /24 IPv4 networks: it is the smallest unit of measuring the SAV deployment used so far by the existing methods [4,19]. We later show that even at this level some results are inconsistent.

5.2   Global Scans

In December 2019, we performed the spoofing and open resolver scans. During the spoofing scan, we observed 14 761 484 A requests on our authoritative DNS server. It has been shown that DNS resolvers tend to issue repetitive queries due to proactive caching or premature querying [26]. Thus, we leave only unique tuples of the source IP address and the domain name, which results in 9 558 190 unique requests (64.75% of all the received requests and 0.34% of all the requests sent by the scanner).

Table 2 presents the statistics gathered from the spoofing scan. From each request received on our authoritative name server, we retrieve the queried domain, extract its hexadecimal part (the destination of our original DNS A query) and convert it to an IP address. We then compare it to the source IP of the query and identify 6 530 799 DNS proxies (local resolvers that forwarded their queries to other recursive resolvers) and 415 983 non-proxies (local resolvers that performed resolutions themselves). We identify that 35.49% of forwarders and 9.60% of non-forwarders are open resolvers.

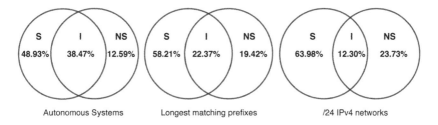

Fig. 2. Filtering inconsistencies (S: vulnerable to inbound spoofing, NS: non-vulnerable to inbound spoofing, and I: inconsistent)

The address encoded in the domain name identifies the originator network. We map every IP address to the corresponding prefix and the autonomous system number. They originate from 32 673 autonomous systems and correspond to 197 641 prefixes (49.34% and 23.61% out of all ASes and longest matching prefixes present in the BGP routing table, respectively) and 959 666/24 blocks.

For the open resolver scan, we retrieve query responses with the NOERROR reply code, meaning that we reached an open resolver. Note that for this study, we do not check the integrity of those responses. In total, we identify 4 022 711 open resolvers, 956 969 of which (23.79%) are forwarders.

5.3 Inferring Absence and Presence of Inbound Filtering

We compare the results of spoofing and open resolver scans to reveal the absence and the *presence* of inbound SAV. For every detected open resolver, we check whether this particular resolver resolved a spoofed query. If it did not, we assume that this resolver is inside a network performing inbound SAV. We note, however, that due to inconsistent filtering policies inside networks and possible packet losses, we may obtain contradictory results for a single AS or a network. We define ASes and networks as inconsistent if we have at least two measurements with a different outcome.

Figure 2 shows the number of vulnerable to inbound spoofing (S), non-vulnerable to inbound spoofing (NS), and inconsistent (I) ASes, prefixes, and/24 networks. As expected, the most inconsistent results are for ASes with 14 382 (38.47%) of them revealing both the absence and presence of inbound SAV. The smaller the network size, the more consistent results we obtain, as it can be seen for the longest matching prefixes and/24 networks. While/24 is a common unit of network filtering policy measurement, it still exhibits a high level of inconsistency with 154 704 (12.30%) networks belonging to both groups. Importantly, after our initial scan, we ascertained that one of our three upstream providers performed source address validation of outbound traffic. This means that all packets with spoofed source IP addresses routed by this provider were dropped, while those routed by other two upstream providers were forwarded. This has significantly affected the measurements and resulted in a very high number of inconsistent results. By disabling this provider before the main scan, the number of inconsistent/24 networks decreased more than two-fold.

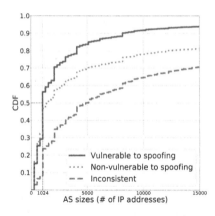
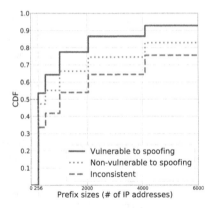

Fig. 3. Sizes of autonomous systems

Fig. 4. Sizes of longest matching prefixes

Figure 3 presents the cumulative distribution of vulnerable to spoofing, non-vulnerable to spoofing, and inconsistent AS sizes (the number of announced IPv4 addresses in the BGP routing table). Around 80% of vulnerable to spoofing ASes have 4 096 addresses and less, meaning that small ASes are less likely to perform packet filtering at the network edge. Figure 4 shows the longest matching prefix sizes. We can observe that almost 90% of vulnerable to spoofing prefixes have 4 096 addresses and less. The sizes of inconsistent ASes and prefixes are significantly larger compared to vulnerable and non-vulnerable ones.

Larger ASes are more likely to peer with a larger number of other ASes and sub-allocate the address space to their customers and therefore, have less consistent filtering policies. To further understand the complexity of the ASes, we use the CAIDA AS relationship data [7] to compute the number of relationships of all ASes in our dataset. We find that inconsistent ASes maintain relationships with 29 other ASes on average, while vulnerable to spoofing and non-vulnerable to spoofing ASes connect to around 7 ASes on average.

The AS relationship data and the AS size give us some initial insights into understanding inconsistencies in ASes. Another possible reason for inconsistent results for a single AS or a network is packet losses. To test this hypothesis, we sampled 1000/24 networks from the inconsistent group and re-scanned them. 48 networks out of 1000 did not respond to any query. Most importantly, 464 became consistent (all vulnerable to spoofing). The remaining/24s were still inconsistent.

Furthermore, we repeated the same test once per day, three days in a row, to estimate the persistence of the results. More than two-thirds of the networks belonged to the same group (inconsistent, vulnerable to spoofing, non-vulnerable, or no data) during all three measurements. Interestingly, half of those were inconsistent. For most of the networks, the exact set of the responding resolver IP addresses changed every day, due to the IP address churn of resolvers [14]. Regarding the remaining one-thirds, it is unlikely that provider filtering policies change so rapidly. Therefore, apart from packet losses, we may be dealing with other issues such as different filtering policies at upstream providers for multi-homed customer ASes.

Table 3. Geolocation results

Rank	Country	Resolvers (#)	Country	Vulnerable to spoofing/24 networks (#)	Country	Vulnerable to spoofing/24 networks (%)
1	China	2 304 601	China	271 160	Cocos Islands	100.0
2	Brazil	687 564	USA	157 978	Kosovo	81.82
3	USA	678 837	Russia	55 107	Comoros	57.89
4	Iran	373 548	Italy	32 970	Armenia	52.16
5	India	348 076	Brazil	29 603	Western Sahara	50.00
6	Algeria	252 794	Japan	28 660	Christmas Island	50.00
7	Indonesia	249 968	India	27 705	Maldives	39.13
8	Russia	229 475	Mexico	24 195	Moldova	38.66
9	Italy	108 806	UK	18 576	Morocco	37.85
10	Argentina	103 449	Morocco	18 135	Uzbekistan	36.17

These experiments show that even though the number of inconsistent/24s decreased almost two-fold, such networks are not uncommon. We plan to contact several network providers to validate our results and gain some insights into their motivation for inconsistent filtering at the network level.

5.4   Geographic Distribution

Identifying the countries that do not comply with the SAV standard is the first step in mitigating the issue by, for example, contacting local CSIRTs. We use the MaxMind database[3] to map every resolver IP address of the spoofed query retrieved from the domain name to its country. Table 3 summarizes the results.

In total, we identified 237 countries and territories vulnerable to spoofing of incoming network traffic. We first compute the number of DNS resolvers per country and map the resolvers to the nearest/24 IP address blocks to evaluate the number of vulnerable to spoofing/24 networks per country. We see that the top 10 countries by the number of DNS resolvers are not the same as the top 10 for vulnerable to spoofing/24 networks because a large number of individual DNS resolvers by itself does not indicate how they are distributed across different networks.

Such absolute numbers are still not representative as countries with a large Internet infrastructure may have many DNS resolvers and therefore reveal many vulnerable to spoofing networks that represent a small proportion of the whole. For this reason, we compute the fraction of vulnerable to spoofing vs. all/24 IPv4 networks per country. To determine the number of all the/24 networks per country, we map all the individual IPv4 addresses to their location, then to the nearest/24 block and keep the country/territory where most addresses of a given network belong to. Figure 5 (in Appendix) presents the resulting world map. We can see in Table 3 that the top 10 ranking has changed. Small countries such as Cocos Islands and Western Sahara, which have one identified resolver each,

---
[3] https://dev.maxmind.com/geoip/geoip2/geolite2/.

suffer from a high proportion of vulnerable to spoofing networks. The only/24 network of Cocos Islands allows inbound spoofing. On the other hand, Morocco is a country with a large Internet infrastructure (47 915/24 networks in total) and with a large relative number of vulnerable to spoofing networks.

5.5 Outbound vs. Inbound SAV Policies

We retrieve the Spoofer data to infer the absence and the presence of outbound SAV. The Spoofer client sends packets with the IP address of the machine on which the client is running as well as packets with a spoofed source address. The results are anonymized per/24 IP address blocks. Spoofer identifies four possible states: *blocked* (only an unspoofed packet was received, the spoofed packet was blocked), *rewritten* (the spoofed packet was received, but its source IP address was changed on the way), *unknown* (neither packet was received), *received* (the spoofed packet was received by the server).

In December 2019, we collected and aggregated the results of the latest measurements to infer outbound SAV compliance. During this period, tests were run from 3 251 distinct/24 networks. In some cases, tests from the same IP address block show different results due to possible changes in the filtering policies of the tested networks, so we kept the latest result for every/24 network. We identified 1 910 networks blocking spoofed outbound traffic and 316 that allow spoofing.

We deploy the forwarders-based technique on our scanning server and analyze the responses in which the originally queried IP address is not the same as the responding one, as described in Sect. 4.2. Interestingly, 3 147 responses arrived from the private ranges of IP addresses. Previous work has shown that this behavior is related to NAT misconfiguration [19]. To detect misbehaving forwarders inside networks vulnerable to outbound spoofing, we check that the IP address of the forwarder, the source IP address of the response, and the scanner IP address belong to different ASes. In this way, we identify 456 816 misbehaving forwarders originated from 20 889/24 IP networks vulnerable to outbound spoofing. In total, the two methods identify 21 203/24 networks without outbound filtering and 1 910/24 networks with outbound SAV in place.

The results obtained by running our scans and using the data of the Spoofer project let us evaluate the filtering policies of networks in both directions (inbound and outbound). We aggregated all the datasets and found 4 541/24 networks with no filtering in any direction and only 151 networks deploying both inbound and outbound SAV. To further understand the filtering preferences of network operators, we analyze how many of them do not filter only outbound or only inbound traffic. Note however, that the coverage of inbound filtering scans is much larger than the one of outbound SAV (forwarders-based method and especially the Spoofer data). To make the datasets comparable, we find the intersection between the networks covered by inbound filtering scans (only those showing consistent results) and all the networks tested with the Spoofer client. In the resulting set of 559/24 networks, there are 298 networks with no filtering for inbound traffic only and 15 with no outbound SAV only. It shows that inbound filtering is less deployed than outbound, which is consistent with previous work [19]. We do the same comparison of our inbound filtering scans and the forwarders-based method. Among 16 839 common/24 networks (all vulnerable to outbound spoofing), 12 393 are also vulnerable to inbound spoofing.

6   Limitations

While we aimed at designing a universal method to detect the deployment of inbound SAV at the network edge, our approach has certain limitations that may impact the accuracy of the obtained results. We rely on one main assumption—the presence of an (open or closed) DNS resolver or a proxy in a tested network. In case of the absence of one of them, we cannot conclude on the filtering policies. If the probed resolver is closed, our method may only confirm that a particular network does not perform SAV for inbound traffic, at least for some part of its IP address space. Only the presence of an open DNS resolver may reveal the SAV presence assuming that the transit networks do not deploy SAV.

From our results, we often cannot unequivocally conclude on the general policies of operators of, for example, larger autonomous systems. Some parts of an AS, a BGP prefix, or even a/24 network may be configured to allow spoofed packets to enter one subnetwork and to filter spoofed packets in another one.

The scanner sending spoofed packets should itself be located in the network not performing SAV for outgoing traffic. Still, even if a spoofed query leaves our network, it may be filtered by some transit networks and never reach the tested destination. Therefore, we plan to test our method from different vantage points.

There are several reasons, apart from deploying SAV, why we have no data for certain IP address blocks. Packet losses and temporary network failures are some of the reasons for not receiving queries from all the target hosts [14]. To overcome this limitation, we plan to repeat our measurements regularly and study the persistence of this vulnerability over time.

7   Conclusion

The absence of ingress filtering at the network edge may lead to important security issues such as DDoS and DNS zone or cache poisoning attacks. Even if network operators are aware of these risks, they choose not to filter traffic, or do it incorrectly because of deployment and maintenance costs or implementation issues. There is a need for identifying and enumerating networks that do not comply with RFC 2827 to understand the scale of the problem and find possible ways to mitigate it.

In this paper, we have presented a novel method for inferring the SAV deployment for inbound traffic and discussed the results of the first Internet-wide measurement study. We have obtained significantly more test results than other methods: we cover over 49% of autonomous systems and 23% of the longest matching BGP prefixes.

The next step for this work is to start longitudinal measurements to infer the SAV deployment in both IPv4 and IPv6 address spaces from different vantage points. Finally, we plan to notify all parties affected by the vulnerability.

Acknowledgments. The authors would like to thank the anonymous reviewers and our shepherd Ramakrishna Padmanabhan for their valuable feedback. This work has been carried out in the framework of the PrevDDoS project funded by the IDEX Université Grenoble Alpes "Initiative de Recherche Scientifique (IRS)".

Appendix

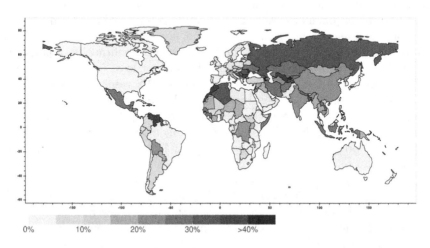

Fig. 5. Fraction of vulnerable to spoofing (inbound traffic) vs. all/24 networks per country

References

1. Baker, F., Savola, P.: Ingress Filtering for Multihomed Networks. RFC 3704, March 2004. https://rfc-editor.org/rfc/rfc3704.txt
2. Beverly, R., Berger, A., Hyun, Y., Claffy, K.: Understanding the efficacy of deployed Internet source address validation filtering. In: Internet Measurement Conference. ACM (2009)
3. Beverly, R., Bauer, S.: The Spoofer project: inferring the extent of source address filtering on the Internet. In: USENIX Steps to Reducing Unwanted Traffic on the Internet (SRUTI) Workshop, July 2005
4. CAIDA: The Spoofer Project. https://www.caida.org/projects/spoofer/
5. The Closed Resolver Project. https://closedresolver.com
6. Deccio, C.: Private Communication
7. Dimitropoulos, X., Krioukov, D., Fomenkov, M., Huffaker, B., Hyun, Y., Riley, G., et al.: AS relationships: inference and validation. ACM SIGCOMM Comput. Commun. Rev. **37**(1), 29–40 (2007)
8. Dittrich, D., Kenneally, E.: The Menlo report: ethical principles guiding information and communication technology research. Technical report, U.S. Department of Homeland Security, August 2012

9. Durumeric, Z., Wustrow, E., Halderman, J.A.: ZMap: fast Internet-wide scanning and its security applications. In: USENIX Security Symposium (2013)
10. Kaminsky, D.: It's the end of the cache as we know it. https://www.slideshare.net/dakami/dmk-bo2-k8
11. Korczyński, M., Król, M., van Eeten, M.: Zone poisoning: the how and where of non-secure DNS dynamic updates. In: Internet Measurement Conference. ACM (2016)
12. Kottler, S.: February 28th DDoS Incident Report. https://github.blog/2018-03-01-ddos-incident-report/
13. Krenc, T., Feldmann, A.: BGP prefix delegations: a deep dive. In: Internet Measurement Conference, pp. 469–475. ACM (2016)
14. Kührer, M., Hupperich, T., Bushart, J., Rossow, C., Holz, T.: Going wild: large-scale classification of open DNS resolvers. In: Internet Measurement Conference. ACM (2015)
15. Kührer, M., Hupperich, T., Rossow, C., Holz, T.: Exit from hell? Reducing the impact of amplification DDoS attacks. In: USENIX Conference on Security Symposium (2014)
16. Lichtblau, F., Streibelt, F., Krüger, T., Richter, P., Feldmann, A.: Detection, classification, and analysis of inter-domain traffic with spoofed source IP addresses. In: Internet Measurement Conference. ACM (2017)
17. Lone, Q., Luckie, M., Korczyński, M., Asghari, H., Javed, M., van Eeten, M.: Using crowdsourcing marketplaces for network measurements: the case of Spoofer. In: Traffic Monitoring and Analysis Conference (2018)
18. Lone, Q., Luckie, M., Korczyński, M., van Eeten, M.: Using loops observed in traceroute to infer the ability to spoof. In: Kaafar, M.A., Uhlig, S., Amann, J. (eds.) PAM 2017. LNCS, vol. 10176, pp. 229–241. Springer, Cham (2017). https://doi.org/10.1007/978-3-319-54328-4_17
19. Luckie, M., Beverly, R., Koga, R., Keys, K., Kroll, J., Claffy, K.: Network hygiene, incentives, and regulation: deployment of source address validation in the Internet. In: Computer and Communications Security Conference (CCS). ACM (2019)
20. Mauch, J.: Spoofing ASNs. http://seclists.org/nanog/2013/Aug/132
21. Müller, L.F., Luckie, M.J., Huffaker, B., Claffy, K., Barcellos, M.P.: Challenges in inferring spoofed traffic at IXPs. In: Conference on Emerging Networking Experiments And Technologies (CoNEXT), pp. 96–109. ACM (2019)
22. Rossow, C.: Amplification hell: revisiting network protocols for DDoS abuse. In: Network and Distributed System Security Symposium (NDSS) (2014)
23. University of Oregon Route Views Project. http://www.routeviews.org/routeviews/
24. Scheffler, S., Smith, S., Gilad, Y., Goldberg, S.: The unintended consequences of email spam prevention. In: Beverly, R., Smaragdakis, G., Feldmann, A. (eds.) PAM 2018. LNCS, vol. 10771, pp. 158–169. Springer, Cham (2018). https://doi.org/10.1007/978-3-319-76481-8_12
25. Senie, D., Ferguson, P.: Network ingress filtering: defeating denial of service attacks which employ IP source address spoofing. RFC 2827, May 2000. https://rfc-editor.org/rfc/rfc2827.txt
26. Shue, C., Kalafut, A.: Resolvers revealed: characterizing DNS resolvers and their clients. ACM Trans. Internet Technol. **12**, 1–17 (2013)
27. Vixie, P., Thomson, S., Rekhter, Y., Bound, J.: Dynamic updates in the domain name system (DNS UPDATE). Internet RFC 2136, April 1997

MUST, SHOULD, DON'T CARE: TCP
Conformance in the Wild

Mike Kosek[1]([✉])[iD], Leo Blöcher[1], Jan Rüth[1][iD], Torsten Zimmermann[1],
and Oliver Hohlfeld[2][iD]

[1] Communication and Distributed Systems, RWTH Aachen University,
Aachen, Germany
{kosek,bloecher,rueth,zimmermann}@comsys.rwth-aachen.de
[2] Chair of Computer Networks, Brandenburg University of Technology,
Cottbus, Germany
oliver.hohlfeld@b-tu.de

Abstract. Standards govern the SHOULD and MUST requirements for
protocol implementers for interoperability. In case of TCP that carries
the bulk of the Internets' traffic, these requirements are defined in RFCs.
While it is known that not all optional features are implemented and
non-conformance exists, one would assume that TCP implementations
at least conform to the minimum set of MUST requirements. In this
paper, we use Internet-wide scans to show how Internet hosts and paths
conform to these basic requirements. We uncover a non-negligible set
of hosts and paths that do not adhere to even basic requirements. For
example, we observe hosts that do not correctly handle checksums and
cases of middlebox interference for TCP options. We identify hosts that
drop packets when the urgent pointer is set or simply crash. Our publicly
available results highlight that conformance to even fundamental protocol requirements should not be taken for granted but instead checked
regularly.

1 Introduction

Reliable, interoperable, and secure Internet communication largely depends on
the adherence to standards defined in RFCs. These RFCs are simple text documents, and any specifications published within them are inherently informal,
flexible, and up for interpretation, despite the usage of keywords indicating the
requirement levels [20], e.g., SHOULD or MUST. It is therefore expected and
known that violations—and thus non-conformance—do arise unwillingly. Nevertheless, it can be assumed that Internet hosts widely respect at least a minimal
set of mandatory requirements. To which degree this is the case is, however,
unknown.

In this paper, we shed light on this question by performing Internet-wide
active scans to probe if Internet hosts and paths are conformant to a set of
minimum TCP requirements that any TCP speaker MUST implement. This
adherence to the fundamental protocol principles is especially important since

© Springer Nature Switzerland AG 2020
A. Sperotto et al. (Eds.): PAM 2020, LNCS 12048, pp. 122–138, 2020.
https://doi.org/10.1007/978-3-030-44081-7_8

TCP carries the bulk of the data transmission in the Internet. The basic requirements of a TCP host are defined in RFC 793 [47]—the core TCP specification. Since its over 40 years of existence, it has accumulated over 25 accepted errata described in RFC 793bis-Draft14 [27], which is a draft of a planned future update of the TCP specification, incorporating all minor changes and errata to RFC 793. We base our selection of probed requirements on formalized MUST requirements defined in this drafted update to RFC 793.

The relevance of TCP in the Internet is reflected in the number of studies assessing its properties and conformance. Well studied are the interoperability of TCP extensions [21], or within special purpose scenarios [40,41], and especially non-conformance introduced by middleboxes on the path [24,35]. However, the conformance to basic mandatory TCP features has not been studied in the wild. We close this gap by studying to which degree TCP implementations in the wild conform to MUST requirements. Non-conformance to these requirements limits interoperability, extensibility, performance, or security properties, leading to the essential necessity to understand who does not adhere to which level of non-conformance. Uncovering occurrences of non-conformities hence reveal areas of improvement for future standards. A recent example is QUIC, where effort is put into the avoidance of such misconceptions during standardization [46].

With our large scale measurement campaign presented in this paper, we show that while the majority of end-to-end connections are indeed conforming to the tested requirements, a non-trivial number of end-hosts as well as end-to-end paths show non-conformities, breaking current and future TCP extensions, and even voiding interoperability thus reducing connectivity. We show that

▶ In a controlled lab study, non-conformance already exists at the OS-level: only two tested stacks (Linux and lwIP) pass all tests, where, surprisingly, others (including macOS and Windows) fail in at least one category each. Observing non-conformance in the wild can therefore be expected.
▶ In the wild, we indeed found a non-negligible amount of non-conformant hosts. For example, checksums are not verified in ~3.5% cases, and middleboxes inject non-conformant MSS values. Worrisome, using reserved flags or setting the urgent pointer can render the target host unreachable.
▶ At a infrastructure level, 4.8% of the Alexa domains with and without www. prefix show different conformance levels (e.g., because of different infrastructures: CDN vs. origin server), mostly due to flags that limit reachability. The reachability of websites can thus depend on the www. prefix.

Structure. In Sect. 2 we present related work followed by our methodology and its validation in Sect. 3. The design and evaluation of our Internet-wide TCP conformance scans are discussed in Sect. 4 before we conclude the paper.

2   Related Work

Multiple measurement approaches have focused on the conformance of TCP implementations on servers, the presence of middleboxes and their interference on TCP connections, and non-standard conform behavior. In the following, we discuss similarities and differences of selected approaches to our work.

TCP Stack Behavior. One line of research aims at characterizing remote TCP stacks by their behavior (e.g., realized in the TCP Behavior Inference Tool (TBIT) [45] in 2001). One aspect is to study the deployment of TCP tunings (e.g., the initial window configuration [48–50]) or TCP extensions (e.g., Fast Retransmit [45], Fast Open [39,44], Selective Acknowledgment (SACK) [36,43,45], or Explicit Congestion Notification (ECN) [18,36,37,42,43,45] and ECN++ [38] to name a few). While these works aim to generally characterize stacks by behavior and to study the availability and deployability of TCP extensions, our work specifically focuses on the *conformance* of *current* TCP stacks to *mandatory* behavior every stack must implement. A second aspect concerns the usage of behavioral characterizations to *fingerprint* TCP stacks (e.g., via active [30] or passive [19] measurements) and mechanisms to defeat fingerprinting (e.g., [53]).

Middlebox Interference. The end-to-end behavior of TCP not only depends on the stack implementations, but also on on-path middleboxes [22], which can tune TCP performance and security but also (negatively) impact protocol mechanisms and extensions (see e.g., [18,42,43]). Given their relevance, a large body of work studies the impact within the last two decades and opens the question if TCP is still extensible in today's Internet. Answering this question resulted in a methodology for middlebox inference which is extended by multiple works to provide middlebox detection tools to assess their influence; By observing the differences between sent and received TCP options at controlled endpoints (TCPExposure [32]), it is observed that 25% of the studied paths tamper with TCP options, e.g., with TCP's SACK mechanism. Similarly, tracebox [24] also identifies middleboxes based on modifications of TCP options, but as client-side only approach without requiring server control. Besides also identifying the issues with TCP's SACK option, they highlight the interference with TCP's MSS option and the incorrect behavior of TCP implementations when probing for MPTCP support. PATHSpider [35] extends tracebox to test more TCP options, e.g., ECN or differentiated services code point (DSCP). They evaluate their tool in an ECN support study, highlighting that some intermediaries tamper with the respective options, making a global ECN deployment a challenging task. Further investigating how middleboxes harm TCP traffic, a tracebox-based study [28] shows that more than a third of all studied paths cross at least one middlebox, and that on over 6% of these paths TCP traffic is harmed. Given the negative influence of transparent middleboxes, proposals enable endpoints to identify and negotiate with middleboxes using a new TCP option [34] and to generally cooperate with middleboxes [23]. While we focus on assessing TCP conformance to mandatory behavior, we follow tracebox's approach to differentiate non-conforming stacks from middlebox interference causing non-conformity.

Takeaway: While a large body of work already investigates TCP behavior and middlebox inference, a focus on conformance to mandatory functionality required to implement is missing—a gap that we address in this study.

3 Methodology

We test TCP conformance by performing active measurements that probe for mandatory TCP features and check adherence to the RFC. We begin by explaining how we detect middleboxes before we define the test cases and then validate our methodology in controlled testbed experiments.

3.1 Middlebox Detection

Middleboxes can alter TCP header information and thereby cause non-conformance, which we would wrongly attribute to the probed host without performing a middlebox detection. Therefore, we use the tracebox approach [24] to detect interfering middleboxes by sending and repeating our probes with increasing IP TTLs. That is, in every test case (see Sect. 3.2), the first segment is sent multiple times with increasing TTL values from 1 to 30 in parallel while capturing ICMP time exceeded messages. We limit the TTL to 30 since we did not observe higher hop counts in our prior work for Internet-wide scans [51]. To distinguish the replied messages and determine the hop count, we encode the TTL in the IPv4 ID and in the TCP acknowledgment number, window size, and urgent pointer fields. We chose to encode the TTL in multiple header fields since middleboxes could alter every single one. These repetitions enable us to pinpoint and detect (non-)conformance within the end-to-end path if ICMP messages are issued by the intermediaries quoting the expired segment. Please note that alteration or removal of some of our encodings does *not* render the path or the specific hop non-conformant. A non-conformance is only attested, if the actual tested behavior was modified as visible through the expired segment. Further, since only parts of the fields—all 16 or 32 bits in size—may be altered by middleboxes (e.g., slight changes to the window size), we repeat each value as often as possible within every field. Our TTL value of at most 30 can be encoded in 5 bits, and thus be repeated 3 to 6 times in the selected fields. Additionally, the TCP header option No-Operation (NOOP) allows an opaque encoding of the TTL. Specifically, we append as many NOOPs as there are hops in the TTL to the fixed-size header. Other header fields are either utilized for routing decisions (e.g., port numbers in load balancers) or are not opaque (e.g., sequence numbers), rendering them unsuitable. Depending on the specific test case, some of the fields are not used for the TTL encoding. For example, when testing for urgent pointer adherence, we do not encode the TTL in the urgent pointer field.

3.2 TCP Conformance Test Cases

Our test cases check for observable TCP conformance of end-to-end connections by actively probing for a set of *minimum* requirements that any TCP must implement. We base our selection on 119 explicitly numbered requirements specified in RFC 793bis-Draft14 [27], of which 69 are absolute requirements (i.e., *MUSTs* [20]). These MUSTs resemble minimum requirements for *any* TCP connection participating in the Internet—not only for hosts, but also for intermediate elements within the traversed path. The majority of these 69 MUSTs address internal state-handling details, and can therefore not be observed or verified via active probing. To enable an Internet-wide assessment of TCP conformance, we thus focus on MUST requirements whose adherence is *observable* by communicating with the remote host. We synthesize eight tests from these requirements, which we summarize in Table 1, and discuss them in the following paragraphs. Each test is in some way critical to interoperability, security, performance, or extensibility of TCP. The complexity involved in verifying conformance to other advanced requirements often leads to the exclusion of these seemingly fundamental properties in favor of more specialized research.

Table 1. Requirements based on the MUSTs (number from RFC shown in brackets) as defined in RFC 793bis, Draft 14 [27]. Further, we show the precise test sequence and the condition leading to a PASS for the test.

Checksum	PASS Condition
ChecksumIncorrect (2,3)	▶ When sending a SYN or an ACK segment with a non-zero but invalid checksum, a target must respond with a RST segment or ignore it
ChecksumZero (2,3)	▶ As above but with an explicit zeroed checksum

Options	PASS Condition
OptionSupport (4)	▶ When sending a SYN segment with EOOL and NOOP options, a target must respond with a SYN/ACK segment
OptionUnknown (6)	▶ When sending a SYN segment with an unassigned option (# 158), a target must respond with a SYN/ACK segment
MSSSupport (4,14,16)	▶ When sending a SYN segment with an MSS of 515 byte, a target must not send segments exceeding 515 byte
MSSMissing (15,16)	▶ When sending a SYN segment without an MSS, a target must not send segments exceeding 536 byte (IPv4) or 1220 byte (IPv6, not tested)

Flags	PASS Condition
Reserved (no MUST)	▶ When Sending a SYN segment with a reserved flag set (# 2), a target must respond with a SYN/ACK segment with zeroed reserved flags ▶ Subsequently, when sending an ACK segment with a reserved flag set (# 2), a target must not retransmit the SYN/ACK segment
UrgentPointer (30,31)	▶ When sending a sequence of segments flagged as urgent, a target must acknowledge them with an ACK segment

TCP Checksum. The TCP checksum protects against segment corruption in transit and is mandatory to both calculate and verify. Even though most Layer 2 protocols already protect against segment corruption, it has been shown [55] that software or hardware bugs in intermediate systems may still alter packet data, and thus, high layer checksums are still vital. Checksums are an essential requirement to consider due to the performance implications of having to iterate over the entire segment after receiving it, resulting in an incentive to skip this step even though today this task is typically offloaded to the NIC. Both the *ChecksumIncorrect* and the *ChecksumZero* test (see Table 1) verify the handling of checksums in the TCP header. They differ only in the kind of checksum used; the former employs a randomly chosen incorrect checksum while the latter, posing as a special case, zeroes the field instead, i.e., this could appear as if the field is unused.

TCP Options. TCP specifies up to 40 bytes of options for future extensibility. It is thus crucial that these bytes are actually usable and, if used, handled correctly. According to the specification, any implementation is required to support the End of option list (EOOL), NOOP, and Maximum Segment Size (MSS) option. We test these options due to their significance for interoperability and, in the general case, extensibility and performance. The different, and sometimes variable, option length makes header parsing somewhat computationally expensive (especially in hardware), opening the door for non-conformant performance enhancements comparable to skipping checksum verification. Further, an erroneous implementation of either requirement can have security repercussions in the form of buffer overflows or resource wastage, culminating in a denial of service. The *OptionSupport* test validates the support of EOOL and NOOP, while the *OptionUnknown* test checks the handling of an unassigned option. The *MSSSupport* test verifies the proper handling of an explicitly stated MSS value, while the *MSSMissing* test tests the usage of default values specified by the RFC in the absence of the MSS option.

TCP Flags. Alongside the stated TCP options, TCP's extensibility is mainly guaranteed by (im-)mutable control flags in its header, of which four are currently still reserved for future use. The most prominent "recent" example is ECN [29], which uses two previously reserved bits. Though not explicitly stated as a numbered formal MUST[1], a TCP must zero (when sending) and ignore (when receiving) unknown header flags, which we test with the *Reserved* test, as incorrect handling can considerably block or delay the adoption of future features.

The *UrgentPointer* test addresses the long-established URG flag. Validating the support of segments flagged as urgent, the test splits around 500 bytes of urgent data into a sequence of three segments with comparable sizes. Each segment is flagged as urgent, and the urgent pointer field caries the offset from its current sequence number to the sequence number following the urgent data, i.e., to the sequence number following the payload. Initially intended to speed up segment processing by indicating data which should be processed imme-

---

[1] RFC 793bis-Draft14 states: *"Must be zero in generated segments and must be ignored in received segments, if corresponding future features are unimplemented by the sending or receiving host."* [27].

Table 2. Results of testbed measurements stating PASS (✓) and F$_{Target}$ (✗)

MUST Test as defined in Table 1	Linux 5.2.10	Windows 1809	macOS 10.14.6	uIP 1.0	lwIP 2.1.2	Seastar 19.06
ChecksumIncorrect	✓	✓	✓	✓	✓	✗
ChecksumZero	✓	✓	✓	✓	✓	✗
OptionSupport	✓	✓	✓	✓	✓	✓
OptionUnknown	✓	✓	✓	✓	✓	✓
MSSSupport	✓	✗	✓	✓	✓	✓
MSSMissing	✓	✓	✗	✓	✓	✓
Reserved	✓	✓	✓	✓	✓	✓
UrgentPointer	✓	✓	✓	✗	✓	✓

diately, the widely-used Berkeley Software Distribution (BSD) socket interface instead opted to interpret the urgent data as out-of-band data, leading to diverging implementations. As a result, the urgent pointer's usage is discouraged for new applications [27]. Nevertheless, TCP implementations are still required to support it with data of arbitrary length. As the requirement's inclusion adds computational complexity, implementers may see an incentive to skip it.

Pass and Failure Condition Notation. For the remainder of this paper, we use the following notation to report passing or failing of the above-described tests. Connections that unmistakably conform are denoted as *PASS*, whereas not clearly determinable results (applies only to some tests) are conservatively stated as *UNK*. UNKs may have several reasons such as, e.g., hosts ceasing to respond to non-test packets after having responded to a liveness test. Non-conformities raised by the target host are denoted as F_{Target}, and non-conformities raised by middleboxes on the path rather than the probed host are denoted as F_{Path}.

3.3 Validation

To evaluate our test design, we performed controlled measurements using a testbed setup, thereby eliminating possible on-path middlebox interference. Thus, only F$_{Target}$ can occur in this validation, but not F$_{Path}$. To cover a broad range of hosts, we verified our test implementations by targeting current versions of the three dominant Operating Systems (OSs) (Linux, Windows, and macOS) as well as three alternative TCP stacks (uIP [13], lwIP [7], and Seastar [8]).

We summarize the results in Table 2. As expected, we observe a considerable degree of conformance. Linux, as well as lwIP, managed to achieve full conformance to the tested requirements. Surprisingly, all other stacks failed in at least one test each. That is, most stacks do not fully adhere to these minimum requirements. uIP exposed the most critical flaw by crashing when receiving a segment with urgent data, caused by a segmentation fault while attempting to read beyond the segment's size (see Sect. 3.2). Since the release of the tested Version of uIP, the project did not undergo further development, but instead moved to the Contiki OS project [3], where it is currently maintained in Contiki-NG [2]. Following up on Contiki, it was uncovered that both distributions are still vulnerable. Their intended deployment platform, embedded microcontrollers, often lack the memory access controls present in modern OSs, amplifying the risk that this flaw poses. Addressing this issue, we submitted a Pull request to Contiki-NG [1]. The remaining F_{Target} have much less severe repercussions. Seastar, which bypasses the Linux L4 network stack using *Virtio* [15], fails both checksum tests. While hardware offloading is enabled by default, Seastar features software checksumming, which should take over if offloading is disabled or unsupported by the host OS. However, host OS support of offloaded features is not verified, which can lead to mismatches between believed to be and actually enabled features. We reported this issue to the authors [9]. The tests pass if the unsupported hardware offloads are manually deselected. The F_{Target} failure for macOS in the *MSSMissing* test is a consequence of macOS defaulting to a 1024 bytes MSS regardless of the IP version, thereby exceeding the IPv4 TCP default MSS, and falling behind that of IPv6. Windows 10 applies the MSS defaults defined in the TCP specification as a lower bound to any incoming value, overwriting the 515 bytes advertised in the *MSSSupport* test. Both MSS non-conformities could be mitigated by path maximum transmission unit (MTU) discovery, dynamically adjusting the segment size to the real network path.

Takeaway: *Only two tested stacks (Linux and lwIP) pass all tests and show full conformance. Surprisingly, all other stacks failed in at least one category each. That is, non-conformance to basic mandatory TCP implementation requirements already exists in current OS implementations. Even though our testbed validation is limited in the OS diversity, we can already expect to find a certain level of host non-conformance when probing TCP implementations in the wild.*

4   TCP Conformance in the Wild

In the following, we move on from our controlled testbed evaluation and present our measurement study in the Internet. Before we present and discuss the obtained results, we briefly focus on our measurement setup and our selected target sets.

4.1   Measurement Setup and Target Hosts

Measurement Setup. Our approach involves performing active probes against target hosts in the Internet to obtain a representative picture of TCP conformance in the wild. All measurements were performed using a single vantage point within the IPv4 research network of our university between August 13 and 22, 2019. As we currently do not have IPv6-capable scan infrastructure at our disposal, we leave this investigation open for future work. Using a probing rate of 10k pps on a distinct 10 GBit/s uplink, we decided to omit explicit loss detection and retransmission handling due to the increased complexity, instead stating results possibly affected by loss as UNK if not clearly determinable otherwise.

Target Hosts. To investigate a diverse set of end-to-end paths as well as end hosts, a total of 3,731,566 targets have been aggregated from three sources: *(i)* the HTTP Archive [33], *(ii)* Alexa Internet's top one million most visited sites list [17,52], and *(iii)* Censys [25] port 80 and 443 scans.

The **HTTP Archive** regularly crawls about 5M domains obtained from the Chrome User Experience Report to study Web performance and publishes the resulting dataset. We use the dataset of July 2019. For this, we were especially interested in the Content Delivery Network (CDN) tagged URLs, as no other source provides URL-to-CDN mappings. Since no IP addresses are provided, we resolved the 876,835 URLs to IPv4 addresses through four different public DNS services of Cloudflare, Google, DNS.WATCH, and Cisco's OpenDNS. Some domains contain multiple CDN tags in the original dataset. For these cases, we obtained the CDN mapping from the chain of CNAME resource records in the DNS responses and excluded targets that could still not be linked to only a single CDN. Removing duplicates on a per-URL basis, one target per resolved IPv4 address was selected. The resulting 4,116,937 targets were sampled to at most 10,000 entries per CDN, leading to 147,318 hosts in total. Removing duplicate IP addresses and blacklist filtering, we derived the final set of 27,795 CDN targets.

As recent research has shown [16], prefixing www. to a domain might not only provide different TLS security configurations and certificates than their non-www counterparts, but might also (re-)direct the request to servers of different Content Providers (CPs). To study this implications on TCP conformance, we used the **Alexa 1M list** published on August 10th, 2019, and resolved every domain with and without www-prefix according to the process outlined in the HTTP Archive. The resulting 3,297,849 targets were further sampled, randomly selecting one target with and without www-prefix per domain, removing duplicate IP addresses and blacklist filtering, leading to 466,685 Alexa targets.

Censys provided us research access to their data of Internet-wide port scans, which represent a heterogeneous set of globally distributed targets. In addition to the IPv4 address and successfully scanned port, many targets include information on host, vendor, OS, and product. Using the dataset compiled on August 8th, 2019, 10,559,985 Censys targets were identified with reachable ports 80 or 443, including, but not limited to, IoT devices, customer-premises equipment, industrial control systems, remote-control interfaces, and network infrastructure appliances. By removing duplicate IP addresses and blacklist filtering we arrive at 3,237,086 Censys target hosts.

Ethical Considerations. We aim to minimize the impact of our active scans as much as possible. First, we follow standard approaches [26] to display the intent of our scans in rDNS records of our scan IPs and on a website with an opt-out mechanism reachable via each scan IP. Moreover, we honor opt-out requests to our previous measurements and exclude these hosts. We further evaluated the potential implications of the uIP/Contiki crash observed in Sect. 3.3. Embedded microcontrollers, commonly used in IoT devices, are the primary use-case of uIP/Contiki. We could not identify hosts using this stack in the Censys device type data to exclude IPs, but assume little to very little use of this software stack within our datasets. We thus believe the potential implications to be minimal. We confirm this by observing that 100% of failed targets in the CDN as well as the Alexa dataset, and 99.35% of failed targets in the Censys dataset, are still reachable following *UrgentPointer* test case execution. We thus argue that our scans have created no harm to the Internet at large.

4.2   Results and Discussion

We next discuss the results of our conformance testing, which we summarize in Table 3. The table shows the relative results per test case for all reachable target hosts, excluding the unreachable ones. As the target data was derived from the respective sources multiple days before executing the tests (see Sect. 4.1), unreachable targets are expected. Except for minor variations, which can be explained by dynamic IP address assignment and changes to host configurations during test execution, ~12% of targets could not be reached in each test case and are removed from the results. While the CDN and Alexa datasets were derived from sources featuring popular websites, we expect a large overlap of target hosts, which is confirmed by 15,387 targets present in both datasets. Alexa and Censys share only 246 target hosts, while CDN and Censys do not overlap. All datasets are publicly available [5]. The decision to classify a condition as PASS, UNK, F_{Target}, or F_{Path}, does vary between test cases as a result of their architecture (see Sect. 3.2) and are discussed in detail next.

TCP Checksum. We start with the results of our checksum tests that validate correct checksum handling. As Table 3 shows, CDNs have a low failure rate

Table 3. Overview of relative results (in %) per test case per dataset. Here, n denotes the number of targets in each dataset. For better readability, we do not show the PASS results and highlight excessive failure rates in bold.

MUST Test as defined in Table 1	CDN $n = 27{,}795$			Alexa $n = 466{,}685$			Censys $n = 3{,}237{,}086$		
	UNK	F_{Target}	F_{Path}	UNK	F_{Target}	F_{Path}	UNK	F_{Target}	F_{Path}
ChecksumIncorrect	0.234	0.374	-	0.441	**3.224**	0.002	3.743	**3.594**	0.003
ChecksumZero	0.253	0.377	-	0.455	**3.210**	0.001	3.873	**3.592**	0.003
OptionSupport	-	0.040	-	-	0.470	0.009	-	1.410	0.313
OptionUnknown	-	0.026	0.011	-	0.585	0.053	-	1.477	0.019
MSSSupport	-	0.018	-	-	0.728	0.002	-	0.412	0.004
MSSMissing	0.026	-	0.018	0.303	0.299	0.136	1.423	0.388	0.416
Reserved	-	**2.194**	0.011	-	**6.689**	0.293	-	**2.791**	0.048
Reserved-SYN	-	0.138	0.011	-	1.297	0.309	-	1.849	0.049
UrgentPointer	0.150	0.330	0.022	0.804	**3.179**	0.208	3.815	**7.300**	0.042

for both tests, and we do not find any evidence for on-path modifications. In contrast, hosts from the Alexa and the Censys dataset show over ~3% F_{Target} failures. Drilling down on these hosts, they naturally cluster into two classes when looking at the AS ownership. On the one hand, we find AS (e.g., Amazon), where roughly 7% of all hosts fail both tests. Given the low share, these hosts could be purpose build high-performance VMs, e.g., for TCP-terminating proxies that do not handle checksums correctly. On the other hand, we find hosts (e.g., hosted in the QRATOR filtering AS) where nearly all hosts in that AS fail the tests. Since QRATOR offers a DDoS protection service, it is a likely candidate for operating a special purpose stack.

Takeaway: *We find cases of hosts that do not correctly handle checksums. While incorrect checksums may be a niche problem in the wild, these findings highlight that attackers with access to the unencrypted payload, but without access to the headers, could alter segments and have the modified data accepted.*

TCP Options. We next study if future TCP extensibility is honored by the ability to use TCP options. In our four option tests (see Table 3 for an overview), we observe overall the lowest failure rates—a generally good sign for extensibility support. Again, the Censys dataset shows the most failures, and especially the *OptionSupport* and the *MSSMissing* test have the highest F_{Path} (middlebox failures) across all tests. Both tests show a large overlap in the affected hosts and have likely the same cause for the high path failure rates. We observe that these hosts are all located in ISP networks. For the *MSSMissing* failures, we observe that an MSS is inserted at these hosts—likely due to the ISPs performing MSS clamping, e.g., due to PPPoE encapsulation by access routers. These routers need to rewrite the options header (to include the MSS option), and as the *OptionSupport* fails when, e.g., some of the EOOL and NOOP are stripped, the exact number of EOOL and NOOP are likely not preserved. Still, inserting the MSS option alters the originally intended behavior of the sender, i.e., having an MSS of 536 byte for IPv4. In this special case, the clamping did actually increase the MSS, and thereby strip some of the EOOL and NOOP options.

Looking at the *OptionUnknown* test, where we send an option with an unallocated codepoint, we again see low F_{Path} failures, but still, a non-negligible number of F_{Target} fails. There is no single AS that stands out in terms of the share of hosts that fail this test. However, we observe that among the ASes with the highest failure rates are ISPs and companies operating Cable networks.

Lastly, the *MSSSupport* test validating the correct handling of MSS values shows comparably high conformance. As we were unable to clearly pinpoint the failures to specific ASes, the most likely cause can be traced to the non-conformant operating systems as shown by our validation (see Sect. 3.3), where Windows fails this test and likely others that we did not test in isolation.

Takeaway: Our TCP options tests show the highest level of conformance of all tests, a good sign for extensibility. Still, we find cases of middlebox inference, mostly MSS injectors and option padding removers—primarily in ISP networks hinting at home gateways. Neither is inherently harmful due to path MTU discovery and the voluntary nature of option padding.

TCP Flags. Besides the previously tested options, TCP's extensibility is mainly guaranteed by (im-)mutable control flags in its header to toggle certain protocol behavior. In the *Reserved* test, we identify the correct handling of *unknown* (future) flags by sending an unallocated flag and expect no change in behavior. Instead, we surprisingly observe high failure rates across all datasets, most notable CDNs. When inspecting the CDN dataset, we found ~10% of Akamai's hosts to show this behavior. We contacted Akamai, but they validated that their servers do *not* touch this bit. Further analysis revealed that the reserved flag on the SYN was truthfully ignored, but *our test* failed as the final ACK of the 3-way handshake (second part of the test, see Table 1), which also contains the reserved flag, was seemingly dropped as we got SYN/ACK retransmissions. However, this behavior originates from the usage of Linux's *TCP_DEFER_ACCEPT* socket option, which causes a socket to only wakeup the user space process if there is data to be processed [10]. The socket will wait for the first data segment for a specified time, re-transmitting the SYN/ACK when the timer expires in the hope of stimulating a retransmission of possibly lost data. Since we were not sending any data, we eventually received a SYN/ACK retransmission, seemingly due to the dropped handshake-completing ACK with the reserved flag set. Hence, we credited the retransmission to the existence of the reserved flag at first, later uncovering that the retransmission was unrelated to the reserved flag, but actually expected behavior using the *TCP_DEFER_ACCEPT* socket option. Following up with Akamai, they were able to validate our assumption by revealing that parts of their services utilize this socket option. While it is certainly debatable if deliberately ignoring the received ACK is a violation of the TCP specification, our test fails to account for this corner case. Thus, connectivity is *not* impaired.

In contrast, connectivity *is* impaired in the cases where our reserved flag SYN fails to trigger a response at all, leaving the host unreachable (see *Reserved-SYN* in Table 3). The difference between both failure rates thus likely denotes hosts using the defer accept mechanism, as CDNs, in general, seem to comply with the standard. We also observe a significant drop in failures in the Alexa targets. While our results are unable to show if *only* defer accepts are the reason for this drop, they likely contribute significantly as TCP implementations would need to differentiate between a reserved flag on a SYN and on an ACK, which we believe is less likely. Our results motivate a more focused investigation of the use of socket options and the resulting protocol configurations and behavioral changes.

Lastly, the URG flag is part of TCP since the beginning to indicate data segments to be processed immediately. With the *UrgentPointer* test we check if segments that are flagged as urgent are correctly received and acknowledged. To confirm our assumption of this test having minimal implications on hosts due to the uIP/Contiki crash (see Sect. 3.3), we checked if the F_{Target} instances were still reachable after test execution. Our results show that of these failed targets, 99.35% of Censys, and 100% of CDN and Alexa, did respond to our following connection requests, which were part of the subsequent test case executed several hours later. While we argue that these unresponsive hosts can be explained by dynamic IP address assignment due to the fluctuating nature of targets in the Censys dataset, we recognize that the implicit check within the subsequent test case is problematic due to the time period between the tests and the possibility of devices and services being (automatically) restarted after crashing. We thus posit, that future research should include explicit connectivity checks directly following test case execution on a per target basis, and skip subsequent tests if a target's connectivity is impaired.

Surprisingly, the *UrgentPointer* test shows the highest failure rate among all tests. That is, segments flagged as urgent are *not correctly* processed. In other words, flagging data as urgent limits connectivity. We find over ~7% of hosts failing in the Censys dataset, where ISPs again dominate the ranking. Only about 1.2% of these failures actively terminated the connection with a RST, while the vast majority silently discarded the data without acknowledging it. Looking at Alexa and CDNs, we again find an Amazon AS at the top. Here, we randomly sampled the failed hosts to investigate the kind of services offered by them. At the top of the list, we discovered services that were proxied by a *Vegur* [14], respective *Cowboy* [4], proxy server that seem to be used in tandem with the *Heroku* [6] cloud platform. Even though we were unable to find how Heroku precisely operates, we suspect a high-performance implementation that might simply not implement the urgent mechanism at all.

Takeaway: *While unknown flags are often correctly handled, they can reduce reachability, especially when set on SYNs. The use of the urgent pointer resulted in the highest observed failure rate by hosts that do not process data segments flagged as urgent. Thus, using the reserved flags or setting the urgent pointer limits connectivity in the Internet.*

We therefore posit to remove the mandatory implementation requirement of the urgent pointer from the RFC to reflect its deprecation status, and thus explicitly state that its usage can break connectivity. Future protocol standards should therefore be accompanied by detailed socket interface specifications, e.g., as has been done for IPv6 [31,54], to avoid RFC misconceptions. Moreover, we started a discussion within the IETF, addressing the issue encountered with the missing formal MUST requirement of unknown flags, which potentially led and/or will lead to diverging implementations [11]. Additionally, we proposed a new MUST requirement, removing ambiguities in the context of future recommended, but not required, TCP extensions which allocate reserved bits [12].

Alexa: Does www. matter? It is known that `www.domain.tld` and `domain.tld` can map to different hosts [16], e.g., the CDN host vs. the origin server, where it is often implicitly assumed that both addresses exhibit the same behavior. However, 4.89% (11.4k) of the Alexa domains with and without www. prefix show different conformance levels to at least one test. That is, while the host with the www. prefix can be conformant, the non-prefixed host could not, and vice versa. Most of these non-conformance issues are caused by TCP flags, for which we have seen that they can impact the reachability of the host. That is, 53.3% of these domains failed the reserved flags test, and 58% the urgent pointer test (domains can be in both sets). Thus, a website can be unreachable using one version and reachable by the other.

Takeaway: *While the majority of Alexa domains are conformant, the ability to reach a website can differ whether or not the www. prefix is used.*

5 Conclusion

This paper presents a broad assessment of TCP conformance to mandatory MUST requirements. We uncover a non-negligible set of Internet hosts and paths that do not adhere to even basic requirements. Non-conformance already exists at the OS-level, which we uncover in controlled testbed evaluations: only two tested stacks (Linux and lwIP) pass all tests. Surprisingly, others (including macOS and Windows) fail in at least one category each. A certain level of non-conformance is therefore expected in the Internet and highlighted by our active scans. First, we observe hosts that do not correctly handle checksums. Second, while TCP options show the highest level of conformance, we still find cases of middlebox inference, mostly MSS injectors and option padding removers—primarily in ISP networks hinting at home gateways. Moreover, and most worrisome, using reserved flags or setting the urgent pointer can render the target host unreachable. Last, we observe that 4.8% of Alexa-listed domains show different conformance levels when the www. prefix is used, or not, of which more than 50% can be attributed to TCP flag issues—which can prevent connectivity. Our results highlight that conformance to even fundamental protocol requirements should not be taken for granted but instead checked regularly.

Acknowledgments. This work has been funded by the DFG as part of the CRC 1053 MAKI within subproject B1. We would like to thank Akamai Technologies for feedback on our measurements, Censys for contributing active scan data, and our shepherd Robert Beverly and the anonymous reviewers.

References

1. Contiki-NG TCP URG Pull Request. https://github.com/contiki-ng/contiki-ng/pull/1173
2. Contiki-NG: The OS for Next Generation IoT Devices. https://github.com/contiki-ng
3. Contiki OS. https://github.com/contiki-os
4. Cowboyku. https://github.com/heroku/cowboyku
5. Dataset to "MUST, SHOULD, DON'T CARE: TCP Conformance in the Wild". https://doi.org/10.18154/RWTH-2020-00809

6. Heroku platform. https://www.heroku.com/
7. lwIP - A Lightweight TCP/IP stack. http://savannah.nongnu.org/projects/lwip/
8. Seastar. https://github.com/scylladb/seastar
9. Seastar: Virtio device reports features not supported by the OS. https://github.com/scylladb/seastar/issues/719
10. tcp(7) - Linux man page. https://linux.die.net/man/7/tcp
11. TCPM Mailinglist: RFC793bis draft 14 reserved bits: problem statement. https://mailarchive.ietf.org/arch/msg/tcpm/s0LtY3Ce3QBBAkJ_DuSH5VDNFMY
12. TCPM Mailinglist: RFC793bis draft 14 reserved bits: proposal. https://mailarchive.ietf.org/arch/msg/tcpm/_jpUQx0AjByR3UOgyX88RWoTxL0
13. uIP. https://github.com/adamdunkels/uip
14. Vegur: Http proxy library. https://github.com/heroku/vegur
15. Virtio: Paravirtualized drivers for KVM/Linux. https://www.linux-kvm.org/page/Virtio
16. Alashwali, E.S., Szalachowski, P., Martin, A.: Does "www." mean better transport layer security? In: ACM International Conference on Availability, Reliability and Security (ARES) (2019). https://doi.org/10.1145/3339252.3339277
17. Alexa Internet: About us. https://www.alexa.com/about
18. Bauer, S., Beverly, R., Berger, A.: Measuring the state of ECN readiness in servers, clients, and routers. In: ACM Internet Measurement Conference (IMC) (2011). https://doi.org/10.1145/2068816.2068833
19. Beverly, R.: A robust classifier for passive TCP/IP fingerprinting. In: Barakat, C., Pratt, I. (eds.) PAM 2004. LNCS, vol. 3015, pp. 158–167. Springer, Heidelberg (2004). https://doi.org/10.1007/978-3-540-24668-8_16
20. Bradner, S.O.: Key words for use in RFCs to indicate requirement levels. RFC 2119, March 1997. https://doi.org/10.17487/RFC2119
21. Cardwell, N., et al.: packetdrill: Scriptable network stack testing, from sockets to packets. In: USENIX Annual Technical Conference (ATC) (2013). https://www.usenix.org/conference/atc13/technical-sessions/presentation/cardwell
22. Carpenter, B., Brim, S.: Middleboxes: taxonomy and issues (2002). https://doi.org/10.17487/RFC3234
23. Craven, R., Beverly, R., Allman, M.: A middlebox-cooperative TCP for a non end-to-end internet. In: ACM SIGCOMM (2014). https://doi.org/10.1145/2619239.2626321
24. Detal, G., Hesmans, B., Bonaventure, O., Vanaubel, Y., Donnet, B.: Revealing middlebox interference with tracebox. In: ACM Internet Measurement Conference (IMC) (2013). https://doi.org/10.1145/2504730.2504757
25. Durumeric, Z., Adrian, D., Mirian, A., Bailey, M., Halderman, J.A.: A search engine backed by internet-wide scanning. In: ACM Conference on Computer and Communications Security (CCS) (2015). https://doi.org/10.1145/2810103.2813703
26. Durumeric, Z., Wustrow, E., Halderman, J.A.: ZMap: Fast Internet-wide scanning and its security applications. In: USENIX Security Symposium (2013). https://www.usenix.org/conference/usenixsecurity13/technical-sessions/paper/durumeric
27. Eddy, W.: Transmission control protocol specification. Internet-draft draft-ietf-tcpm-rfc793bis-14. Internet Engineering Task Force, July 2019. https://datatracker.ietf.org/doc/html/draft-ietf-tcpm-rfc793bis-14. Work in Progress
28. Edeline, K., Donnet, B.: A bottom-up investigation of the transport-layer ossification. In: Network Traffic Measurement and Analysis Conference (TMA) (2019). https://doi.org/10.23919/TMA.2019.8784690

29. Floyd, S., Ramakrishnan, D.K.K., Black, D.L.: The addition of explicit congestion notification (ECN) to IP. RFC 3168, September 2001. https://doi.org/10.17487/RFC3168

30. Fyodor: Remote OS detection via TCP/IP stack fingerprinting (1998). https://nmap.org/nmap-fingerprinting-article.txt

31. Gilligan, R.E., McCann, J., Bound, J., Thomson, S.: Basic socket interface extensions for IPv6. RFC 3493, March 2003. https://doi.org/10.17487/RFC3493

32. Honda, M., Nishida, Y., Raiciu, C., Greenhalgh, A., Handley, M., Tokuda, H.: Is it still possible to extend TCP? In: ACM Internet Measurement Conference (IMC) (2011). https://doi.org/10.1145/2068816.2068834

33. HTTP Archive: About HTTP Archive. https://httparchive.org/about

34. Knutsen, A., Ramaiah, A., Ramasamy, A.: TCP option for transparent middlebox negotiation (2013). https://tools.ietf.org/html/draft-ananth-middisc-tcpopt-02

35. Kühlewind, M., Walter, M., Learmonth, I.R., Trammell, B.: Tracing internet path transparency. In: Network Traffic Measurement and Analysis Conference (TMA) (2018). https://doi.org/10.23919/TMA.2018.8506532

36. Kühlewind, M., Neuner, S., Trammell, B.: On the state of ECN and TCP options on the internet. In: Roughan, M., Chang, R. (eds.) PAM 2013. LNCS, vol. 7799, pp. 135–144. Springer, Heidelberg (2013). https://doi.org/10.1007/978-3-642-36516-4_14

37. Langley, A.: Probing the viability of TCP extensions (2008). http://www.imperialviolet.org/binary/ecntest.pdf

38. Mandalari, A.M., Lutu, A., Briscoe, B., Bagnulo, M., Alay, O.: Measuring ECN++: good news for ++, bad news for ECN over mobile. IEEE Commun. Mag. **56**(3), 180–186 (2018). https://doi.org/10.1109/MCOM.2018.1700739

39. Mandalari, A.M., Bagnulo, M., Lutu, A.: TCP Fast Open: initial measurements. In: ACM CoNEXT Student Workshop (2015)

40. Marinos, I., Watson, R.N., Handley, M.: Network stack specialization for performance. In: ACM SIGCOMM (2014). https://doi.org/10.1145/2619239.2626311

41. Marinos, I., Watson, R.N., Handley, M., Stewart, R.R.: Disk, Crypt, Net: rethinking the stack for high-performance video streaming. In: ACM SIGCOMM (2017). https://doi.org/10.1145/3098822.3098844

42. Medina, A., Allman, M., Floyd, S.: Measuring interactions between transport protocols and middleboxes. In: ACM Internet Measurement Conference (IMC) (2004). https://doi.org/10.1145/1028788.1028835

43. Medina, A., Allman, M., Floyd, S.: Measuring the evolution of transport protocols in the internet. SIGCOMM Comput. Commun. Rev. **35**(2), 37–52 (2005)

44. Paasch, C.: Network support for TCP fast open. Presentation at NANOG 67 (2016)

45. Padhye, J., Floyd, S.: On inferring TCP behavior. In: ACM SIGCOMM (2001). https://doi.org/10.1145/383059.383083

46. Piraux, M., De Coninck, Q., Bonaventure, O.: Observing the evolution of QUIC implementations. In: ACM CoNEXT Workshop on the Evolution, Performance, and Interoperability of QUIC (EPIQ) (2018). https://doi.org/10.1145/3284850.3284852

47. Postel, J.: Transmission control protocol. RFC 793, September 1981. https://doi.org/10.17487/RFC0793

48. Rüth, J., Hohlfeld, O.: Demystifying TCP initial window configurations of content distribution networks. In: Network Traffic Measurement and Analysis Conference (TMA) (2018). https://doi.org/10.23919/TMA.2018.8506549

49. Rüth, J., Bormann, C., Hohlfeld, O.: Large-scale scanning of TCP's initial window. In: ACM Internet Measurement Conference (IMC) (2017). https://doi.org/10.1145/3131365.3131370

50. Rüth, J., Kunze, I., Hohlfeld, O.: TCP's initial window—deployment in the wild and its impact on performance. IEEE Trans. Netw. Serv. Manag. (TNSM) (2019). https://doi.org/10.1109/TNSM.2019.2896335

51. Rüth, J., Zimmermann, T., Hohlfeld, O.: Hidden treasures – recycling large-scale internet measurements to study the internet's control plane. In: Choffnes, D., Barcellos, M. (eds.) PAM 2019. LNCS, vol. 11419, pp. 51–67. Springer, Cham (2019). https://doi.org/10.1007/978-3-030-15986-3_4

52. Scheitle, Q., et al.: A long way to the top: significance, structure, and stability of internet top lists. In: ACM Internet Measurement Conference (IMC) (2018). https://doi.org/10.1145/3278532.3278574

53. Smart, M., Malan, G.R., Jahanian, F.: Defeating TCP/IP stack fingerprinting. In: USENIX Security Symposium (2000)

54. Stevens, W.R., Thomas, M., Nordmark, E., Jinmei, T.: Advanced sockets application program interface (API) for IPv6. RFC 3542, June 2003. https://doi.org/10.17487/RFC3542

55. Stone, J., Partridge, C.: When the CRC and TCP checksum disagree. In: ACM SIGCOMM (2000). https://doi.org/10.1145/347059.347561

Domain Names

Extortion or Expansion? An Investigation into the Costs and Consequences of ICANN's gTLD Experiments

Shahrooz Pouryousef[1(✉)], Muhammad Daniyal Dar[2], Suleman Ahmad[3], Phillipa Gill[1], and Rishab Nithyanand[2]

[1] University of Massachusets, Amherst, MA, USA
{shahrooz,phillipa}@cs.umass.com
[2] University of Iowa, Iowa, IA, USA
{mdar,rishab-nithyanand}@uiowa.edu
[3] University of Wisconsin-Madison, Madison, WI, USA
suleman.ahmad@wisc.edu

Abstract. Since October 2013, the Internet Corporation of Assigned Names and Numbers (ICANN) has introduced over 1K new generic top-level domains (gTLDs) with the intention of enhancing innovation, competition, and consumer choice. While there have been several positive outcomes from this expansion, there have also been many unintended consequences. In this paper we focus on one such consequence: the gTLD expansion has provided new opportunities for malicious actors to leverage the trust placed by consumers in trusted brands by way of typosquatting. We describe gTLDtm (The gTLD typosquatting monitor) – an open source framework which conducts longitudinal Internet-scale measurements to identify when popular domains are victims of typosquatting, which parties are responsible for facilitating typosquatting, and the costs associated with preventing typosquatting. Our analysis of the generated data shows that ICANN's expansion introduces several causes for concern. First, the sheer number of typosquatted domains has increased by several orders of magnitude since the introduction of the new gTLDs. Second, these domains are currently being incentivized and monetarily supported by the online advertiser and tracker ecosystem whose policies they clearly violate. Third, mass registrars are currently seeking to profit from the inability of brands to protect themselves from typosquatting (due to the prohibitively high cost of doing so). Taken as a whole, our work presents tools and analysis to help protect the public and brands from typosquatters.

1 Introduction

With the stated goal of improving the choice of domain names for brand holders, since 2013, ICANN approved the delegation of over 1.2K new generic Top Level Domains (gTLDs). Since its initial expansion, the new gTLD program has been experiencing continuous growth with processes for adding new gTLDs being more codified and streamlined [1]. We provide a brief history of the gTLD

© Springer Nature Switzerland AG 2020
A. Sperotto et al. (Eds.): PAM 2020, LNCS 12048, pp. 141–157, 2020.
https://doi.org/10.1007/978-3-030-44081-7_9

expansion in the Appendix of this paper (Sect. A.1). While these new gTLDs have been a boon for organizations seeking to gain relevant domain names for their brands, they also present exciting opportunities for malicious actors. Previous work examined the types of content hosted on the domains using the new gTLDs and found higher incidence rates of malicious content such as malware, in comparison with domain names using the old gTLDs [1–3]. The problem is exacerbated by the fact that domain names are a source of trust with sites using HTTPS and certificates linked to them and cyber criminals have exploited this trust placed by users in safe domain names by utilizing visually similar domain names [4] or typos of these safe domain names [5–7] to launch attacks – a practice generally referred to as typosquatting. Despite many studies analyzing the incidence rates of typosquatting in the context of the original gTLDs [5–10], there has been little attention on typosquatting using the new gTLDs. What remains unknown, specifically, is how ICANN's gTLD expansion has impacted established and trusted brands seeking protection from typosquatting. In this paper, we fill this gap. Our overall objective is to understand how ICANN's gTLD expansion impacts brands trusted by Internet users. To achieve this objective, we develop techniques to reliably identify and monitor typosquatting and understand the challenges and costs facing organizations seeking to protect their brands from typosquatters. More specifically, we make the following contributions.

gTLDtm: The gTLD Typosquatting Monitor. We develop a framework, called the gTLD typosquatting monitor (gTLDtm), which routinely performs Internet-scale measurements to identify when popular domains are victims of typosquatting, which parties are facilitating the typosquatting – on old and new gTLDs, and what the cost is to prevent typosquatting. gTLDtm is open source and available at https://sparta.cs.uiowa.edu/projects/auditing.html. Periodic dumps of gTLDtm gathered data and inferences are also available for download. The data gathered by this framework forms the basis of the analysis conducted in this paper and will serve many communities seeking to understand the abuse of user trust in established brands online – e.g., studies characterizing typosquatting for fake news and propaganda dissemination, malware distribution, and online scams, amongst many others. The framework may also be used by organizations seeking to identify instances of typosquatting on their brands. During construction of this framework, we also identify several inconsistencies in records maintained by ICANN and gTLD registries.

Characterizing Perpetrators and Victims of Typosquatting. We uncover the mechanics of typosquatting – e.g., types of content and domains that are targeted by typosquatters, the role of advertisers and mass registrars in the typosquatting ecosystem, the extent of knowledge of typosquatters by web intelligence sources such as McAfee [11], as well as the intent behind typosquatting and the cost for a victim to defend against typosquatting. Our characterization explicitly focuses on identifying the differences in these mechanics for each generation of gTLDs. This allows us to understand how the typosquatting ecosystem has changed as a consequence of ICANN's gTLD expansions.

2   The gTLDtm Framework

In order to understand the ecosystem of typosquatting, we construct a measurement framework called the gTLD typosquatting monitor (gTLDtm). gTLDtm consists of several components: a URL curator, typo generator, data generator, typosquatting detector, and a defense cost estimator. The interaction between these components is illustrated in Fig. 1 and described in this section.

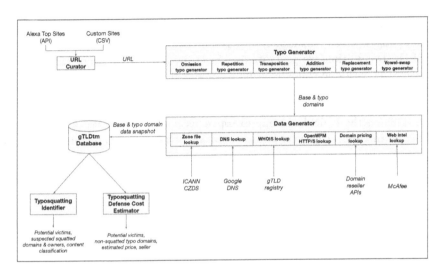

Fig. 1. The gTLDtm architecture.

2.1   URL Curation and Typosquatting Candidate Generation

The URL curator periodically fetches a list of URLs whose typos will be monitored by our system. The current implementation grabs a list of 231 most popular URLs in the News, Business, Society, and Shopping categories using the Alexa top sites API. It also has the capability of accepting custom lists of URLs. Given a base domain (obtained by our URL curator), we need to generate domain names likely to be targeted by typosquatters seeking to exploit user trust in the base domain. We do this by leveraging six typosquatting generation techniques: omissions, repetitions, transpositions, additions, replacements, and vowel-swaps. These techniques are applied to the second-level domains (SLDs) only. *For each second-level domain typo generated, we use every possible gTLD to form a typosquatting candidate.* We explain each of the six second-level domain typo generation techniques using the SLD "icann-example" as an example: (1) **Omission:** We generate new SLDs by excluding a single character in the base SLD. This method yields `cann-example`, `iann-example`, ..., and `icann-exampl` as

typo SLDs; (2) **Repetition:** We generate new SLDs by repeating a single character in the base SLD. This method yields `iicann-example`, `iccann-example`,
..., `icann-examplee` as typo SLDs; (3) **Transposition:** We generate new SLDs
by swapping two adjacent characters in the base SLD. This method yields
`ciann-example`, `iacnn-example`, ..., `icann-exampel` as typo SLDs; (4) **Addition:** We generate new SLDs by inserting an additional character at the end
of the base SLD. This method yields `icann-examplea`, ..., `icann-examplez`
as typo SLDs; (5) **QWERTY- and visually- adjacent replacements** [12]:
We generate new SLDs by replacing a single character in the base SLD with
one which is adjacent to it on the QWERTY keyboard. This method yields
`ocann-example`, `ucann-example`, ..., `icann-examplw` as candidate typosquatting SLDs. In addition, we generate new SLDs by replacing a single character in
the base SLD with one which is visually similar to it (using the sans-serif font).
This method yields `lcann-example` as a typo SLD; and (6) **Vowel-swap** [13]:
We generate new SLDs by replacing the vowel in the base SLD with another
vowel. This method yields `acann-example` as a typo SLD. We are currently
working on incorporating new typo-generation strategies into our measurement
framework.

2.2   Domain Intelligence and Data Gathering

For each base and typo domain, gTLDtm gathers domain intelligence and
domain metadata from a variety of Internet authorities. These are described
below.

Zone Files. ICANN mandates that all open gTLD registries make their up-to-
date zone files available to the public via ICANN's CZDS, after the user is able to
identify themselves via a physical and IP address [14]. gTLDtm downloads all the
zone files made available by the ICANN CZDS repository [15] each day. Given
a domain name as input, gTLDtm verifies that it is present in the appropriate
zone file. This helps us infer the registration status of a domain.

DNS and WHOIS Records. Given a domain name as input, gTLDtm gathers
`A`, `AAAA`, `MX`, and `NS` records by querying Google's public DNS server at `8.8.8.8`.
Similarly, it also fetches WHOIS records from the corresponding gTLD registry.
Data extracted include the *domain registration date, registrar, organization,* and
contact emails. This data helps us infer ownership information of a domain.

Web Content. Given a domain name, we also attempt to make connections via
HTTP and HTTPS to them. We utilize the OpenWPM [16] crawler to visit the
domain and gather data associated with the content hosted on it. This includes
page content, content sources, cookies, and certificates. This data helps us make
inferences about content type and registration intent.

Domain Pricing Data. Domain resellers are third-party organizations that
offer domain name registrations through authorized registrars such as GoDaddy
and Namecheap. gTLDtm is registered as a domain reseller with one of the

Table 1. Data gathered by gTLDtm for 231 base domains between 03–10/2019.

	pre-2000	2000-12	post-2012
gTLDs	7	15	1.2K
w/access to zone file	1	7	715
Typosquatting candidates	22K	47.8K	3.9M
Owned domains	8.8K	7.5K	353.4K
w/WHOIS records	8.6K	6.1K	195.6K
w/DNS records	7.4K	3.8K	300.9K
w/Zone file entry	6.7K	198	10.3K
w/HTTP(S)	625	555	9.6K
w/TLS certificate	152	437	3.8K
Categorized by Mcafee	579	335	1.4K
Unowned domains	13.2K	40.3K	3.5M
w/ pricing data (randomly sampled)	352	514	29.7K

most popular mass registrars – GoDaddy. gTLDtm uses the domain reseller API exposed by this registrar [17,18] to obtain data regarding the availability of the input domain name and the associated cost of purchase. This data helps us estimate the cost of registering an typo domain.

Web Intelligence Data. gTLDtm also seeks to gather intelligence about a domain name from existing domain categorization services. Given an input domain name, gTLDtm makes a request for the domain category (if available) to the McAfee categorization service [11]. This data helps us make inferences about the content type and registration intent.

All together, the data gathered by gTLDtm can be used to make inferences about the ownership of a domain, the type of content it serves, the intent behind its registration, and the cost associated with its purchase. gTLDtm currently repeats this data gathering once every fortnight. A summary of the data gathered by gTLDtm that was used is shown in Table 1. The data shows that there are numerous inconsistencies in the data made available by gTLD registries – e.g., one would expect every domain with a WHOIS record would have a zone file record, but this is not the case. We note that the registries of the post-2012 gTLDs have been the most inconsistent. To deal with this challenge, we categorize domains which have either a valid WHOIS, DNS, or zone file record to be "owned" and those with no WHOIS, DNS, or zone file record to be "unowned".

2.3 Typosquatting Identification and Domain Cost Estimation

At a high-level, we say that a typo domain is being squatted on if the entity owning the base domain does not also own the typo domain.

Identifying Domain Owners. In order to uncover the owner of an owned domain, we rely on the organization details (i.e., *name* and *email*) reported by the WHOIS record. In rare cases (<200) where a WHOIS record does not exist but a DNS or zone record does (due to inconsistent records), we use the owners of the DNS infrastructure (i.e., NSes) reported by DNS records or zone files.

Recognizing Typosquatting. We identify when the owner of a base domain is different from the owner of a typo domain, as different owners imply typosquatting. This process is complicated as simply checking for inequality of strings is insufficient for identifying differences in ownership due to inconsistencies in the domain registration process – e.g., we observed the organization names Name.com, Inc., Name.com, and Name, Inc. in the WHOIS records for domains are all owned by the same mass registrar (name.com). To circumvent this, we use a conservative approach for each (base, typo) domain pair: (1) if both domains list identical organization contact details in their WHOIS records, we conclude that they have the same owners; (2) for remaining domain pairs, we find the longest contiguous subsequence of the organization name for each domain (e.g., Name.com, Name.com, and Name in our previous example) and check if the similarity of the extracted sequence is high (>50: determined through a manual pilot study involving 200 randomly sampled pairs to have a false-positive rate of .01), we say they have the same owner; (3) any remaining domain pairs are said to have different owners. We note that a similar approach has been leveraged in previous work seeking to identify owners of ASes and their siblings [19]. We do not rely on comparisons of hosting infrastructure due to the possibilities of inaccurate conclusions brought by the widespread use of popular CDNs by popular websites and typosquatters. Similarly, we are currently unable to identify inaccuracies caused by the practice of outsourcing defensive domain registrations to organizations such as MarkMonitor.

Unowned Domain Cost Estimation. To identify the cost of an unowned domain, we randomly sampled unowned typo domains that had SLDs which were up to a Damerau-Levenshtein edit-distance of three away from the base domain. Random sampling was performed due to constraints on the number of queries that our reseller API permitted us to make (60 queries/minute). Given the cost distributions for typo domains at a particular edit distance, we extrapolate the estimated cost for purchasing all domains at that edit distance.

3 Results

In total, our method identified 188K typosquatted domains (from 4M candidate domains). Of these, 176K domains were from the post-2012 gTLD era (with 6.8K (pre-2000) and 5.4K (2000–2012) across the other eras respectively). We attribute this large skew towards post-2012 gTLDs to the fact that there are over 1.2K post-2012 gTLDs in comparison to just 22 pre-2012 gTLDs. This has two major consequences: (1) post-2012 gTLDs present more opportunities for typosquatting due to the larger number of typosquatting candidate domains

Table 2. Relationships between base domain characteristics and $risk_{norm}$. ** and *** indicate F-test p-values of $<10^{-2}$ and $<10^{-3}$ for our linear regressions. •

	Length	Rank	Category {shop, news, biz, soc}
Linear regression fit on $risk_{norm}$			
R^2 score	.76***	.70**	NA
Pearson correlation coefficient	.57	−.79	NA
Logistic regression classifier			
Accuracy: 81%			
Log-odds ratios	−3.4	−5.3	{−4.0, −3.1, −3.3, −2.9}
Decision tree classifier			
Accuracy: 97%			
Gini feature importance	.23	.56	{.02, .03, .02, .04}

and (2) due to the large number of candidates described in (1), it is increasingly expensive for brands to protect themselves by defensive registrations. We note that although ICANN provides Trademark Clearinghouse (TMCH) [20] which allows brands to perform defensive registrations on new gTLDs before they are open to public registration, the TMCH limits access only to paying members (up to \$750 per trademark) and only allows registration of domains which exactly match the brand trademark (e.g., for the organization registered as ICANN Example: `icannexample.money` and `icann-example.money` may be pre-emptively registered with TMCH, but registration of any typos such as `icann-examples.money` are not allowed). These consequences are further compounded by the non-uniform release of new gTLDs which prevent a single effort to register all trademarked domains – instead forcing constant monitoring and action.

3.1   Characteristics of Typosquatting Victims

Our 231 base domains were found to have 188K typosquatted domains. We now analyze the characteristics of the base domains which make them vulnerable to being typosquatted on. We refer to the number of typosquatting candidates for a base domain as $risk_{potential}$, the number of typosquatted domains for a base domain as $risk_{realized}$, and their ratio as $risk_{norm}$. To explore the relationships between characteristics of the base domains (i.e., length, rank, and category) and risk outcomes, we rely on two approaches: (1) linear regressions and correlations to measure the dependence and statistical significance of the variables and (2) using interpretable machine learning models on base domain characteristics and domain risk to measure the predictive nature of each characteristic. Our intuition with the latter approach is that if an interpretable classifier (e.g., logistic regression or decision tree classifier) can achieve a reasonable high classification

success rate, then interpreting their feature importance will yield domain characteristics that* are predictive of the likelihood of a domain being typosquatted on.
For our classification task, models were built to predict the level of normalized
risk associated with the domain (each level was associated with a quartile from
the distribution of all risks). In order to interpret the logistic regression model,
we computed the estimated weights for each feature and their corresponding
log-odds ratio. If the log-odds ratio of a feature f is x, it means that a unit
increase in f changes the odds of our outcome variable y by a factor of e^x when
all other features remain the same. Therefore, higher values are indicative of
more predictive features. These log-odds for the length and rank features are
shown in Table 2. In order to interpret the decision tree model, we computed
the Gini importance score for each feature. At a high-level, the Gini importance
counts the number of times a feature is used as a splitting variable in proportion
with the fraction of samples it splits. We expect higher scores to represent more
important features.

Our results are shown in Table 2. Here we see that there are statistically significant relationships between base domain lengths and ranks with the associated
$risk_{norm}$. Our 10-fold cross-validated interpretable classifier models, whose task
was to classify a base domain into its correct $risk_{norm}$ quartile, also found these
characteristics strongly predictive of the quartile range of $risk_{norm}$. Interestingly,
our analysis showed that the category of the base domain was not predictive of
its $risk_{norm}$.

Takeaway. A domain's normalized typosquatting risk ($risk_{norm}$) is predictable
using off-the-shelf interpretable classifiers. When considering individual features,
the rank of the domain is the most predictive feature, while the domain category
contains little predictive information. This suggests that higher ranked domains
are the most common target for typosquatters.

3.2   Characteristics of Typosquatted Domains

We now analyze characteristics of typosquatted domains which use different era
gTLDs with a specific focus on how they are selected, used, monetized, and
understood by the web.

Table 3. Typosquatted domain intent by gTLD era (as a percentage of all non-error
pages). A suffix of '-3rd' indicates that the inferred intent was associated with a third-
party and '-orig' indicates that the intent was associated with the original base domain.

gTLD era	Content-3rd	Parked-3rd	Parked-orig	Redirect-3rd	Redirect-orig	Sale	Unused
pre-2000	26.91	12.43	0.68	0.82	5.61	45.41	8.14
2000–2012	23.12	8.35	0.41	0.61	6.46	55.41	5.65
post-2012	37.23	12.82	0.72	0.77	3.74	38.74	6.20

How are Typosquatted Domains Selected by Squatters? As shown by our six typosquatting candidate generation methods, there are millions of targets for typosquatters to select with each having relatively short edit distances (less than 3) from a base domain. To understand the predictive nature of the edit-distance, gTLD era, and typo generation method on the is_domain_squatted_on variable, we use interpretable logistic regression and decision tree classifiers to find the most predictive features of typosquatted domains. We convert each of our inputs into binary features (e.g., is_pre2000_gTLD, is_post_2012_gTLD, etc.) and use a 10-fold cross-validation evaluation. Our classifiers had accuracies of 62% and 69% in identifying typosquatted domains from all candidates, respectively. Our analysis of the predictiveness of each feature finds that domains with lower edit distances from the base and using the 'omission' typo generation method are most likely to be squatted on. Figure 2a shows number of registered typo domains as a function of edit distance from base domains in each gTLD era. As it is clear, most of the typo domains (%80) have a short edit distance (less than 2) from a base domain. Amongst the different eras of gTLDs, pre-2000 gTLDs are most likely to be squatted on (followed closely by post-2012 gTLDs, while 2000–2012 era gTLDs are not predictive of squatting). We note that our analysis tool may be leveraged for brands to identify which domains need to be targeted for pre-emptive defensive registration.

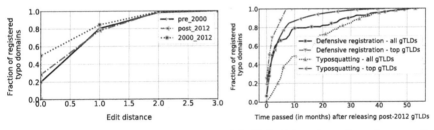

(a) CDF of typosquatting domain registrations as a function of edit distance from base domain.

(b) CDF of domain registrations as a function of time since release of the post-2012 gTLD.

Fig. 2. CDF of domain registrations as a function of edit distance and time of gTLD release.

How are Typosquatted Domains Being Used by Squatters? In order to understand how typosquatted domains are being used, we relied on a three-step process: similarity computation, clustering, and tagging. First, we compute the semantic pairwise-similarity of the textual content in each html page fetched by our framework's OpenWPM crawling module. To make this process scalable, we rely on Jenks natural breaks optimization to find ideal clusters based on the one-dimensional parameter: file size. The intuition here is that the similarity between files belonging to different Jenks clusters will be low owing to the large differences in their file sizes. We then compute the similarity matrix such that the similarity of files in different Jenks clusters is set to zero and only intra-Jenks-cluster similarities are computed. Using this similarity matrix, we use k-means clustering to identify clusters of similar pages. k was determined by iterating through all possible values and selecting the candidate value with the highest silhouette score. Our clusters achieved a silhouette score of 0.48 with $k = 54$ clusters. Finally, we manually inspected and tagged 25 randomly sampled pages from each cluster to verify similarity. One of nine tags was then assigned to each cluster: content-original, content-third-party, parked-original, parked-third-party, redirect-original, redirect-third-party, sale, unused, and error.

Our results, broken down by gTLD era, are shown in Table 3. Here we notice that approximately 75% of all typosquatted domains identified by our framework were either hosting third-party content (i.e., content not provided by the base domain) or listed for sale. On average, less than 4% of all typosquatted domains were parked by or redirected to their base domains. Broken down by gTLD era, we see that the typosquatted domains using post-2012 gTLDs are indeed more likely to host content from parties unrelated to the base domain. While we do not currently study the nature of the differences in content in this study, it is clear that this often results in negative impact for users and brands. For example, post-2012 gTLD typos of the cbsnews base domain were frequently used to spread political misinformation during the 2016 US Presidential elections – simultaneously harming public discourse and brand reputation.

How are Typosquatted Domains Monetized? While our analysis of the domain intent yields some insights into how typosquatted domains are being used, we also seek to understand how the advertising and tracking ecosystem fuels the typosquatting economy. To this end, we analyzed the incidence rates of different advertising and tracking services using the Easylist and Easyprivacy filter lists [21]. We notice several interesting trends here. First, 67% of all the post-2012 gTLD typosquatters hosting third-party content served ads or hosted trackers in comparison to 53% of the other typosquatted domains. Interestingly, the ad and tracker networks participating in the typosquatting ecosystem vary by the gTLD era. Over 1.6K unique networks were observed in the post-2012 gTLD typosquatted domains in comparison to 1.2K and 384 in the pre-2000 and 2000–2012 eras gTLD typosquatted domains. We identified 103 unique domains serving ads only in the post-2012 gTLD typosquatted domains, including vertamedia, adsnative, and others. We note that the top 20 ad providers for the base domains were all observed in large fractions of typosquatted domains. This suggests the absence of enforcing policies that are meant to prevent the monetization of harmful practices such as typosquatting – e.g., Google's adsense (which was the most prevalent advertising service in our typosquatted domains) policy prohibits using their program to place ads on sites which have 'misrepresentative content' including content which 'misrepresents, misstates, or conceals information about you, your content or the primary purpose of your web destination' or 'falsely implies having an affiliation with, or endorsement by, another individual, organization, product, or service' [22].

How Quickly Do Brands Perform Defensive Registrations? Using the "creation date" entry in each typosquatting candidate domain WHOIS record and knowledge of the release dates for each gTLD (gTLD's delegation date based on ICANN), we seek to understand the amount of time that passes between the availability of a typosquatting candidate domain (using a post-2012 gTLD) and its registration by brands and typosquatters. Figure 2b shows the domains registered by typosquatters and organizations with post-2012 gTLDs as a function of time since release of the post-2012 gTLDs. We find that in the cases where brands do make defensive registrations to prevent typosquatting, a majority occur within the first year of the domains availability (85% of the time when considering all post-2012 gTLDs and 98% of the time when considering only the most popular post-2012 gTLDs observed in our dataset of registered typosquatting candidates (i.e., `app`, `media`, `mobi`, `xxx`, and `agency`)). Typosquatters are rarely left behind. In fact 30% and 98% of all typosquatted domains using the most popular gTLDs are registered within the first month and year of their public availability, respectively. When considering all post-2012 gTLDs however, we observe that there is no landrush – only 45% are registered within the first year of their availability. Our results show that brands are generally able to outpace typosquatters in registering typosquatting candidate domains. Despite this, our previous results show that typosquatting is extremely common. This points to a barrier in either resources or interest in pre-emptive defensive registrations by brands.

How Are Typosquatted Domains Viewed by the Web? Web intelligence services such as OpenDNS [23], VirusTotal [24], and McAfee's domain categorizer [11] play a crucial role in protecting users from deceptive online practices. Our measurements of their coverage of typosquatted domains yielded underwhelming results. In total, only 6.6%, 4.5%, and 0.4% of all pre-2000, 2000–2012, and post-2012 gTLD typosquatted domains were found to be categorized. Besides the overall poor coverage of typosquatted domains, these results also suggest that web intelligence services have not yet begun covering domains utilizing new gTLDs to the same extent of those using older gTLDs – leaving users of their services vulnerable to deception from them.

3.3 Cost of Brand Protection

We now focus on understanding the costs associated with defensive registration of typosquatting candidates by brands.

What is the Cost of Complete Protection from Typosquatters? To measure the monetary resources required to register typosquatting candidate domains, we registered as domain resellers on GoDaddy domain registrar which have access to 385 of the all 1230 currently open gTLDs. Since the total number of unregistered typosquatting candidate domains is over $4M and our reseller API are rate limited to 60 queries/minute, we randomly sampled domains with edit distances of less than three from the base domain. In total we received 33K

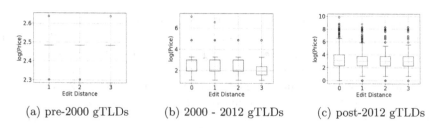

(a) pre-2000 gTLDs   (b) 2000 - 2012 gTLDs   (c) post-2012 gTLDs

Fig. 3. Distribution of unowned typosquatting domain prices within 3 edit distances of base domains, broken down by gTLD era.

responses to our queries – 352, 514, and 29.7K for queries on candidates using pre-2000, 2000–2012, and post-2012 gTLDs, respectively.

Figure 3 illustrates the cost for each of our queried domains, broken down by gTLDs and edit-distance from the base SLD. Comparing across all gTLD eras, we see that the typo domains with post-2012 gTLDs are generally more expensive than all other eras – regardless of the edit distance from the base domain. Comparing within eras, our results show that typo domains with exact matches of the base domains are also significantly more expensive than higher edit distance domains – i.e., edit-distance 0 domains with post-2012 gTLDs cost $138 on average while edit-distance 1 and edit-distance 2 domains average $95 and $96, respectively. The median of cost of queried domains, broken down by gTLDs and edit-distance 0 from the base SLD for 2000–2012 and post-2012 gTLDs is $17.99 and $21.99, respectively. We also note that GoDaddy advertises these exact match domains as "premium". This suggests that there is knowledge of trademark value of the domain and the increased price and lack of restrictions on domain purchase suggests that there is a willful effort to profit off of typosquatting.

From our analysis so far, we can estimate the cost that a brand needs to pay in order to protect itself from typosquatting as a result of the 2012 gTLD expansion. To get the lower bound, we only consider the cost of purchasing domains with open gTLDs (643). To only purchase domains with exactly identical SLDs, a brand would require $63K. Our earlier results suggesting that the majority of typosquatting occurs at an edit-distance of one away from the base SLD indicate that $63K is far from sufficient for meaningful protection from typosquatting. Considering that the average cost of a domain with a post-2012 gTLD and edit-distance of one is $95 and there are hundreds of possible typos with each individual gTLD, it is safe to say that it is not feasible or reasonable to expect brands to be able to protect their domains from typosquatters. Our most conservative estimates show the cost of typosquatting protection against edit-distance 0–1 and open post-2012 gTLD typosquatting to be in the millions of dollars (exact values depend on the length of the base domain SLD).

4 Related Work

ICANNs gTLD Expansion. ICANN's gTLD expansion has been the subject of much research over the past several years. Previous research has focused on the economics of the gTLD expansion from the perspective of registries purchasing the new gTLDs. Halvorson et al. [1] found that only a half of the new gTLD-owning registries had recovered their $185K registration costs two years after the expansion. In other work, Halvorson et al. [3] performed specific measurements of the xxx gTLD and found that the gTLD was primarily used for defensive registration with only 4% of the listed domains actually hosting content. In more recent work, the focus has been on how domains with new gTLDs increase security vulnerabilities. Korczyński et al. [2] conducted an investigation of the abuse rates observed in domains using the pre-2012 and post-2012 gTLDs. They found that the incidence rate of spam-domains in the post-2012 gTLD domains was a whole order of magnitude higher than in the pre-2012 gTLD domains. Further, the authors showed an upward trend in the number of spam domains in using the post-2012 gTLDs. Osterweil et al. [25] quantified Man in the Middle (MitM) attacks on web browsing caused due to internal namespace WPAD query leakage. They found that almost all leaked queries are for new gTLD domains and 10% of these highly-vulnerable domains have been registered.

Typosquatting on the Web. The incidence of typosquatting on the Internet has been extensively discussed in previous literature. However, the focus has generally been on the pre-2012 gTLDs or on the general behaviours of typosquatters. Agten et al. [5] conducted a longitudinal study on the Alexa top 500 websites and showed that 95% of these websites were actively targeted by typosquatters and that only a handful pursued measures to protect themselves through pre-emptive registrations of candidate domains. Khan et al. [7] demonstrated methods to quantify the harm of typosquatting on the Internet by using time lost for users and visitors lost to brands as their primary metrics. Nikiforakis et al. [26] found a "Typosquatting Cross-site Scripting" (TXSS) vulnerability that exploited typosquatted domains. Wang et al. [27] proposed Strider – a system designed for detecting and discovering large-scale and systematic typosquatters by monitoring neighboring domains. Banerjee et al. [9,10] analyzed phony sites and their network layer behavior, e.g., number of http redirections. While the relationship of domain parking services and malicious domains and parking services has been analyzed in other researches such as [28,29], these papers do not specifically target domain names registered with new released gTLDs.

5 Discussion

Taken in completeness, our study shows that typosquatting incidence rates continue to remain high and that the sheer number of typosquatted domains has significantly increased since ICANN's 2012 gTLD expansion. In fact, typosquatting candidate domains using post-2012 gTLD are already being used by third-parties for content hosting and being monetized at higher rates than any previous gTLD era. Further, our findings highlight a simultaneous failure of multiple entities in the typosquatting ecosystem: (1) advertisers and trackers have failed to enforce their own policies regarding acceptable publishers, therefore presenting monetary incentives for typosquatters and (2) mass registrars, rather than protecting trademarked domains, are themselves seeking to monetize both trademarked and typo domains. These failures have a cost not only to the brands for whom it is unreasonably expensive to defend against typosquatting, but also to the public whose trust in them is more easily exploited by malicious entities – e.g., the 2016 US Presidential election showed that fake news was spread via websites spoofing major media outlets [30]. Finally, our work also shows the cost for brands to protect their own trademarks from typosquatters to be unreasonably high. Taken together, our study suggests that the gTLD expansion has in fact resulted in an ecosystem which facilitates extortion of trusted brands and organizations. We are currently expanding gTLDtm to automatically identify occurrences of typosquatting for the purpose of mis- and dis-information during the 2020 US Presidential election and also seeking to build tools to enable brands to identify which domains should be targeted for pre-emptive registration.

Appendix

A.1   ICANN and gTLD Expansions

In this section, we provide a high-level overview of how gTLDs have been expanded over the years and the role that ICANN plays in regulating these expansions. Since 1998, the Internet Corporation for Assigned Names and Numbers (ICANN), has been responsible for administering the Internet Domain Name System (DNS). This role has included the authority for establishing new top-level domains (TLDs). TLDs have historically been classified into: (1) TLDs reserved for countries and territories (country-code TLDs or ccTLDs), (2) a TLD reserved for Internet infrastructure (infrastructure TLD: .arpa), and (3) TLDs that may be used for other purposes (generic TLDs or gTLDs).

gTLD Expansion Between 1984 and 2012. Between 1984 and 2000, the number of gTLDs increased from five to seven with .net and .int added to the "core" set (.com, .edu, .gov, .mil, and .org). Of these seven, three TLDs – .com, .net, and .org – have always been open to public registration with the other TLDs being reserved for use by specific organizations such as universities (.edu) and government entities (.gov). Starting in 1998, ICANN began considering a more "open" gTLD program which would allow private entities to act as registries and manage new gTLDs. Following a public call for proposals in August 2000 and a two-month period for public comment, ICANN announced seven new gTLDs in November 2000 (.aero, .biz, .coop, .info, .museum, .name, and .pro). The process was repeated again in 2004, resulting in the introduction of six new gTLDs (.asia, .cat, .jobs, .mobi, .tel, and .travel). Between 2004 and 2012, only two other gTLDs – .xxx and .post –

were added. By the end of 2012, the Internet had 22 gTLDs – of which 15 were open to public registration. As of August 2013, the 15 additions to the 7 core gTLDs accounted for 3% of all domain registrations while the 7 core gTLDs accounted for 51% of all domain registrations on the Internet (ccTLD domain registrations accounted for 35%) [31].

The 2012–2013 gTLD Expansion. In 2008, citing the success of the previous gTLD expansions in 2000 and 2004, ICANN approved new policies to facilitate the large-scale creation of new gTLDs with the stated goal of "enhancing innovation, competition, and consumer choice" [32]. Following the creation and multiple revisions of a guide for the application process of new gTLDs, in 2011 steps were taken to enable the registration of new gTLDs. These guidelines are still applicable today. In order to register a new gTLD, a registry needs to demonstrate capabilities to handle technical, operational, and business operations related to the handling of registrar relationships and submit a $185K application and evaluation fee [33]. Applications for new gTLDs were opened in 2012 following criticism and protest from Internet societies, including Harvard's Berkman Center for Internet & Society [34], the Association of National Advertisers [35], and the United States Federal Trade Commission [36] which primarily cited the lack of transparency in the evaluation process, potential for trademark infringement and other generally malicious conduct. By 2013, over 1,900 applications were received of which 1,543 were granted and 1,208 are still active today. Contested gTLD registration applications were resolved by a bidding process. As of July 2016, the ICANN netted a profit of $233M from the bidding process alone [37]. As of August 2018, the 1,208 active new gTLDs accounted for 9% of all domain registrations on the Internet [31]. We note that statistics regarding the registration of new gTLD domains have not been updated on the ICANN website since 2015 and are only available through other third-party services.

Registry Responsibilities and Guidelines. Following the delegation of a gTLD, a registry is required to perform certain responsibilities related to maintenance of the gTLD. A full specification of these requirements is available online [38]. We summarize the requirements that are relevant to our study below.

- *WHOIS services.* Registries are required to maintain a fully responsive and searchable WHOIS service available via port 43 and through a web-based interface.
- *Zone files.* Registries are required to provide public access to their *current* zone files via the Centralized Zone Data Access (CZDA) provider [14]. In order for a member of the public to gain access to the zone file, they need to provide "information sufficient to correctly identify and locate" themselves. These may include an organization name and address, IP address, *etc. There is no specified time within which a registry is required to provide a response.*
- *Protected domains.* All registries owning and operating an *open* gTLD are subject to a *sunrise* period of 30 days. During this period, domains may only be registered by organizations registered with ICANNs Trade Mark Clearing House (TMCH). Following this period, all domains are open for public registration – regardless of their trademark status and any trademark disputes

are to be resolved using ICANN services. All costs associated with disputes, trademark verification, and TMCH registration are to be paid by the trade mark holder. Further, the TMCH will only accept domains as trademarked if the following criteria are met (examples are demonstrated with the organization "ICANN Example"): (1) exact match rule—`icannexample.org` is a valid trademark domain, (2) hyphen for spaces/special characters rule—`icann-example.org` is a valid trademark domain. *All other domain variations, including plurals are considered invalid (e.g.,* `icann-examples.org`).

We note that we were unable to find documents relating to how compliance with these responsibilities were to be monitored or enforced.

References

1. Halvorson, T., Der, M.F., Foster, I., Savage, S., Saul, L.K., Voelker, G.M.: From .academy to .zone: an analysis of the new TLD land rush. In: Proceedings of the 2015 Internet Measurement Conference, pp. 381–394. ACM (2015)
2. Korczyński, M., et al.: Cybercrime after the sunrise: a statistical analysis of DNS abuse in new gTLDs. In: Proceedings of the 2018 on Asia Conference on Computer and Communications Security, pp. 609–623. ACM (2018)
3. Halvorson, T., Levchenko, K., Savage, S., Voelker, G.M.: XXXtortion? Inferring registration intent in the. XXX TLD. In: Proceedings of the 23rd International Conference on World Wide Web, pp. 901–912. ACM (2014)
4. Dhamija, R., Tygar, J.D., Hearst, M.: Why phishing works. In: Proceedings of the SIGCHI Conference on Human Factors in Computing Systems, pp. 581–590. ACM (2006)
5. Agten, P., Joosen, W., Piessens, F., Nikiforakis, N.: Seven months' worth of mistakes: a longitudinal study of typosquatting abuse. In: Proceedings of the 22nd Network and Distributed System Security Symposium (NDSS 2015). Internet Society (2015)
6. Szurdi, J., Kocso, B., Cseh, G., Spring, J., Felegyhazi, M., Kanich, C.: The long "taile" of typosquatting domain names. In: USENIX Security Symposium, pp. 191–206 (2014)
7. Khan, M.T., Huo, X., Li, Z., Kanich, C.: Every second counts: quantifying the negative externalities of cybercrime via typosquatting. In: 2015 IEEE Symposium on Security and Privacy (SP), pp. 135–150. IEEE (2015)
8. Nikiforakis, N., Van Acker, S., Meert, W., Desmet, L., Piessens, F., Joosen, W.: Bitsquatting: exploiting bit-flips for fun, or profit? In: Proceedings of the 22nd International Conference on World Wide Web, pp. 989–998. ACM (2013)
9. Banerjee, A., Barman, D., Faloutsos, M., Bhuyan, L.N.: Cyber-fraud is one typo away. In: IEEE INFOCOM 2008: The 27th Conference on Computer Communications, pp. 1939–1947. IEEE (2008)
10. Banerjee, A., Rahman, Md.S., Faloutsos, M.: SUT: quantifying and mitigating URL typosquatting. Comput. Netw. **55**(13), 3001–3014 (2011)
11. McAfee (2019). https://www.mcafee.com/en-us/index.html. Accessed 20 Oct 2019
12. Holgers, T., Watson, D.E., Gribble, S.D.: Cutting through the confusion: a measurement study of homograph attacks. In: USENIX Annual Technical Conference, General Track, pp. 261–266 (2006)

13. Stout, B., McDowell, K.: System and method for combating cybersquatting. US Patent App. 13/612,603, 3 January 2013
14. ICANN Centralized Zone Data Service (2019). https://www.icann.org/resources/pages/zfa-2013-06-28-en. Accessed 20 July 2019
15. ICANN-CZDS (2019). https://czds.icann.org/home. Accessed 20 Oct 2019
16. Englehardt, S., Narayanan, A.: Online tracking: a 1-million-site measurement and analysis. In: Proceedings of the 2016 ACM SIGSAC Conference on Computer and Communications Security, pp. 1388–1401. ACM (2016)
17. GoDaddy (2018). https://www.godaddy.com/. Accessed 20 Aug 2018
18. NameCheap (2018). https://www.namecheap.com/. Accessed 20 Aug 2018
19. Nithyanand, R., Starov, O., Gill, P., Zair, A., Schapira, M.: Measuring and mitigating AS-level adversaries against Tor. In: 23rd Annual Network and Distributed System Security Symposium, NDSS 2016, San Diego, California, USA, 21–24 February 2016 (2016)
20. Trade Mark Clearing House (2019). https://www.trademark-clearinghouse.com/. Accessed 29 Oct 2019
21. EasyList (2018). https://easylist.to/. Accessed 20 Aug 2018
22. Google AdSense (2019). https://www.google.com/adsense/. Accessed 20 Oct 2019
23. OpenDNS (2018). www.opendns.com. Accessed 20 Aug 2018
24. Virustotal (2018). www.virustotal.com. Accessed 20 Aug 2018
25. Chen, Q.A., Osterweil, E., Thomas, M., Mao, Z.M.: MitM attack by name collision: cause analysis and vulnerability assessment in the new gTLD era. In: 2016 IEEE Symposium on Security and Privacy (SP), pp. 675–690. IEEE (2016)
26. Nikiforakis, N., et al.: You are what you include: large-scale evaluation of remote Javascript inclusions. In: Proceedings of the 2012 ACM Conference on Computer and Communications Security, pp. 736–747. ACM (2012)
27. Wang, Y.-M., Beck, D., Wang, J., Verbowski, C., Daniels, B.: Strider typo-patrol: discovery and analysis of systematic typo-squatting. In: SRUTI 2006, pp. 31–36 (2006)
28. Vissers, T., Joosen, W., Nikiforakis, N.: Parking sensors: analyzing and detecting parked domains. In: Proceedings of the 22nd Network and Distributed System Security Symposium (NDSS 2015), pp. 53–53. Internet Society (2015)
29. Plohmann, D., Yakdan, K., Klatt, M., Bader, J., Gerhards-Padilla, E.: A comprehensive measurement study of domain generating malware. In: 25th USENIX Security Symposium (USENIX Security 2016), pp. 263–278 (2016)
30. The Media Trust (2018). https://mediatrust.com/media-center/real-fake-news-spoofed-domains-are-targeting-major-media-outlets. Accessed 20 Aug 2019
31. Domain Name Stat. Domain name registration's statistics. https://domainname stat.com/
32. ICANN. About the program: ICANN new gTLDs. https://newgtlds.icann.org/en/about/program
33. ICANN: gTLD Applicant Guidebook, June 2012
34. Burkert, H., et al.: Accountability and transparency at ICANN: an independent review (2010)
35. Association National of Advertisers: ICANN generic top level domain developments: ANA. http://www.ana.net/content/show/id/icann
36. Leibowitz, J., Rosch, T., Ramirez, E., Brill, J.: Consumer protection concerns regarding new gTLDs, December 2011
37. ICANN: New gTLD auction proceeds: ICANN new gTLDs. https://newgtlds. icann.org/en/applicants/auctions/proceeds
38. ICANN: Base registry agreement, July 2017

Counterfighting Counterfeit: Detecting and Taking down Fraudulent Webshops at a ccTLD

Thymen Wabeke[1]([⊠]), Giovane C. M. Moura[1,3], Nanneke Franken[2],
and Cristian Hesselman[1,4]

[1] SIDN Labs, Arnhem, The Netherlands
{thymen.wabeke,giovane.moura,cristian.hesselman}@sidn.nl
[2] SIDN, Arnhem, The Netherlands
nanneke.franken@sidn.nl
[3] TU Delft, Delft, The Netherlands
[4] University of Twente, Enschede, The Netherlands

Abstract. Luxury goods such as sneakers and bags are in high demand. Many websites offer them at high discounts, which, in many cases, are simply cheap counterfeit versions of the original product. Online shoppers, however, may be unaware they are buying a counterfeit product and end up being scammed and having to deal with financial losses, as has been widely reported by various news outlets. This work presents a multiyear effort of The Netherlands' .nl country-code top-level domain (ccTLD) in detecting and removing counterfeit online shops from the .nl DNS zone. We have developed two detection systems and partnered with registrars and a large credit card issuer, which ultimately led to more than 4,400 counterfeit online shops being taken down.

1 Introduction

Counterfeit or fake goods are unauthorized replicas of products that attempt to pass as legitimate ones. They cover a large array of goods, such as pharmaceuticals [17], electronics [1], aircraft parts [37], and books [31].

Luxury goods, from brands such as Nike and Louis Vuitton, are among the most popular counterfeit products. Their popularity originates from the consumer's high demand, leading to high-profit margins [37] for those who sell them. In the U.S. alone, seizures at the border of counterfeit goods in 2017 had an estimated value of US$1.2 billion [36], had these products been genuine. In the EU, 2016 border seizures were valued at €670 million (US$ 743 million) [33]. In both cases, most shipments originated from China, which has been also found as a major source of counterfeit shoes [28].

To be able to sell online, counterfeiters first have to attract potential buyers, and they have been using various tactics. In a previous study, Wang *et al.* [38] have shown how counterfeiters often employ search engine optimization (SEO) in an attempt to improve rankings in search engines. In addition, social networking

© Springer Nature Switzerland AG 2020
A. Sperotto et al. (Eds.): PAM 2020, LNCS 12048, pp. 158–174, 2020.
https://doi.org/10.1007/978-3-030-44081-7_10

websites have been also employed [22]: in 2016, a large number of Instagram accounts were dedicated to disseminating counterfeit luxurious goods—roughly 20% of the 150k analyzed posts [35], which contained links to stores dedicated to selling these type of products. Last, market places such as Amazon [31] and Ebay have been exploited by counterfeiters.

Buyers of these goods are often *unaware* that they are buying from a counterfeit webshop and in many cases, they end up not receiving any product, or receiving a lower quality version—being scammed either way. Moreover, they may become victims of ID theft, given that they have to provide their credit card details and address information. Financial losses to online shoppers have also been widely reported by several media outlets in The Netherlands [21–23], where they have been known to exist since 2016 in the .nl zone (Figs. 11 and 12 in Appendix A and [5]). This is not only observed in .nl: Germany's .de was found to have more than 16.000 counterfeit shops, many active for several years [24].

In this paper, we focus on a subset of the counterfeit industry—the so-called *luxury goods* that are sold *online*, that often leads to shoppers experiencing financial loss. We leverage our centralized vantage point as the country-code top-level domain (ccTLD) registry for The Netherlands (.nl), operated by SIDN [30]. Centralized, in this context, refers to access we have to historical registration data of all .nl domain names, which also includes registrants' contact details. Given that most webshops in The Netherlands are registered under the .nl ccTLD (and are available in Dutch language), counterfeiters would have incentives to register their domains under .nl as well, to mimic what most legitimate webshops do. As such, our centralized vantage point allow us to leverage this strong association between ccTLD, country, and language.

This paper presents the results of a multiyear effort in detecting such webshops, which led to 4455 domain names being removed from the .nl zone. We present two detection systems—BrandCounter (Sect. 3) and FaDe (Sect. 4), which have been used in production over the past three years by our Abuse Handling Analysts to evaluate .nl domain names and notify registrars and/or registrants. BrandCounter, the first system from 2017, employs a very *simple* but *effective* heuristic. We used its results in a case study with Registrar A, that ultimately led to the removal of ∼3.7k counterfeit webshops from the .nl zone (Sect. 3.1). FaDe (Sect. 4), in turn, was developed in early 2019 to cope with the new tactics employed by counterfeiters (Sect. 4.2), who adapted after the initial take downs based on BrandCounter's results. We carried out another case study with the results from FaDe together with International Credit Cards (*ICS*, [11]), a major credit card issuer in The Netherlands with more than 3.5 million clients. This study led to the removal of an additional 747 domain names (Sect. 4.1). Lastly, we infer the popularity of the counterfeit domains among users by analyzing the volume of DNS queries to the .nl authoritative servers (Sect. 5).

2   Background

Domain Name Registration: Registering a domain name is the process of creating a unique name that is added to a DNS zone file. Next, we describe this process under .nl. It usually involves a *registrant*, *registrar* (or reseller), and *registry*. The registrant (a user) requests an accredited registrar to register an available domain name at the registry. The registrar only executes this request once certain requirements are met, such as registrant information and payment being cleared, as shown in the left part of Fig. 1.

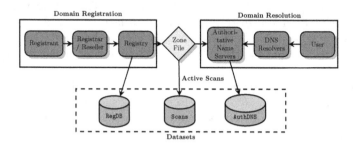

Fig. 1. TLD operations: registration (left), domain resolution (right), and datasets.

Domains are registered for a period of one year, which will be automatically renewed at .nl. If the domain is cancelled, it will expire and is put on hold for 40 days and right after that made available for a new registration by any registrant. The list of valid domain names is then used to generate a DNS *Zone File* (Fig. 1) that contains the list of all domains under .nl, and their respective DNS records. These Zone Files are used as input on the *authoritative name servers*, which are used to answer queries on .nl domain names.

Domain Name Resolution: Domain name resolution consists of resolving a domain name into, ultimately, its IP address or other specific types of DNS records [18]. To do that, a user's application contacts the stub DNS resolver (Fig. 1) on his/her computer, which, in turn, sends a DNS request to its DNS *resolver* [10]. The DNS resolver will, on behalf of the user, recursively resolve the requested domain name, and ultimately contact the appropriate authoritative name server. Caching on DNS resolvers [19,20] is used to eliminate frequently issued queries, improving response times.

2.1   Datasets

We leverage three types of datasets available at the .nl registry. Two of them are passive data, while one is obtained through active measurements:

- RegDB: We have access to the historical database of registration and removal of .nl second-level domains (such as example.nl), which covers 20+ years. This dataset contains complete information about registrant and registrar (and resellers, if applicable), as well as some of the DNS records of the respective domains [18].

- **Scans**: We crawl all domains under .nl on a monthly basis. We scan for four types of application: DNS records, HTTP pages, SMTP and TLS (and its certificates on web pages). We employ DMap [40], an application we have developed to carry out these scans. Besides that, the .nl zone is scanned daily by OpenIntel [26], a research project that crawls daily multiple TLD zones for various DNS record types.

- **AuthDNS**: We have access to historical query data from two out of the four authoritative name servers for .nl. This data provides a centralized but sampled view (due to caching on the resolvers) of all queries issued to .nl. We use our open-source Hadoop-based ENTRADA [41] to store and process this dataset.

3 BrandCounter

While detecting phishing domains in the .nl zone in 2016 [5], we came across the first suspicious luxury goods webshops, which advertised goods at high discount, as shown in Fig. 11, in Appendix A. Upon inspection, we observed that they shared one common feature: long page titles (HTML element `<title>`) that listed a series of luxury brands—in an attempt to improve rankings on search engines [38].

That provided us with a simple but effective way to detect such shops in the entire .nl zone: we crawl the zone for web pages and, for each page, we compare how many words in the page title match the words from our 1,100+ pre-compiled list of luxury brands and discount-related words, such as "discount", "sale", in both English and Dutch. We determined empirically a threshold of $t \geq 5$ matching words to classify webpages as suspicious. We automated this process into a single tool (BrandCounter), and ran it roughly once a month, for over 1.5+ years, as shown Fig. 2. In total, BrandCounter detected 18952 suspicious webshops.

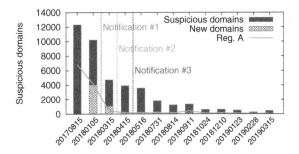

Fig. 2. BrandCounter suspicious domain results for .nl zone.

Results and Analysis: Eighteen thousand allegedly counterfeit webshops seems like a large number—0.3% of the entire of .nl zone. We analyzed these domains, and observe the following characteristics:

Domains are Cheap and Disposable: Given that it is relatively cheap to register a .nl domain (less than €10 in 2020), counterfeiters may choose to register a large number of domains, and even if some are taken down, the profits made from the remaining ones are enough to sustain the operation. The relatively short lifetime also indicates that domains are disposable (Fig. 6).

Registrar Concentration: Out of 18952 domains, 16512 are registered by 10 registrars, as can be seen in Fig. 3. The top registrar—Reg. A—is alone responsible for 8017 (42.3%) of all detected shops. One of the reasons for that may be the fact that Reg. A ranks among the cheapest registrars and provides an API that allows for bulk registration of domains, which is very handy in case of automated registrations. Given such concentration, we carried a case study with Reg. A (Sect. 3.1), in which a large part of these domains were suspended.

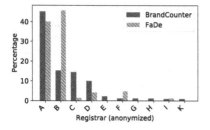

Fig. 3. Top 10 registrars with suspicious domains.

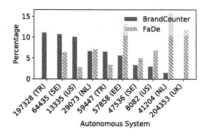

Fig. 4. Top 10 ASes (countries) hosting suspicious domains.

Similar But Yet Different Website Templates: We analyzed the home pages of some of these webshops and found out that they are different, but seem to be using a few content-management systems (CMS). The webshops do not support HTTPS, and have a single image in the page footer that contains icons of most credit card companies with no link or a broken link. Such designs also suggest use of automated tools to create such websites. Wang *et al.* [38] describe many *doorway pages*, which are non-shopping sites that are specifically designed to improve SEO results and *redirect* users to the real websites. In our work we do not see such pages since we do not rely on search engine results—we see the actual automatically generated pages listing the counterfeit goods, always with large discounts.

Most Domains were Drop-Catch: 15242 shops are hosted on domains that expired and were re-registered by the counterfeiters (80.4%). The majority of these domains are immediately registered when they became available (Fig. 5), a practice known as "drop-catch" [7]. By registering freshly expired domains to host counterfeit webshops, counterfeiters can benefit from their previously built reputation [14]. This timely precision in registering domains—and the fact that they seem indifferent to the name of the domain itself, as many were previously used by small businesses such as bakeries, beauty parlors—supports the idea of automation in the registration process.

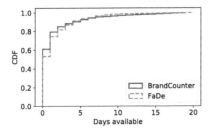

Fig. 5. Suspicious domains: days in between domain expiration and re-registration.

Fig. 6. Suspicious domains lifetime: most domains are not renewed after one year—the registration period.

Chinese e-mails and Chinese Diurnal Registration Timing: Registrants are required to provide their e-mail address to register a domain with .nl. Out of 18925 suspicious domains, 4696 are registered using 163.com (24.81%), a well-known Chinese e-mail provider which is particularly not popular in The Netherlands (Fig. 7). Moreover, the registration diurnal patterns coincide with east China working hours (Fig. 8).

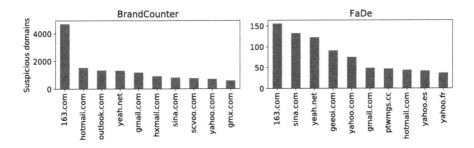

Fig. 7. Number of shops by the registrant's e-mail domain.

Hosting Provider Concentration: We see that 66.59% of the counterfeit webshops are hosted in 10 ASes—as can be seen in Fig. 4—and none of them are located in China. We also see that most of them, however, use default DNS services provided by their registrars during registration. We inspected a sample of websites

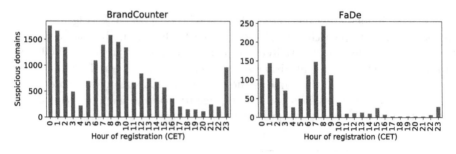

Fig. 8. Number of shops by registration hour.

from the `.com` zone hosted under some of the same IP addresses of AS197328. Some were counterfeit webshops in other languages, but we also found websites that seemed legitimate, such as small businesses in Turkey.

3.1   Registrar Notification Case Study

Counterfeiters employed Registrar A to register 8017 suspicious domains (Fig. 2), from the more than 15k detected, for the entire period covered. Given this concentration, we partner with Reg. A in a case study of three months in which we provided them with a list of domains that were labeled as suspicious by BrandCounter. In these three months, we sent 4106 domains to Reg. A.

Reg. A, in turn, would verify the identity of the registrants and take appropriate measures according to their regulations. While other registrars were also notified—and many also removed suspicious domain names—we single out Reg. A in this section, because we only tracked results for this registrar.

Table 1 shows the number of domains we notified to Reg. A—more than four thousand in the three notifications. Upon receiving the list of domains, Reg. A determined the accuracy of the registrant data and judged each domain individually. The column "Suspended" shows the number of suspended domains by Reg. A—meaning they changed their NS records to sinkhole-like authoritative name servers (*e.g.,* `sinkhole.example.nl`), which they typically use for their suspended domains. To determine when the suspension occurs, we use daily crawls provided by OpenIntel [26].

Table 1. Registrar A notification and suspension results.

Date	Domains	Suspended-NS	Online
2018-01-18	3560	3174 (89.16%)	386 (10.84%)
2018-03-16	399	387 (97.24%)	12 (3.02%)
2018-05-02	148	147 (99.32%)	1 (0.68%)
Total	4107	3708 (90.31%)	398 (9.69%)

We can see the effects from this notification in Fig. 2: first, a drop in the number of domains labeled as "suspicious" originated from Reg A, followed by an overall drop of detected suspicious domains. We also see the effectiveness of this intervention in the same figure: as domains started to be suspended by registrars, and we see a drop in the number of domains classified as suspicious. After October 2018, we see very little change in the volume of such domains. Overall, our notification study lead to more than 3708 domains being ultimately suspended by Registrar A, potentially protecting users from scams.

4   FaDe

BrandCounter was initially effective in detecting counterfeit webshops, but after a first round of takedowns, we observed a sharp decrease in the number of suspicious domains (Fig. 2). Why was that? Have the counterfeiters given up or have they learned to avoid detection by BrandCounter? Given that, we set out to develop a new detector FaDe—Fake Detector—which does not rely on the words in the web page title. Instead we utilize a Support Vector Machine (SVM) [32] that employs nine features related to the registration itself and the infrastructure. We chose SVM because it is a robust method that has been successfully applied to classify various types of malicious activity [4,12,13].

SVM is a supervised learning method and relies upon labeled data for training. For that, we collaborated with the Abuse Department of *ICS*, a major credit card issuer in The Netherlands. *ICS* provided us with a list of 231 .nl domains labeled as fraudulent (Nov 2018–Jan 2019). We also randomly sampled 229 webshops from our zone which we manually labelled as a trustworthy webshop. This resulted in a data set of 460 samples.

Feature Selection: We employ nine features in FaDe that characterize counterfeit webshops (Table 2). The first three were inspired on the work by Hao *et al.* [6]—which we also observed with BrandCounter (Sect. 3). Re-registration indicates if the domain has been previously registered or not, Registration Hour represents the *hour of the day* in which the domain was registered, and the third was the registrar used.

The remaining six features (highlighted in Table 2) are based on other patterns we have seen with the domains detected by BrandCounter (Sect. 3) and the training set provided by ICS. E-mail provider indicates whether a suspicious e-mail domain is used by the registrant, given we have seen a high concentration of unusual mail providers (Fig. 7). The fifth feature—reported domains score—is the ratio of malicious domains reported via the Netcraft abuse list [15] divided by all the domains registered by a given registrar in 2018 on the .nl zone. The sixth feature captures the ratio of lowercase characters in the registrant's name, given that we noticed that many counterfeit webshops register with lowercase only. We observed that 227 of the 231 webshops reported by ICS did not configure mail servers (defined by their MX record [18]), which we also then use as a feature. The eighth feature is the issuer of the TLS certificate, because we observed that 3 issuers are responsible for 156 of the 183 webshops that were labeled by ICS as fraudulent and have TLS configured (websites have also been found employing TLS [27]). Finally, we consider the autonomous system of the A record and of the domain, *i.e.*, the AS of the hosting provider, given the high concentration of certain ASes (Fig. 4). All features are normalized to the same scale ([0, 1]) to ensure they all have the same influence on the distance metric.

Table 2. Features used by FaDe.

Dataset	Feature	Importance
	1. Re-registration	2
	2. Registration Hour	4
RegDB	3. Registrar	6
	4. Suspicious e-mail provider of registrant	1
	5. Reported domains score	5
	6. Registrant name lowercase	9
	7. Existence of a MX record	3
Scans	8. Issuer of TLS certificate (if any)	7
	9. Autonomous System of A Record	8

Model Training: To train our model, we start by randomly splitting our dataset with 460 samples into two categories: training set (367 samples, 80%) and test set (93 samples, 20%). We then use grid search [2] to find the optimal SVM parameters (*i.e.*, kernel, C and γ). We employ cross-validation [8] so that we can use the full training set for both training and validation. The best scores over all folds—mean precision of 0.98 and mean recall of 0.97—were obtained using the RBF kernel with $C = 10$ and $\gamma = 0.1$. Next, we train our final model using these parameters and the full training set. This model was then applied to the test set yielding a precision of 1.00 and recall of 1.00. Although the test set is small, it at least indicates that our model performed well.

Feature Importance: To estimate feature importance, we use the coefficients of the best SVM classifier with a linear kernel. We omit the exact coefficients because we do not want to help counterfeiters with exact values and show the relative importance in Table 2.

Results and Analysis: After training our model, we apply it to a subset of the .nl zone: only domains that are automatically classified as *eCommerce* by our crawler DMap [40]. We focus on this subset to prevent many false positives that could discourage abuse analysts. For this purpose, the crawler extracts technologies used on webpages using Wappalyzer [39] and some regular expressions that look at specific HTTP headers, HTML content and cookies. A domain is classified as eCommerce if it has at least one eCommerce related technology (e.g., Zen Cart or WooCommerce).

Ultimately, we evaluated 30k domains of our zone that were classified as eCommerce and were registered at most 365 days ago, using data crawled in January 2019. Table 3 shows the results. In total, FaDe classifier detected 1407 suspicious domains.

Table 3. FaDe results and validation.

Category	Domains
Suspicious	1407
Unreachable	181 (13%)
Reachable	1226 (87%)
True positive	894 (73%)
False positive	332 (27%)

Table 4. Notification and take down results.

Registrar	Notified	Webshop-down	NX-domain	NS-change
A	505	248	57	244
B	576	433	9	438
C	21	11	12	0
D	55	31	0	31
F	64	11	39	0
Others	63	13	16	0
Total	894	747 (84%)	133 (15%)	713 (80%)

To validate the results, we shared the lists of suspicious domains with *ICS*, where analysts manually verified every single domain in the period between 2019-01-29 and 2019-02-04—including evaluating the payment provider used by the website. Out of the 1407 domains, 181 domains (Table 4) were not reachable anymore by the time of the validation—in 14 cases analysts report a DNS error, 167 domains are annotated with a generic 'no response' label which could indicate failure at the DNS or server level. This left us with 1226 domains that were both suspicious and reachable. Out of these, 894 were confirmed as true positives (72.92% precision). *ICS* analysts reported notes on a few false positives: 38 were redirects to legitimate webshops and 8 were adult websites.

4.1   Registrar Notification and Takedown

Being able to detect these counterfeit webshops is just the first step. To protect .nl users, we need to act upon these domains, and preferably take them down.

We then split the true positives per registrar, as can be seen in Table 4, and notified the respective registrars of these domains, via two channels: *ICS* carried out their notifications and the registration department at SIDN also notified registrars. After receiving notifications, registrars can individually decide, according to their policies and processes, to suspend the domain—a process that we were not involved in.

To determine which domains were taken down, we could use the same approach shown in Sect. 3.1. However, different registrars may employ different take down methods: web page content changes, domain suspension, DNS records changes, among others. Given that we notify multiple registrars, we analyze changes in the content of web pages, domain cancellations, and nameserver changes in the period starting from the notification date until 01-05-2019. We use RegDB data and Scans data (Sect. 2.1) for this purpose.

Table 4 shows the results. Out of the 894 domains that we notified to registrars, 747 (83.56%) were effectively taken down, as measured by a change of webpage content. We can also see in the same table the method employed by the registrar: 133 (14.88%) domains are cancelled resulting in an NX domain and 713 (79.75%) changed their NS records [18], which point to the authoritative name server of a domain. We manually checked the name server changes. 677 domains changed to a sinkhole name server and 36 to a regular name server. This indicates that registrars employ different strategies to take down counterfeit webshops. For example, Reg. B suspended most domains by changing name servers whereas all Reg. F domains were cancelled. 147 (16.44%) of the notified domains were not taken down. In the majority of those cases the registrar did not respond and the registrant details were legitimate, giving us no ground to remove the domain from our zone.

4.2 BrandCounter vs FaDe Compared: Evolving Tactics

Given that BrandCounter was effective with such a simple heuristic, we can deduct that counterfeiters were likely facing very little defensive pressure—they did not seem to make any efforts to hide the suspicious characteristics of their websites, or at least not in early 2017. We could expect counterfeiters to *adapt* to our detection methods, especially because thousands of domains were taken down.

To determine why BrandCounter's performance reduces over time (Fig. 2), we apply BrandCounter to the true positives generated by FaDe. Out of the 894 domains, 707 had a score of 0 matching words—and no domain had a score above 3. Given we use a threshold of $t > 5$, counterfeiters evaded BrandCounter detection. In other words, they *adapted* to BrandCounter. Upon inspection, we see that they have essentially removed references to popular brands and inserted generic product titles, colors, type of garment, and targeted age group/gender, ultimately evading BrandCounter—which is surprising, given that up to that point we have not disclosed how we detected these websites.

Registrar and Email Provider Diversification: We have shown in Sect. 3.1 how Registrar A took down more than 3700 domain names upon our notifications.

We could expect counterfeiters to respond to that. We see that in Fig. 3, in which registrar B becomes the number 1 registrar employed by counterfeiters. More prominently, we see a diversification of e-mail providers used by registrants (Fig. 7)—moving from the dominant 163.com for BrandCounter detected domains, to a more diverse distribution for domains detected by FaDe.

Hosting Diversification: We still observe that counterfeit webshops are hosted on a small number of ASes. However, the ASes themselves did change over the years as can be seen in Fig. 4. AS 41204 and AS 204353 were frequently observed during the second study based on FaDe, while no shops were later hosted on AS 197328. Interestingly, the hosting infrastructure still does not map to Chinese IP addresses.

5   How Popular Are the Counterfeit Webshops?

Our notification campaigns led to 4.5k domains being removed or suspended. In this section, we explore the popularity of these counterfeit webshops.

We can indirectly infer a counterfeit webshop popularity by analyzing incoming queries for the `.nl` authoritative server—leveraging our `AuthDNS` dataset described in Sect. 2.1. For each domain name d, we extract the number of queries and unique IP addresses of resolvers we observed one week before the notification dates. (we chose one week given the known weekly diurnal patterns of Internet traffic [25]). While the number of queries and resolvers do not correspond to the number of unique shoppers (due to caching at DNS resolvers), it provides an indication of how diverse the population of the resolver is.

Figure 9 shows the average number of daily queries for the domains taken down before the notification, while Fig. 10 shows the average daily number of resolvers. The baseline consists of a random set of 500k domain names that serve a website (defined by a `200 OK` HTTP status code). We see a significant discrepancy in counterfeit webshops popularity: 50% of them have, on average, 100 daily queries prior to the notification, from ∼70 unique resolvers. However, there are *some* domains that are *very* popular: 55 domains had an average

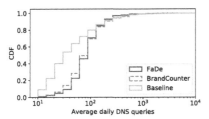
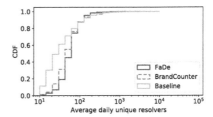

Fig. 9. Average number of daily DNS queries for counterfeit shops one week prior notification and a random subset of 500k domains that serve a website.

Fig. 10. Average number of daily unique resolvers for counterfeit shops one week prior notification and a random subset of 500k domains that serve a website.

1000 daily queries from 653 resolvers. We manually analyzed the queries of the top 10 counterfeit webshops and found that most queries originated from public resolvers and local ISPs, which is similar to normal query behavior. This suggests variability in domains' popularity, which may coincide with their advertisement strategies.

6   Privacy and Legal Considerations

Together with our legal department, we have developed a publicly available data privacy framework [3] that conforms to both EU and Dutch [3,9] legislation. This framework has been implemented, including a privacy board that oversees SIDN Labs' research. For the purpose of this research, only domain names and their associated labels—either legitimate or suspicious—were shared between SIDN Labs research and respectively *ICS* and the registrars. This collaboration was formalised using a data sharing agreement.

Note that domains with counterfeit webshops were mostly taken down by registrars. SIDN only takes down domains based on content if it is clearly criminal or unlawful. However, .nl regulations [29] determines that registrant data must be legitimate. Failure to conform to the regulation may result in domain name removal from the zone—the legal instrument that has been used in some take down procedures.

7   Related Work

Counterfeit Market: Counterfeit industry has been previously studied by criminology researchers [37]. However, they focus on sales in the streets and not online. The online world of counterfeit stores have been extensively studied and mapped by [38]. The authors' starting point was Google search results. Our work, however, is based on 5.8M domains issued by .nl, and with a focus on non-English results. Besides, we cover years of continuous efforts to mitigate such webshops and we carry out notification campaigns with domain registrars and a credit card issuer, which lead to 4.5k domains being taken down (and more belonging to other registrars, which our colleagues of the registration department notified but we did not cover in this study). We also show how counterfeiters adapted to our first classifier, once their domains started being taken down.

Payment Systems: McCoy et al. [16] cover payment systems in abuse-advertised goods, and in 2018 they focused on bullet-proof payment systems [34]. We do not cover payment systems in this paper, but we collaborated with *ICS*, which is a major credit card provider that deals with payment systems themselves.

8   Conclusions

Counterfeit luxury goods are a very profitable business, and employ high levels of automation in both registration and hosting. Our results suggest most registrations are supposedly done from China, but most hosting is not. We show that counterfeiters operate not only in English and in .com, as in previous works, but also in Dutch and on .nl, which illustrates how professional this industry is.

We have developed and used two systems to detect counterfeit webshops in production at .nl, detecting more than 20k suspicious webshops over a period of more than two years. By notifying registrars and teaming up with *ICS*, we carried out notification campaigns that resulted in 4455 domains being suspended, ultimately protecting users of the .nl zone from possible scams. Both detectors are relatively simple but at the same time effective, suggesting that counterfeiters were suffering little defensive pressure. As such, we can expect they will try to evade our detection systems again—as they have done with BrandCounter— which requires us to continuously adapt to evolving tactics.

Acknowledgments. We thank very much the collaboration involved in this study: the (anonymized) registrars that collaborated in removing counterfeit webshops, as well as ICS and their analysts for manually validating our results.

We also would like to thank Geoff Voelker, Moritz Müller, Damon McCoy, Elmer Lastdrager for reviewing on various paper drafts, as well as the anonymous reviewers of PAM2020, and our shepherd, Dave Levin.

SIDN and the University of Twente received funding from the European Union's Horizon 2020 Research and Innovation program under Grant Agreement No 830927. Project website: https://www.concordia-h2020.eu/.

A   Appendix: Screenshots of Counterfeit Webshops

Figure 11 shows the screenshot of a counterfeit webshop captured in 2016 on the .nl zone, also shown in [5]. Figure 12 shows the screenshot of a counterfeit webshop captured in 2019.

Fig. 11. Example of counterfeit webshop detected in 2016.

Fig. 12. Example of counterfeit webshop detected in 2019.

References

1. Ahi, K., Asadizanjani, N., Shahbazmohamadi, S., Tehranipoor, M., Anwar, M.: Terahertz characterization of electronic components and comparison of terahertz imaging with x-ray imaging techniques, vol. 9483, April 2015. https://doi.org/10.1117/12.2183128
2. Bergstra, J., Bengio, Y.: Random search for hyper-parameter optimization. J. Mach. Learn. Res. **13**(Feb), 281–305 (2012)
3. Hesselman, C., Jansen, J., Wullink, M., Vink, K., Simon, M.: A privacy framework for DNS big data applications. Technical report (2014). https://www.sidnlabs.nl/downloads/yBW6hBoaSZe4m6GJc_0b7w/2211058ab6330c7f3788141ea19d3db7/SIDN_Labs_Privacyraamwerk_Position_Paper_V1.4_ENG.pdf
4. Drucker, H., Wu, D., Vapnik, V.: Support vector machines for spam categorization. IEEE Trans. Neural Netw. **10**(5), 1048–1054 (1999). https://doi.org/10.1109/72.788645
5. Moura, G.C.M., Muller, M., Wullink, M., Hesselman, C.: nDEWS: a new domains early warning system for TLDs. In: IEEE/IFIP International Workshop on Analytics for Network and Service Management (AnNet 2016), Co-Located with IEEE/IFIP Network Operations and Management Symposium (NOMS 2016), April 2016
6. Hao, S., Kantchelian, A., Miller, B., Paxson, V., Feamster, N.: PREDATOR: proactive recognition and elimination of domain abuse at time-of-registration. In: Proceedings of the 2016 ACM SIGSAC Conference on Computer and Communications Security, CCS 2016, pp. 1568–1579. ACM, New York (2016). https://doi.org/10.1145/2976749.2978317
7. Hao, S., et al.: Understanding the domain registration behavior of spammers. In: Proceedings of the 2013 Conference on Internet Measurement Conference, IMC 2013, pp. 63–76. ACM, New York (2013). https://doi.org/10.1145/2504730.2504753
8. Hastie, T., Tibshirani, R., Friedman, J.: The Elements of Statistical Learning. Springer, New York (2009). https://doi.org/10.1007/978-0-387-84858-7

9. Hesselman, C., Moura, G.C.M., Schmidt, R.O., Toet, C.: Increasing DNS security and stability through a control plane for top-level domain operators. IEEE Commun. Mag. **55**(1), 197–203 (2017). https://doi.org/10.1109/MCOM.2017.1600521CM
10. Hoffman, P., Sullivan, A., Fujiwara, K.: DNS terminology. RFC 8499, IETF, November 2018. http://tools.ietf.org/rfc/rfc8499.txt
11. ICS: International Credit Card Services (2020). https://icscards.nl
12. Kazemian, H., Ahmed, S.: Comparisons of machine learning techniques for detecting malicious webpages. Expert Syst. Appl. **42**(3), 1166–1177 (2015). https://doi.org/10.1016/j.eswa.2014.08.046
13. Kruczkowski, M., Szynkiewicz, E.N.: Support vector machine for malware analysis and classification. In: 2014 IEEE/WIC/ACM International Joint Conferences on Web Intelligence (WI) and Intelligent Agent Technologies (IAT). IEEE, August 2014. https://doi.org/10.1109/wi-iat.2014.127
14. Lever, C., Walls, R., Nadji, Y., Dagon, D., McDaniel, P., Antonakakis, M.: Domain-Z: 28 registrations later measuring the exploitation of residual trust in domains. In: 2016 IEEE Symposium on Security and Privacy (SP), pp. 691–706, May 2016. https://doi.org/10.1109/SP.2016.47
15. Netcraft Ltd.: Netcraft, 10 October 2019. https://www.netcraft.com/
16. McCoy, D., Dharmdasani, H., Kreibich, C., Voelker, G.M., Savage, S.: Priceless: the role of payments in abuse-advertised goods. In: Proceedings of the 2012 ACM Conference on Computer and Communications Security, CCS 2012, pp. 845–856. ACM, New York (2012). https://doi.org/10.1145/2382196.2382285
17. McCoy, D., et al.: PharmaLeaks: understanding the business of online pharmaceutical affiliate programs. In: Proceedings of the 21st USENIX Security Symposium. USENIX Association, Bellevue, August 2012
18. Mockapetris, P.: Domain names - concepts and facilities. RFC 1034, IETF, November1987. http://tools.ietf.org/rfc/rfc1034.txt
19. Moura, G.C.M., Heidemann, J., Schmidt, R.O., Hardaker, W.: Cache me if you can: effects of DNS time-to-live. In: Proceedings of the 2019 ACM Internet Measurement Conference, October 2019. https://doi.org/10.1145/3355369.3355568
20. Moura, G.C.M., Heidemann, J., Müller, M., Schmidt, R.O., Davids, M.: When the dike breaks: dissecting DNS defenses during DDoS. In: Proceedings of the ACM Internet Measurement Conference, October 2018. https://doi.org/10.1145/3278532.3278534
21. Nieuws, R.: Dit jaar al 307 nep-webwinkels offline gehaald door politie (in Dutch), 12 December 2018. https://www.rtlnieuws.nl/geld-en-werk/artikel/4520646/dit-jaar-al-307-nep-webwinkels-offline-gehaald-door-politie
22. NOS: Consumenten voor 5 miljoen euro opgelicht via nepwinkels op sociale media (in Dutch), 12 December 2018. https://nos.nl/artikel/2258095-consumenten-voor-5-miljoen-euro-opgelicht-via-nepwinkels-op-sociale-media.html
23. NOS: Waar komen al die nep-webshops toch vandaan? (in Dutch), 5 May 2018. https://nos.nl/artikel/2230087-waar-komen-al-die-nep-webshops-toch-vandaan.html
24. Peter, H.: Gefälschte Sneaker von der FDP? (In German) (2019). https://www.tagesschau.de/wirtschaft/fakeshops-plagiate-sneaker-china-101.html
25. Quan, L., Heidemann, J., Pradkin, Y.: When the internet sleeps: correlating diurnal networks with external factors. In: Proceedings of the 2014 Conference on Internet Measurement Conference, IMC 2014, pp. 87–100. ACM, New York (2014). https://doi.org/10.1145/2663716.2663721

26. van Rijswijk-Deij, R., Jonker, M., Sperotto, A., Pras, A.: A high-performance, scalable infrastructure for large-scale active DNS measurements. IEEE J. Sel. Areas Commun. **34**(6), 1877–1888 (2016)
27. Roberts, R., Goldschlag, Y., Walter, R., Chung, T., Mislove, A., Levin, D.: You are who you appear to be: a longitudinal study of domain impersonation in TLS certificates. In: Proceedings of the 2019 ACM SIGSAC Conference on Computer and Communications Security, CCS 2019, pp. 2489–2504 (2019). https://doi.org/10.1145/3319535.3363188
28. Schmidle, N.: Inside the Knockoff-Tennis-Shoe factory. The New York Times (2010). http://www.nytimes.com/2010/08/22/magazine/22fake-t.html
29. SIDN: General terms and conditions for .nl registrants, 19 May 2019. https://www.sidn.nl/downloads/d_7zdiiDQvOGbSo1FGCcqw/6d8b113b06e293bd9af55fb11a66c499/General_Terms_and_Conditions_for_nl_Registrants.pdf
30. SIDN: Stichting internet domein nederland, 30 Ago 2019. https://sidn.nl/en
31. Streitfeld, D.: What happens after Amazon's domination is complete? Its bookstore offers clues. New York Times, 23 June 2019. https://www.nytimes.com/2019/06/23/technology/amazon-domination-bookstore-books.html
32. Suykens, J.A., Vandewalle, J.: Least squares support vector machine classifiers. Neural Process. Lett. **9**(3), 293–300 (1999). https://doi.org/10.1023/A:1018628609742
33. Taxation and Customs Union: Customs Union: EU customs seized over 41 million fake goods at EU borders last year (2016). https://ec.europa.eu/taxation_customs/node/976_en
34. Tian, H., Gaffigan, S.M., West, D.S., McCoy, D.: Bullet-proof payment processors. In: 2018 APWG Symposium on Electronic Crime Research (eCrime), pp. 1–11, May 2018. https://doi.org/10.1109/ECRIME.2018.8376208
35. Turner, K.: That Chanel bag on your Instagram feed may not be a Chanel bag (2016). https://www.washingtonpost.com/news/the-switch/wp/2016/05/26/that-chanel-bag-on-your-instagram-feed-may-not-be-a-chanel-bag
36. U.S. Customs and Border Protection Office of Trade: Intellectual Property Rights - Fiscal Year 2017 Seizure Statistics (2017). https://www.cbp.gov/document/stats/fy-2017-ipr-seizure-statistics
37. Wall, D.S., Large, J.: Jailhouse frocks: locating the public interest in policing counterfeit luxury fashion goods. Br. J. Criminol. **50**(6), 1094–1116 (2010). http://ssrn.com/abstract=1649773
38. Wang, D.Y., et al.: Search + Seizure: the effectiveness of interventions on SEO campaigns. In: Proceedings of the 2014 Conference on Internet Measurement Conference, IMC 2014, pp. 359–372. ACM, New York (2014). https://doi.org/10.1145/2663716.2663738
39. Wappalyzer: Identify technology on websites, 19 October 2019. https://www.wappalyzer.com/
40. Wullink, M., Moura, G.C., Hesselman, C.: Dmap: automating domain name ecosystem measurements and applications. In: 2018 Network Traffic Measurement and Analysis Conference (TMA), pp. 1–8. IEEE, June 2018
41. Wullink, M., Moura, G.C., Müller, M., Hesselman, C.: ENTRADA: a high-performance network traffic data streaming warehouse. In: 2016 IEEE/IFIP Network Operations and Management Symposium (NOMS), pp. 913–918. IEEE, April 2016

When Parents and Children Disagree: Diving into DNS Delegation Inconsistency

Raffaele Sommese[1]([✉]), Giovane C. M. Moura[2], Mattijs Jonker[1],
Roland van Rijswijk-Deij[1,3], Alberto Dainotti[4], K. C. Claffy[4],
and Anna Sperotto[1]

[1] University of Twente, Enschede, The Netherlands
r.sommese@utwente.nl
[2] SIDN Labs, Arnhem, The Netherlands
[3] NLnet Labs, Amsterdam, The Netherlands
[4] CAIDA, San Diego, USA

Abstract. The Domain Name System (DNS) is a hierarchical, decentralized, and distributed database. A key mechanism that enables the DNS to be hierarchical and distributed is *delegation* [7] of responsibility from parent to child *zones*—typically managed by different entities. RFC1034 [12] states that authoritative nameserver (NS) records at both parent and child should be "consistent and remain so", but we find inconsistencies for over 13M second-level domains. We classify the type of inconsistencies we observe, and the behavior of resolvers in the face of such inconsistencies, using RIPE Atlas to probe our experimental domain configured for different scenarios. Our results underline the risk such inconsistencies pose to the availability of misconfigured domains.

1 Introduction

The Domain Name System (DNS) [12] is one of the most critical components of the Internet, used by virtually every user and application. DNS is a distributed, hierarchical database that maps hosts, services and applications to IP addresses and various other types of records. A key mechanism that enables the DNS to be hierarchical and distributed is *delegation* [7]. In order for delegation to work, the DNS hierarchy is organized in parent and child zones—typically managed by different entities—that need to share common information (NS records) about which are the authoritative name servers for a given domain. While RFC1034 [12] states that the NS records at both parent and child should be "consistent and remain so", there is evidence that this is not always the case [10]. However, a full and systematic analysis of the extent of this problem is still missing.

In this paper, we analyze this issue by *(i)* providing a broad characterization of inconsistencies in DNS delegations, and *(ii)* investigating and shedding light on their practical consequences. Specifically, we first evaluate if there are inconsistencies between parent and child sets of NS records (NSSet) for all active second-level domain names of three large DNS zones: `.com`, `.net`, and `.org`

A. Sperotto et al. (Eds.): PAM 2020, LNCS 12048, pp. 175–189, 2020.
https://doi.org/10.1007/978-3-030-44081-7_11

(Sect. 3)—together comprising of more than 166M domain names (50% of the DNS namespace), as well as all top-level domains (TLDs) from the Root DNS zone [22]. We show that while 80% of these domain names exhibit consistency, 8% (i.e., 13 million domains) do not. These inconsistencies affect even large and popular organizations, including Twitter, Intel and AT&T. Overall we find that at least 50k .com, .net, and .org domains of the Alexa Top 1M list are affected.

We then classify these inconsistencies into four categories (Sect. 3): the cases (i) in which the parent and child NSSets are *disjoint* sets, (ii) the parent NSSet is a *subset* of the child NSSet, (iii) the parent NSSet is a *superset* of the child NSSet and (iv) the parent and child NSSet have a non-empty intersection but do not match (ii) or (iii). These inconsistencies are not without harm. Even in the case in which disjoint sets of NS records resolve to the same IP addresses, case (i) introduces fragility in the DNS infrastructure, since operators need to maintain different information at different levels of the DNS hierarchy, which are typically under separate administrative control. Case (ii) may lead to unresponsive name servers, while case (iii) points to a quite understandable error of modifying the child zone while forgetting the parent, but it offers a false sense of resilience and it results in improper load balancing among the name servers. Finally, case (iv), which we see happening in more than 10% of the cases in which parent and child have a non-empty intersection, suffers all the aforementioned risks.

To understand the practical consequences of such inconsistencies, we emulate all four categories (Sect. 4) by setting up a test domain name and issuing DNS queries from more than 15k vantage points. Our experiment highlights the consequences of delegation inconsistency on query load distribution in the wild. We then investigate how popular DNS resolvers from different vendors deal with such inconsistencies (Sect. 5), and find that some resolvers do not comply with RFC specifications.

Finally, we conclude the paper discussing our findings and offering recommendations for domain name operators to manage the inconsistencies we identified.

2   Background and Related Work

DNS uses a *hierarchical name space* [12], in which the root node is the *dot* (.). Zones under the root—the top-level domains such as .org—are referred to as *delegations* [7]. These delegations have second-level delegations of their own such as example.org. To create delegations for a *child* zone (such as example.org), DNS NS records [12] are added to the *parent* zone (.org in Fig. 1). In this example, the NS records are [a,b].iana-servers.net, which, in practice, means that these records are the *authoritative* name servers for example.org, i.e.,servers that have definitive information about the example.org zone.

RFC1034 states that the NSSet should be consistent between parent and child authoritative servers. This, however, is far from trivial. Parent and child zones and servers are almost always maintained by different organizations across administrative boundaries. The most common case is where the parent is a TLD. Delegation changes in the parent go through the so-called Registry-Registrar-Registrant (RRR) channel for almost all TLDs. In this model, the Registry

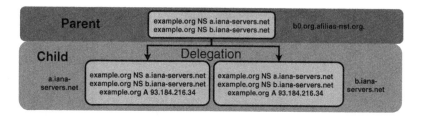

Fig. 1. Domain name delegation: parent and child authoritative servers.

operates the TLD, the Registrar sells domain names under the TLD and the Registrant is the domain holder. If the domain holder wants to change the delegation, they can make the change in their child zone, but need to file a request with the Registry through the Registrar. This process currently always happens via an out-of-band channel (not through the DNS) and in some cases may even require forms on paper. Add to this that domain holders may not always be aware of this complexity and the requirement to keep parent and child in sync, and it is clear to see that keeping the DNS consistent is prone to human errors.

The problem of Parent-Child consistency is addressed in RFC7477 [6], which introduces a method to automatically keep records in the parent in sync through a periodical polling of the child using SOA records and a new type of record (CSYNC). Unfortunately, RFC7477 lacks deployment.

Pappas *et al.* [17] analyzed divergence between parent and child delegations on sample domains (∼6M) from multiple zones and found inconsistencies in 21% of the DNS zones evaluated, in three different years. Kristoff [10] analysed delegations in .edu and finds that 25% of .edu delegations suffer some form of inconsistency. In his work, he considers 3 types of inconsistency: superset, subset and disjoint-set. Our work significantly expands on both studies by considering both the largest generic TLDs .com, .net and .org and the root zone of the DNS (∼166 million domains, Sect. 3) and evaluating implications for resolvers in the wild (Sect. 4).

Liu *et al.* show that dangling delegation records referring to expired resources (e.g., cloud IP addresses or names) left in the parent or child pose a significant risk [11]. An attacker can obtain control of these records through the same cloud services by randomly registering new services, and in this way take control of the domain. Finally, Moura *et al.* [14] have looked into the consistency of time-to-live values [12] of parent and child NS records.

3 Parent and Child NSSet: Are They Consistent?

DNS NS records must be configured at both parent and child zones [5,12].

We compare NS records at parents and children in the wild considering all second-level domains (SLDs) under .com, .net, and .org, on 2019-10-16. We also evaluate the records in the Root DNS zone on 2019-10-30. We make use of OpenINTEL, a large-scale DNS measurement platform [23]. OpenINTEL collects

Table 1. Parent (P) and Child (C) NSSet consistency results. "IP" refers to A records of the NSSet of P and C.

	.com SLD	.org SLD	.net SLD	Root TLD	.com Ratio	.org Ratio	.net Ratio
Total domains	142,302,090	9,998,488	13,181,091	1528			
Unresponsive	19,860,226	949,137	1,663,403	0	14.0%	9.5%	12.6%
$P = C$	111,077,299	8,291,257	10,443,314	1476	78.0%	82.9%	79.2%
$P \neq C$	11,364,565	758,094	1,074,374	52	8.0%	7.6%	8.2%
$P \cap C = \emptyset$	6,594,680	418,269	548,718	16	58.0%	55.2%	51.0%
$IP(P) = IP(C)$	3,046,075	216,130	245,936	16	48.2%	53.9%	46.7%
$IP(P) \neq IP(C)$	3,265,171	184,885	280,988	0	51.8%	46.1%	53.3%
$IP(P) \cap IP(C) = \emptyset$	1,415,838	83,720	137,913	0	43.3%	45.3%	49.1%
$IP(P) \cap IP(C) \neq \emptyset$	1,849,333	101,165	143,075	0	56.7%	54.7%	51.9%
$P \cap C \neq \emptyset$	4,769,885	339,825	525,656	36	42.0%	44.8%	49.0%
$P \subset C$	3,506,090	236,257	369,442	18	73.5%	69.5%	70.2%
$P \supset C$	681,082	64,161	98,345	10	14.3%	18.9%	18.7%
Rest	582,713	39,407	57,869	8	12.2%	11.6%	11.1%

daily active measurements of over 60% of the global DNS namespace every day. For each SLD, we extract the sets of NS records from the parent and child authoritative servers, respectively indicated as P and C.

Table 1 shows the results of our comparative analysis. The first row shows the total number of SLDs for each TLD zone on the date considered. For the three zones, ~80% of SLDs have a consistent set of NS records at both the parent and the child zones. However, ~8% of SLDs (~13M) do not. For comparison, consider that 13M is almost as many domain names as some of the largest country-code TLDs (Germany's .de, one of the largest, has 16M SLDs [3]). The remaining 12% of domains are unresponsive to our queries. This could happen for different reasons, i.e. misconfigurations, failure, etc., not addressed in this work. We even see that 52 TLDs in the Root zone have inconsistent NSSets. Out of these, 26 are country-code TLDs (ccTLDs). We are currently notifying these ccTLD operators, in order to resolve these non-conforming setups, since they can have an adverse effect, among others, on load balancing.

Inconsistent NSSets Classification: We classify inconsistent domain names into four categories: the cases in which (i) the parent and child NSSets are *disjoint*, (ii) the parent NSSet is a *subset* of the child NSSet, (iii) the parent NSSet is a *superset* of the child NSSet and (iv) the parent and child NSSet have a non-empty intersection but do not match (ii) or (iii).

For case (i), we observe that 51–58% of domains have completely *disjoint NSSets* ($P \cap C = \emptyset$). Depending on if resolvers are parent or child-centric, in this case resolvers will trust different NS records.

Given the surprising results for disjoint sets, we investigate the IP addresses of the NS records (IP(P, C, lines 4–7 in Table 1).[1] We discover that in half of the

---

[1] This covers 96% of names with disjoint NSSets, the remaining 4% are indeterminate due to unresolvable names in the NSSets.

cases, domains have disjoint NSSets that point to the same addresses, *i.e.*,there is an inconsistency of names but addresses match. In the other half, there is inconsistency also in addresses. Of these, ∼45% have completely disjoint sets of IP addresses, for the remaining 55% there is some sort of overlap.

Disjoint sets may increase the risk of human error even in the case of name servers resolving to the same IP address, since operators would need to maintain redundant information in the parent and child, thus introducing fragility in the DNS data. Disjoint sets also may lead to lame delegations [7], *i.e.*,pointing resolvers to servers that may no longer be authoritative for the domain name.

Finally disjoint sets can be related to another malpractice: *CNAME configured on the Apex* [1]. However, further analysis shows that only a negligible percentage of cases are related to this.

Considering partially matching SLDs ($P \cap C \neq \emptyset$), we observe that 69–73% belong to case (ii), where the parent NSSet is a *subset* of the child NSSet. This may be intentional, e.g. an operator may want to first update the child and observe traffic shifts, and then later update the parent. Alternatively, operators may forget to update the delegation at the parent after updating the child.

Case (iii) where the parent NSSet forms a *superset* of the child NSSet ($P \supset C$) occurs in 14–18% of cases. This situation may introduce latency in the resolution process due to unresponsive name servers. Finally, the *Rest* category is case (iv), where the NSSets form neither a superset nor a subset, yet they have a non-empty intersection. Between 11–12% of SLDs fall in this category, and are susceptible to the range of operational issue highlighted for the previous categories.

Note that the OpenINTEL platform performs the measurements choosing *one* of the child authoritative nameservers. To verify how often sibling name servers have different configurations (child-child delegation inconsistency), we execute a measurement on a random sample of ∼1% of .org domains (10k domains). The measurement suggests that ∼2% of total parent-child delegation inconsistency cases also have child-child delegation inconsistencies, meaning that our results give a lower bound for the problem of parent-child mismatch. In fact, the Open-INTEL resolver could randomly choose a server configured correctly, while the others are not.

4   Implications of NSSet Differences in the Wild

We observed that roughly 8% of studied domains have parent/child inconsistencies. In this section, we investigate the consequences of such inconsistencies, by emulating the four categories of NSSet mismatches. We configure parent and child authoritative servers in eight different configurations (Table 2), and explore the consequences in terms of query load distribution. Our goal is to study these consequences in a controlled environment, where the authoritative name servers are in the same network. In the real-world, the authoritative name servers are often distributed geographically and the query load can depend on external factors, e.g. nearest server, popularity of a domain in a certain region, etc.

We emulate an operator that (i) has full control over its child authoritative name servers and (ii) uses the same zone file on all authoritative name servers (zones are synchronized). We place all child authoritative servers in the same network, thus, having similar latencies. We expect this to result in querying resolvers distributing queries evenly among child authoritatives [15].

As vantage points, we use RIPE Atlas [20, 21], measuring each unique resolver as seen from their probes physically distributed around the world (3.3k ASes). Many Atlas probes have multiple recursive resolvers, so we treat each combination of probe and unique recursive resolver as a vantage point (VP), since potentially each represents a different perspective. We therefore see about 15k VPs from about 9k Atlas probes, with the exact number varying by experiment due to small changes in probe and resolver availability.

Table 2. Experiments to compare differents in Parent/Child NSSet

	Disjoint		Subset		Superset		Rest	
Experiment	Min-Off	Min-On	Min-Off	Min-On	Min-Off	Min-On	Min-Off	Min-On
Measurement ID	23020789	23019715	23113087	23113622	23114128	23115432	23117852	23116481
Frequency	600s							
Duration	2h							
Query	A $probeid-$timestamp.marigliano.xyz with 30 seconds TTL							
NSSet Parent	[ns1, ns3]		[ns1, ns3]		[ns1, ns2, ns3, ns4]		[ns1, ns2, ns3, ns4]	
NSSet Child	[ns2, ns4]		[ns1, ns2, ns3, ns4]		[ns2, ns4]		[ns2, ns4, ns5, ns6]	
TTL NS Parent	3600s							
TTL NS Child	3600s							
Date	20191003	20191003	20191025	20191025	20191025	20191026	20191027	20191027
Probes	9028	9031	8888	8883	8892	8879	8875	8875
VPs	15956	15950	15639	15657	15647	15611	15557	15586
Queries	190434	190333	184364	185706	186960	185015	182992	186472
Answers	178428	178416	169224	175200	175080	174804	174288	174504
From ns1, ns3	109661	175124	132179	169482	52233	83607	53944	84709
From ns2, ns4	65527	322	31753	1557	118835	86804	83100	85739
From ns5, ns6	N/A	N/A	N/A	N/A	N/A	N/A	31740	1545
fail	3240	2970	5292	4161	4012	4393	5504	2511

4.1 Disjoint Parent and Child NSSet

We have configured our test domain (marigliano.xyz) for the disjoint NSSet experiment as shown in Fig. 2. For this experiment, we set the NSSet at the

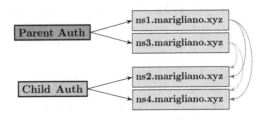

Fig. 2. Disjoint NSSset experiment for marigliano.xyz

parent to [ns1, ns3].`marigliano.xyz`, while on the child authoritative servers, we set the NSSet to [ns2, ns4].`marigliano.xyz` (Table 2).

Zone files: we then configure the zone files of [ns1–ns4] to answer NS queries with [ns2, ns4], if explicitly asked, *i.e.,*the same records pointed to by the child authoritative servers. By doing that, we are able to single out resolvers that are *parent-centric*, since they will only contact [ns1, ns3].

As vantage points, we use ~9k Atlas probes, and configure them to send A queries through each of their resolvers for \$probeid-\$timestamp.`marigliano`. `xyz`, which encodes the unique Atlas probe ID and query timestamp, thus avoiding queries of multiple probes interfering with each other. We also set the TTL value of the record to 30 s, and probe every 600 s, so resolver caches are expected to be empty for each round of measurements [13].

Our goal is to determine, *indirectly*, which NS records were used to answer the queries. To do that, we configure [ns1, ns3] to answer our A queries with the IP 42.42.42.42, and [ns2, ns4] with the IP 43.43.43.43. We use this approach instead of inspecting the query log on the server-side to speed up parsing and to avoid duplicated detection.

Figure 3a shows the results of the experiment. In round 0 of the measurements, we have a warm-up phase of RIPE Atlas probes, where not all the probes participate. Furthermore, we expect resolvers to have a cold cache and to use the NSSet provided by the parent. As the figure shows, this is mostly the case although 253 unique resolver IPs (different probes can share the same resolver) do contact the child name servers. This can be either due to them sending explicit NS queries (and thus learning about [ns2, ns4]) or because some probes share upstream caches. In subsequent rounds, we expect more traffic to go to the child name servers [ns2, ns4]. This is because resolvers learn about the child delegation from the "authority section" included in the response to the A query to ns1 or ns3. According to RFC2181 resolvers may prefer this information over the delegation provided by the parent. Indeed, in rounds [1–11] we see traffic also going to the child name servers. However, not all traffic goes to servers in the child NSSet, because not all resolvers trust data from the "authority section" due to mitigations against the so-called Kaminsky attack [8]. A key takeaway of this experiment is that domain owners may mistakenly assume traffic to go to the name servers in the child NSSet if they change it, whereas for this change to be effective, they must also update the parent NSSet.

The situation is even worse in our second experiment. Here, we configure [ns1–ns4] to answer with *minimal responses*, which prevents these servers from including "extra" records in the authority and additional sections of DNS answers. This means we do not expect resolvers to learn about the existence of [ns2, ns4] at all, since they are no longer present in the "authority section" of responses to the A queries. Only if resolvers perform explicit NS queries will they learn about [ns2, ns4]. As Fig. 3b shows, as expected, almost all resolvers exclusively send their queries to the name servers in the NSSet of the parent. Only about 40 vantage points receive data from the name servers in the child NSSet, indicating

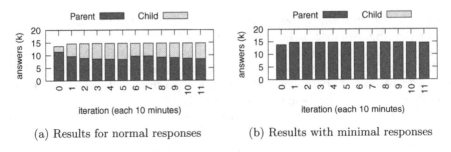

(a) Results for normal responses   (b) Results with minimal responses

Fig. 3. Disjoint NSSet experiments

their resolvers likely performed explicit NS queries. Authoritative name servers are increasingly configured to return minimal responses to dampen the effect of DNS amplification attacks, especially for DNSSEC-signed domains [19]. A key takeaway from this experiment is with this configuration becoming more and more prevalent, it becomes even more important to keep parent and child NSSets correctly synchronized.

Real-World Case: On 2019-10-30, we notified India's .in, given they had ns[1-6].neustar.in as NS records at the parent, and [ns1-ns6].registry.in at the child. However, altogether, both NSSets pointed to the same A/AAAA records and, as such, resolvers ended up reaching the same machines. After our notification, .in fixed this inconsistency on 2019-11-02 (we analyzed DNS OARC's root zone file repository [4]). Besides .in, 15 other internationalized ccTLDs run by India had the same issue with their NSset, and were also fixed.

4.2   Parent NSSet Is a Subset of Child

Recall from Table 1 that the majority (69–73%) of cases in which parent and child NSSets differ fall into the category where the child NSSets contains one or more additional NS records not present in the parent NSSet. A common reason to add additional NS records is to spread load over more name servers, and we assume this to be one of the reasons for this common misconfiguration.

We set up experiments to determine the consequences on query distribution if you have this setup. In other words: how many queries will eventually be answered by the extra NS record? We configure our test domain with [ns1, ns3] at the parent and [ns1, ns2, ns3, ns4] at the child. Like in the previous section, we configure [ns1, ns3] to give a different response to the A queries sent by the Atlas probes than [ns2, ns4], so we learn how many queries were answered by the name servers that are only in the child NSSet.

Figure 4a shows the results. Similary to the results shown in Sect. 4.1, most resolvers will use the NS records provided by the parent. Given that the child NSSet includes the NSSet at the parent, we see that the extra name servers

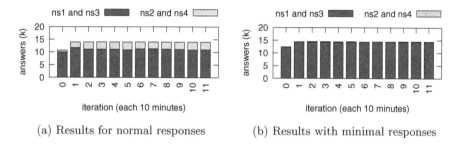

(a) Results for normal responses   (b) Results with minimal responses

Fig. 4. Subset NS sets experiments

receive only ∼24% of the queries. If in addition we configure the name servers to return minimal responses, we see that, just as in Sect. 4.1 virtually no resolvers contact the extra name servers in the child NSSet (Fig. 4b). A key takeaway from these two experiments is that the, perhaps, expected even load distribution domain owners are hoping to see will not occur if only the child NSSet is updated. This again underlines the importance of keeping parent and child in sync.

Real-World Case: `att.com`: A real-world example that demonstrates that this type of misconfiguration also occurs for prominent domains is the case of `att.com`. We discovered that AT&T's main domain `att.com` had a parent NSSet containing [`ns1...ns3`]`.attdns.com`, whereas the child had [`ns1...ns4`]`.attdns.com`. We notified AT&T of this misconfiguration and on 2019-10-24 the issue was resolved when the fourth name server (`ns4.attdns.com`) was also added to the parent.

4.3 Parent NSSet Is a Superset of Child

Roughly 14–18% of domain names that have different NSSet at parent and child have, one or more extra NS records at the *parent* ($P \supset C$ in Table 1). This could be due to operators forgetting to remove name servers that are no longer in use at the parent, but also the reverse case of the previous section in which a new name server is added at the parent but not added at the child.

To investigate the consequences of this for resolvers, we carry out experiments using Atlas VPs, setting four NS records at the parent ([ns1, ns2, ns3, ns4], as in Table 2) and only two at the child ([ns2, ns4]). Our goal is to identify the ratio of queries answered by the extra NS records at the parent.

Figure 5a shows the results for the experiment. As can be seen, the servers listed both in the parent and in the child ([ns2, ns4]) answer, on average, 68% of the queries. In case minimal responses are configured (Fig. 5b), we see the queries being distributed evenly among the NS records in the parent. Consequently, having authoritative servers include an authority section in their answer to the A queries seems to cause *some* resolvers to prefer the child NSSet over the one in the parent. For example, Atlas VP (21448, 129.13.64.5) distributes queries

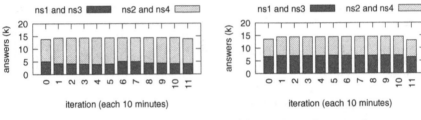

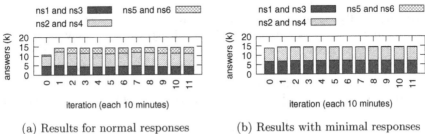

Fig. 5. Superset NS sets experiments

(a) Results for normal responses   (b) Results with minimal responses

Fig. 6. Rest NS sets experiments

only among ns2 and ns4, in the case of normal responses, instead it distributes queries among all name servers in case of minimal responses.

These measurements then confirm that including "authority data" in the authoritative server responses will cause *some* resolvers to prefer only the child authoritative servers.

4.4   Mixed NSSets (Rest)

We have shown in Table 1 that in 11% of cases, the NSSet of the parent and child do not have a subset/superset relationship. Instead, some elements are present in both, but both parent and child have at least one NS that is not available in the other. To simulate this scenario, as shown in Table 2, we set four NS records at the parent: [*ns1*,ns2,*ns3*,ns4]. Then, at the child, we set [ns2, ns4, *ns5*, *ns6*], where the highlighted names show the ones not shared.

Figure 6a shows the experiment results. We see that [ns2, ns4], which are listed at both parent and child receive most queries. Then, records set only at the parent ([ns1, ns3]) are second to receive more queries. Finally, records set only at the child ([ns5, ns6]) receive the least amount of queries. In case of minimal responses (Fig. 6b), the name servers only present at the child ([ns5, ns6]) receive virtually no traffic.

Table 3. O.S. and resolver versions evaluated (N/available, N/covered)

	Bind	Unbound	Knot	PowerDNS	Windows-DNS
Ubuntu-18-04	9.11.3-1	1.6.7	2.1.1	4.1.1	N/A
Ubuntu-16.04	9.10.3-P4	1.5.8	1.0.0	4.0.0	N/A
CentOS 7	9.9.4	1.6.6	2.4.1	4.1.9	N/A
CentOS 6	9.8.2rc1	1.4.20	N/C	3.7.4	N/A
Source	9.14.0	1.9.0	N/C	4.1.9	N/A
Windows	N/C	N/C	N/C	N/C	2008r2, 2012, 2016, 2019

4.5   Discussion

Having inconsistent NSSets in parent and child authoritative servers impacts how queries are distributed among name servers, which plays an important role in DNS engineering. Overall, for all evaluated cases, queries will be unevenly distributed among authoritative servers – and the servers listed at the parent zone will receive more queries than then ones specified in the child.

5   Resolver Software Evaluation

The experiments carried out in Sect. 3 evaluates DNS resolver behavior in the wild. Since we use RIPE Atlas, we do not know what resolver software is used, if probes use DNS forwarders, or what kind of cache policies they use. We, however, see the aggregated behavior among a large set of configurations.

In this section, we focus on evaluating specific DNS resolver software instead, in a controlled environment, in order to understand how they behave towards DNS zones that are inconsistent with regards to their parent/child NSSet. Our goal is to identify which vendors conform to the standards. In particular, we pay attention as to whether resolvers follow RFC2181 [5], which specifies *how* resolvers should rank data in case of inconsistency: child authoritative data should be preferred.

We evaluate four popular DNS resolver implementations: *BIND* [9], *Unbound* [16], *Knot* [2], and *PowerDNS* [18]. We do this under popular Linux server distribution releases, using default packages and configurations. In addition, we evaluate resolvers shipped with various Windows server releases. Table 3 shows which vendors and versions we evaluate.

Experiments: We configure the authoritative name servers for our test domain (marigliano.xyz) as a *disjoint* NSSet, as in Sect. 4.1. We configure the parent zone with [ns1 ,ns3].marigliano.xyz, and the child with [ns2, ns4].marigliano.xyz.

Each experiment includes the four tests described in Table 4(i–iv), in which we vary query types and query sequence. In (i), we ask the resolver for an A

Table 4. Expected resolver behavior

	(i) A Query	(ii) NS Query	(iii) A Query Then NS Query		(iv) NS Query Then A Query	
Query			First	Second	First	Second
Answer	C(A)	C(NS)	C(A)	C(NS)	C(NS)	C(A)
Cache	C(A); C(NS)	C(NS)	C(A); C(NS)	C(A); C(NS)	C(NS)	C(NS); C(A)
Minimal response enabled						
Answer	C(A)	C(NS)	C(A)	C(NS)	C(NS)	C(A)
Cache	C(A); P(NS)	C(NS)	C(A); P(NS)	C(A); C(NS)	C(NS)	C(NS); C(A)
Information provided by: C⇒ Child, P⇒ Parent						

record of a subdomain in our test zone. In test (ii), we ask for the NS record of the zone. In (iii) we send first an A query followed by an NS query, to understand if resolvers use non-authoritative cached NS information to answer to the following query violating (§5.4.1 of RFC2181 [5]). In (iv) we invert this order to understand if authoritative record are overwritten by non-authoritative ones in the cache.

We dump the cache of the resolver after each query, and show which records are in cache and received by our client (we clear the cache after each query). Table 4 shows the expected NS usage by the resolvers, if they conform to the RFCs.

5.1   Results

We evaluate five resolver vendors and multiple versions. In total, we found that out of 22 resolvers/vendors evaluated, 13 conform to the RFCs. Next, we report the non-confirming resolver vendors/versions.

For experiment (i), in which we query for A records, we found that BIND packaged for Ubuntu did not conform to the standards: it caches only information from the parent and does not override it with information from the authoritative section provided by the child (which comes as additional section). This, in turn, could explain part of results of parent centricity observed in Sect. 4.

For experiment (i) and (iii), if we compile the latest *BIND* from source it also does not behave as expected: it sends the parent an explicit NS query before performing the A query. This is not a bad behavior, *i.e.,*it does not violate RFCs, instead it tries to retrieve more authoritative information. However, either if the name server information retrieved and used in the following query is the one provided by the child, *BIND* caches the data from the parent. This behavior of BIND could be one explanation of the small number of child-centric resolvers shown in Sect. 4 with Minimal Responses.

We are in the process of notifying BIND developers about this issue.

For experiment (iii), *PowerDNS* packaged for CentOS 6 and Ubuntu Xenial, and Windows (all) use the cached non-authoritative information to answer the *NS* query in the test, not conforming to RFC2181.

PowerDNS Notification. We reached out to the developers of *PowerDNS*, who have confirmed the behavior. They do not maintain older versions anymore and the fix will not be backported due to the low severity of the problem. Our suggestion to the package maintainers of the distributions is to update the software to a newer version of the software.

6   Conclusions and Recommendations

Given a domain name, its NSSet in the parent and child DNS zones should be consistent [12]. This is the first study that shows, across the .com, .net and org zones (50% of the DNS namespace), that roughly 8% (13M) domains do not conform to that. We also show that DNS resolvers in the wild differ in behavior in returning information from the parent or child.

Inconsistency in parent and child NSSets have consequences for the operation of the DNS, such as improper load balancing among the name servers, increased resolution latency and unresponsive name servers. We strongly advise operators to verify their zones and follow RFC1034. To automate this process, we advise zone operators to consider supporting CSYNC DNS records (RFC7477) or other automated consistency checks, so the synchronization can be done in an automated fashion.

Finally, we also recommend that resolver vendors conform to the authoritative information ranking in RFC2181 (taking into account the recommendations to mitigate the Kaminsky attack as specified in RFC5452), and when possible, to *explicitly* ask for the child's NS records, similarly to what is done in DNSSEC, where signed records are only available at the child (Sect. 5).

Acknowledgments. We thank John Heidemann, Ólafur Guðmundsson and Ülrich Wisser for feedback provided in the early stages of this research. We also thank the PAM2020 anonymous reviewers, our shepherd, Steve Uhlig, and Philip Homburg, from RIPE NCC. This work uses measurements from RIPE Atlas (https://atlas.ripe.net), an open measurements platform operated by RIPE NCC.

This work is partially funded by the NWO-DHS MADDVIPR project (Grant Agreement 628.001.031/FA8750-19-2-0004), the PANDA project (NSF OAC-1724853) and the EU CONCORDIA project (Grant Agreement 830927). This material is based on research sponsored by Air Force Research Laboratory under agreement number FA8750-18-2-0049. The U.S. Government is authorized to reproduce and distribute reprints for Governmental purposes notwithstanding any copyright notation thereon. The views and conclusions in this paper are those of the authors and do not necessarily reflect the opinions of a sponsor, Air Force Research Laboratory or the U.S. Government.

A   Longitudinal View on Inconsistency

A.1   NS Inconsistency over Time

The results presented in Table 1 show NS inconsistency for a single day. However, it is also interesting to understand how this misconfiguration evolves over time.

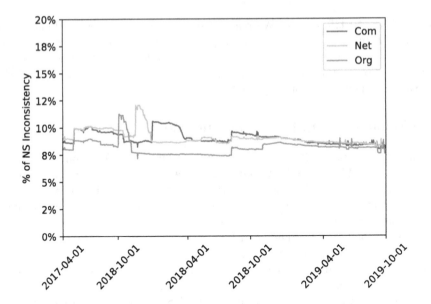

Fig. 7. NS inconsistency $(P \neq C)$ from 2017-04-01 until 2019-10-01

We analyzed NS inconsistency for the case $P \neq C$ over the two and a half year-period preceding the date of the analysis presented in Table 1. Figure 7 shows the results of this analysis. The figure clearly demonstrates that the fraction of domains affected by this misconfiguration remains similar over time. This result suggests that NS inconsistency is a long-term misconfiguration in the DNS ecosystem.

References

1. Almond, C.: CNAME at the apex of a zone. https://www.isc.org/blogs/cname-at-the-apex-of-a-zone/
2. CZ.NIC: Knot Resolver. https://www.knot-resolver.cz
3. DENIC AG: Statistics of .de domains, 22 October 2019. https://www.denic.de/en/know-how/statistics/1
4. DNS OARC: Root zone archive. https://www.dns-oarc.net/oarc/data/zfr/root (Jan 2020)
5. Elz, R., Bush, R.: Clarifications to the DNS specification. RFC 2181, IETF, July 1997. http://tools.ietf.org/rfc/rfc2181.txt
6. Hardaker, W.: Child-to-parent synchronization in DNS. RFC 7477, IETF, March 2015. http://tools.ietf.org/rfc/rfc7477.txt
7. Hoffman, P., Sullivan, A., Fujiwara, K.: DNS terminology. RFC 8499, IETF, November 2018. http://tools.ietf.org/rfc/rfc8499.txt
8. Hubert, A., Mook, R.: Measures for making DNS more resilient against forged answers. RFC 5452, IETF, January 2009. http://tools.ietf.org/rfc/rfc5452.txt
9. Internet Systems Consortium: BIND: Berkeley Internet Name Domain. https://www.isc.org/bind/

10. Kristoff, J.: DNS inconsistency (2018). https://blog.apnic.net/2018/08/29/dns-inconsistency/
11. Liu, D., Hao, S., Wang, H.: All your DNS records point to us: understanding the security threats of dangling DNS records. In: Proceedings of the 2016 ACM SIGSAC Conference on Computer and Communications Security, CCS 2016, pp. 1414–1425. ACM, New York (2016). https://doi.org/10.1145/2976749.2978387
12. Mockapetris, P.: Domain names - concepts and facilities. RFC 1034, IETF, November 1987. http://tools.ietf.org/rfc/rfc1034.txt
13. Moura, G.C.M., Heidemann, J., Müller, M., de Schmidt, R.O., Davids, M.: When the dike breaks: dissecting DNS defenses during DDoS. In: Proceedings of the ACM Internet Measurement Conference, October 2018. https://doi.org/10.1145/3278532.3278534
14. Moura, G.C.M., Heidemann, J., de Schmidt, R.O., Hardaker, W.: Cache me if you can: effects of DNS time-to-live (extended). In: Proceedings of the ACM Internet Measurement Conference. ACM, Amsterdam, October 2019. https://doi.org/10.1145/3355369.3355568. p. to appear
15. Müller, M., Moura, G.C.M., de Schmidt, R.O., Heidemann, J.: Recursives in the wild: engineering authoritative DNS servers. In: Proceedings of the ACM Internet Measurement Conference, London, UK, pp. 489–495 (2017). https://doi.org/10.1145/3131365.3131366
16. NLnet Labs: Unbound, March 2019. https://unbound.net/
17. Pappas, V., Wessels, D., Massey, D., Lu, S., Terzis, A., Zhang, L.: Impact of configuration errors on DNS robustness. IEEE J. Sel. Areas Commun. **27**(3), 275–290 (2009)
18. PowerDNS: PowerDNS Recursor. https://www.powerdns.com/recursor.html
19. van Rijswijk-Deij, R., Sperotto, A., Pras, A.: DNSSEC and its potential for DDoS attacks: a comprehensive measurement study. In: Proceedings of the 2014 ACM Conference on Internet Measurement Conference, IMC, pp. 449–460. ACM, November 2014
20. RIPE Ncc Staff: RIPE Atlas: a global internet measurement network. Internet Protocol J. (IPJ) **18**(3), 2–26 (2015)
21. RIPE Network Coordination Centre: RIPE Atlas (2015). https://atlas.ripe.net
22. Root Zone file: Root, February 2019. http://www.internic.net/domain/root.zone
23. van Rijswijk-Deij, R., Jonker, M., Sperotto, A., Pras, A.: A high-performance, scalable infrastructure for large-scale active DNS measurements. IEEE J. Sel. Areas Commun. **34**(6), 1877–1888 (2016). https://doi.org/10.1109/JSAC.2016.2558918

Topology and Routing

A First Comparative Characterization of Multi-cloud Connectivity in Today's Internet

Bahador Yeganeh[1(✉)], Ramakrishnan Durairajan[1], Reza Rejaie[1],
and Walter Willinger[2]

[1] University of Oregon, Eugene, USA
{byeganeh,ram,reza}@cs.uoregon.edu
[2] NIKSUN Inc., Boston, USA
wwillinger@niksun.com

Abstract. Today's enterprises are adopting multi-cloud strategies at an unprecedented pace. Here, a multi-cloud strategy specifies end-to-end connectivity between the multiple cloud providers (CPs) that an enterprise relies on to run its business. This adoption is fueled by the rapid build-out of global-scale private backbones by the large CPs, a rich private peering fabric that interconnects them, and the emergence of new third-party private connectivity providers (*e.g.,* DataPipe, HopOne, etc.). However, little is known about the performance aspects, routing issues, and topological features associated with currently available multi-cloud connectivity options. To shed light on the tradeoffs between these available connectivity options, we take a cloud-to-cloud perspective and present in this paper the results of a cloud-centric measurement study of a coast-to-coast multi-cloud deployment that a typical modern enterprise located in the US may adopt. We deploy VMs in two regions (*i.e.,* VA and CA) of each one of three large cloud providers (*i.e.,* AWS, Azure, and GCP) and connect them using three different options: (i) transit provider-based best-effort public Internet (BEP), (ii) third-party provider-based private (TPP) connectivity, and (iii) CP-based private (CPP) connectivity. By performing active measurements in this real-world multi-cloud deployment, we provide new insights into variability in the performance of TPP, the stability in performance and topology of CPP, and the absence of transit providers for CPP.

1 Introduction

Modern enterprises are adopting multi-cloud strategies at a rapid pace. Defined here as end-to-end connectivity between multiple cloud providers (CPs)[1], multi-cloud strategies are critical for supporting distributed applications such as geo-distributed analytics [33, 35, 57, 68, 69] and distributed genome sequencing studies

---

[1] This is different from hybrid cloud computing, where a direct connection exists between a public cloud and private on-premises enterprise server(s).

© Springer Nature Switzerland AG 2020
A. Sperotto et al. (Eds.): PAM 2020, LNCS 12048, pp. 193–210, 2020.
https://doi.org/10.1007/978-3-030-44081-7_12

at universities [12,25]. Other benefits that result from pursuing such strategies are competitive pricing, vendor lockout, global reach, and requirements for data sovereignty. According to a recent industry report, more than 85% of enterprises have already adopted multi-cloud strategies [39].

Fueled by the deployment of multi-cloud strategies, we are witnessing two new trends in Internet connectivity. First (see Fig. 1(bottom)), there is the emergence of new Internet players in the form of third-party private connectivity providers (*e.g.,* DataPipe, HopOne, among others [5,29,51]). These entities offer direct, secure, private, layer 3 connectivity between CPs (henceforth referred to as *third-party private* or TPP), at a cost of a few hundreds of dollars per month[2]. TPP routes bypass the public Internet at Cloud Exchanges [19,21,71] where they operate virtualized routers allowing their customers to form virtualized peering sessions with the participating CPs and offer additional benefits to users (*e.g.,* enterprise networks can connect to CPs without owning an Autonomous System Number, or ASN, or physical infrastructure). Second (see Fig. 1(top)), the large CPs are aggressively expanding the footprint of their serving infrastructures, including the number of direct connect locations where enterprises can reach the cloud via direct, private connectivity (henceforth referred to as *cloud-provider private* or CPP) using either new CP-specific interconnection services (*e.g.,* [4,28,50]) or third-party private connectivity providers at colocation facilities. Of course, as shown in Fig. 1 (middle), a multi-cloud user can forgo the TPP and CPP options altogether and rely instead on the traditional, best effort connectivity over the public Internet—henceforth referred to as *(transit provider-based) best-effort public (Internet)* (BEP). In terms of routing, CPP and BEP connectivity is offered through default route configurations while TPP routes are enforced via BGP configurations that customers of the TPP network install on their virtual routers.

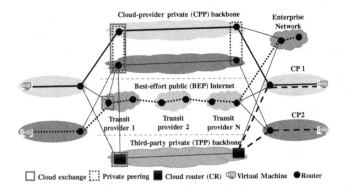

Fig. 1. Overview of three different multi-cloud strategies. Sample end-to-end measurement paths highlighted using thicker solid, dashed, and dotted lines for CPP, TPP, and BEP options.

---

[2] See Sect. 3.4 for more details.

With multi-cloud connectivity being the main focus of this paper, we note that existing measurement techniques are a poor match in this context. For one, they fall short of providing the data needed to infer the type of connectivity (*i.e.*, TPP, CPP, and BEP) between (two or more) participating CPs. Second, they are largely incapable of providing the visibility needed to study the topological properties, performance differences, or routing strategies associated with different connectivity options. Third, while mapping the connectivity from cloud/content providers to users has been considered in prior work (*e.g.*, [9,15–17,20,60] and references therein), multi-cloud connectivity from a cloud-to-cloud (C2C) perspective has remained largely unexplored to date.

This paper aims to empirically examine the different types of multi-cloud connectivity options that are available in today's Internet and investigate their performance characteristics using non-proprietary cloud-centric, active measurements. In the process, we are also interested in attributing the observed characteristics to aspects related to connectivity, routing strategy, or the presence of any performance bottlenecks. To study multi-cloud connectivity from a C2C perspective, we deploy and interconnect VMs hosted within and across two different geographic regions or availability zones (*i.e.*, CA and VA) of three large cloud providers (*i.e.*, Amazon Web Services (AWS), Google Cloud Platform (GCP) and Microsoft Azure) using the TPP, CPP, and BEP option, respectively.

Using this experimental setup as a starting point, we first compare the stability and/or variability in performance across the three connectivity options using metrics such as delay, throughput, and loss rate over time. We find that CPP routes exhibit lower latency and are more stable when compared to BEP and TPP routes. CPP routes also have higher throughput and exhibit less variation compared to the other two options. Given that using the TPP option is expensive, this finding is puzzling. In our attempt to explain this observation, we find that inconsistencies in performance characteristics are caused by several factors including border routers, queuing delays, and higher loss-rates of TPP routes. Moreover, we attribute the CPP routes' overall superior performance to the fact that each of the CPs has a private optical backbone, there exists rich inter-CP connectivity, and that the CPs' traffic *always* bypasses (*i.e.*, is invisible to) BEP transits. In summary, this paper makes the following contributions:

- To the best of our knowledge, this is one of the first efforts to perform a comparative characterization of multi-cloud connectivity in today's Internet. To facilitate independent validation of our results, we will release all relevant datasets [1] (properly anonymized; *e.g.*, with all TPP-related information removed).

- We identify issues, differences, and tradeoffs associated with three popular multi-cloud connectivity options and elucidate/discuss the underlying reasons. Our results highlight the critical need for open measurement platforms and more transparency by the multi-cloud connectivity providers.

2 Background and Related Work

Measuring and understanding the connectivity ecosystem of the Internet has been the subject of a large number of studies over the years [52, and references therein]. Efforts include mapping the (logical) connectivity of the public Internet at the router level (*e.g.,* [10,11,13,44,64]), the POP-level (*e.g.,* [62,63,65]), and the Autonomous System or AS-level (*e.g.,* [45,73]). Other efforts have focused on issues such as the rise of Internet Exchange Points (IXPs) and their effects on inaccuracies of network-layer mapping (*e.g.,* [2,11]), the "flattening" of the Internet's peering structure (*e.g.,* [22,27,40]), and the Internet's physical infrastructure (building repositories of point of presence (POP), colocation, and datacenter locations (*e.g.,* [37,61]), the long-haul and metro connectivity between them (*e.g.,* [23,24,38]), and interconnections with other networks (*e.g.,* [3,43,46]).

More recently, enterprise networks have been able to establish direct connectivity to cloud providers—even without owning an AS number—at Open Cloud Exchanges [19,21] (shown in the red box in Fig. 1) via a new type of interconnection service offering called virtual private interconnections [71]. With the advent of such interconnection services, today's large cloud (and content) providers (*e.g.,* Google, Facebook, Microsoft) have experienced enormous growth in both their ingress (*i.e.,* Internet-facing) and mid-gress (*i.e.,* inter-datacenter) traffic. To meet these demands, they are not only aggressively expanding their presence at new colocation facilities but are also simultaneously building out their own private optical backbones [26,36] (see CPP in Fig. 1). In addition, connectivity to the CPs at colocation facilities are also available via third-party providers [5,29,51] (TPP in Fig. 1) for additional costs (*e.g.,* thousands of dollars for a single, dedicated, private link to CP).

While measuring the peering locations, serving infrastructures and routing strategies of the large content providers has been an active area of research [9,15–17,20,60,70] and comparing the performance of CPs and their BEP properties has been the focus of prior efforts [14,18,30,41,74], to the best of our knowledge, ours is one of the first studies to (a) examine and characterize the TPP, CPP, and BEP connectivity options from a C2C perspective, and (b) elucidate their performance tradeoffs and routing issues.

3 Measurement Methodology

In this section, we describe our measurement methodology to examine the various multi-cloud connectivity options, the cloud providers under consideration, and the performance metrics of interest.

3.1 Measurement Setting

As shown in Fig. 1, we explore three different types of multi-cloud connectivity options: *TPP* connectivity between CP VMs that bypasses the public Internet,

CPP connectivity enabled by private peering between the CPs, and *BEP* connectivity via transit providers. To establish TPPs, we deploy cloud routers via a third-party connectivity provider's network. At a high level, this step involves (i) establishing a virtual circuit between the CP and a connectivity partner, (ii) establishing a BGP peering session between the CP's border routers and the partner's cloud router, (iii) connecting the virtual private cloud gateway to the CP's border routers, and (iv) configuring each cloud instance to route any traffic destined to the overlay network towards the configured virtual gateway. To establish CPP connectivity, participating CPs automatically select private peering locations to stitch the multi-cloud VMs together. Finally, we have two measurement settings for BEP. The first setting is between a non-native colocation facility in Phoenix AZ and our VMs through the BEP Internet; the second form of measurement is through the BEP Internet towards Looking Glasses (LGs) residing in the colocation facility hosting our cloud routers.

We conduct our measurements in a series of rounds. Each round consists of path, latency, and throughput measurements between all pairs of VMs (in both directions to account for route asymmetry). Furthermore, the measurements are performed over the public BEPs as well as the two private options (*i.e.,* CPP and TPP). Each connectivity path is enforced by the target address for our measurements (i.e., public IP address for BEP and CPP paths and private IPs VM instances in the TPP case). We avoid cross-measurement interference by tracking the current state of ongoing measurements and limit measurement activities to one active measurement per cloud VM.

3.2   Measurement Scenario and Cloud Providers

For this study, we empirically measure and examine one coast-to-coast, multi-cloud deployment in the US. Our study focuses on connectivity between three major CPs (AWS, Azure, and GCP) as they collectively have a significant market share and are used by many clients concurrently [72]. Using these CPs, we create a realistic multi-cloud scenario by deploying two cloud routers using one of the top third-party connectivity providers' networks; one of the cloud routers is in the Santa Clara, CA region, and one is in the Ashburn, VA region. These cloud routers are interconnected with native cloud VMs from the three CPs. The cloud VMs are all connected to cloud routers with 50 Mb/s links. We select the colocation facility hosting the cloud routers based on two criteria: (i) CPs offer native cloud connectivity within that colo, and (ii) geo-proximity to the target CPs datacenters. Cloud routers are interconnected with each other using a 150 Mb/s link capacity that supports the maximum number of concurrent measurements that we perform (*i.e.,* 3 concurrent measurements in total to avoid more than 1 ongoing measurement per VM). Each cloud VM has at least 2 vCPU cores, 4 GB of memory, and runs Ubuntu server 18.04 LTS. Our VMs were purposefully over-provisioned to reduce any measurement noise within virtualized environments. Throughout our measurement experiments, the VMs CPU utilization always remained below 2%. We also cap the VM interfaces at 50 Mb/s to have a consistent measurement setting for both public (BEP) and private

(TPP and CPP) routes. We perform measurements between all CP VMs within regions (intra-region) and across regions (inter-region). Additionally, we also perform measurements between our cloud VMs and two LGs that are located within the same facility as our cloud routers in California and Virginia, respectively, and use these measurements as baselines for BEP[3] comparisons.

3.3 Data Collection and Performance Metrics

We conducted our measurements for about a month-long period in the Spring of 2019. The measurements were conducted in 10-min rounds. In each round, we performed latency, path, and throughput measurements between all pairs of relevant nodes. For each round, we measure and report the latency using 10 *ping* probes paced in 1 s intervals. We refrain from using a more accurate one-way latency measurement tool such as OWAMP as the authors of OWAMP caution its use within virtualized environments [34]. Similarly, paths are measured by performing 10 attempts of *paris-traceroute* using *scamper* [42] towards each destination. We used ICMP probes for path discovery as they maximized the number of responsive hops along the forward path. Lastly, throughput is measured using the *iperf3* tool, which was configured to transmit data over a 10-s interval using TCP. We discard the first 5 s of our throughput measurement to account for TCP's *slow-start* phase and consider the median of throughput for the remaining 5 s. These efforts resulted in about 48k samples of latency, path, and throughput measurements between each unique src/dst pair and connectivity option.

To infer inter-AS interconnections, the resulting traceroute hops from our measurements were translated to their corresponding AS paths using BGP prefix announcements from Routeviews and RIPE RIS [59,67]. Missing hops were attributed to their surrounding ASN if the prior and next hop ASNs were identical. The existence of IXP hops along the forward path was detected by matching hop addresses against IXP prefixes published by PeeringDB [56] and Packet Clearing House (PCH) [55]. We mapped each ASN to its corresponding ORG number using CAIDA's AS-to-ORG mapping dataset [32]. Lastly, the inter-AS interconnection segments are identified using the latest version of bdrmapIT [3].

3.4 Limitations and Ethical/Legal Considerations

Our study is US-centric and limited by the geographic span of our multi-cloud deployment as well as the number of third-party connectivity providers that we examine. The high cost for connecting multiple clouds using TPP connections prevents us from having a global-scale deployment and performing experiments that involve different TPP providers. For example, for each 1 Gbps link to a CP network, third-party providers charge anywhere from about 300 to 700 USD per

---

[3] In Sect. 5 we highlight that our inter-cloud measurements do not exit the source and destination CP's network.

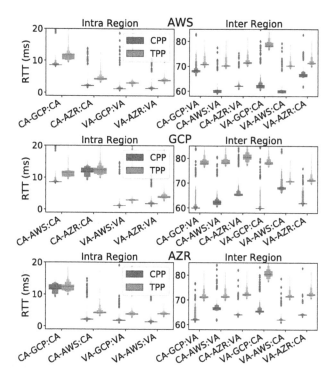

Fig. 2. Distribution of RTT between AWS, GCP, and Azure for intra (left) and inter (right) region paths. (Color figure online)

month [48,53,58][4]. While limited in scale, the deployment that we consider in this study is nevertheless representative of a typical multi-cloud strategy adopted by modern enterprises with a US-wide footprint [49].

Our study does not raise any ethical issues. Overall, since the goal of this study is to measure and improve multi-cloud connectivity without attributing particular features to any of the utilized third-party providers and CPs, we are not in violation of any of their terms of service. In particular, we obfuscate, and wherever possible, we omit all information that can be used to identify the colocation and third-party connectivity providers. This information includes names, supported measurement APIs, costs, time and date of measurements, topology information, and any other potential identifiers.

4   Characteristics of C2C Routes

In this section, we characterize the performance of C2C routes (*i.e.*, latency and throughput) and attribute the observed characteristics to connectivity and routing.

---

[4] Note that these price points do not take into consideration the additional charges that are incurred by CPs for establishing connectivity to their network.

4.1   Latency Characteristics

CPP Routes Exhibit Lower Latency Than TPP Routes and Are Stable. Figure 2 depicts the distribution of RTT values (using letter-value plots [31]; see Appendix A.1) between different CPs across different connectivity options. The rows (from top to bottom) correspond to AWS, GCP, and Azure as the source CP, respectively. Intra-region (inter-region) measurements are shown in the left (right) columns, and CPP (TPP) paths are depicted in blue (orange).

The first two characters of the x-axis labels encode the source CP region and the remaining characters encode the destination CP and region. From these figures, we see that CPP routes typically exhibit lower medians of RTT compared to TPP routes, suggesting that CPP routes traverse the CP's optical private backbone. We also observe a median RTT of ~2 ms between AWS and Azure VMs in California which is in accordance with the relative proximity of their datacenters for this region. The GCP VM in California has a median RTT of 13 ms to other CPs in California, which can be attributed to the geographical distance between GCP's California datacenter in LA and the Silicon Valley datacenters for AWS and Azure. Similarly, we notice that the VMs in Virginia all exhibit low median RTTs between them. We attribute this behavior to the geographical proximity of the datacenters for these CPs. At the same time, the inter-region latencies within a CP are about 60 ms with the exception of Azure which has a higher median of latency of about 67 ms. Finally, the measured latencies (and hence the routes) are asymmetric in both directions albeit the median of RTT values shows latency symmetry (<0.1 ms). Also, the median of the measured latency between our cloud routers is in line with the published values by third-party connectivity providers, but the high variance of latency indicates that the TPP paths are in general a less reliable connectivity option compared to CPP routes. Lastly, BEP routes for cloud to LG measurements always have an equal or higher median of latency compared to CPP paths with much higher variability (order of magnitude larger standard deviation; results are omitted for brevity).

Why Do CPP Routes Have Better Latency than TPP Routes? In our path measurements, we observe that intra-cloud paths always have a single organization, indicating that regardless of the target region, the CP routes traffic internally towards the destination VM. More interestingly, the majority of inter-cloud paths only observe two organizations corresponding to the source and destination CPs. Only a small fraction (<4%) of paths involves three organizations, and upon closer examination of the corresponding paths, we find that they traverse IXPs and involve traceroutes that originate from Azure and are destined to Amazon's network in another region. We reiterate that single organization inter-CP paths correspond to traceroutes which are originated from GCP's network and do not reveal any internal hops of its network. For the cloud-to-LG paths, we observe a different number of organizations depending on the source CP as well as the physical location of the target LG. The observations range from only encountering the target LG's organization to seeing intermediary IXP hops as points of peering. Lastly, we measure the stability of routes at the AS-level and observe that all paths remain consistently stable over time with the exception of

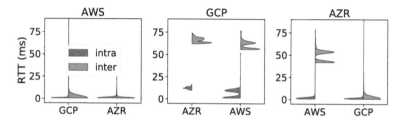

Fig. 3. Distribution of RTT between source CP and the peering hop. (Color figure online)

routes sourced at Azure California and destined to Amazon Virginia. The latter usually pass through private peerings between the CPs, and only less than 1% of our path measurements go through an intermediary IXP. In short, we did not encounter any transit providers in our measured CPP routes.

By leveraging the AS/organization paths described in Sect. 3, we next identify the peering points between the CPs. Identifying the peering point between two networks from traceroute measurements is a challenging problem and the subject of many recent studies [3,43,46]. For our study, as mentioned in Sect. 3 above, we utilized *bdrmapIT* [3] to infer the interconnection segment on the collection of traceroutes that we have gathered. Additionally, we manually inspected the inferred peering segments and, where applicable, validated their correctness using (i) IXP address to tenant ASN mapping and (ii) DNS names such as AMAZON.SJC-96CBE-1A.NTWK.MSN.NET which is suggestive of peering between AWS and Azure. We find that *bdrmapIT* is unable to identify peering points between GCP and the other CPs since GCP only exposes external IP addresses for paths destined outside of its network, *i.e., bdrmapIT* is unaware of the source CPs network as it does not observe any addresses from that network on the initial set of hops. For these paths, we choose the first hop of the traceroute as the peering point only if it has an ASN equal to the target IP addresses ASN. Using this information, we measure the RTT between the source CP and the border interface to infer the geo-proximity of the peering point from the source CP. Using this heuristic allows us to analyze each CP's inclination to use hot-potato routing.

Figure 3 shows the distribution of RTT for the peering points between each CP. From left to right, the plots represent AWS, GCP, and Azure as the source CP. Each distribution is split based on intra (inter) region values into the left/blue (right/orange) halves, respectively. We observe that AWS' peering points with other CPs are very close to their networks and therefore, AWS is employing hot-potato routing. For GCP, we find that hot-potato routing is never employed and traffic is always handed off near the destination region. The bi-modal distribution of RTT values for each destination CP is centered at around 2 ms, 12 ms, 58 ms, and 65 ms corresponding to the intra-region latency for VA and CA, and inter-region latency to other CPs, respectively. Finally, Azure exhibits mixed routing behavior. Specifically, Azure's routing behavior

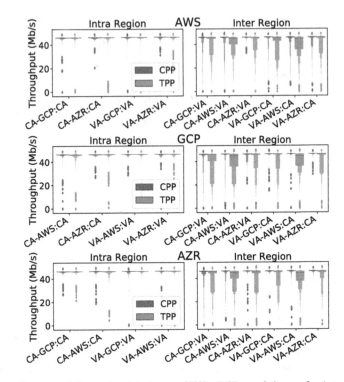

Fig. 4. Distribution of throughput between AWS, GCL, and Azure for intra (left) and inter (right) region paths.

depends on the target network – Azure employs hot-potato routing for GCP and cold-potato routing for AWS. More specifically, intra-region traffic destined to AWS is delivered through a local peering point while its Virginia-California traffic destined to AWS is handed off in Los Angeles, and for inter-region paths from California to AWS Virginia, the traffic is usually (99%) handed off in Dallas TX and for the remainder is being exchanged through Digital Realty Atlanta's IXP. From these observations, the routing behavior for each path can be modeled with a simple threshold-based method. More concretely, for each path i with an end-to-end latency of l_{ei} and a border latency of l_{bi}, we can infer if source CP employs hot-potato routing if $l_{bi} < \frac{1}{10}l_{ei}$. Otherwise, the source CP employs cold-potato routing (*i.e.*, $l_{bi} > \frac{9}{10}l_{ei}$). The fractions (*i.e.*, $\frac{1}{10}$ and $\frac{9}{10}$) are not prescriptive and are derived based on the latency distributions depicted in Fig. 3.

4.2   Throughput Characteristics

CPP Routes Exhibit Higher and More Stable Throughput than TPP Routes. Figure 4 depicts the distribution of throughput values between different CPs using different connectivity options. While intra-region measurements

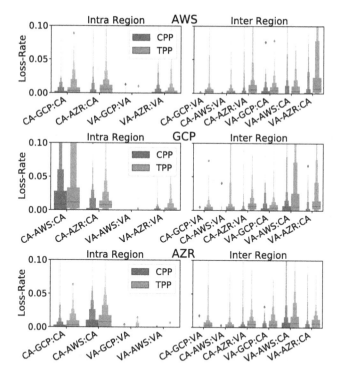

Fig. 5. Distribution of loss-rate between AWS, GCL, and Azure for intra (left) and inter (right) region paths.

tend to have a similar median and variance of throughput, we observe that for inter-region measurements, TPPs exhibit a lower median throughput with higher variance. Degradation of throughput seems to be directly correlated with higher RTT values as shown in Fig. 2. Using our latency measurements, we also approximate loss-rate to be 10^{-3} and 10^{-4} for TPP and CPP routes, respectively. Using the formula of Mathis et al. [47] to approximate TCP throughput[5], we can obtain an upper bound for throughput for our measured loss-rate and latency values.

Using Mathis et al. model, the upper bound of throughput for an MSS of 1460 bytes, a 70 ms latency and loss-rate of 10^{-3} (corresponding to the average measured values for TPP routes between two coasts) is about 53 Mb/s. While this value is higher than our interface/link bandwidth cap of 50 Mb/s, bursts of packet loss or transient increases in latency could easily lead to sub-optimal TCP throughput for TPP routes.

Why Do CPP Routes Have Better Throughput than TPP Routes? Our initial methodology for measuring loss-rate relied on our low-rate *ping* probes

---

[5] We do not have access to parameters such as TCP timeout delay and number of acknowledged packets by each ACK to use more elaborate TCP models (*e.g.*, [54]).

(outlined in Sect. 3.3). While this form of probing can produce a reliable estimate of average loss-rate over a long period of time [66], it doesn't capture the dynamics of packet loss at finer resolutions. We thus modified our probing methodology to incorporate an additional *iperf3* measurement using UDP probes between all CP instances. Each measurement is performed for 5 s and packets are sent at a 50 Mb/s rate.[6] We measure the number of transmitted and lost packets during each second and also count the number of packets that were delivered out of order at the receiver. We perform these loss-rate measurements for a full week. Based on this new set of measurements, we estimate the overall loss-rate to be $5*10^{-3}$ and 10^{-2} for CPP and TPP paths, respectively. Moreover, we experience 0 packet loss in 76% (37%) of our sampling periods for CPP (TPP) routes, indicating that losses for CPP routes tend to be more bursty than for TPP routes. The bursty nature of packet losses for CPP routes could be detrimental to real-time applications which can *only* tolerate certain levels of loss and should be factored in by the client. The receivers did not observe any out-of-order packets during our measurement period. Figure 5 shows the distribution of loss rate for various paths.

The rows (from top to bottom) correspond to AWS, GCP, and Azure as the source CP, respectively. Intra-region (inter-region) measurements are shown in the left (right) columns, and CPP (TPP) paths are depicted in blue (orange). We observe consistently higher loss-rates for TPP routes compared to their CPP counterparts and lower loss-rates for intra-CP routes in Virginia compared to California. Moreover, paths destined to VMs in the California region show higher loss-rates regardless of where the traffic has been sourced from, with asymmetrically lower loss-rate on the reverse path indicating the presence of congested ingress points for CPs within the California region. We also notice extremely low loss-rates for intra-CP (except Azure) CPP routes between the US east and west coasts and for inter-CP CPP routes between the two coasts for certain CP pairs (*e.g.,* AWS CA to GCP VA or Azure CA to AWS VA).

4.3   Main Findings

Our measurement experiments reveal two interesting findings. First, CPP routes are better than TPP routes in terms of latency as well as throughput. Within a multi-cloud setting, TPPs can serve multiple purposes, including providing connectivity towards CPs from colo facilities that CPs aren't present, lowering inter-cloud traffic costs [7,8], and providing private inter-cloud connectivity over private address spaces. Second, the better performance of CPP routes as compared to their TPP counterparts can be attributed to (a) the CPs' rich (private) connectivity in different regions with other CPs (traffic is by-passing the BEP Internet altogether) and (b) more stable and better provisioned CP (private) backbones.

---

[6] In an ideal setting, we should not experience any packet losses as we are limiting our probing rate at the source.

5 Discussion

CPs Are Heterogeneous in Handling Path Measurements. Measuring the number of observed AS/organizations (excluding hops utilizing private IP addresses) for inter-cloud, intra-cloud, and cloud-to-LG routes, we observed that of the three CPs, only AWS used multiple ASNs (*i.e.,* ASes 8987, 14618, and 16509) and that there are striking difference between how CPs respond to traceroute probes. In particular, GCP does not expose any of its routers unless the target address is within another GCP region; Azure does not expose its internal routers except for their border routers that are involved in peering with other networks; and AWS relies heavily on private/shared IP addresses for its internal network.

CPs Are Tightly Interconnected with Each Other in the US. To check the absence of transit ASes along our measured C2C paths more thoroughly, we conducted a more extensive measurement study by launching VM instances within all US regions for our three target CP networks and performing UDP and ICMP *paris-traceroutes* between all VM instances using *scamper*. After annotating the traceroutes as described in Sect. 3.3, in terms of AS/organization-level routes, we only observe organizations corresponding to the three target CPs as well as IXP ASNs for Coresite Any2 and Equinix. All organization-level routes passing through an IXP correspond to paths that are sourced from Azure and are destined to AWS. These measurements further confirm our initial observation regarding the rich connectivity of our three large CPs and their tendency to avoid exchanging traffic through the public Internet.

Taking an Enterprise-to-Cloud (E2C) Perspective. Instead of the C2C perspective shown in Fig. 1, we also considered an enterprise-to-cloud (E2C) perspective and report preliminary results for this scenario in Appendix A.2.

6 Summary

In this paper, we perform a first-of-its-kind measurement study to understand the tradeoffs between three popular multi-cloud connectivity options (CPP vs. TPP vs. BEP). Based on our cloud-centric measurements, we find that CPP routes are better than TPP routes in terms of latency as well as throughput. The better performance of CPPs can be attributed to (a) CPs' rich connectivity in different regions with other CPs (by-passing the BEP Internet altogether) and (b) CPs' stable and well-designed private backbones. In addition, we find that TPP routes exhibit better latency and throughput characteristics when compared with BEP routes. The key reasons include shorter paths and lower loss rates compared to the BEP transits. Although limited in scale, our work highlights the need for more transparency and access to open measurement platforms by all the entities involved in interconnecting enterprises with multiple clouds.

A   Appendices

A.1   Representation of Results

Distributions in this paper are presented using letter-value plots [31]. Letter-value plots, similar to boxplots, are helpful for summarizing the distribution of data points but offer finer details beyond the quartiles. The median is shown using a dark horizontal line and the $1/2^i$ quantile is encoded using the box width, with the widest boxes surrounding the median representing the quartiles, the 2nd widest boxes corresponding to the octiles, etc. Distributions with low variance centered around a single value appear as a narrow horizontal bar while distributions with diverse values appear as vertical bars.

Throughout this paper we try to present full distributions of latency when it is illustrative. Furthermore, we compare latency characteristics of different paths using the median and variance measures and specifically refrain from relying on minimum latency as it does not capture the stability and dynamics of this measure across each path.

A.2   Preliminary results on E2C perspective

We emulate an enterprise leveraging multi-clouds by connecting a cloud router in the Phoenix, AZ region to a physical server hosted within a colocation facility in Phoenix, AZ.

TPP Routes Offer Better Latency than BEP Routes. Figure 6a shows the distribution of latency for our measured E2C paths. We observe that TPP routes consistently outperform their BEP counterparts by having a lower baseline of latency and also exhibiting less variation. We observe a median latency of 11 ms, 20 ms, and 21 ms for TPP routes towards GCP, AWS, and Azure VM instances in California, respectively. We also observe symmetric distributions on the reverse path but omit the results for brevity. In the case of our E2C paths, we always observe direct peerings between the upstream provider (*e.g.,* Cox Communications (AS22773)) and the CP network. Relying on *bdrmapIT* to infer the peering points from the traceroutes associated with our E2C paths, we measure the latency on the peering hop. Figure 6b shows the distribution of the latency for the peering hop for E2C paths originated from the CPs' instances in CA towards our enterprise server in AZ. While the routing policies of GCP and Azure for E2C paths are similar to our observations for C2C paths, Amazon seems to hand-off traffic near the destination which is unlike their hot-potato tendencies for C2C paths. We hypothesize that this change in AWS' policy is to minimize the operational costs via their Transit Gateway service which provide finer control to customers and peering networks over the egress/ingress point of traffic to their network [6]. In addition, observing an equal or lower minimum latency for TPP routes as compared to BEP routes suggests that TPP routes are shorter than BEP paths[7]. We also find (not shown here) that the average

---

[7] In the absence of information regarding the physical fiber paths, we rely on latency as a proxy measure of path length.

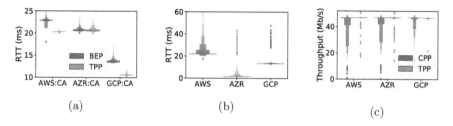

Fig. 6. (a) Distribution of latency for E2C paths between our server in AZ and CP instances in California through TPP and BEP routes. Outliers on the Y-axis have been deliberately cut-off to increase the readability of distributions. (b) Distribution of RTT on the inferred peering hop for E2C paths sourced from CP instances in California. (c) Distribution of throughput for E2C paths between our server in AZ and CP instances in California through TPP and BEP routes.

loss rate on TPP routes is $6 * 10^{-4}$ which is an order of magnitude lower than the loss rate experienced on BEP routes ($1.6 * 10^{-3}$).

TPP Offers Consistent Throughput for E2C Paths. Figure 6c depicts the distribution of throughput for E2C paths between our server in AZ and CP instances in CA via TPP and BEP routes, respectively. While we observe very consistent throughput values near the purchased link capacity for TPP paths, BEP paths exhibit higher variability which is expected given the best effort nature of public Internet paths. Similar to the latency characteristics, we attribute the better throughput of TPP routes to the lower loss rates and shorter fiber paths from the enterprise server to the CPs' instances in CA. Moreover, compared to the CPs' connect locations, the third-party providers are often present in additional, distinct colocation facilities closer to the edge and partially answers the question we posed earlier in Sect. 4.3.

References

1. A first comparative characterization of multi-cloud connectivity in today's internet (2020). https://gitlab.com/onrg/multicloudcmp
2. Ager, B., Chatzis, N., Feldmann, A., Sarrar, N., Uhlig, S., Willinger, W.: Anatomy of a large European IXP. In: SIGCOMM. ACM (2012)
3. Alexander, M., Luckie, M., Dhamdhere, A., Huffaker, B., Claffy, K., Jonathan, S.M.: Pushing the boundaries with bdrmapIT: mapping router ownership at internet scale. In: Internet Measurement Conference (IMC). ACM (2018)
4. Amazon: AWS direct connect. https://aws.amazon.com/directconnect/
5. Amazon: AWS direct connect partners. https://aws.amazon.com/directconnect/partners/
6. Amazon: AWS transit gateway. https://aws.amazon.com/transit-gateway/
7. Amazon: AWS direct connect pricing (2019). https://aws.amazon.com/directconnect/pricing/
8. Amazon: EC2 instance pricing - Amazon web services (2019). https://aws.amazon.com/ec2/pricing/on-demand/

9. Anwar, R., Niaz, H., Choffnes, D., Cunha, Í., Gill, P., Katz-Bassett, E.: Investigating interdomain routing policies in the wild. In: Internet Measurement Conference (IMC). ACM (2015)
10. Augustin, B., et al.: Avoiding traceroute anomalies with paris traceroute. In: Internet Measurement Conference (IMC). ACM (2006)
11. Augustin, B., Krishnamurthy, B., Willinger, W.: IXPs: mapped? In: Internet Measurement Conference (IMC). ACM (2009)
12. Ausmees, K., John, A., Toor, S.Z., Hellander, A., Nettelblad, C.: BAMSI: a multicloud service for scalable distributed filtering of massive genome data. BMC Bioinf. **19**, 240 (2018)
13. CAIDA: the skitter project (2007). http://www.caida.org/tools/measurement/skitter/
14. Calder, M., Fan, X., Hu, Z., Katz-Bassett, E., Heidemann, J., Govindan, R.: Mapping the expansion of Google's serving infrastructure. In: Internet Measurement Conference (IMC). ACM (2013)
15. Calder, M., Flavel, A., Katz-Bassett, E., Mahajan, R., Padhye, J.: Analyzing the performance of an anycast CDN. In: Internet Measurement Conference (IMC). ACM (2015)
16. Calder, M., et al.: Odin: Microsoft's scalable fault-tolerant {CDN} measurement system. In: NSDI. USENIX (2018)
17. Chiu, Y.C., Schlinker, B., Radhakrishnan, A.B., Katz-Bassett, E., Govindan, R.: Are we one hop away from a better internet? In: Internet Measurement Conference (IMC). ACM (2015)
18. CloudHarmony: Cloudharmony, transparency for the cloud. https://cloudharmony.com/
19. CoreSite: The Coresite open cloud exchange. https://www.coresite.com/solutions/cloud-services/open-cloud-exchange
20. Cunha, Í., et al.: Sibyl: a practical internet route oracle. In: NSDI. USENIX (2016)
21. Demchenko, Y., et al.: Open Cloud Exchange (OCX): architecture and functional components. In: International Conference on Cloud Computing Technology and Science. IEEE (2013)
22. Dhamdhere, A., Dovrolis, C.: The Internet is flat: modeling the transition from a transit hierarchy to a peering mesh. In: CoNEXT. ACM (2010)
23. Durairajan, R., Barford, P., Sommers, J., Willinger, W.: InterTubes: a study of the US long-haul fiber-optic infrastructure. In: SIGCOMM. ACM (2015)
24. Durairajan, R., Ghosh, S., Tang, X., Barford, P., Eriksson, B.: Internet Atlas: a geographic database of the Internet. In: HotPlanet. ACM (2013)
25. Elshazly, H., Souilmi, Y., Tonellato, P.J., Wall, D.P., Abouelhoda, M.: MC-GenomeKey: a multicloud system for the detection and annotation of genomic variants. BMC Bioinf. **18**, 49 (2017)
26. Facebook: Building express backbone: Facebook's new long-haul network (2017). https://code.fb.com/data-center-engineering/building-express-backbone-facebook-s-new-long-haul-network/
27. Gill, P., Arlitt, M., Li, Z., Mahanti, A.: The Flattening Internet topology: natural evolution, unsightly barnacles or contrived collapse? In: Claypool, M., Uhlig, S. (eds.) PAM 2008. LNCS, vol. 4979, pp. 1–10. Springer, Heidelberg (2008). https://doi.org/10.1007/978-3-540-79232-1_1
28. Google: GCP direct peering. https://cloud.google.com/interconnect/docs/how-to/direct-peering
29. Google: Google supported service providers. https://cloud.google.com/interconnect/docs/concepts/service-providers

30. Haq, O., Raja, M., Dogar, F.R.: Measuring and improving the reliability of wide-area cloud paths. In: WWW. ACM (2017)
31. Hofmann, H., Kafadar, K., Wickham, H.: Letter-value plots: boxplots for large data. Technical report. had.co.nz (2011)
32. Huffaker, B., Keys, K., Fomenkov, M., Claffy, K.: AS-to-organization dataset (2018). http://www.caida.org/research/topology/as2org/
33. Hung, C.C., Ananthanarayanan, G., Golubchik, L., Yu, M., Zhang, M.: Wide-area analytics with multiple resources. In: EuroSys Conference. ACM (2018)
34. Internet2: One-Way Ping (OWAMP) (2019). http://software.internet2.edu/owamp/
35. Iyer, A.P., Panda, A., Chowdhury, M., Akella, A., Shenker, S., Stoica, I.: Monarch: gaining command on geo-distributed graph analytics. In: Hot Topics in Cloud Computing (HotCloud). USENIX (2018)
36. Khalidi, Y.: How Microsoft builds its fast and reliable global network (2017). https://azure.microsoft.com/en-us/blog/how-microsoft-builds-its-fast-and-reliable-global-network/
37. Klöti, R., Ager, B., Kotronis, V., Nomikos, G., Dimitropoulos, X.: A comparative look into public IXP datasets. In: SIGCOMM CCR (2016)
38. Knight, S., Nguyen, H.X., Falkner, N., Bowden, R.A., Roughan, M.: The Internet topology zoo. In: JSAC. IEEE (2011)
39. Krishna, A., Cowley, S., Singh, S., Kesterson-Townes, L.: Assembling your cloud orchestra: a field guide to multicloud management. https://www.ibm.com/thought-leadership/institute-business-value/report/multicloud
40. Labovitz, C., Iekel-Johnson, S., McPherson, D., Oberheide, J., Jahanian, F.: Internet inter-domain traffic. In: SIGCOMM. ACM (2010)
41. Li, A., Yang, X., Kandula, S., Zhang, M.: CloudCmp: comparing public cloud providers. In: Internet Measurement Conference (IMC). ACM (2010)
42. Luckie, M.: Scamper: a scalable and extensible packet prober for active measurement of the Internet. In: Internet Measurement Conference (IMC). ACM (2010)
43. Luckie, M., Dhamdhere, A., Huffaker, B., Clark, D., et al.: bdrmap: inference of borders between IP networks. In: Internet Measurement Conference (IMC). ACM (2016)
44. Madhyastha, H.V., et al.: iPlane: an information plane for distributed services. In: OSDI. USENIX (2006)
45. Mao, Z.M., Rexford, J., Wang, J., Katz, R.H.: Towards an accurate AS-level traceroute tool. In: SIGCOMM. ACM (2003)
46. Marder, A., Smith, J.M.: MAP-IT: multipass accurate passive inferences from traceroute. In: Internet Measurement Conference (IMC). ACM (2016)
47. Mathis, M., Semke, J., Mahdavi, J., Ott, T.: The macroscopic behavior of the TCP congestion avoidance algorithm. In: SIGCOMM CCR (1997)
48. Megaport: Megaport pricing (2019). https://www.megaport.com/pricing/
49. Megaport: Nine Common Scenarios of multi-cloud design (2019). https://knowledgebase.megaport.com/megaport-cloud-router/nine-common-scenarios-for-multicloud-design/
50. Microsoft: Azure ExpressRoute. https://azure.microsoft.com/en-us/services/expressroute/
51. Microsoft: Expressroute partners and peering locations. https://docs.microsoft.com/en-us/azure/expressroute/expressroute-locations
52. Motamedi, R., Rejaie, R., Willinger, W.: A survey of techniques for Internet topology discovery. Commun. Surv. Tutor. **17**, 1044–1065 (2014)

53. PacketFabric: Cloud Connectivity (2019). https://www.packetfabric.com/packetcor#pricing
54. Padhye, J., Firoiu, V., Towsley, D., Kurose, J.: Modeling TCP throughput: a simple model and its empirical validation. In: SIGCOMM CCR (1998)
55. PCH: Packet Clearing House (2019). https://www.pch.net/
56. PeeringDB: PeeringDB (2019). https://www.peeringdb.com/
57. Pu, Q., et al.: Low latency geo-distributed data analytics. In: SIGCOMM CCR (2015)
58. Pureport: Pricing - Pureport (2019). https://www.pureport.com/pricing/
59. RIPE: RIPE RIS (2019)
60. Schlinker, B., et al.: Engineering egress with edge fabric: steering oceans of content to the world. In: SIGCOMM. ACM (2017)
61. Sermpezis, P., Nomikos, G., Dimitropoulos, X.A.: Re-mapping the Internet: bring the IXPs into play. CoRR (2017)
62. Shavitt, Y., Shir, E.: DIMES: let the internet measure itself. In: SIGCOMM CCR. ACM (2005)
63. Sherwood, R., Bender, A., Spring, N.: Discarte: a disjunctive internet cartographer. In: SIGCOMM. ACM (2008)
64. Sherwood, R., Spring, N.: Touring the Internet in a TCP sidecar. In: SIGCOMM Conference on Measurement. ACM (2006)
65. Spring, N., Mahajan, R., Wetherall, D.: Measuring ISP topologies with Rocketfuel. In: SIGCOMM (2002)
66. Tariq, M.M.B., Dhamdhere, A., Dovrolis, C., Ammar, M.: Poisson versus periodic path probing (or, does pasta matter?). In: Internet Measurement Conference (IMC). ACM (2005)
67. University of Oregon: Route views project. http://www.routeviews.org/
68. Viswanathan, R., Ananthanarayanan, G., Akella, A.: {CLARINET}: WAN-aware optimization for analytics queries. In: Operating Systems Design and Implementation ({OSDI}). USENIX (2016)
69. Vulimiri, A., et al.: Wanalytics: geo-distributed analytics for a data intensive world. In: SIGMOD. ACM (2015)
70. Wohlfart, F., Chatzis, N., Dabanoglu, C., Carle, G., Willinger, W.: Leveraging interconnections for performance: the serving infrastructure of a large CDN. In: SIGCOMM. ACM (2018)
71. Yeganeh, B., Durairajan, R., Rejaie, R., Willinger, W.: How cloud traffic goes hiding: a study of Amazon's peering fabric. In: Internet Measurement Conference (IMC). ACM (2019)
72. ZDNet: Top cloud providers (2019). https://tinyurl.com/y526vneg
73. Zhang, B., Liu, R., Massey, D., Zhang, L.: Collecting the Internet AS-level topology. In: SIGCOMM CCR. ACM (2005)
74. Zhang, H., et al.: Guaranteeing deadlines for inter-data center transfers. Trans. Netw. (TON) **25**, 579–595 (2017)

Unintended Consequences: Effects of Submarine Cable Deployment on Internet Routing

Rodérick Fanou$^{(\boxtimes)}$, Bradley Huffaker, Ricky Mok, and K. C. Claffy

CAIDA/UC San Diego, San Diego, USA
{roderick,bhuffake,cskpmok,kc}@caida.org

Abstract. We use traceroute and BGP data from globally distributed Internet measurement infrastructures to study the impact of a noteworthy submarine cable launch connecting Africa to South America. We leverage archived data from RIPE Atlas and CAIDA Ark platforms, as well as custom measurements from strategic vantage points, to quantify the differences in end-to-end latency and path lengths before and after deployment of this new South-Atlantic cable. We find that ASes operating in South America significantly benefit from this new cable, with reduced latency to all measured African countries. More surprising is that end-to-end latency to/from some regions of the world, including intra-African paths towards Angola, <u>increased</u> after switching to the cable. We track these unintended consequences to suboptimally circuitous IP paths that traveled from Africa to Europe, possibly North America, and South America before traveling back to Africa over the cable. Although some suboptimalities are expected given the lack of peering among neighboring ASes in the developing world, we found two other causes: (*i*) problematic intra-domain routing within a single Angolese network, and (*ii*) suboptimal routing/traffic engineering by its BGP neighbors. After notifying the operating AS of our results, we found that most of these suboptimalities were subsequently resolved. We designed our method to generalize to the study of other cable deployments or outages and share our code to promote reproducibility and extension of our work.

1 Introduction

The underlying physical infrastructure of the Internet includes a mesh of submarine cables, generally shared by network operators who purchase capacity from the cable owners [8,48]. Little academic research has tried to isolate performance changes induced by the deployment of new submarine cables, although a few studies have investigated the end-to-end performance impacts of disruptions to existing cable operations [21,23]. Recently Bischof *et al.* [8,9] made a case for a new research agenda focused on characterizing the fundamental role these cables play in inter-continental connections. We agree with this aspiration and undertook a study that represents a step toward it.

A. Sperotto et al. (Eds.): PAM 2020, LNCS 12048, pp. 211–227, 2020.
https://doi.org/10.1007/978-3-030-44081-7_13

In 2018, Angola Cables, Inc. (AC) deployed the first trans-Atlantic under-sea cables (SACS) crossing the South Hemisphere [56], linking Fortaleza, Brazil to Sangano, Angola [24,26,56,57]. We developed a methodology to analyze the impact of a specific cable launch on observed end-to-end round-trip latencies and paths across different regions of the world, and applied it to the case of the new SACS cable. The initial challenge in such a task is to identify the cable of interest using IP-layer traceroute measurements. Transit providers often do not publicly disclose cable details, e.g., IP addresses, and existing measurement techniques cannot easily distinguish multiple co-terminating (or nearly co-terminating) par-allel cable systems [9]. The unique landing points of SACS created an opportu-nity to identify it in large-scale traceroute datasets: besides the fact that SACS is the first South-Atlantic cable system linking Africa to the Americas, only two cable systems (WACS and SACS) anchor at Sangano post-SACS, versus 18 to Fortaleza, the second landing point of the new cable.

Our high-level approach was to analyze traceroutes paths that crossed SACS from mid-Sep 2018 to late Jan 2019, to the paths those same endpoints tra-versed before the cable activation. This comparison revealed significantly reduced latency from ASes operating in South America toward Africa. However, we were surprised to find 21.3% of observed paths, with sources in Europe and Asia, as well as intra-African paths, experienced worse performance – in terms of higher RTTs across the corresponding endpoints – after SACS. Even more surprising, the median RTT of intra-African paths towards Angola doubled. We analyzed the root causes of these unintended consequences – suboptimal circuitous paths that unnecessarily crossed continents e.g., from Africa/Europe toward Angola.

This work makes three contributions. First, we introduce a methodology to investigate submarine cable-related events, and second, we applied it to the case of the first operational South-Atlantic submarine cable to Africa. Finally, we suggest ways operators can avoid/mitigate suboptimal routing post-cable acti-vation during future deployments. We emphasize that as third-party observers, we do not have access to traffic data: the observed suboptimalities may occur on paths traversed by little to no traffic. In other words, this analysis does not necessarily reflect the performance of most traffic actually using that link. That said, these circuitous paths lasted the whole period considered in our analysis (i.e., 3.5 months post-SACS) until we notified the provider.

We believe this work is the first attempt to evaluate the macroscopic impact of a new submarine cable on end-to-end paths and performance, and our results reveal how lack of diagnostic tools and exercises can amplify the existing rout-ing inefficiencies involving the developing world, that derive from investment decisions, peering strategies [7,10,29,32,34], or traffic engineering [55].

2   Methodology

Our method requires first identifying the link of interest and its terminating IP addresses. We use these IP addresses to extract relevant paths from historical traceroute archives and then use this subset of paths to study the effects of the event on AS topology and performance (Sect. 2.1). We assume there is, and the method requires identifying, a cable of interest [1,2], and its IP addresses, which we call **link IPs**. The method also requires some meta-data about the event of interest, including date, duration, and the AS(es) operating the cable. We believe our method generalizes to the study of other cable deployments, and cable failures/outages. If the cable supports the use of layer-2 tunnels or wavelengths by different operators, identifying these link IPs is more complex and requires further study.

Step 1: Collect Candidate IP Paths That Could Have Crossed the Cable. We conduct traceroute measurements from vantage points (VPs) near the two cable endpoints toward each other; these are **candidate IP paths** that possibly traversed or rerouted through the link/cable after the event. Researchers can use public sea cable databases/maps [1,2,41,58] to inform the scheduling and execution of targeted traceroutes on existing measurement platforms [11,18,51].

Step 2: Identify Router IP Interfaces on Both Sides of the Cable. This task requires disambiguating the IP addresses terminating the cable of interest from those terminating other cable systems. We combine two approaches: an RTT-threshold based on speed-of-light constraints and IP geolocation. We analyze only the traceroute hops inferred (using bdrmapIT [42]) to be owned by the AS of interest. For these hops, we look for an RTT difference gap between consecutive hops in traceroute, using a threshold of $t = \frac{2 \times l}{(2/3) \times c}$, where l is the physical length of the cable, and $\frac{2}{3}c$ is the speed of light traveling in fiber optics.

At this point, we can narrow down the set of consecutive hops to the ones that match the landing sites of the cable of interest. We use IP geolocation databases (*e.g.*, NetAcuity [25], MaxMind [43]) to map IP addresses to countries. Given the low accuracy of such geolocation databases for router infrastructure [33,35,49], we also apply hostname-based geolocation. We validate the inferred location of IP addresses adjacent to these IPs by measuring the RTTs from VPs located in the inferred country. We consider the geolocation correct if the minimum RTT is less than 10 ms. We then resolve the router aliases of the selected IPs using CAIDA's MIDAR [16], Vela `aliasq` [19], and ITDK [20]. We obtain two lists of IP addresses of the router interfaces at the two ends of the cable denoted by $\mathcal{R}_\mathcal{A}$ and $\mathcal{R}_\mathcal{B}$. We call these two lists **link IPs**.

Step 3: Search for Comparable Historical Traceroutes. We use $\mathcal{P}$ to denote all source IP/destination prefix pairs, $<s,d>$, where s is the VP's source IP address and d is the longest-match prefix for the destination in the BGP routing table. We use longest-match because existing measurement platforms (Ark and Atlas) randomly probe within prefixes [17,52], and thus probing an exact destination IP address twice within a short period of time is unlikely. Furthermore, in many cases, only some IPs within a prefix respond to measurement probes [45]. We first look for a set of traceroutes, $\mathcal{T}_{<s,d>}, \forall <s,d> \in \mathcal{P}$, that contain either $\mathcal{R}_\mathcal{A} \rightarrow \mathcal{R}_\mathcal{B}$ or $\mathcal{R}_\mathcal{B} \rightarrow \mathcal{R}_\mathcal{A}$ *after* the occurrence of the event. With this list of prefix pairs, we search for pre-event traceroutes from the same $<s,d>$ pairs, $\mathcal{T}'_{<s,d>}$, for comparison.

Step 4: Annotate Collected Paths. For every hop in the traceroute sets $\mathcal{T}_{<s,d>}$ and $\mathcal{T}'_{<s,d>}$, we resolve the hostname and AS number, perform country-level IP geolocation, and compute the difference in RTT from that of the previous hop. To accurately map IP addresses appearing in traceroutes to AS numbers, we run bdrmapIT [42] on the traceroutes collected on each day from both Ark and Atlas, using as inputs *daily RIB from Routeviews and RIPE RIS* [44,53], CAIDA's *AS relationship file* [13,40] from the first five days of the month, a *daily dump of IXP prefixes from peeringDB* [39,46], and *WHOIS delegation files* collected in the middle of the period of the study. To resolve IP addresses to hostnames, we use zdns [28] and qr [37]. Next, we collect a combined list of Internet eXchange Points (IXPs) prefixes from CAIDA's IXP Dataset [14], compare them to the prefix corresponding to every hop in the traceroute sets $\mathcal{T}_{<s,d>}$ and $\mathcal{T}'_{<s,d>}$, and single out traces for which an IXP prefix matches the prefix of the IP hop. By doing so, we identify the IXPs through which the cable operator received/routed the packets pre and post-event.

We then group the traceroutes of each set by $<s,d>$ pair and, based on their corresponding timestamps of execution, we cluster them per week. For every IP hop of each traceroute, we include its inferred annotations. These annotated traceroutes enable us to compare the AS paths and latency before and after the event using metrics described in Sect. 2.1.

2.1   Metrics for Quantifying the Impact of the Event

We compare the performance and AS paths between $\mathcal{T}_{<s,d>}$ and $\mathcal{T}'_{<s,d>}$ using three metrics.

1: RTTs to the Common IP Hops Closest to the Traceroute Destinations. This metric compares RTT values to reveal the change in latency across the network paths before and after cable deployment. Figure 1 illustrates the identification of traceroutes in sets $\mathcal{T}_{<s,d>}$ and $\mathcal{T}'_{<s,d>}$ between the same $<s,d>$ pair that share at least one IP address. Among all traceroutes run toward a destination prefix, we locate the common IP hop, h_c, closest to the destination IP and extract the RTTs from s to h_c in $\mathcal{T}_{<s,d>}$ and $\mathcal{T}'_{<s,d>}$, denoted as d_c and d'_c, respectively. We only consider the subset $\hat{\mathcal{P}}$ of $<s,d>$,

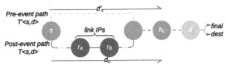

Fig. 1. Pre&post-event path comparison. Orange circles indicate common IP hops in $\mathcal{T}_{<s,d>}$ and $\mathcal{T}'_{<s,d>}$. s is the source IP address, and h_c is the common IP hop closest to the destination IP. The red circles $r_A \in \mathcal{R}_A$ and $r_B \in \mathcal{R}_B$ are the router interfaces of the two ends of the submarine cable (Step 2). (Color figure online)

such that $\hat{\mathcal{P}} \subseteq \mathcal{P}$ and $h_c \neq \emptyset$ (*i.e.*, that contains non-empty h_c) in our analysis. For each $<s,d>$ pair, we then compute the medians of all d_c and d'_c per week and choose their respective minimum values over the periods pre and post-event to mitigate noise.

2: AS-Centrality of Transit ASes in Paths. We use bdrmapIT [42] to infer AS paths from the IP paths and compute from $T_{<s,d>}$ and $T'_{<s,d>}$ the AS-centrality of each observed transit AS. This metric is defined as the percentage of $<s,d>$ pairs for which the AS path with the minimum observed RTT d_c (or d'_c for pre-event) contains the considered AS, and where that AS is neither the source nor the destination [29]. A higher AS-centrality of an AS post-event indicates increased transit importance, *i.e.*, more ASes use that AS for transit.

3: Length of AS Paths Crossing Cable Operator's Network Pre and Post-event. We analyze the length of AS paths between source AS/destination prefix pairs observed to cross the cable operator's network in RouteViews and RIPE RIS [44,53] data pre and post-event. Similar to previous work [13,40], we consider paths collected on the first five days of the month before and after the event.

3 Data Collection: Case Study of SACS Cable Deployment

We collected candidate IP paths that crossed SACS (Sect. 3.1) on Mar 25–26, 2019. We identified the link IPs from those candidate IP paths and ITDK [20] (Sect. 3.2). We used those link IPs to search in Ark and RIPE Atlas historical data for matching traceroutes post-SACS (Jan–mid-Sep 2018) and the traceroutes with the same $<s,d>$ pairs pre-SACS (mid-Sep 2018–Jan 2019) (Sect. 3.3). Next, we annotated these traceroutes with supplementary information for its analysis (Sect. 3.4).

3.1 Collecting Candidate IP Paths Crossing SACS

At the beginning of this study (Mar 2019) there were eight active Ark VPs in South America, but none in Angola. AC hosted a looking-glass (LG) server [5] connected to the Sangano landing point [26,27,36]: An LG server allows BGP and traceroute queries by third-parties. Using both CAIDA's *Vela* interface [18] to execute measurements on the Ark infrastructure, and the AC LG server [5], we collected traceroutes from VPs located in South America toward the AC LG server (and in the reverse direction) to obtain IP paths that possibly crossed SACS, *i.e.*, candidate IP paths.

3.2 Identifying Link IPs

Based on the length of the cable, we estimate the round-trip time to cross SACS to be about $t_{SACS} = \frac{6,165km \times 2}{(2/3) \times c} = 62$ ms. By inspecting the candidate IP paths, we found a pair of AC IP addresses (170.238.232.146 and 170.238.232.145) in the same /30, which had RTT differences with preceding and subsequent IPs that matched our latency heuristics. We could not resolve their hostnames, but the hostnames of their adjacent hops contained geolocation hints ao.sgn and br.ftz. Because of the small differential RTTs between the two IPs and their adjacent hops, we inferred that 170.238.232.146 and 170.238.232.145 were in

Sangano, Angola and Fortaleza, Brazil, respectively. We leveraged VPs in Angola and Brazil to conduct latency measurements toward these two IPs to confirm our inference. Using the two IP addresses, we obtained a set of aliases of SACS routers in Angola ($\mathcal{R}_\mathcal{A}$) and Brazil ($\mathcal{R}_\mathcal{B}$) from ITDK [20] of Jan 2019. We found that $\mathcal{R}_\mathcal{A}$ and $\mathcal{R}_\mathcal{B}$ contained respectively 29 and 18 MIDAR-observed IP addresses aliases of the same router.

3.3   Fetching Matching Traceroutes Paths

We analyzed CAIDA's Ark [11] and RIPE Atlas data [51]. We considered the *on-going IPv4 Routed /24 Topology measurements* [17] from 178 Ark VPs that execute ICMP Paris-traceroute [6] toward a random destination in every routed /24 prefix. Using CAIDA's *Henya* [15] interface to search Ark traceroute data, we split historical Ark traceroutes into two sets. ARK-AFTER includes traceroutes going through SACS from mid-Sep 2018 to late Jan 2019 (after SACS) and which had an IP of $\mathcal{R}_\mathcal{A}$ followed by an IP of $\mathcal{R}_\mathcal{B}$ or vice-versa; and ARK-BEFORE includes traceroutes from early Jan 2018 to mid-Sep 2018 between the same $<s, d>$ pairs as those measured in ARK-AFTER. Of the 8,035 $<s, d>$ pairs common to both ARK-BEFORE and ARK-AFTER, we enumerate 6,778 (84.3%) $<s, d>$ pairs that contained a common IP hop.

RIPE Atlas (Atlas) had more VPs (10,196 vs 178) than CAIDA's Ark project, but far fewer usable $<s, d>$ pairs (823 vs. 6,778). Although both platforms probe the full set of routed prefixes, Atlas divides its prefix list across 10,196 VPs [52], while Ark divides /24 prefixes across its 178 VPs. Thus, an Ark probe has a larger probability of probing the same prefix. The set of common pairs did not change despite our attempts to augment our dataset with targeted traceroutes between and toward Atlas VPs in Angola and Brazil post-SACS.

3.4   Adding Supplementary Datasets

We annotated each IP address with its operating AS, router hostname, and geographic information. Using bdrmapIT [42], we mapped 95% of our IPs into ASes. We used zdns [28] and qr [37] to resolve 35% of those IPs to hostnames. We geolocated IP addresses using the methodology described in Sect. 2. We mapped IP hops to their corresponding AS's country if either: (*i*) the AS had no customers and NetAcuity [25] geolocated more than 50% of its IP addresses (*i.e.*, those it originates into BGP) to the country, or (*ii*) 50% of its AS customers geolocated to the same country (by the same process as in *(i)*). We marked all IP addresses whose hostnames contained geographic hints and updated the city and country they refer to. For cases where we found suboptimal routing (Sect. 4.2), we manually cross-checked the geographic hints and the RTT difference to validate the inferred locations. We then identified IXPs at which AC peered pre and post-event, using IXP prefixes in CAIDA's IXPs dataset [14] as described in Sect. 2.

The cable deployment, although entirely within AC's network, could have triggered a substantial change in the number of BGP paths traversing this AS, since other ASes would have incentive to leverage it, especially those who route traffic between the connected countries/continents. To explore this hypothesis, we analyzed BGP-observed AS paths traversing AC pre and post-SACS. For computation and evaluation of the AS path length, we gathered AS paths (without loops or private ASes) collected from Routeviews [44] and RIS [53] during the first five days of Aug and Oct 2018 and included AC (AS37468). To check the post-SACS path stability, we collected new IP paths using Ark and LG servers in AC transit providers and customers between mid-May and end-June 2019.

4   Results and Validation

4.1   Effects on Performance

We quantified the observed RTT changes for packets sent from ASes hosting Ark and Atlas VPs that crossed the cable. We discovered cases of both performance improvements and degradations on paths used pre vs. post-SACS (Figs. 2 and 3). Our results confirm Prior's claim [50] that the new cable "reduced latency to the Americas substantially, including a reduction from 338 ms to 163 ms between Cape Town and Miami". VPs in South America also experienced lower latencies

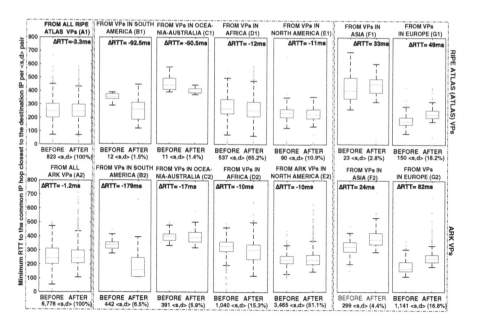

Fig. 2. Boxplots of minimum RTTs from Ark and Atlas VPs to the common IP hops closest to the destination IPs. Sets BEFORE or AFTER are defined in Sect. 2. We present $\Delta RTT_{AFTER-BEFORE}$ per sub-figure. RTT changes are similar across platforms. Paths from South America experienced a median RTT decrease of 38%, those from Oceania-Australia, a smaller decrease of 8%, while those from Africa and North-America, roughly 3%. Conversely, paths from Europe and Asia that crossed SACS after its deployment experienced an average RTT increase of 40% and 9%, respectively.

to Africa, with a median RTT decrease of 38% toward all measured African countries. Our findings confirm the drop of latencies from Europe/Africa toward Brazil and those from Brazil to Angola as claimed in [27,36], except for VPs in North America and Asia, which experienced higher latencies to Brazil (Fig. 3). However, our data does not confirm the claim that latencies to Angola generally experienced an improvement [27,36,57] – on the contrary, paths from VPs in Africa, Asia, and Europe had median latency increases!

Figure 2 shows a boxplot of minimum RTT values observed between Ark/Atlas source IP/destination prefix ($<s, d>$) pairs. After fetching matching traceroutes (Sect. 3.3), half of the 6,778 Ark $<s, d>$ pairs were sourced from North America, while most (65.2%) of the 823 Atlas ones were sourced from Africa. For both measurements platforms, at least 16% of the $<s, d>$ pairs were sourced from Europe. Figure 3 presents a heatmap of RTT differences pre vs. post-SACS, for continent/destination country pairs. For statistical significance, we considered only such pairs for which we had at least 20 IP paths. Each box contains the number of observed $<s, d>$ pairs (Sect. 2.1). The x-axis shows the VP locations, while the y-axis the destination prefix countries. The countries on the y-axis are all direct customers of AC. None of Angola's direct geographic neighbors (Zambia, Zimbabwe, Botswana, Namibia, or Democratic Republic of Congo) are represented on the y-axis. Neither are those neighbors in the 1,034 ASes of AC's AS customer cone [12,54].

Figure 2 highlights that the Ark and Atlas platforms show similar trends in RTT performance pre to post-SACS per region, as one would expect. In fact, 64% of countries and 89% of $<s, d>$ pairs represented in Fig. 3 are already present in the same matrix inferred only from Ark data. Overall, RTT values on IP paths observed by Atlas VPs as crossing SACS are statistically stable (from 249 ms to 246 ms) with a decrease of the interquartile range (IQR) of 10% (from 102 ms to 92 ms). The trend for Ark VPs is similar: median RTT drops from 245 ms to 243 ms, and the IQR drops 18%.

One would expect the greatest performance improve-

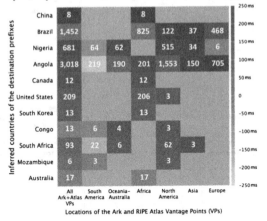

Fig. 3. $\Delta RTT_{AFTER-BEFORE}$ of the medians of minimum RTTs per week pre&post SACS for observed $<s, d>$ pairs. We sort the x-axis by the average change per region and the y-axis by ΔRTT for all VPs. **Each cell contains the number of observed $<s, d>$ pairs**, and is colored according to the corresponding ΔRTT; a grey cell means data non-available. The highest performance improvements are observed from South America to Angola or South Africa, while the worst degradations are from Africa to Angola or North-America to Brazil.

ments for VPs in Africa and South America, *i.e.*, close to the cable. Figure 2B1 and 2B2 show that this is the case for communications from South America crossing SACS. For example, before SACS launch, traffic from Brazil to Angola via AC visited São Paulo, London/Lisbon, and Sangano via the WACS cable [59], traversing double the great-circle distance between Brazil and Angola, before reaching Luanda (AO) with an RTT of at least 279 ms. The use of SACS dropped this RTT to a low of 108 ms. These statistics are consistent with those AC presented in [36].

In contrast, Fig. 2D1 and 2D2 reveal only a slight RTT decrease (10 ms *i.e.*, 3%) for VPs in Africa, comparable to that of VPs in North America (Fig. 2E1 and 2E2). While Fig. 3 shows that the most significant RTT drops are on paths from South America to Angola (226 ms a 67% drop), South Africa (199 ms, a 55% drop), and Nigeria (138 ms, a 46% drop), it shows that these are all at least twice the percent drop observed on paths from Africa to Brazil (73 ms, a 21% drop). In fact, IP paths from, for instance, Dar-es-Salam (TZ) traversed Mombassa (KE), London (UK), Paris (FR), Amsterdam (NL), Miami (US) to reach Brazil before SACS deployment, and switched to Mombassa (KE), Marseille (FR), Madrid (ES), Lisbon (PT), Sangano (AO), and Brazil after SACS. We inspect these circuitous paths and their causes in Sect. 4.2.

Our dataset confirms that, for $<s, d>$ pairs from South Africa toward Brazil that benefited from SACS, observed minimum RTTs decreased from 298 ms to 116 ms (highlighted in [60]). Minimum RTTs decreased 44% for $<s, d>$ pairs from Zambia, 35% for those from Nigeria and 3.5% from Ghana toward prefixes in Brazil. The dataset also reveals performance degradations *e.g.*, for RTTs from most VPs in Europe and Asia (Fig. 2G and F). From the inspection of performance per continents/countries destination, we learned that the biggest RTT increase occurred for $<s, d>$ pairs sourced from Africa to Angola (241 ms *i.e.*, 161%), which surprisingly crossed SACS after its launch (Fig. 3). This is followed by cases of paths from North America to Brazil (189 ms increase *i.e.*, 123%), Europe to Angola (102 ms – 69%), and Africa to China (24%).

4.2   Effects on Country Paths and Transit ASes Serving Forward Paths

We investigated the change in forward paths from South America, Africa, and Europe to Angola. Before using SACS, packets from South America to Angola first traveled to Europe, and then went through the existing WACS cable [59] to Angola (inferred via hostnames that indicate WACS landing points). AC served 46% of $<s, d>$ pairs observed by both Ark and Atlas VPs. After SACS, paths for all observed $<s, d>$ pairs transited through AC, leveraging SACS for lower latency (Fig. 4A). Figure 4B shows paths from Europe to Angola, where the forward paths crossed SACS instead of the existing WACS. In this case, the use of SACS <u>increased</u> latency due to higher propagation delay and an increase in the number of transited routers (Fig. 2G1 and G2).

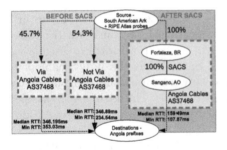 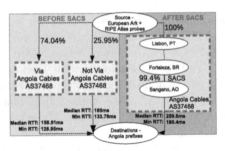

(A) Partial AS paths from South America to Angola. Before using SACS, paths between 46% of < s, d > pairs crossed Europe and then Angola via AC. SACS provided to all measured < s, d > pairs a more direct path between these two continents and improved performance.

(B) Partial AS paths from Europe to Angola. AC was the major transit provider for traffic from Europe to Angola throughout the entire period of study. However, the use of SACS within AC significantly lengthened the physical path, and thus the latency of the forward path.

Fig. 4. Impact of SACS deployment on the set of transit cases on observed paths going from South America to Angola (RTT improvement) and from Europe to Angola (RTT degradation). The white ovals inside AC are part of traceroutes post-SACS we manually geolocated using hints in hostnames.

Figure 5 illustrates how, after SACS, a high proportion of observed paths for certain continent/destination country pairs followed circuitous paths within AC's network, crossing the sea multiple times.

We computed the AS-centrality (Sect. 2.1) of ASes within the forward paths and inferred the top three transit ASes that serve most <s, d> pairs (Table 1). After SACS, the same top two ASes remained, although the AS-centrality of AC shifted to 90%. However, observed packets routed within AC took a suboptimal route: for 27.2% of <s, d> pairs, packets routed within AC via Cape Town/Johannesburg (ZA) traveled a great-circle distance of 13,502 km more than before SACS, while for another 55% of <s, d> pairs, packets entering AC through London traveled 7,081 km more than before SACS. Suboptimal paths from Africa (through Europe, possibly North America, and Brazil) to Angola inducing the RTT increase of Fig. 3 (241 ms) post-SACS were either due to suboptimality within AC itself or to neighbors that were routing packets towards AC even though going through SACS was not the shortest route anymore. Figure 5A depicts how 55% of paths originating in different African countries entered AC either through South Africa, via Europe down to Brazil, and crossed SACS before landing in Angola.

The next largest median RTT increase was for paths from North America to Brazil, which rose 187 ms (123%) for observed <s, d> pairs of this category. Figure 5 shows two trajectories used by 25% of these paths: from North America, packets crossed Europe or Asia, enter AC PoPs at IXPs in South Africa, then all went to Angola before crossing SACS to Brazil: this proves the existence of a direct link from South Africa to Angola (via WACS), making the suboptimal African paths previously mentioned even more curious. All three most-central

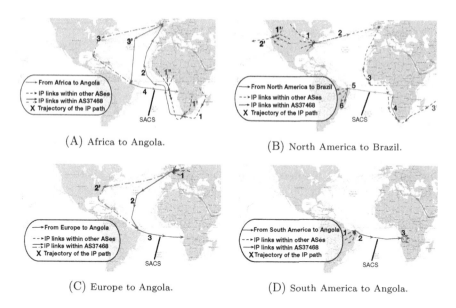

(A) Africa to Angola.

(B) North America to Brazil.

(C) Europe to Angola.

(D) South America to Angola.

Fig. 5. Examples of suboptimal trajectories followed post-SACS by most paths from Africa to Angola (at least 55%), North America to Brazil (25%), and Europe to Angola (99.3%) *within AC's network (AS37468)* or within other ASes in the paths vs. straightforward trajectory *within AC* or other ASes of most paths from South America to Angola (≃100%), explaining the values of ΔRTT_{A-B} in Fig. 2. We use the same colors to code stages (1, 2, 3, 4, 5, and 6) regardless of the subfigure.

Table 1. Top three transit ASes serving $<s, d>$ pairs from continents to destination countries. The categories for which we noticed suboptimal routing and RTT increase post-SACS are in italic. Although all our pre-selected paths post-SACS cross SACS, AC may still have an AS-centrality lower than 100%, since the AS-centrality does not account for cases where the AS is either the source or the destination of the AS path.

Category ($\#< s, d >$)	CC	Before AS-centrality	Before Transit AS	After Transit AS	After AS-centrality	CC
From Africa to Angola (201)	AO	66.7%	Angola Cables (AS37468)		90.1%	AO
	ZA	32.3%	Internet Solutions (AS3741)		22.4%	ZA
	BG	20.9%	Sofia Connect (AS47872)	WIOCC-AS (AS37662)	16.4%	MU
				IPPLANET (AS12491)	16.4%	IL
From North America to Brazil (122)	US	44.4%	ATT-Internet4 (AS7018)	Angola Cables (AS37468)	100%	AO
	BR	30.1%	NipBr (AS27693)	Chinanet-B. (AS4134)	60.2%	CN
	US	23%	Nitel (AS53828)	Abilene (AS11537)	58.3%	US
From Europe to Angola (705)	AO	62.9%	Angola Cables (AS37468)		78.1%	AO
	BG	18.6%	Sofia-Connect (AS47872)	Telianet (AS1299)	17.6%	EU
	EU	14.2%	Telianet (AS1299)	TWTC (AS4323)	9.9%	US
From Asia to Brazil (141)	AO	50.3%	Angola Cables (AS37468)		90.1%	AO
	US	28.4%	TATA (AS6453)	TWTC (AS4323)	31.9%	US
	JP	24.1%	KDDI (AS2516)		26.2%	JP
From South America to Angola (212)	AO	45.7%	Angola Cables (AS37468)		96.2%	AO
	BR	36.8%	Terremark do Brasil (AS28625)	Cilnet (AS28580)	18.4%	BR
	US	36.3%	Cogent (AS174)	CO.PA.CO. (AS27768)	11.8%	PY

ASes for the same pairs changed after SACS launch, with a higher AS-centrality and 100% of $<s, d>$ pairs were served by AC post-SACS (Table 1).

Paths from Europe to Angola showed a median increase of 102 ms (69%). Figure 5 shows the trajectory of such paths sourcing from Europe and entering AC in Europe before going to Brazil and crossing SACS, on their way to their destinations in Angola. We learned from our dataset that after SACS, 99% of paths went through Fortaleza within AC's network vs. none before. Since using the WACS cable was an option for AC post-SACS, there was suboptimal routing within AC for this category. Packets routed this way traveled roughly 6,435 km more than when they went from London (UK) to Luanda (AO) through WACS. Conversely, the largest median RTT <u>decrease</u> (38%) corresponds to paths from South America to Angola: 99% of observed paths directly traversed SACS when routed within AC, enabling packets to travel a great-circle distance of 6,641 km less than before. This case shows that optimal routing within AC's network can indeed substantially improve end-to-end performance for AS paths it serves.

We saw only a third of such improvement from Africa to Brazil (a drop of 73 ms *i.e.*, 21%). Further investigation revealed cases of suboptimal interdomain routing for paths going notably from Mauritius, Ghana, Tanzania, South Africa, or Zambia to Brazil via cities on other continents, which result from the persistent lack of peering among neighboring ASes [29,30,32,34].

We then used Fig. 3 and Table 1 to check whether SACS introduced new backup IP paths between the regions AC connected. No observed $<s, d>$ pairs hinted the existence of paths from South America to Europe/Asia via SACS and Africa. Instead, paths from North America toward destinations in Africa via SACS benefit from an RTT decrease of at least 20 ms; SACS could thus play the role of a valid backup path for North American ASes to reach African countries or could be used for load balancing purposes. We also checked whether AC received/routed packets post-SACS through new IXPs. Before the SACS launch, AC was present at public peering points spanning five continents [3,4,47]. We observed AC peering at five additional IXPs (in UK, US, BR, and RU) post-SACS for the same set of $<s, d>$ pairs, *i.e.*, and expanded interconnection footprint.

4.3   Impact on AS Paths Lengths

From Routeviews and RIPE RIS BGP snapshots of Aug 1st–5th and Oct 1st–5th, 2018 (the months before and after SACS launch), we extracted all AS paths through AC post-SACS (Set AFTER), and all AS paths between the same source AS/destination prefix routed pre-SACS (Set BEFORE). We found 2,115,761 unique AS paths that crossed AC in both snapshots. Since

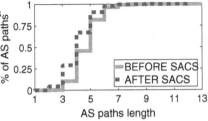

Fig. 6. Distribution of the length of AS paths between same source AS/destination prefix pairs served via AC (AS37468) pre&post SACS, showing the increase of paths of lengths 2–7.

the number of observed AS paths differed in each set and the measurements windows are not strictly identical, we computed the average AS path length per source ´AS/destination prefix pairs: the percentage of outliers *i.e.*, paths of lengths 10–13 (max) was ≈1%. We noticed the AS path length distribution shifted, with AS paths of length 2–7 generally increasing, reflecting the fact that more neighboring ASes preferred AS paths via AC after the SACS launch (Fig. 6). Interestingly, AC apparently announced many paths to prefixes owned by multiple ASes 2–3 months before the SACS launch [22], perhaps preparing for the launch.

4.4 Validation with the ISP

In Jul 2019, we successfully contacted AC and were able to validate the inferred set of SACS link IPs and their respective locations. AC distinguished cases where the anomalous routes occurred outside their network, and tromboning occurred due to lack of local peering, or where neighbor ASes were circuitously routing traffic toward AC after SACS. During our exchange with them, we took subsequent measurements that showed some AC neighbors had modified their routing configurations in ways that improved performance. Although AC did not validate cases of suboptimal routing within their network, most observed IP paths (from North America/Asia to Brazil or Europe/Asia to Angola) switched to more optimal paths after our conversation. AC also explained that internal link failures could account for the performance degradations. For example, if the MONET cable [3,59] (which AC's router in Miami crosses to reach Fortaleza) becomes unavailable, the router may re-route traffic through London. They also noted that no customers had complained, so if there were any suboptimal routing, it was unlikely to be affecting any routes that carried any traffic. That said, we found that a few (≈4%) <*s, d*> pairs used remarkably suboptimal paths as late as Jul 12, 2019, *e.g.*, from Africa to prefixes in Angola served via Europe and Brazil or those from North America to Angola routed by AC via SACS and Lisbon. Finally, AC informed us that most traffic crossing SACS through AC goes from either South America to Angola or South Africa to Brazil, cases where our results show a pronounced decrease post-SACS (Sect. 4.1).

4.5 Potential Root Causes of Suboptimal Routing

We confirmed the occurrence of the routing suboptimalities described in this paper using two measurements platforms that revealed similar trends per region. We tried to obtain insights from the ISP operating the cable (AC) into potential causes, without success. We conjecture that these suboptimalities derived from multiple causes (potentially concurrent): (*i*) misconfigurations of either the Internal or External Gateway Protocol (IGP/EGP), due to typos, errors, etc, [10] (*ii*) slow IGP or EGP convergence [38], (*iii*) some ASes routing packets through AC although it is not the optimal path to the destination, (*iv*) the persistent lack of peering among local ASes in Africa (despite ongoing efforts for more local interconnections) [30,32] and frequent use of default routes via international transit providers in developing regions.

5 Conclusion

It is generally assumed that deployment of undersea cables between continents improves performance, at least for paths that cross a cable once it is deployed. We present a reproducible scientific method by third-parties to investigate the performance impact of a cable deployment, and we apply it to the case of the first South-Atlantic cable, connecting Brazil to Angola. We used traceroute and BGP data from global measurement platforms, and geolocation data and inferences to find that this new cable had at least initially reduced RTTs asymmetrically: the median RTT decrease from Africa to Brazil was roughly a third of that from South America to Angola (226 ms). More surprising is that latency statistics to/from other regions of the world, including paths within Africa, increased post-activation due to circuitous IP paths that suboptimally crossed continents and the cable. We uncovered other potential sources of suboptimality: slow BGP route updates/lack of traffic engineering after a major event occurring in a neighboring AS, and problematic intra-domain routing within a single network. Our results suggest ways operators can avoid suboptimal routing post-activation of cables in the future: (i) informing BGP neighbors of the launch to allow time for appropriate changes in advance; (ii) ensuring optimal iBGP configurations post-activation, not only for pairs of ASes/countries expected to route most traffic through the cable, but also for served intra-regional and cross-regional traffic; and (iii) collaborate with measurements platforms or research institutions to verify path optimality. Our methodology is general enough to apply to other cable deployments, as well as cable failures, and contributes to a toolbox to support further scientific study of the global submarine cable network [8,9]. We share our code [31] to promote reproducibility and extension of our work.

Acknowledgment. We thank the anonymous reviewers and our shepherd, Fabian Bustamante, for their insightful comments. We also thank Angola Cables, especially their IP services department, for their cooperation, despite their tight schedule and Stephen Strowes for the introductions. This research was supported by the National Science Foundation (NSF) grant OAC-1724853.

References

1. Submarine Cable Networks, January 2020. https://www.submarinenetworks.com/en/
2. Subsea World News, January 2020. https://subseaworldnews.com
3. Angola Cables: Angola Cables Network, January 2020. https://www.angolacables.co.ao/en/network/
4. Angola Cables: SACS, January 2020. https://sacs.angolacables.co.ao
5. Angonix: Angonix - BIRD Looking Glass, January 2019. http://lg.angonix.net/

6. Augustin, B., Cuvellier, X., Orgogozo, B., Viger, F., Friedman, T., Latapy, M., Magnien, C., Teixera, R.: Avoiding traceroute anomalies with Paris traceroute. In: Proceedings of the ACM SIGCOMM Internet Measurement Conference (IMC), pp. 153–158. ACM, October 2006

7. Berenguer, S.S., Carisimo, E., Alvarez-Hamelin, J.I., Pintor, F.V.: Hidden Internet topologies info: truth or myth? In: Proceedings of the 2016 Workshop on Fostering Latin-American Research in Data Communication Networks, pp. 4–6 (2016)

8. Bischof, Z.S., Fontugne, R., Bustamante, F.E.: Submarine Cables and Internet Resiliency (2018). https://www.iij.ad.jp/en/dev/iir/pdf/iir_vol41_focus2_EN.pdf

9. Bischof, Z.S., Fontugne, R., Bustamante, F.E.: Untangling the world-wide mesh of undersea cables. In: Proceedings of the 17th ACM Workshop on Hot Topics in Networks (HotNets), pp. 78–84. ACM (2018)

10. Bischof, Z.S., Rula, J.P., Bustamante, F.E.: In and out of Cuba: characterizing Cuba's connectivity. In: Proceedings of the 2015 Internet Measurement Conference, pp. 487–493 (2015)

11. CAIDA: Archipelago (Ark) Measurement Infrastructure, January 2020. https://www.caida.org/projects/ark/

12. CAIDA: AS Rank, January 2020. http://as-rank.caida.org

13. CAIDA: AS Relationships, January 2020. http://www.caida.org/data/as-relationships

14. CAIDA: CAIDA Internet eXchange Point (IXP) Dataset, January 2020. http://www.caida.org/data/ixps/

15. CAIDA: Henya, January 2020. https://www.caida.org/tools/utilities/henya/

16. CAIDA: MIDAR, January 2020. http://www.caida.org/tools/measurement/midar/

17. CAIDA: The IPv4 Routed /24 Topology Dataset, January 2020. http://www.caida.org/data/active/ipv4_routed_24_topology_dataset.xml

18. CAIDA: Vela, January 2020. https://vela.caida.org

19. CAIDA: Velasq, January 2020. https://www.caida.org/projects/ark/vela/aliasq-api/

20. Center for Applied Internet Data Analysis (CAIDA): Macroscopic Internet Topology Data Kit (ITDK), January 2019. http://www.caida.org/data/internet-topology-data-kit/

21. Chang, R., Chan, E., Li, W., Fok, W., Luo, X.: Could ash cloud or deep-sea current overwhelm the Internet? In: Proceedings of USENIX Workshop on Hot Topics in System Dependability (HotDep), October 2010

22. Chung, T., Aben, E., Bruijnzeels, T., Chandrasekaran, B., Choffnes, D., Levin, D., Maggs, B.M., Mislove, A., Rijswijk-Deij, R.V., Rula, J., et al.: RPKI is coming of age: a longitudinal study of RPKI deployment and invalid route origins. In: Proceedings of the Internet Measurement Conference, pp. 406–419 (2019)

23. Clark, B.: Undersea cables and the future of submarine competition. Bull. Atom. Sci. **72**(4), 234–237 (2016)

24. Dawn-Hiscox, T.: Angola cables lights up world's first submarine cable linking Africa to the Americas, September 2019. https://www.datacenterdynamics.com/news/angola-cables-lights-up-worlds-first-submarine-cable-linking-africa-to-the-americas/

25. Digital Element: Netacuity, January 2020. http://www.digital-element.net/ip_intelligence/ip_intelligence.html

26. Doug, M.: First Subsea Cable Across South Atlantic Activated, September 2018. https://internetintel.oracle.com/blog-single.html?id=First+Subsea+Cable+Across+South+Atlantic+Activated

27. Doug, M., Darwin, C., Humberto, G.: South Atlantic Cable System the Impact on the Internet LACNIC 30 - Lightning Talk, September 2018. https://www.lacnic. net/innovaportal/file/3209/1/sacs_lightning_talk_lacnic30.pdf
28. Durumeric, Z., Pearce, P.: Fast CLI DNS Lookup Tool, September 2019. https:// github.com/zmap/zdns
29. Fanou, R., Francois, P., Aben, E.: On the diversity of interdomain routing in Africa. In: Mirkovic, J., Liu, Y. (eds.) PAM 2015. LNCS, vol. 8995, pp. 41–54. Springer, Cham (2015). https://doi.org/10.1007/978-3-319-15509-8_4
30. Fanou, R., Francois, P., Aben, E., Mwangi, M., Goburdhan, N., Valera, F.: Four years tracking unrevealed topological changes in the African interdomain. Comput. Commun. **106**, 117–135 (2017)
31. Fanou, R., Huffaker, B., Mok, R.K., Claffy, K.: Submarine Cable Impact Analysis: Public Codebase, January 2020. https://github.com/CAIDA/submarine-cable-impact-analysis-public
32. Formoso, A., Chavula, J., Phokeer, A., Sathiaseelan, A., Tyson, G.: Deep Diving into Africa's Inter-Country Latencies. In: IEEE Conference on Computer Communications (INFOCOM) (2018)
33. Gharaibeh, M., Shah, A., Huffaker, B., Zhang, H., Ensafi, R., Papadopoulos, C.: A look at router geolocation in public and commercial databases. In: Proceedings of the ACM Internet Measurement Conference (IMC) (2017)
34. Gupta, A., Calder, M., Feamster, N., Chetty, M., Calandro, E., Katz-Bassett, E.: Peering at the Internet's Frontier: a first look at ISP interconnectivity in Africa. In: International Conference on Passive and Active Network Measurement (PAM), March 2014
35. Huffaker, B., Fomenkov, M., Claffy, K.: Geocompare: a comparison of public and commercial geolocation databases. In: Proceedings of NMMC, pp. 1–12 (2011)
36. Humberto, G.: South Atlantic Cable System - SACS The Impact on the Internet WTR POP-BA/RNP 2018 - Lightning Talk (2018). https://wtr.pop-ba.rnp.br/ 2018/files/apresentacoes/10-WTR2018-LT02-AngolaCables-HumbertoGaliza.pdf
37. Hyun, Y.: Dolphin: Bulk DNS Resolution Tool, June 2014. http://www.caida.org/ publications/presentations/2014/dolphin_dhs/dolphin_dhs.pdf
38. Labovitz, C., Ahuja, A., Bose, A., Jahanian, F.: Delayed Internet routing convergence. ACM SIGCOMM Comput. Commun. Rev. **30**(4), 175–187 (2000)
39. Lodhi, A., Larson, N., Dhamdhere, A., Dovrolis, C., Claffy, K.: Using PeeringDB to understand the peering ecosystem. ACM SIGCOMM Comput. Commun. Rev. **44**(2), 20–27 (2014)
40. Luckie, M., Huffaker, B., Dhamdhere, A., Giotsas, V., Claffy, K.: AS relationships, customer cones, and validation. In: Proceedings of the 2013 Conference on Internet Measurement Conference, pp. 243–256 (2013)
41. Mahlknecth, G.: Greg Mahlknecth's Cable Map, January 2020. https://cablemap. info/_default.aspx
42. Marder, A., Luckie, M., Dhamdhere, A., Huffaker, B., Smith, J.M., et al.: Pushing the boundaries with bdrmapIT: mapping router ownership at Internet scale. In: Proceedings of the ACM Internet Measurement Conference (IMC) (2018)
43. MaxMind: GeoIP, August 2019. https://dev.maxmind.com/geoip/geoip2/geoip2-city-country-csv-databases/
44. Mayer, D.: University of Oregon Route-Views Archive Project, January 2020. http://routeviews.org
45. Padmanabhan, R., Schulman, A., Levin, D., Spring, N.: Residential links under the weather. In: ACM Proceedings of the ACM Special Interest Group on Data Communication (SIGCOMM), pp. 145–158 (2019)

46. PeeringDB, April 2019. https://www.peeringdb.com/
47. PeeringDB: Angola Cables, January 2020. https://www.peeringdb.com/net/4894
48. Phil, E.: A Map of all the Underwater Cables that Connect the Internet, November 2015. https://www.vox.com/2015/3/13/8204655/submarine-cables-internet
49. Poese, I., Uhlig, S., Kaafar, M.A., Donnet, B., Gueye, B.: IP geolocation databases: unreliable? ACM SIGCOMM Comput. Commun. Rev. **4**(2), 53–56 (2011)
50. Prior, B.: Teraco Data Centres Will Benefit from SACS Cable, November 2018. https://mybroadband.co.za/news/cloud-hosting/284682-teraco-data-centres-will-benefit-from-sacs-cable.html
51. RIPE NCC: Global RIPE Atlas Network Coverage, January 2020. https://atlas.ripe.net/results/maps/network-coverage/
52. RIPE NCC: RIPE Atlas: Built-in Measurements, January 2020. https://atlas.ripe.net/docs/built-in/
53. RIPE NCC: RIPE RIS, January 2020. https://www.ripe.net/analyse/internet-measurements/routing-information-service-ris/
54. RIPE NCC: RIPE Stats, January 2020. https://stat.ripe.net/
55. Shah, A., Fontugne, R., Papadopoulos, C.: Towards characterizing international routing detours. In: Proceedings of the ACM Asian Internet Engineering Conference (AINTEC) (2016)
56. Submarine Cable Networks: SACS, March 2018. https://www.submarinenetworks.com/systems/brazil-africa/sacs
57. Subsea World News: South Atlantic Cable System Launched in Angola, August 2019. https://subseaworldnews.com/2017/08/09/south-atlantic-cable-system-launched-in-angola/
58. Telegeography: Submarine Cable Frequently Asked Questions, January 2020. https://www2.telegeography.com/submarine-cable-faqs-frequently-asked-questions
59. Telegeography: Telegeography Submarine Cable Map, January 2020. https://www.submarinecablemap.com/
60. Vermeulen, J.: From Brazil to South Africa and Back in 98ms, April 2019. https://mybroadband.co.za/news/broadband/303574-from-brazil-to-south-africa-and-back-in-98ms.html

Topology: Alias Resolution

Alias Resolution Based on ICMP Rate Limiting

Kevin Vermeulen[1](✉), Burim Ljuma[1](✉), Vamsi Addanki[1](✉),
Matthieu Gouel[1](✉), Olivier Fourmaux[1](✉), Timur Friedman[1](✉),
and Reza Rejaie[2](✉)

[1] Sorbonne Université, Paris, France
{kevin.vermeulen,burim.ljuma,vamsi.krishna,matthieu.gouel,
olivier.fourmaux,timur.friedman}@sorbonne-universite.fr
[2] University of Oregon, Eugene, USA
reza@cs.uoregon.edu

Abstract. Alias resolution techniques (e.g., MIDAR) associate, mostly through active measurement, a set of IP addresses as belonging to a common router. These techniques rely on distinct router features that can serve as a signature. Their applicability is affected by router support of the features and the robustness of the signature. This paper presents a new alias resolution tool called Limited Ltd. that exploits ICMP rate limiting, a feature that is increasingly supported by modern routers that has not previously been used for alias resolution. It sends ICMP probes toward target interfaces in order to trigger rate limiting, extracting features from the probe reply loss traces. It uses a machine learning classifier to designate pairs of interfaces as aliases. We describe the details of the algorithm used by Limited Ltd. and illustrate its feasibility and accuracy. Limited Ltd. not only is the first tool that can perform alias resolution on IPv6 routers that do not generate monotonically increasing fragmentation IDs (e.g., Juniper routers) but it also complements the state-of-the-art techniques for IPv4 alias resolution. All of our code and the collected dataset are publicly available.

1 Introduction

Route traces obtained using `traceroute` and similar tools provide the basis for generating maps that reveal the inner structure of the Internet's many autonomously administered networks, but not necessarily at the right level of granularity for certain important tasks. Designing network protocols [42] and understanding fundamental properties of the Internet's topology [18] are best done with router-level maps. Rather than revealing routers, `traceroute` only provides the IP addresses of individual router interfaces. The process of grouping IP addresses into sets that each belong to a common router is called *alias resolution*, and this paper advances the state of the art in alias resolution.

A common approach to alias resolution is to send probe packets to IP addresses, eliciting reply packets that display a feature that is distinctive enough

A. Sperotto et al. (Eds.): PAM 2020, LNCS 12048, pp. 231–248, 2020.
https://doi.org/10.1007/978-3-030-44081-7_14

to constitute a signature, allowing replies coming from a common router to be matched. This paper describes a new type of signature based upon a functionality, *ICMP rate limiting*, in which an Internet-connected node (router or end-host) limits the ICMP traffic that it sends or receives within a certain window of time. This new signature enjoys much broader applicability than existing ones for IPv6 alias resolution, thanks to ICMP rate limiting being a required function for IPv6 nodes. The signature also complements IPv4 existing signatures.

Our contributions are: (1) The Limited Ltd. algorithm, a new signature-based alias resolution technique that improves alias resolution coverage by 68.4% on Internet2 for IPv6 and by 40.9% on SWITCH for IPv4 (2) a free, open source, and permissively licensed tool that implements the algorithm.

We evaluate Limited Ltd. by comparing its performance to two state-of-the-art alias resolution tools: Speedtrap [29] for IPv6, and MIDAR [26] for IPv4, using ground truth provided by the Internet2 and SWITCH networks.

The remainder of this paper is organized as follows: Sect. 2 provides technical background and related work for both alias resolution and ICMP rate limiting. Section 3 describes the Limited Ltd. technique in detail. Section 4 presents the evaluation. Section 5 discusses ethical considerations and Sect. 6 summarizes our conclusions and points to future work.

2   Background and Related Work

Limited Ltd. is the latest in a long line of alias resolution methods stretching back over twenty-plus years. An inventory of all previously known techniques (Table 1) shows that there are only four techniques known to work for IPv6. Of these, there is a publicly-available tool for only one: Speedtrap [29]. But Speedtrap has a known limitation of only working on routers that generate monotonically increasing IPv6 fragmentation IDs, whereas there is an entire class of routers, such as those from Juniper, that do not generate IDs this way. Relying upon monotonically increasing IP IDs for IPv4, as does state-of-the-art MIDAR [26], presents a different issue: fewer and fewer routers treat IPv4 IP IDs this way due to a potential vulnerability [2,15]. Limited Ltd. is a publicly available tool that does not rely upon monotonically increasing IDs, thereby enabling IPv6 alias resolution on Juniper routers for the first time and IPv4 alias resolution on a growing class of routers for which MIDAR will no longer work.

Regarding ICMP, the Internet Control Message Protocol: its IPv4 and IPv6 variants [13,34] allow routers or end-hosts to send error and informational messages. The RFC for ICMPv6 [13] cites the "bandwidth and forwarding costs" of originating ICMP messages to motivate the need to limit the rate at which a node originates ICMP messages. It also recommends the use of a token bucket mechanism for rate limiting. It explicitly calls for compatibility with `traceroute` by stating that "Rate-limiting mechanisms that cannot cope with bursty traffic (e.g., traceroute) are not recommended". Furthermore, it states that, in the case of "ICMP messages [being] used to attempt denial-of-service attacks by sending back to back erroneous IP packets", an implementation that correctly deploys

Table 1. Alias resolution methods

Year	Basis (s) = signature (t) = topology (o) = other	Algorithms and tools	Condition of applicability	IPv4 (τ) = tool (δ) = dataset	IPv6
1998 [32]	Source IP address (s)	Pansiot and Grad [32]	Respond with a common IP address in ICMP Destination Unreachable messages	Yes	
		Mercator [16]		Yes (τ) (δ)	
2002 [40]	IP ID (s)	Ally [40]	Send replies with a shared IP ID counter that increases monotonically with each reply	Yes (τ)	
		RadarGun [7]		Yes (τ)	
		MIDAR [26]		Yes (τ) (δ)	
2002 [40]	Reverse DNS (o)	Rocketfuel [40] AROMA [28]	IP address resolves to a name	Yes	Yes
2006 [17]	traceroute (t)	APAR [17]	Respond with ICMP Time Exceeded messages	Yes	
		kapar [25]		Yes (τ) (δ)	
2010 [38]	IP Prespecified Timestamp option (s)	Sherry et al. [38] Pythia [30]	Fill in timestamps as specified by the option	yes	
2010 [36]	IPv6 source routing (s)	Qian et al. [35,36]	Source routing must be enabled		Yes
2013 [29]	IPv6 fragmentation identifier (s)	Speedtrap [29]	IDs elicited from responses increase monotonically		Yes (τ) (δ)
2013 [39]	IP Record Route option (t)	DisCarte [39]	Fill in IP addresses as specified by the option	Yes	
2015 [31]	IPv6 unused address (s)	Padman-abhan et al. [31]	126 prefixes on a point to point link		Yes
2019	ICMP rate limiting (s)	Limited Ltd.	ICMP rate limiting shared by interfaces of the router	Yes (τ) (δ)	Yes (τ) (δ)

the recommended token bucket mechanism "would be protected by the ICMP error rate limiting mechanism". The RFC makes ICMP rate limiting mandatory for all IPv6 nodes. ICMP rate limiting is a supported feature on all modern routers but its implementation may vary by vendor [9,11,12,14,20,22–24] based on ICMP message type and IP version. ICMP rate limiting can be performed on incoming traffic or generated replies. Limited Ltd. makes no distinction between the two. It works whenever multiple interfaces of a router are subject to a common ICMP rate limiting mechanism, i.e., when there is a shared token bucket across multiple interfaces. Vendor documentation [11,20,23,24], indicates that `ping` packets are more likely to trigger shared ICMP rate limiting behavior. We validated this observation in a prior survey and in a lab environment. In particular on Juniper (model J4350, JunOS 8.0R2.8), we observed a shared ICMP rate limiting mechanism for Echo Reply, Destination Unreachable and Time Exceeded packets across all of its interfaces by default. But on Cisco (model 3825, IOS 12.3), we observed that the rates for Time Exceeded and Destination Unreachable packets are limited on individual interfaces by default, and only the rate for Echo Reply packets is shared across different interfaces [10]. Therefore, we adopted the `ping` Echo Request and Echo Reply mechanism in our tool to maximize the chances of encountering shared ICMP rate limits across router interfaces.

A few prior studies have examined ICMP rate limiting behavior in the Internet. Ravaioli et al. [37] identified two types of behavior when triggering ICMP rate limiting of Time Exceeded messages by an interface: on/off and non on/off. Alvarez et al. [4] demonstrated that ICMP Time Exceeded rate limiting is more widespread in IPv6 than in IPv4. Guo and Heidemann [19] later proposed an algorithm, FADER, to detect ICMP Echo Request/Reply rate limiting at very low probing rates, up to 1 packet per second. They found rate limiting at those rates for very few /24 prefixes. Our work is the first one that exploits the shared nature of ICMP rate limiting across different interfaces of a router as a signature to relate these interfaces for alias resolution.

3 Algorithm

The main intuition behind our approach is that two interfaces of a router that implements shared ICMP rate limiting, should exhibit a similar loss pattern if they are both probed by ICMP packets at a cumulative rate that triggers rate limiting. The key challenges are to efficiently trigger rate limiting and reliably associate aliases based on the similarity of their loss patterns despite the noise due to independent losses of probes and replies.

Pseudo code 1 describes how Limited Ltd. divides a set of input IP addresses into subsets that should each be an alias set. It proceeds iteratively, taking the following steps in each iteration: First, a random IP address from the input set is selected as a *seed*, with all remaining members of the input set being *candidate* aliases for the seed. The seed is probed at incrementally higher rates until the rate r_s that induces ICMP rate limiting is identified (`find_rate()`). Then, the seed is probed at that rate of r_s while all of the candidates interfaces are simultaneously probed at low rates. All probing takes place from a single vantage point. Loss traces for reply packets from the seed and each of the candidate interfaces are gathered. It is very challenging to infer that two interfaces are aliases by directly correlating their loss traces. Instead, the algorithm extracts a set of features from each loss trace and collectively uses these as the signatures of the corresponding interfaces(`signatures()`). Using a classification technique (`classify()`), the algorithm examines whether the signatures of candidate and seed are sufficiently similar to classify them as aliases, in which case the candidate is added to an alias set (A_s). Each identified alias set is refined through further testing in order to reduce the chance of false positives (`refine()`). Finally, the alias set is removed from the input set, and iterations continue until the input set is empty. The remainder of this section further details these steps.

Algorithm 1 `Limited Ltd.`

Input
    S: a set of IP addresses
Output
    A: a set of alias sets
  $K \leftarrow \texttt{controls}(S)$: set of controls
  $A \leftarrow \emptyset$
while $S \neq \emptyset$ **do**
    choose at random a seed $s \in S$
    $C_s \leftarrow S \setminus \{s\}$: candidate aliases for s
    $r_s \leftarrow \texttt{find\_rate}(s)$: rate limiting rate for s
    $\Sigma_s \leftarrow \texttt{signatures}(s, r_s, C_s, K)$: set of signatures
    $A_s \leftarrow \{s\}$: alias set for s
    for $c \in C_s$ **do**: for each candidate c
      $\sigma_{s,c} \in \Sigma_s$ is the pairwise signature for s and c
      if $\texttt{classify}(\sigma_{s,c}) == \textbf{true}$ **then**
        s and c are aliases
        $A_s \leftarrow A_s \cup \{c\}$: add c to the alias set
    $A_s \leftarrow \texttt{refine}(A_s)$: try to reduce false positives
    $A \leftarrow A \cup \{A_s\}$: add the new alias set to A
    $S \leftarrow S \setminus A_s$: remove the aliases of s from S
  return A

3.1 Triggering ICMP Rate Limiting

The goal of `find_rate`(s) is to efficiently determine r_s, the probing rate that triggers ICMP rate limiting at the router to which seed s belongs. It proceeds by probing the seed with ICMP Echo Request probes across multiple rounds, increasing the probing rate with each round until the loss rate of observed ICMP Echo Replies enters a target range. The target loss range should be sufficiently large to minimize the effect of random independent losses and also relatively small to minimize the load on the router. To satisfy these two opposing conditions, we empirically set the range at 5 to 10%. The probing rate remains constant during each round. The rate is low (64 pps) for the first round, and exponentially increases in consecutive rounds until the loss rate falls within (or exceeds) the target range.[1] If the observed loss rate is within the target range, the probing is concluded and the last rate is reported as r_s. But if the loss rate is higher than the target range, up to eight additional rounds are launched in a binary search between the last two rates. If the loss rate still does not fall within the target range, the probing rate that generates the loss rate closest to the range

---

[1] We have explicitly verified that the actual probing rate is not limited by the network card or other factors.

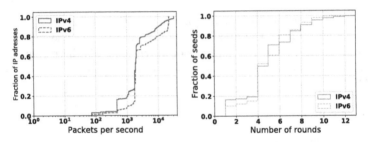

Fig. 1. CDF of the probing rate r_s (left) and the number of probing rounds (right) to trigger ICMP rate limiting for 2,277 IPv4 and 1,099 IPv6 addresses.

is chosen. If the target loss range is not reached as the probing reaches a maximum rate (32,768 pps), the probing process ends without any conclusion. The duration of each round of probing should be sufficiently long to reliably capture the loss rate while it should also be limited to control the overhead of probing. We experimentally set the duration of each round of probing to 5 s, followed by a period, of equal length, of no probing. The right plot of Fig. 1 presents the CDF of the number of probing rounds to trigger the target loss rate for thousands of IPv4 and IPv6 interfaces (using our dataset from Sect. 3.3). We observe that for 90% of IPv4 or IPv6 interfaces, the ICMP rate limiting is triggered in less than 8 rounds of probing. The left plot of Fig. 1 shows the CDF of the probing rate that triggered the target loss rate (i.e., the inferred rate for triggering the ICMP rate limiting) across the same IPv4 and IPv6 interfaces. This figure indicates that for 70% (80%) of IPv6 (IPv4) interfaces, ICMP rate limiting is triggered at less than 2k pps. This result confirms that our selected min and max probing rate covers a proper probing range for more than 99% of interfaces. We note that the binary search process failed to reach the target loss rate for fewer than 1% of the interfaces. All the parameters of our probing strategy are empirically determined. Section 5 elaborates on the ethical considerations associated with the probing scheme.

3.2 Generating Interface Signatures

A signature based on the loss traces of individual interfaces is obtained by probing the seed interface at its target rate (r_s) while simultaneously probing each candidate interface at the low rate of R_c pps. Probing a large number of candidate interfaces in each round may lead to a better efficiency, but the aggregate probing rate should remain low so that it does not independently trigger ICMP rate limiting even if all those candidates are in fact aliases. To address these two constraints, we set the number of candidate interfaces that are considered in each round to 50 and R_c to 10 pps. In an unlikely scenario that all of these 50 candidate interfaces are aliases, this strategy leads to a 500 pps probing rate

Table 2. Selected features for a Signature.

	Seed s	Candidate c	Control κ_s	Control κ_c
Loss rate	x	x	x	x
Change point	x	x		
gap → gap transition probability	x	x		
burst → burst transition probability	x	x		
Pearson correlation coefficient	x			

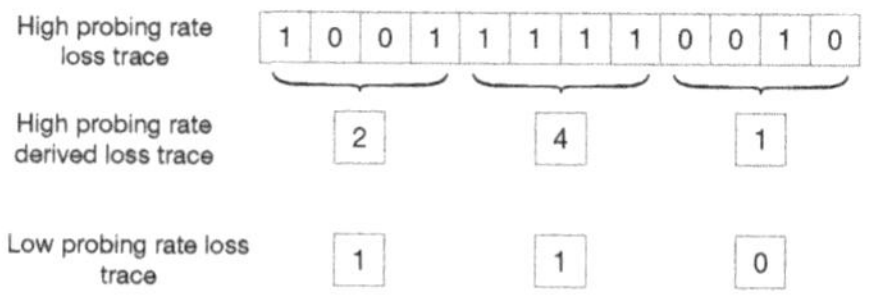

High probing rate loss trace: 1 0 0 1 1 1 1 1 0 0 1 0

High probing rate derived loss trace: 2 4 1

Low probing rate loss trace: 1 1 0

Fig. 2. Mapping between loss traces with different length.

for the corresponding router that does not trigger ICMP rate limiting in 90% of routers, as we showed in the left plot of Fig. 1.[2]

Control Interface. In order to distinguish the observed losses in the loss traces for the target interfaces (i.e., seed s and individual candidate c) that are not related to ICMP rate limiting, we also consider another interface along the route to each target interface and concurrently probe them at a low rate (10 pps). These interfaces are called the *controls*, κ_s and κ_c. The control κ_i for target interface i is identified by conducting a Paris Traceroute [6] towards i and selecting the last responsive IP address prior to i.[3] The loss rate for κ_i also forms part of i's signature. In practice, the *controls* are identified at the beginning of the Limited Ltd. procedure by conducting route traces to all IP addresses in the input set S. This corresponds to controls() and K is the resulting set of controls.

Inferring Alias Pairs. The above probing strategy produces a separate loss trace for each interface. We have found that when losses occur simultaneously at pairs of alias interfaces, they can do so in multiple ways, as the five examples in Fig. 4 illustrate. The black and white strokes in each trace correspond respectively to received and lost ICMP Echo Replies, and their varied patterns defy attempts to find simple correlations. We therefore use a machine learning classifier to identify pairs of aliases. It is based on the following features extracted from loss traces that, intuitively, we believe capture the temporal pattern of the losses in each trace. (See also Table 2.)

1. Loss rate: This is simply the number of losses in the trace divided by the total number of probes in the trace.

---

[2] The largest reported alias set by MIDAR and Speedtrap has 43 interfaces. Therefore, the likelihood of observing 50 candidate interfaces that are all aliases is low.

[3] Limited Ltd. maintains the flow ID necessary to reach κ_s in subsequent probing of s and κ_s.

238   K. Vermeulen et al.

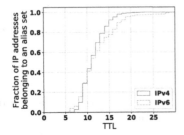

Fig. 3. CDF of the TTL distance from the Limited Ltd. vantage point of the IP addresses belonging to an alias set in our training data.

Fig. 4. Raw times series of loss traces of pairs of aliases.

2. Change point detection: This is the point in a time series (such as our loss traces) when the probability distribution of a time series changes [5]. We adopt a method based on the variation of the mean and the variance [27].
3. Transition probabilities: These are obtained by using each loss trace to train a Gilbert-Elliot two-state Markov model, in which losses occur in the burst state and no losses occur in the gap state. The P(gap → gap) and P(burst → burst) transition probabilities are sufficient to fully describe the model since other two probabilities can be easily calculated from these. For example, P(gap → burst) = 1 − P(gap → gap).
4. Correlation coefficient: The Pearson correlation coefficient between the two loss traces is used as a measure of similarity between them. Calculating this coefficient requires both time series to have the same number of values but our loss traces do not meet this condition since we use a higher probing rate for the seed. To address this issue, we condition the seed's loss trace to align it with the loss trace of other interfaces as shown in Fig. 2. In this example, the length of the loss trace of the seed is four times longer than the ones from the other interfaces. We consider groups of four consecutive bits in the seed loss trace and convert it to the sum of the 1's. The resulting loss trace has a lower rate and can be directly correlated with other loss traces.

3.3 Classifying the Signatures

We use the *random forest* classifier from the scikit-learn Python machine learning library [33]. If it identifies two interfaces as aliases based on their signatures, classify() returns true; otherwise, false. There are several challenges to building such a classifier: (1) it must learn from training data that represents the diversity of possible loss traces generated by pairs of aliases; (2) it should be able to distinguish between losses triggered by ICMP rate limiting and unrelated losses; (3) it should have a high precision, so that Limited Ltd. minimizes false positives; and (4) if the training data come from other alias resolution techniques, such as MIDAR and Speedtrap, it must be able to generalize to pairs that they cannot find. We tackled these challenges as follows.

Training and Testing Data. We have access to ground truth router-level topology for two networks, Internet2 and SWITCH, but these do not suffice to capture the richness of router behaviors in the Internet as a whole. We therefore randomly selected routable IPv4 and IPv6 prefixes from the RIPE registry [3], and conducted multipath Paris Traceroute [41] from PlanetLab Europe [1] nodes towards the first address in each prefix. This procedure yielded 25,172 IPv4 addresses in 1,671 autonomous systems (ASes) and 18,346 IPv6 addresses in 1,759 ASes from 6,246 and 4,185 route traces, respectively. We use MIDAR and Speedtrap to identify IPv4 and IPv6 alias sets, respectively, since both tools are known to have low false positive rates. Pairs of interfaces from these sets are used as labeled as `true`. For the `false` labels, we take the conservative approach of selecting pairs of IP addresses that are more than 6 hops from each other in a given route trace. The 6 hop value is empirically set, as 99.9% of the alias pairs identified by MIDAR and Speedtrap are fewer than 6 hops apart. This labeling process identified 70,992 unique IPv4 and 7,000 unique IPv6 addresses. 15,747 of IPv4 and 1,616 IPv6 addresses are labeled as aliases forming 2,277 IPv4 and 1,099 IPv6 alias sets, respectively. Figure 3 shows the CDF of hop count distance between our vantage point and selected IP addresses and indicates that these targets are 7–17 hops away from the vantage point. For each alias set, one address is chosen at random to play the role of the seed s, and the candidate set is composed of all of the other aliases in the set that are rounded up with some randomly selected non-aliases to make a C_s of size between 2 (minimum one alias and one non-alias) and 50 (our cap for the number of addresses to be simultaneously probed at a low rate). The high rate r_s at which to probe the seed is found through `find_rate`(s), and the signatures are generated through `signatures`(s, r_s, C_s, K).

Note that while our classifier is trained on alias sets identified by alias resolution techniques with known limitations, it is nonetheless able to identify new alias sets. We argue that this is because the training set is sufficiently rich due to its size and random selection of interfaces, providing considerable diversity and heterogeneity of loss traces across aliases. Our evaluation in Sect. 4 confirms this observation and confirms the ability of our technique to generalize patterns in the training dataset, i.e., the fourth aforementioned challenge.

Choice of Classifier. We compared the performance of four classifiers that `scikit-learn` library offers, namely random forest, multilayer perceptron, k-nearest neighbors (KNN), and support vector machines (SVM). To this end, we evenly divided our dataset into a training and a test set, and compared these classifiers based on their precision, recall, and F1 score for both IPv4 and IPv6 datasets. Since `true` labels are only provided from aliases identified by MIDAR and Speedtrap, the recall values correspond to the portion of pairs of aliases in our training set that are detectable by both MIDAR and Limited Ltd. (IPv4) or by both Speedtrap and Limited Ltd. (IPv6). Table 3 presents the averaged result of this comparison after performing 10 randomized splits of the training and test sets. All classifiers exhibit relatively good performance. We have decided to use

Table 3. Classifier performance on our test set averaged over ten training/testings.

	IPv4			IPv6		
	Precision	Recall	F1 score	Precision	Recall	F1 score
Random forest	0.990	0.499	0.652	0.992	0.647	0.782
Multilayer perceptron	0.993	0.431	0.591	0.978	0.641	0.769
KNN	0.952	0.638	0.764	0.970	0.622	0.756
SVM	0.986	0.478	0.642	0.988	0.599	0.743

Table 4. The five most important features of our random forest classifiers.

	Gini index	
Feature	IPv4	IPv6
loss rate for the candidate c	0.169	0.192
burst $\rightarrow$ burst transition probability for the candidate c	0.113	0.125
burst $\rightarrow$ burst transition probability for the seed s	0.101	0.121
Pearson correlation coefficient	0.091	0.109
loss rate for κ_c, the control of the candidate c	0.077	0.104

the random forest classifier, which is composed of 500 trees, as it has the highest precision for both IPv4 and IPv6, and the best F1 score for the IPv6 dataset.

Finally, Table 4 shows the five most important features of our random forest classifiers based on the Gini index [8] that describes the weight of individual features in the classifier's decision. This table reveals a few important points. First, no single feature dominates the classifier's decision, particularly for IPv6. This confirms the complexity of the patterns for relating loss traces of aliases, as they cannot be accurately learned by a small number of features or simple threshold-based rules. Second, this table also illustrates that most of our engineered features are indeed very important in distinguishing loss traces of aliases. Third, the use of κ_c as one of the main features suggests that the classifier distinguishes losses related to rate limiting from other losses.

3.4 Refining the Alias Set

Independent network loss could accidentally result in classifying unrelated interfaces as aliases, i.e., generating false positives. To reduce the chance of this, Limited Ltd. incorporates a refinement step, `refine`(A_s), that involves repeating `signature()` and `classify()` on the previously-identified alias set A_s. If a candidate c fails to be (re)classified as an alias of the seed s, it is removed from the alias set. This step is repeated until the alias set remains unchanged over two iterations. Section 4 evaluates the resulting reduction of false positives.

4 Evaluation

We evaluate Limited Ltd. with regards to its ability (i) to identify alias pairs that state-of-the-art techniques, namely MIDAR and Speedtrap, are unable to identify, and (ii) to maintain a low rate of false positives.

Table 5. Evaluation on ground truth networks.

		IPv4			IPv6		
		MIDAR	ltd ltd	MIDAR ∪ ltd ltd	Speedtrap	ltd ltd	Speedtrap ∪ ltd ltd
Internet2	Precision	1.000	1.000	1.000	N/A	1.000	1.000
	Recall	0.673	0.800	0.868	N/A	0.684	0.684
SWITCH	Precision	1.000	1.000	1.000	1.000	1.000	1.000
	Recall	0.090	0.499	0.599	0.384	0.385	0.772

Dataset. We evaluate Limited Ltd. on ground truth data from the Internet2 and SWITCH networks. For Internet2, router configuration files were obtained on 10 April, with measurements conducted on 11 and 12 April 2019. There were 44 files, each corresponding to a single router. All are Juniper routers. The files concern 985 IPv4 and 803 IPv6 addresses/interfaces, from which we removed 436 IPv4 addresses and 435 IPv6 addresses that did not respond to any probes sent by either MIDAR, Speedtrap, or Limited Ltd. The resulting dataset consists of 6,577 IPv4 and 2,556 IPv6 alias pairs. For SWITCH, a single file was obtained on 3 May, with measurements conducted 3–5 May 2019. The file identified 173 Cisco routers running either IOS or IOS-XR. From the 1,073 IPv4 and 706 IPv6 addresses listed in the file, we removed 121 IPv4 and 29 IPv6 unresponsive addresses. The resulting dataset consists of 4,912 IPv4 and 2,641 IPv6 alias pairs.

Reducing False Positives. We computed the distribution of number of rounds for `refine()` to finalize the alias set for each seed in our dataset: For 79% (98%) of all seeds, `refine()` takes 2 (3) more rounds. Note that the minimum of two rounds is required by design (Sect. 3.4). This basically implies that `refine()` only changed the alias set for 20% of the seeds in a single round.

Results. Table 5 presents the precision and recall of MIDAR, Speedtrap, Limited Ltd., and the union of both tools on IPv4 and IPv6 ground truth data from the Internet2 and SWITCH networks. Note that it is possible for recall from the union of both tools to be greater than the sum of recall values for individual tools, as we observe in the SWITCH results. This arises from the transitive closure of alias sets identified from the two tools that leads to the detection of additional alias pairs. The main findings of Table 5 can be summarized as follows:

1. Limited Ltd. exhibits a high precision in identifying both IPv4 and IPv6 alias pairs from both networks with zero false positives.
2. Limited Ltd. can effectively discover IPv6 aliases that state-of-the-art Speedtrap is unable to find. In the Internet2 network that uses Juniper routers, Limited Ltd. was able to identify 68.4% of the IPv6 alias pairs while Speedtrap was unable to identify any. In the SWITCH network that deploys Cisco routers, Limited Ltd. and Speedtrap show comparable performance by identifying 38.5% and 38.4% of the IPv6 alias pairs, respectively. The results were

complementary, with the two tools together identifying 77.2% of the IPv6 alias pairs, a small boost beyond simple addition of the two results coming from the transitive closure of the alias sets found by each tool.
3. Limited Ltd. can discover IPv4 aliases that state-of-the-art MIDAR is unable to find. In the Internet2 network, Limited Ltd. identifies 80.0% while MIDAR detects 67.3% of aliases. In the SWITCH networks, Limited Ltd. identified 49.9% while MIDAR detects only 9.0% of all aliases.

A couple of detailed observations follow. We conducted follow up analysis on the behavior of Speedtrap and MIDAR to ensure proper assessment of these tools. First, we examined Speedtrap's logs to diagnose Speedtrap's inability to detect any IPv6 aliases for Internet2. We noticed that every fragmentation identifier time series that Speedtrap seeks to use as a signature, was either labeled as random or unresponsive. This was not surprising, as prior work on Speedtrap [29] also reported that this technique does not apply to the Juniper routers that primarily comprise Internet2. Second, we explored MIDAR's logs to investigate the cause of its low recall for SWITCH. We learned that only one third of the IPv4 addresses in this network have monotonically increasing IP IDs.

Limitations and Future Work. Because ICMP rate limiting could be triggered at thousands of packets per second, Limited Ltd. requires the sending of many more packets than other state-of-the-art alias resolution techniques. The maximum observed probing rate during the experiments for this paper was 34,000 pps from a single vantage point during a 5 s round. On Internet2 (SWITCH), MIDAR and Speedtrap sent 164.5k (106k) and 4k (12.7k) probe packets while Limited Ltd. sent about 4,8M (12.7M) packets. In future work, we plan to explore ways to reduce the overhead of probing and make Limited Ltd. more scalable.

5   Ethical Considerations

Limited Ltd. works by triggering limits in routers that are there for protective reasons. This raises ethical concerns, which we discuss below. To evaluate the impact of Limited Ltd., we have taken two steps: experiments in a lab environment (Sect. 5.1 and Appendix A), and feedback from operators (Sect. 5.2).

5.1   Lab Experiments

We have run experiments in a lab environment on conservatively chosen hardware (over 10 years old) to show that Limited Ltd. has a controlled impact. Our findings are that: (1) routers being probed with Echo Requests by the tool remain reachable to others via ping with a high probability; and (2) Router CPUs show a manageable overhead at the highest probing rate, leading us to believe that our measurements are unlikely to impact the control and data planes. (3) Both Limited Ltd. and existing measurement techniques impact troubleshooting efforts (e.g., `ping`, `traceroute`). Limited Ltd. does not stand out in terms of impact compared with other accepted techniques. Appendix A details the experiments which support these conclusions.

5.2   Real-World Operator Feedback

In addition to lab experiments, we conducted joint experiments with SURFNET and SWITCH to evaluate the potential impact of Limited Ltd. The experiment consisted in running Limited Ltd. on their routers while they were monitoring the CPU usage. Each run lasted about 1 min. For SURFNET, we ran Limited Ltd. on two Juniper routers: an MX240 and an MX204. The operator observed a 4% and 2% CPU overhead. The operator also told us that the CPU overhead was observed on the MPC (line modules) CPU and not the central routing engine CPU. For SWITCH, we ran Limited Ltd. on three Cisco routers: an NCS 55A1, an ASR 9001, and an ASR-920-24SZ-M. On the two first routers, the operator told us that there was no observable change in CPU utilization. On the third router, which has a lower CPU capacity than the two others, the operator observed a CPU overhead up to 29%. These results confirm our belief that Limited Ltd. is unlikely to impact the control and data planes.

6   Conclusion

This paper presents Limited Ltd., a new, high-precision alias resolution technique for both IPv4 and IPv6 networks that leverages the ICMP rate limiting feature of individual routers. We have shown that ICMP rate limiting can generate loss traces that can be used to reliably identify aliases from other interfaces. Limited Ltd. enables IPv6 alias resolution on networks composed of Juniper routers that the state-of-the-art Speedtrap technique is not able to identify. As a part of our future work, we plan to enhance the efficiency of Limited Ltd. and explore the use of ICMP rate limiting for fingerprinting individual routers. Both the source code for Limited Ltd. and our dataset are publicly available[4].

Acknowledgments. We thank Niels den Otter from SURFNET and Simon Leinen from SWITCH network for their time in conducting joint experiments of Limited Ltd. We thank people from Internet2 and SWITCH for providing the ground truth of their network. We thank the anonymous reviewers from both the PAM TPC and our shepherd, for their careful reading of this paper and suggestions for its improvement. Kevin Vermeulen, Olivier Fourmaux, and Timur Friedman are associated with Sorbonne Université, CNRS, Laboratoire d'informatique de Paris 6, LIP6, F-75005 Paris, France. Kevin Vermeulen and Timur Friedman are associated with the Laboratory of Information, Networking and Communication Sciences, LINCS, F-75013 Paris, France. A research grant from the French Ministry of Defense has made this work possible.

---

[4] https://gitlab.planet-lab.eu/cartography.

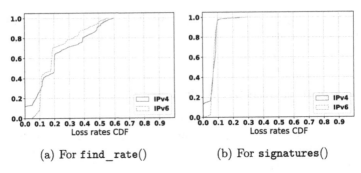

(a) For find_rate()   (b) For signatures()

Fig. 5. Maximum loss rates

A   Ethical Considerations

A.1   Precautions Taken

We take two precautions, that we understand to be community best practice: We sent all probing traffic from IP addresses that were clearly associated via WHOIS with their host locations, either at our institution or others hosting PlanetLab Europe nodes. We have also set up a web server on the probing machines with a contact email, so that any network operators could opt out from our experiment. We received no notice whatsoever from network operators expressing concern about our measurements. Though this is a positive sign, it could be that there are impacts that were not noticed, or that the concerns did not reach us. We therefore pushed our examination further, as detailed in the following sections.

A.2   Impact on Other Measurements

Limited Ltd.'s find_rate() aims to find an ICMP Echo Request probing rate that produces an Echo Reply trace with a loss rate in the $[0.05, 0.10]$ range. While it is searching for this rate, it can induce a loss rate above 0.10. If it does so, it proceeds to a binary search to find a lower probing rate for which traces falls within the desired range. Figure 5 shows that loss rates can go as high as 0.60.

The impact on reachability for the IP addresses of that node is that there is a worst case 0.60 probability that a single ping packet to such an address will not receive a response if it arrives at the node during the five seconds of highest rate probing time. Most pings occur in series of packets, so the worst case probabilities are 0.36 for two ping packets being lost, 0.22 for three, 0.13 for four, 0.08 for five, and 0.05 for six. These are worst case probabilities for the five seconds at highest loss rate. Average reachability failure probabilities are 0.22 for one ping packet, 0.05 for two, 0.01 for three, and so on, while a node is being probed at its highest rate. To judge whether such a level of interference with other measurements is exceptional, we compare it to the impact of the state-of-the-art MIDAR tool. MIDAR has a phase during which it elicits three series of 30 responses each,

```
traceroute to 83.99.240.90 (83.99.240.90), 30 hops max, 60 byte packets
 1  132.227.123.1   0.350 ms  0.308 ms  0.363 ms
 2  134.157.167.125 0.342 ms  0.435 ms  0.415 ms
 3  134.157.254.124 0.495 ms  0.468 ms  0.444 ms
 4  195.221.127.181 0.359 ms  0.350 ms  0.327 ms
 5  193.51.181.102  1.326 ms  1.325 ms  1.303 ms
 6  193.51.180.108  1.395 ms  1.290 ms 193.51.177.117  1.239 ms
 7  83.97.89.9      1.029 ms  1.011 ms  0.989 ms
 8  * * *
 9  62.40.98.36     8.879 ms  8.866 ms  8.951 ms
10  * * *
11  87.245.233.222  38.814 ms  38.846 ms  38.902 ms
12  87.245.242.26   39.142 ms 87.245.242.29  38.878 ms 87.245.242.26  39.012 ms
13  85.254.1.16     39.105 ms 85.254.1.128  39.029 ms 85.254.1.16  39.236 ms
14  82.193.72.232   39.287 ms  39.548 ms 82.193.72.130  39.619 ms
15  83.99.240.90    45.451 ms * *
```

(a) Before and after MIDAR run

```
traceroute to 83.99.240.90 (83.99.240.90), 30 hops max, 60 byte packets
 1  132.227.123.1   0.436 ms  0.341 ms  0.343 ms
 2  * * *
 3  134.157.254.124 0.421 ms  0.457 ms  0.434 ms
 4  195.221.127.181 0.358 ms  0.349 ms  0.319 ms
 5  193.51.181.102  1.209 ms  1.196 ms  1.200 ms
 6  193.51.177.117  8.860 ms 193.51.180.108  0.948 ms 193.51.177.117  0.896 ms
 7  63.97.89.9      0.975 ms  0.973 ms  0.950 ms
 8  * * *
 9  62.40.98.36     8.565 ms  8.607 ms  8.544 ms
10  * * *
11  87.245.233.222  38.801 ms  38.768 ms  38.748 ms
12  87.245.242.29   38.945 ms 87.245.242.26  39.009 ms  38.988 ms
13  85.254.1.16     39.028 ms  39.065 ms  39.070 ms
14  82.193.72.232   39.238 ms  39.426 ms 82.193.72.130  39.400 ms
15  * * *
16  * * *
17  * * *
18  * * *
19  * * *
20  * 83.99.240.90  45.314 ms *
```

(b) While MIDAR is running

Fig. 6. Example erroneous `traceroute` result

using different methods for each series: TCP SYN packets, to elicit TCP RST or TCP SYN-ACK responses; UDP packets to a high port number, to elicit ICMP Destination Unreachable responses; and ICMP Echo Request packets, to elicit ICMP Echo Reply responses [26]. The probing rate is very low compared to Limited Ltd.: a mere 100 packets per second across multiple addresses. This is not a concern for the TCP and ICMP probing. However, the UDP probing taps into an ICMP rate limiting mechanism that tends to be much less robust than the typical ICMP Echo Reply mechanism on some routers. ICMP Destination Unreachable messages are often rate limited at 2 packets per second, which is $1/500^{\text{th}}$ the typical rate at which ICMP Echo Reply messages are rate limited. (For example, the default rate at which Cisco routers limit ICMP Destination Unreachable messages is 1 every 500 ms.)

We found that, when an IP address is a `traceroute` destination, MIDAR can completely block ICMP Destination Unreachable messages coming from that destination. Figure 6 illustrates the impact. The figure shows two `traceroute` results, the top one from before or after MIDAR being run, and the bottom one during MIDAR probing. During the MIDAR run, we see that `traceroute` receives no responses while it is probing hop 15, where the destination is in fact to be found. The normal functioning of `traceroute` is to continue probing at higher and higher hop counts. Only a few seconds later, when `traceroute` is sending probes to hop 20, does it start to receive ICMP Destination Unreachable messages from the destination. The result is an erroneous `traceroute`, indicating that the destination is five hops further away than it actually is. We observed this erroneous `traceroute` effect on 2,196 IP addresses out of a dataset of 10,000 IPv4 addresses collected from across the Internet. For both Limited Ltd. and MIDAR, transient interference with other measurements can be observed for the few seconds during which an IP address is being probed. Our conclusion is not that the diminution in `ping` reachability induced by Limited Ltd. is necessarily anodyne. Care should be taken to circumscribe this effect. But we observe that it does not stand out in terms of its impact on other measurements.

CPU Usage. We now examine the CPU overhead generated by Limited Ltd., and its potential impact on the forwarding plane and other features involving the CPU. We have run an experiment in a local network with our own Cisco (model 3825, IOS 12.3) and Juniper (model J4350, JunOS 8.0R2.8) routers. The experiment consists in measuring three metrics while find_rate() routine of Limited Ltd., which has the highest probing rate, is running. We measured: (1) The CPU usage of the router, (2) the throughput of a TCP connection between the two end hosts, and (3) the rate of BGP updates. ICMP rate limiting is configured on both our Juniper and Cisco routers with an access list [10,21], limiting the ICMP input bandwidth destined to the router to 1,000 packets per second, which is the default configuration on Juniper routers.

TCP throughput was unaffected, at an average of 537 Mbps and BGP updates remained constant at 10 per second. CPU usage was at 5% for Cisco and 15% for Juniper when Limited Ltd. was not probing. During the probing, the maximum overhead was triggered for both at a maximum probing rate of 2,048 packets per second, with a peak at 10% for Cisco and 40% for Juniper during 5 s. Our conclusion is that there is an impact of high probing rates on CPU, but we do not witness a disruptive impact on either the data plane (TCP throughput) or the control plane (BGP update rate).

References

1. PlanetLab Europe. https://www.planet-lab.eu
2. Private communication with CAIDA
3. RIPE Registry. https://www.ripe.net/publications/docs/ripe-508
4. Alvarez, P., Oprea, F., Rule, J.: Rate-limiting of IPv6 traceroutes is widespread: measurements and mitigations. In: Proceedings of IETF, vol. 99 (2017)
5. Aminikhanghahi, S., Cook, D.J.: A survey of methods for time series change point detection. Knowl. Inf. Syst. **51**(2), 339–367 (2017)
6. Augustin, B., et al.: Avoiding traceroute anomalies with Paris Traceroute. In: Proceedings of IMC (2006)
7. Bender, A., Sherwood, R., Spring, N.: Fixing Ally's growing pains with velocity modeling. In: Proceedings of IMC (2008)
8. Breiman, L., Friedman, J., Olshen, R., Stone, C.: Classification and Regression Trees. Wadsworth and Brooks, Monterey (1984)
9. Cisco: Cisco IOS quality of service solutions configuration guide, release 12.2SR. In: Policing and Shaping Overview. https://www.cisco.com/c/en/us/td/docs/ios/qos/configuration/guide/12_2sr/qos_12_2sr_book/polcing_shping_oview.html
10. Cisco: Configure commonly used IP ACLs. https://www.cisco.com/c/en/us/support/docs/ip/access-lists/26448-ACLsamples.html
11. Cisco: Control plane policing implementation best practices. https://www.cisco.com/c/en/us/about/security-center/copp-best-practices.html#7
12. Cisco: IPv6 ICMP rate limiting. https://www.cisco.com/c/en/us/td/docs/ios-xml/ios/ipv6_basic/configuration/xe-3s/ip6b-xe-3s-book/ip6-icmp-rate-lmt-xe.pdf
13. Conta, A., Gupta, M.: RFC 4443, Internet Control Message Protocol (ICMPv6) for the Internet Protocol version 6 (IPv6) specification. IETF (2006)
14. Deal, R.A.: Cisco router firewall security: DoS protection. http://www.ciscopress.com/articles/article.asp?p=345618&seqNum=5

15. Ensafi, R., Knockel, J., Alexander, G., Crandall, J.R.: Detecting intentional packet drops on the Internet via TCP/IP side channels. In: Proceedings of PAM (2014)
16. Govindan, R., Tangmunarunkit, H.: Heuristics for Internet map discovery. In: Proceedings of INFOCOM (2000)
17. Gunes, M.H., Sarac, K.: Resolving IP aliases in building traceroute-based Internet maps. IEEE/ACM Trans. Netw. **17**(6), 1738–1751 (2009)
18. Gunes, M.H., Sarac, K.: Importance of IP alias resolution in sampling Internet topologies. In: Proceedings of GI (2007)
19. Guo, H., Heidemann, J.: Detecting ICMP rate limiting in the Internet. In: Proceedings of PAM (2018)
20. Juniper: Default ICMP rate limit on the system for host inbound connections. https://kb.juniper.net/InfoCenter/index?page=content&id=KB28184&cat=SRX_SERIES&actp=LIST
21. Juniper: IPv6 multicast routing on E series broadband services routers, release 15.1. Access-list. https://www.juniper.net/documentation/en_US/junose15.1/topics/reference/command-summary/access-list.html
22. Juniper: Policer implementation overview. https://www.juniper.net/documentation/en_US/junos/topics/concept/policer-mx-m120-m320-implementation-overview.html
23. Juniper: System management and monitoring feature guide for switches. Internet-options (ICMPv4). https://www.juniper.net/documentation/en_US/junos/topics/reference/configuration-statement/icmpv4-rate-limit-edit-system.html
24. Juniper: System management and monitoring feature guide for switches. Internet-options (ICMPv6). https://www.juniper.net/documentation/en_US/junos/topics/reference/configuration-statement/icmpv6-rate-limit-edit-system.html
25. Keys, K.: Internet-scale IP alias resolution techniques. ACM SIGCOMM Comput. Commun. Rev. **40**(1), 50–55 (2010)
26. Keys, K., Hyun, Y., Luckie, M., Claffy, K.: Internet-scale IPv4 alias resolution with MIDAR. IEEE/ACM Trans. Netw. **21**(2), 383–399 (2013)
27. Killick, R., Eckley, I.A.: changepoint: an R package for changepoint analysis. J. Stat. Softw. **58**(3), 1–19 (2014). http://www.jstatsoft.org/v58/i03/
28. Kim, S., Harfoush, K.: Efficient estimation of more detailed Internet IP maps. In: Proceedings of ICC (2007)
29. Luckie, M., Beverly, R., Brinkmeyer, W., et al.: SpeedTrap: Internet-scale IPv6 alias resolution. In: Proceedings of IMC (2013)
30. Marchetta, P., Persico, V., Pescapè, A.: Pythia: yet another active probing technique for alias resolution. In: Proceedings of CoNEXT (2013)
31. Padmanabhan, R., Li, Z., Levin, D., Spring, N.: UAv6: alias resolution in IPv6 using unused addresses. In: Proceedings of PAM (2015)
32. Pansiot, J.J., Grad, D.: On routes and multicast trees in the Internet. ACM SIGCOMM Comput. Commun. Rev. **28**(1), 41–50 (1998)
33. Pedregosa, F., et al.: Scikit-learn: machine learning in Python. J. Mach. Learn. Res. **12**, 2825–2830 (2011)
34. Postel, J.: RFC 792. Internet Control Message Protocol, IETF (1981)
35. Qian, S., Wang, Y., Xu, K.: Utilizing destination options header to resolve IPv6 alias resolution. In: Proceedings of GLOBECOM (2010)
36. Qian, S., Xu, M., Qiao, Z., Xu, K.: Route positional method for IPv6 alias resolution. In: Proceedings of ICCCN (2010)
37. Ravaioli, R., Urvoy-Keller, G., Barakat, C.: Characterizing ICMP rate limitation on routers. In: Proceedings of ICC (2015)

38. Sherry, J., Katz-Bassett, E., Pimenova, M., Madhyastha, H.V., Anderson, T., Krishnamurthy, A.: Resolving IP aliases with prespecified timestamps. In: Proceedings of IMC (2010)
39. Sherwood, R., Bender, A., Spring, N.: Discarte: a disjunctive Internet cartographer. ACM SIGCOMM Comput. Commun. Rev. **38**(4), 303–314 (2008)
40. Spring, N., Mahajan, R., Wetherall, D.: Measuring ISP topologies with rocketfuel. ACM SIGCOMM Comput. Commun. Rev. **32**(4), 133–145 (2002)
41. Vermeulen, K., Strowes, S.D., Fourmaux, O., Friedman, T.: Multilevel MDA-lite Paris Traceroute. In: Proceedings of IMC (2018)
42. Willinger, W., Alderson, D., Doyle, J.C.: Mathematics and the Internet: a source of enormous confusion and great potential. Not. Am. Math. Soc. **56**(5), 586–599 (2009)

APPLE: Alias Pruning by Path Length Estimation

Alexander Marder[(✉)]

UC San Diego/CAIDA, San Diego, USA
amarder@caida.org

Abstract. Uncovering the Internet's router graph is vital to accurate measurement and analysis. In this paper, we present a new technique for resolving router IP aliases that complements existing techniques. Our approach, Alias Pruning by Path Length Estimation (APPLE), avoids relying on router manufacturer and operating system specific implementations of IP. Instead, it filters potential router aliases seen in traceroute by comparing the reply path length from each address to a distributed set of vantage points.

We evaluated our approach on Internet-wide collections of IPv4 and IPv6 traceroutes. We compared APPLE's router alias inferences against router configurations from two R&E networks, finding no false positives. Moreover, APPLE's coverage of the potential alias pairs in the ground truth networks rivals the current state-of-the-art in IPv4, and far exceeds existing techniques in IPv6. We also show that APPLE complements existing alias resolution techniques, increasing the total number of inferred alias pairs by 109.6% in IPv4, and by 1071.5% in IPv6.

1 Introduction

Uncovering the Internet's router graph is vital to accurately analyzing and measuring the Internet. The current tool for uncovering the Internet's topology, traceroute [12], only exposes the IP addresses of router interfaces. Collapsing that to a router-level topology requires first resolving the IP address aliases for each router, a process known as *alias resolution*.

The current state-of-the-art alias resolution techniques rely on exploiting implementations of the IP on routers, such as how a router responds to Destination Unreachable packets [8,14] and populates the IP-ID field [7,15,16,25]. However, implementations can differ between router manufacturers and operating systems, limiting their ability to resolve aliases. Moreover, current RFC recommendations advise against setting the IP-ID field in IPv4 [26], and IPv6 only includes the IP-ID field for fragmented packets.

We present an alternative approach to alias resolution that avoids relying on IP implementations specific to router manufacturers and operating systems, and that resolves aliases in IPv4 and IPv6. Our approach, called Alias Pruning by Path Length Estimation (APPLE), relies only on the fact that routers in

A. Sperotto et al. (Eds.): PAM 2020, LNCS 12048, pp. 249–263, 2020.
https://doi.org/10.1007/978-3-030-44081-7_15

the Internet generally use destination-based forwarding. After inferring potential router aliases in traceroute graphs, we corroborate them with pings from geographically and topologically distributed vantage points (VPs). Our hypothesis, which we validate against ground truth from two networks (Sect. 5), is that path lengths between a router and a VP remain mostly the same regardless of the source address, allowing us to distinguish between valid and invalid router aliases using reply path lengths.

In this paper, we make the following contributions,

- we present APPLE, a novel technique for inferring router aliases using reply path length;
- we compare APPLE's alias resolution inferences against a combined 71 router configurations from two large R&E networks, with no false positives; and
- we show that APPLE complements existing alias resolution techniques, increasing the total number of inferred router alias pairs of addresses by 109.6% in IPv4 and by 1071.5% in IPv6.

2   Previous Work

The earliest reliable alias resolution techniques, Mercator [8] and iffinder, try to induce ICMP Destination Unreachable responses. Some routers report the transmitting interface address when originating Destination Unreachable packets, indicating that the probed and transmitting interface addresses alias the same router. UAv6 [22] extends this idea, sending probes to unused addresses in /30 and /126 subnets. These techniques exploit implementations of ICMP packet generation, but many routers either report the probed address or do not respond to the probes, limiting their effectiveness.

Other approaches draw inferences from the IPv4 IP-ID field, used to aid reassembly of fragmented packets, that some routers populate using a shared counter for all of their interfaces. The Rocketfuel [25] component Ally compares pairs of addresses to see if the IP-IDs increase at similar rates. RadarGun [7] removes the need to compare each pair of addresses separately, sampling and comparing the IP-IDs for all addresses at once. MIDAR [15] also collects and analyzes IP-IDs, but ensures that the IP-IDs of inferred aliases form a monotonically increasing sequence. To address the absence of the IP-ID in normal IPv6 packets, Speedtrap [16] attempts to induce fragmented ICMP Echo Replies with IP-IDs, but some routers do not fragment packets in IPv6. In general, the future of IP-ID-based alias resolution is uncertain, as current IETF recommendations advise against setting the IP-ID in IPv4 packets outside of packet fragmentation [26].

Like APPLE, some techniques derive router aliases from the interface graph generated by traceroute. Spring et al. [24] assumed that most routers report the inbound interface address in response to traceroute probes, inferring aliases when addresses share a common successor. As we describe in Sect. 3, this technique tends to incorrectly infer aliases in the presence of off-path addresses, L3VPN outbound responses, hidden MPLS tunnels, and multipoint-to-point

Fig. 1. Routers typically report the address of the interface that received the traceroute probe (inbound address).

(a) Traceroutes   (b) Router graph.

Fig. 2. The traceroutes in (a) suggest the possible router graph in (b).

links. APAR [10] and kapar [13] try to discover router aliases by aligning traceroutes from multiple vantage points. When multiple ends of the same link appear in different traceroutes, they infer that addresses seen adjacent to the link are aliases of the link routers. Current graph analysis techniques suffer from false router alias inferences.

Furthermore, our technique is not the first to use the TTL in the reply packet (reply TTL) to guide alias resolution. Vanaubel et al. [29] used the reply TTL to fingerprint router manufacturers, and Grailet et al. [9] used those fingerprints to restrict the possible alias pairs inferred via other techniques. Unlike APPLE, they used the reply TTL to restrict the search space, not to identify alias pairs.

Most recently, Hoiho [18] automatically learned regular expressions for extracting router name information from DNS hostnames, with the potential to provide valuable router alias constraints. As future work, we hope to use Hoiho to improve APPLE's router alias inferences.

Our technique avoids many of the pitfalls inherent to prior techniques for three reasons. First, many routers that respond to the traditional pings that we send do not respond to probes specifying unused ports or invalid host addresses, or always report the probe destination address. Second, we do not rely on features of the IP header specific to IPv4 or IPv6, ensuring it generalizes to both IP versions. Third, we make no assumptions about IP link prefixes and do not accept potential aliases indicated by traceroute graphs without additional evidence.

3   Common Successor Alias Resolution

Before describing our technique, we briefly discuss traceroute interpretation and the problems with relying solely on common successors for alias resolution. Conventional traceroute interpretation assumes that when a router responds to a TTL-expiring probe, it reports the address of the interface that received the probe, known as the *inbound* address (Fig. 1). Since an interface often connects its router to exactly one other router, if two addresses both precede a third address in different traceroutes, then the two addresses might belong to the same physical router. This occurs in Fig. 2a, where the addresses a and b

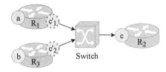

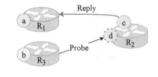

Fig. 3. Multipoint-to-point IP links connect more that two routers.

Fig. 4. Off-path address can appear subsequent to multiple routers.

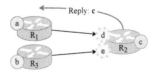

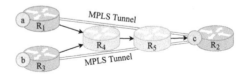

Fig. 5. The L3VPN address creates a common successor for a and b.

Fig. 6. Invisible MPLS tunnels make R_1 and R_3 appear interconnected with R_2.

have the common successor c. Assuming that c is the inbound interface on its router, and that c connects to exactly one other router, we could infer that a and b belong to the same router (Fig. 2b). Unfortunately, many potential problems, most prominently multipoint-to-point links, off-path addresses, Layer 3 Virtual Private Networks (L3VPN), and invisible Multiprotocol Label Switching (MPLS) tunnels, confound common successor alias resolution.

Multipoint-to-Point Links. Common successor alias resolution assumes that router interconnections occur over point-to-point links, but IP links can connect more than two routers. Multipoint-to-point links typically connect routers using layer 2 switches, allowing more than two routers to interconnect using the same IP subnet. In Fig. 3 the switch connects R_1, R_2, and R_3, so a and b belong to different routers but precede the inbound address c. Internet exchange points (IXPs) often use multipoint-to-point links to connect their participant's routers [3,5].

Off-Path Addresses. Even when routers connect over a point-to-point link, off-path addresses can violate the inbound address assumption. While some routers always respond with the inbound address [4], others adhere to RFC 1812 [6] and report the address of the interface used to respond to the traceroute probe. When such a router uses different interfaces to receive and reply to a traceroute probe, the router reports the off-path address instead of the inbound address [11].

In Fig. 4, R_2 received the traceroute probe through interface d but sends the reply through c, and puts c in the source address field in the reply packet. As a result, c appears immediately after b in the traceroute. If in another traceroute R_2 receives and replies to a probe through c, a might also appear prior to c.

Layer 3 Virtual Private Networks. Like off-path addresses, L3VPNs violate the inbound address assumption. When L3VPN exit routers respond to traceroute probes, they report the address of the outbound interface that would have

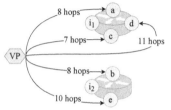
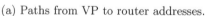
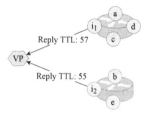

(a) Paths from VP to router addresses.   (b) Paths from routers to VP.

Fig. 7. Paths from a VP to different addresses on a router might differ (a), but the router to VP paths are often the same regardless of source address (b).

continued forwarding the packet toward the destination [17,20], rather than the inbound interface address or a traditional off-path address. Consequently, addresses on any prior router could precede the outbound address in a traceroute. In Fig. 5, R_2 reports the outbound address c, so a and b appear prior to c.

MPLS Tunnels. The fourth prominent reason is that MPLS tunnels might violate the assumption that adjacent hops in traceroute indicate directly connected routers. Invisible MPLS tunnels can cause addresses from unconnected routers to appear adjacent in a traceroute path [27,28]. When a probe packet enters an MPLS tunnel, the entry router encapsulates the probe inside an MPLS packet. Network operators can either configure the router to propagate the TTL from the encapsulated packet, or use a default value. The tunnel routers only decrement the TTL in the MPLS packet header, and not the probe's TTL, so if the entry router does not propagate the TTL, the exit router's response appears immediately after the entry router's response. This occurs in Fig. 6, where R_1 and R_3 do not propagate the probe packet TTL to the MPLS header, so R_2's response appears immediately subsequent to the responses from R_1 and R_3.

4   Methodology

Clearly, the fact that two addresses share a common successor does not always mean that the two addresses belong to the same router. However, common successors can help constrain the process of alias resolution by providing an initial set of possible router aliases. Our goal is to find pairs of addresses that belong to the same router (*alias pairs*) among addresses that share a common successor.

We infer that a pair of addresses belong to the same router by comparing the reply paths from each address to several vantage points (VPs). While the path from a VP to different addresses on the same router might differ significantly (Fig. 7a), especially when the addresses have different longest matching prefixes, all responses from the router to a given VP use the same destination address, and we hypothesize that they often share the same path (Fig. 7b). This follows from the fact that routers primarily forward packets according to their destination

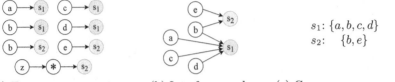

(a) Traceroute segments.   (b) Interface graph.   (c) Common successor sets.

Fig. 8. Based on the traceroutes (a), we create the interface graph (b). We exclude (z, s_2) due to the unresponsive hop between them. Using the incoming edges for s_1 and s_2 we create the potential router alias sets (c).

addresses, so the path from a router to the same destination should mostly remain the same regardless of source address. Thus, we discard potential alias pairs when we infer that a sufficient number of the reply paths differ. We discuss how we make this decision in Sect. 4.2.

When a router originates an IP packet to a VP, that packet does not record the actual path that it traversed, but the packet does include a TTL value that routers decrement as they forward it to the VP. Routers typically initialize that TTL to either 32, 64, 128, or 255 [27,29], and the same router will always initialize the TTLs with the same value. Thus, when a VP receives a reply packet from a router, the TTL value in the packet header (*reply TTL*) indicates the path length from the router to the VP.

Our approach, APPLE, relies on the path length indications given by reply TTLs to evaluate the similarity of reply paths between addresses in potential alias pairs. APPLE performs this alias resolution in two steps. First, APPLE uses traceroutes to group the addresses according to common successors (Sect. 4.1). Second, APPLE evaluates potential alias pairs in each group, filtering unlikely pairs based on their reply TTLs (Sect. 4.2).

4.1 Group Addresses by Common Successor

In order to create the potential alias pairs for evaluation, we group addresses according to common successors. To do so, we represent the traceroutes in our collection with a directed interface-graph. First, we truncate each traceroute at the first occurrence of a repeated address separated by at least one other address. These address cycles [30] indicate forwarding loops, violating our assumption that a traceroute continually moves away from the initiating VP. We also strip the last traceroute hop if it responded with an ICMP Echo Reply, since routers always report the probed address in Echo Replies, violating the inbound interface address assumption [17,19,21]. Then we create an edge from each address to the next hop, provided no unresponsive hops separate the addresses in traceroute.

In Fig. 8, we use the traceroutes in Fig. 8a to create the graph in Fig. 8b. We construct an edge from each address to its successors, except from z to s_2, since an unresponsive hop separates them. Then, we create the sets of possible router

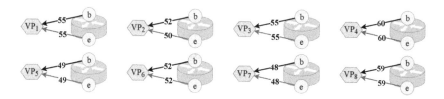

Fig. 9. Reply TTLs to 8 VPs from each address in the possible alias pair (b, e).

aliases in Fig. 8c using the incoming edges for each node. We do not perform the transitive closure on these sets for the reasons in Sect. 3, so both sets contain b.

4.2 Probing and Filtering Alias Pairs

After creating the common successor groups, we evaluate each potential alias pair. First, we ping each address with a possible alias pair from every VP, recording the reply TTLs. This requires $O(numAddresses \times numVPs)$ probes, allowing it to scale to large traceroute collections. We also run the probes from each VP concurrently, reducing the run time to the time required for one VP.

We do not require that reply TTLs from each address in a potential alias pair match at every VP. Instead, we require a minimum number of matches (*minimum match threshold*) designed to limit the impact of random reply TTL collisions, which we set using a generalized solution to the birthday problem [23]. With v total VPs, r unique reply TTLs per VP, and a potential alias pairs, $p(a, r, v) \approx 1 - e^{(a/r^v)}$ computes the probability that any pair of unrelated addresses will have the same combination of values (Appendix A). The ping probes and common successor pairs dictate r and a respectively, so we set the minimum match threshold to the smallest v where $p(a, r, v) < 1/a$. We reject any pair with fewer than v matches.

We also reject alias pairs based on the number of comparisons required to reach the minimum match threshold. For each alias pair, we first sort the pairs of responses according to the minimum RTT to either address. This reflects our assumption that replies to nearby VPs generally encounter fewer network technologies that might confound reply TTL comparison. Next, we compare reply TTLs in sorted order until reaching the minimum match threshold, and prune the alias pair if the ratio of matches to comparisons falls below a predetermined *acceptance threshold*. In Fig. 9, we need eight comparisons to reach the required seven matches, so we discard the pair if $7/8 = 0.875$ falls below the acceptance threshold. Defining the acceptance threshold in terms of the minimum match threshold, and not as a fixed constant, allows it to scale with the required number of matches.

Finally, we create transitive alias pairs based on the transitive closure of the pairs inferred through reply TTLs. We do so by constructing an undirected graph with the common successor alias pairs as edges. Then, we infer alias pairs for every combination of addresses in each graph component, ensuring that our alias pairs cover all inferred aliases of the same router.

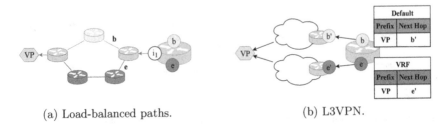

(a) Load-balanced paths.   (b) L3VPN.

Fig. 10. Load-balanced paths of and L3VPNs can misalign reply TTLs.

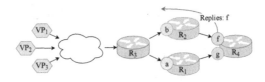

Fig. 11. The off-path address f succeeds both a and b. Both R_1 and R_2 sends replies to the VPs through R_3, so pings to a and b indicate the same reply TTLs.

4.3   Limitations

Addresses on the same router might not always have identical reply TTLs to a VP if network or router configurations cause the replies to traverse a different number of routers, such as load-balanced paths and L3VPN virtual routing and forwarding (VRF) tables (Fig. 10). When load-balanced paths use different numbers of hops, as in Fig. 10a, the reply packets traverse a different number of routers, resulting in different reply TTLs. Similarly, some routers have multiple virtual forwarding tables, known as VRFs, in addition to the default forwarding table. In Fig. 10b, the router includes e in a VRF that uses a different path to reach the VP, so the reply TTLs differ.

Conversely, we might falsely infer alias pairs when a parallel or load-balanced path exists between the VPs and a common successor for a potential alias pair. This occurs in Fig. 11, where R_4 responded with the off-path address f, creating a common successor for a and b. In this case, R_1 and R_2 are on load-balanced paths between R_3 and R_4. Since all responses to the VP first go to R_3, most VPs will receive responses from a and b with the same reply TTL, causing us to incorrectly identify (a, b) as an alias pair.

The transitive nature of alias resolution can cause cascading false inferences, so preventing false alias pairs is paramount. Currently, topologically and geographically distributing the set of VPs provides our only defense against load-balanced and parallel paths. As future work, we hope to investigate how to determine the set of VPs to include and exclude for each pair to maximize the ability of our acceptance threshold to prune incorrect alias pairs. We also plan to experiment with including other alias resolution techniques, such as Hoiho [18], to add additional constraints based router identifiers in DNS hostnames.

Table 1. Statistics from our IPv4 and IPv6 ping probing (a), the ping probing VPs (b), and the alias pairs in the ground truth for Internet2 and R&E visible in our traceroute collections and ping probing (c). In (a) Pairs indicates the potential common successor alias pairs among the responding addresses.

	ITDK	Pings Sent	Probed	Responses	Resp. %	Pairs
IPv4	04-2019	04-2019	366,469	292,141	79.7%	5,022,839
IPv6	01-2019	05-2019	76,098	16,320	78.6%	563,489

(a) Ping probing statistics.

	Total	ASNs	Countries	Cities
IPv4	99	71	37	83
IPv6	78	61	29	63

(b) VP statistics.

	Total		Probed		Responses	
	IPv4	IPv6	IPv4	IPv6	IPv4	IPv6
Internet2	2176	1095	719	616	646	536
R&E	1651	137	352	137	352	137

(c) Ground truth alias pairs.

5   Evaluation

We evaluated APPLE on separate IPv4 and IPv6 traceroute collections (Table 1). For IPv4 we used the traceroutes included in CAIDA's Internet Topology Data Kit (ITDK) for April 2019 [1]. While we ran our ping probes in the same month, human error caused us to only ping 83.4% of the addresses seen prior to a Time Exceeded or Destination Unreachable reply. The ITDK also includes a combination of MIDAR and iffinder alias resolution, allowing us to compare APPLE against existing techniques. For our IPv6 evaluation we use traceroutes from the January 2019 ITDK [2], the most recent ITDK to include IPv6 alias resolution. We pinged 366,052 and 75,979 IPv4 and IPv6 addresses respectively from 99 VPs in 83 different cities for IPv4 and from 78 VPs in 63 cities for IPv6.

We compared APPLE's alias pair inferences against router configurations from Internet2 and another large R&E network in the United States (Table 1c). Our evaluation focuses on the alias pairs that APPLE inferred and those visible in the traceroute collections. First, we set the minimum match threshold, and explore the trade-offs between the positive predictive value (PPV) and the true positive rate (TPR) related to the acceptance threshold. Then, we evaluated APPLE's TPR by comparing it against the ground truth router configurations (Sect. 5.2), and compared the alias pairs generated by APPLE to those found by state-of-the-art alias resolution techniques (Sect. 5.3). Finally, we explore how the number of VPs affects APPLE's accuracy (Sect. 5.4).

5.1   Evaluating Input Parameters

Before evaluating our results, we set the minimum match and acceptance thresholds from Sect. 4.2. To set the minimum match threshold, we first need to determine the possible reply TTLs seen at a given VP. For each VP, we grouped

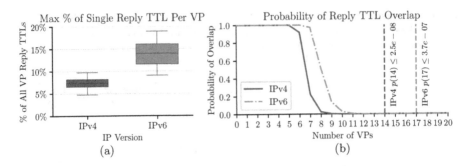

Fig. 12. Using the maximum percentage of all reply TTLs at a VP accounted for by a single value (a), we approximate the probability of reply TTL collision (b).

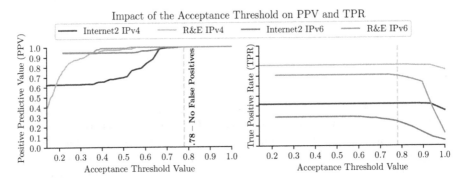

Fig. 13. The acceptance threshold impact on precision and the true positive rate. Lines starts at the first possible acceptance threshold value.

responses by their reply TTL, selected the largest group, and computed the fraction of all responses to the VP included in the group, e.g., for a VP with replies [55, 59, 55, 53], 55 has the most responses, accounting for 50% of the responses seen by that VP.

Figure 12a shows the distribution of these fractions across the VPs in our experiments. No reply TTL accounted for more than 10%/20% of the responses to an individual VP in IPv4/IPv6, so we set the number of possible replies per VP to $r = \frac{1}{0.1} = 10$ in IPv4 and $r = \frac{1}{0.2} = 5$ in IPv6. Using the number of possible alias pairs (a) from Table 1a, we computed the lower bound on the probability of an anomalous match for 1–20 VPs (Fig. 12b). The smallest number of VPs that reduces the probability to less than $\frac{1}{a}$ is 14/17 for IPv4/IPv6, so we set the minimum match threshold to those values in the remaining experiments.

Next, we investigated the trade-off between excluding false alias pairs and discarding valid pairs using the acceptance threshold. When the ratio of matching reply TTLs to comparisons falls below the acceptance threshold, we discard the pair. In this analysis, we exclude transitive pairs, and only evaluate the common successor pairs with at least the minimum number of required matches.

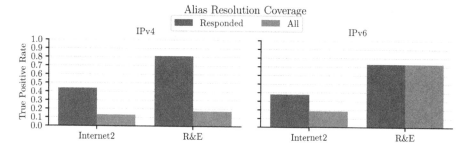

Fig. 14. The TPR for the set of alias pairs where both addresses responded to pings (Responded), and the set of all alias pairs in the traceroute collection (All).

As seen in Fig. 13, increasing the acceptance threshold removes false alias pairs but decreases coverage. Generally, we value increased PPV when inferring alias pairs, rather than increased TPR, since the transitive nature of alias resolution tends to cascade false inferences. We use an acceptance threshold of 0.78 in the remaining evaluation, preventing all false alias pairs in our ground truth.

5.2 Evaluating APPLE's Accuracy

Using the parameters from Sect. 5.1, we validate APPLE's alias pair inferences against our two ground truth networks. These parameter settings eliminated all of the incorrect alias pairs, so we only present the true positive rate (TPR), which indicates the fraction of alias pairs in the ground truth that we detected. In this evaluation, we also include the transitive alias pairs in the results.

Figure 14 shows the TPR for IPv4 and IPv6. The Responded TPR refers to the alias pairs where both addresses responded to the ping probing, indicating the practical ceiling for our performance. APPLE generally performs better for R&E than Internet2, possibly due to the extensive use of L3VPNs in Internet2. For IPv4, the TPR for R&E exceeds 80%, and for Internet2 APPLE found 43.8% of the alias pairs. APPLE achieves worse coverage for IPv6, with TPRs of 73.0% and 37.9% for R&E and Internet2 respectively. We remain unsure what caused the difference in coverage between IPv4 and IPv6, but ruled out insufficient responses to VPs in common.

Figure 14 also provides the coverage for all of the possible alias pairs in the traceroute collections (All TPR). Since the number of inferred alias pairs remained the same, while the number of missing pairs increased, the coverage is worse when considering all visible alias pairs. Overall, APPLE found 13.0%–17.3% of the IPv4 alias pairs and 18.5%–73.0% of the IPv6 alias pairs.

5.3 Comparing APPLE's Coverage to Current Techniques

Next, we show that APPLE complements current alias resolution techniques by finding additional alias pairs. Specifically, we compare APPLE to the alias resolution datasets included in the ITDKs, which analyze all intermediate hop

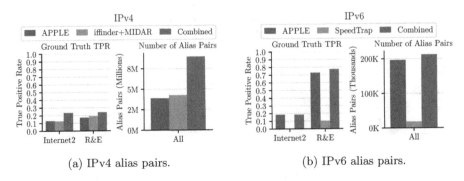

(a) IPv4 alias pairs.   (b) IPv6 alias pairs.

Fig. 15. Comparing APPLE to iffinder+MIDAR in IPv4 (a) and Speedtrap (b) in IPv6, for all addresses seen in the traceroute collections. Each graph shows the TPR for Internet2 and R&E, and the total number of alias pairs.

addresses in the traceroute collection. In IPv4, the ITDK uses a combination of iffinder [14] and MIDAR [15], and in IPv6 it uses SpeedTrap [16]. Both MIDAR and Speedtrap rely on global IP-ID counters, and prioritize minimizing false alias pairs.

As seen in Fig. 15, APPLE adds alias pairs for both networks in IPv4 and IPv6, exceeding the ITDK's alias resolution coverage for all but R&E in IPv4, despite only comparing common successor alias pairs. In total, combining APPLE and the ITDK increased the number of inferred alias pairs for the entire traceroute collection, and not just those seen in the ground truth, by 109.6% in IPv4 and by 1071.5% in IPv6, over the ITDK alias resolution alone. The increased coverage is especially important for IPv6 (Fig. 15b), which does not include the IP-ID in the normal IP packet header. Speedtrap only works when it can induce fragmentation and expose a global IP-ID counter on a router. This does not work for Juniper routers [16], used for all routers in the Internet2 ground truth and three of the R&E routers. It also did not resolve any aliases for the nine Cisco routers in R&E with multiple addresses in the traceroutes. All of Speedtrap's alias pair inferences in our ground truth include addresses on Brocade routers.

5.4   Reducing the Number of VPs

Our final experiment shows the impact of fewer VPs on APPLE's accuracy. We re-ran our experiments for IPv4 with the same parameters, but artificially limited the number of VPs. We experimented with random groups of VPs from 15 to 95 in increments of five, using the same IPv4 parameters as before.

Figure 16 shows the precision and recall of the ten random groups created for each increment, excluding the transitive pairs. APPLE filters out all incorrect R&E alias pairs, but keeps incorrect Internet2 pairs for 50 of the 160 groups. Increasing the acceptance threshold to 0.85 removes all false alias pairs for 32 of those groups with little effect on the TPRs, suggesting that we set the acceptance threshold too low. Interestingly, for the false alias pairs in this experiment, the

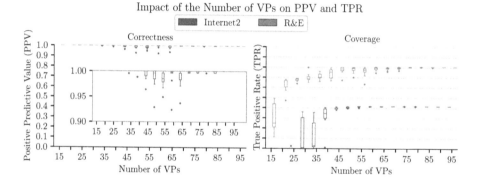

Fig. 16. We re-ran our experiments for IPv4 but limited the available VPs.

VPs with shorter RTTs to the addresses in the false alias pairs generally see mismatched reply TTLs more frequently than those further away. As future work, we plan to investigate weighting VPs according to their relative RTT to the addresses in a potential alias pair.

6   Caveats

Although we found no incorrect alias pairs when validating against our ground truth using the full set of VPs, we have anecdotal evidence that APPLE draws incorrect inferences in some cases. The addresses (`89.149.137.33`, `141.136.108.26`) provide an example of a likely incorrect alias pair outside of our ground truth. Their DNS hostnames `xe-11-0-5.cr2-sjc1.ip4.gtt.net` and `xe-4-1-1.cr1pao1.ip4.gtt.net` indicate that one address is on a router in Palo Alto, while the other is on a router in San Jose. As future work, we hope to improve the precision of our approach by gathering more ground truth and incorporating other constraints, like parsing DNS hostnames [18], in addition to the reply TTL.

7   Conclusion

We presented APPLE, a technique for resolving router aliases seen in traceroute using reply TTLs. We intend for APPLE to complement, rather than replace, existing alias resolution techniques; combining APPLE with existing alias resolution techniques yielded 109.6% and 1071.5% more alias pairs in IPv4 and IPv6 respectively. Despite perfect precision compared to ground truth, we expect some false positives in APPLE's inferred alias pairs. We plan to continue experimenting and improving APPLE to increase its reliability. We also plan to release our source code, allowing other researchers to use and improve on our technique.

Acknowledgments. We thank kc claffy, Matthew Luckie, and Young Hyun for their invaluable feedback. This work was supported by NSF grants OAC-1724853 and OIA-1937165.

A Generalizing the Birthday Problem to Alias Resolution

The birthday problem computes the probability that any combination of n people share the same birthday. A common approximate general solution [23] takes the form,

$$p(n,d) \approx 1 - \exp\left(\frac{n(n-1)}{2d}\right),$$

where d is the number of days in the year. Of note, the $\frac{n(n-2)}{2}$ term corresponds to the number of possible two-person combinations. Using a to represent the number of combinations, the equation takes the form,

$$p(a,d) \approx 1 - \exp\left(\frac{a}{d}\right).$$

Applying this equation to our problem, we first replace the number of combinations with the number of potential alias pairs. Second, we must determine the potential reply space for each address. When an address replies to a VP, the VP sees a reply TTL from the space of possible reply TTLs, r. If we assume that a reply TTL to one VP is independent of all the others, then the potential reply space for an address is r^v. Practically, we consider r^v an upper bound on the possible combinations, since we expect that the network topology and control plane create dependent probabilities. Plugging r^v in for d we get the approximate probability that a pair of addresses will have the same combination of replies to all v VPs,

$$p(a,r,v) \approx 1 - \exp\left(\frac{a}{r^v}\right).$$

To limit collisions, while maximizing the number of true alias pairs, we use the smallest value of v such that $p(a,r,v) < 1/a$.

References

1. Internet topology data kit - April 2019. http://www.caida.org/data/internet-topology-data-kit/. Accessed Apr 2019
2. Internet topology data kit - January 2019. http://www.caida.org/data/internet-topology-data-kit/. Accessed Jan 2019
3. Ager, B., Chatzis, N., Feldmann, A., Sarrar, N., Uhlig, S., Willinger, W.: Anatomy of a large European IXP. In: ACM SIGCOMM CCR (2012)
4. Amini, L.D., Shaikh, A., Schulzrinne, H.G.: Issues with inferring Internet topological attributes. In: Internet Performance and Control of Network Systems III (2002)
5. Augustin, B., Krishnamurthy, B., Willinger, W.: IXPs: mapped? In: IMC (2009)
6. Baker, F.: RFC 1812: requirements for IP version 4 routers. Technical report, Internet Engineering Task Force (1995)
7. Bender, A., Sherwood, R., Spring, N.: Fixing ally's growing pains with velocity modeling. In: IMC (2008)

8. Govindan, R., Tangmunarunkit, H.: Heuristics for Internet map discovery. In: Nineteenth Annual Joint Conference of the IEEE Computer and Communications Societies, Proceedings, INFOCOM 2000. IEEE (2000)
9. Grailet, J.F., Donnet, B.: Towards a renewed alias resolution with space search reduction and IP fingerprinting. In: Network Traffic Measurement and Analysis Conference (TMA) (2017)
10. Gunes, M.H., Sarac, K.: Resolving IP aliases in building traceroute-based Internet maps. IEEE/ACM Trans. Netw. 17, 1738–1751 (2009)
11. Hyun, Y., Broido, A., Claffy, K.: On third-party addresses in traceroute paths. In: PAM (2003)
12. Jacobson, V.: Traceroute. ftp://ftp.ee.lbl.gov/traceroute.tar.gz
13. Keys, K.: Internet-scale IP alias resolution techniques. ACM SIGCOMM Comput. Commun. Rev. (CCR) 40, 50–55 (2010)
14. Keys, K.: iffinder. https://www.caida.org/tools/measurement/iffinder/
15. Keys, K., Hyun, Y., Luckie, M., Claffy, K.: Internet-scale IPv4 alias resolution with MIDAR. IEEE/ACM Trans. Netw. 21, 383–399 (2013)
16. Luckie, M., Beverly, R., Brinkmeyer, W., et al.: Speedtrap: internet-scale IPv6 alias resolution. In: IMC (2013)
17. Luckie, M., Dhamdhere, A., Huffaker, B., Clark, D., Claffy, K.: bdrmap: inference of borders between IP networks. In: IMC (2016)
18. Luckie, M., Huffaker, B., et al.: Learning regexes to extract router names from hostnames. In: IMC (2019)
19. Marder, A., Luckie, M., Dhamdhere, A., Huffaker, B., Claffy, K., Smith, J.M.: Pushing the boundaries with bdrmapIT: mapping router ownership at internet scale. In: IMC (2018)
20. Marder, A., Luckie, M., Huffaker, B., Claffy, K.: vrfinder: finding forwarding addresses in traceroute. In: POMACS (2020)
21. Marder, A., Smith, J.M.: MAP-IT: multipass accurate passive inferences from traceroute. In: IMC (2016)
22. Padmanabhan, R., Li, Z., Levin, D., Spring, N.: UAv6: alias resolution in IPv6 using unused addresses. In: PAM (2015)
23. Sayrafiezadeh, M.: The birthday problem revisited. Math. Mag. 67(3), 220–223 (1994)
24. Spring, N., Dontcheva, M., Rodrig, M., Wetherall, D.: How to resolve IP aliases. Technical report, UW-CSE-TR 04–05-04, University of Washington (2004)
25. Spring, N., Mahajan, R., Wetherall, D.: Measuring ISP topologies with Rocketfuel. ACM SIGCOMM CCR 32, 133–145 (2002)
26. Touch, J.: RFC 6864: updated specification of the ipv4 id field. Technical report, Internet Engineering Task Force, February 2013
27. Vanaubel, Y., Luttringer, J., Mérindol, P., Pansiot, J., Donnet, B.: TNT, watch me explode: a light in the dark for revealing MPLS tunnels. In: Network Traffic Measurement and Analysis Conference, June 2019
28. Vanaubel, Y., Mérindol, P., Pansiot, J.J., Donnet, B.: Through the wormhole: tracking invisible MPLS tunnels. In: IMC (2017)
29. Vanaubel, Y., Pansiot, J.J., Mérindol, P., Donnet, B.: Network fingerprinting: TTL-based router signatures. In: IMC (2013)
30. Viger, F., et al.: Detection, understanding, and prevention of traceroute measurement artifacts. Comput. Netw. 52(5), 998–1018 (2008)

Web

Dissecting the Workload of a Major Adult Video Portal

Andreas Grammenos[1,3]($\boxtimes$), Aravindh Raman[2,3], Timm Böttger[3],
Zafar Gilani[3], and Gareth Tyson[3]

[1] University of Cambridge, Cambridge, UK
ag926@cl.cam.ac.uk
[2] King's College London, London, UK
[3] Queen Mary University of London, London, UK

Abstract. Adult content constitutes a major source of Internet traffic. As with many other platforms, these sites are incentivized to engage users and maintain them on the site. This engagement (*e.g.*, through recommendations) shapes the journeys taken through such sites. Using data from a large content delivery network, we explore session journeys within an adult website. We take two perspectives. We first inspect the corpus available on these platforms. Following this, we investigate the session access patterns. We make a number of observations that could be exploited for optimizing delivery, *e.g.*, that users often skip within video streams.

1 Introduction

The Internet has evolved from a largely web-oriented infrastructure to a massively distributed content delivery system [10]. Video content has become particularly popular, and we have therefore seen a range of studies investigating the usage and access patterns of major portals, *e.g.*, user-generated content (UGC) [5,16], video on demand (VoD) [23], Internet TV (IPTV) [6] and catch-up TV [1,13]. A particularly prevalent form of online video is that of *adult content*, *i.e.*, pornographic material [3]. In the last five years there has been a surge of research activity in this space, attempting to characterize the content corpus of sites [18,20], the workload of sites [3,24] and the use of adult social networks [19]. Despite this, we still lack the breadth and depth of understanding common to many other aspects of online video delivery.

Due to the paucity of data, there is a particular lack of understanding related to the unique workload that such websites place on the infrastructure of a Content Delivery Network (CDN). Particularly, there has been limited work exploring the per-session content request patterns on these portals. Thus, in this paper, we present a large-scale analysis of access patterns for a major adult website, with a focus on understanding how individual viewer decisions (or "journeys") impact the workload observed.

To achieve this, we bring together two key datasets. We have gathered data from a large CDN, covering 1 h of access logs for resources hosted served by the

© Springer Nature Switzerland AG 2020
A. Sperotto et al. (Eds.): PAM 2020, LNCS 12048, pp. 267–279, 2020.
https://doi.org/10.1007/978-3-030-44081-7_16

site. This covers 20.08M access records, 62K users and 3.28 TB of exchanged data. Although this offers fine-grained insight into content request patterns, alone is it insufficient. This is because modern adult websites also consist of a large body of surrounding "meta" interactions, including categories and ranking of content. Hence, we also gather metadata about each access by scraping the web content itself, *e.g.,* content category and upload date.

In this paper, we look into three aspects of operation. First, we inspect the corpus and workload served by the platform (Sect. 4). Despite its prominence as a video portal, the access logs are dominated by image content, primarily serving thumbnail content. That said, we find that the majority of bytes served is actually for video content, primarily due to it voluminous nature. Video content tends to be relatively short, with subtle variations observed across the categories. Popularity across these resources is highly skewed though: the top 10% of videos contribute 73.7% of all accesses. This leads us to explore the specifics of per-session access patterns on the site (Sect. 5). We see that, for instance, the majority of sessions limit accesses to one or two categories. This leads us to inspect *where* accesses come from. The majority of views arrive from the main video page, but we also observe a number of views from the homepage and search function. Finally, we discuss potential implications from our work (Sect. 6). We find that this genre of material is highly cacheable, and briefly test the efficacy of city-wide edge cache deployment. We conclude by proposing simple innovations that could streamline delivery (Sect. 7).

2   Background and Related Work

Pornography is amongst the most searched for content on the web [14,22]. Although this topic remains a taboo in some research fields, there has been an expanding body of research into the video platforms that drive its delivery. We have seen recent work inspecting the content corpus of popular adult websites [18,20] and their workloads [3,12,24,25] as well as various studies that have attempted to estimate the load that they create on the wider Internet. For example, [14] estimates that Porn 2.0 sites such as xHamster and YouPorn can gain up to 16 million views per month.

There have also been a number of related studies that have explored the topic of online pornography more generally, *e.g.,* privacy [21]; automated recognition and classification [9,11]; interest recommendations [17]; and security issues [22]. This paper presents one of the first large-scale studies of an online adult multimedia delivery service. That said, there are a multitude of studies into more traditional video streaming systems that already provide some insight. These include catch-up TV [1,13], user generated content [5,16,26], Video-on-Demand [23] and IPTV [6,7]. These insights have been used to drive a range of modeling and systems research activities, *e.g.,* building content popularity models [8], optimized caching techniques [1] and improved delivery schemes [4]. The paucity of data related to adult video access, however, makes it difficult to appreciate the applicability of these technologies to this particular field. We write this paper to shed insight into the session-level specifics of adult content access patterns.

3   Methodology and Data

The work in this paper relies on two key datasets. First, we utilize a dataset provided by a CDN, which captures access logs to an anonymous major adult video content provider. Second, we compliment this with web metadata surrounding each video in the access logs.

3.1   CDN Data

We first describe the basic features of the CDN data, collected in 2019, as well as the necessary post-processing required to extract sessions.

Data Description. We have been given access logs for web resources hosted by a major adult video website. The data has been collected from the vantage point of a single US-based data center operated by a major Content Delivery Network (CDN). The dataset covers 1 h, and includes 20.08M access entries. Each log entry maps to a single resource request, consisting of:

- Timestamp: The time when the item was requested.
- Client ID: This is a prefix preserving anonymized IP Address (so that we can approximate client location).
- Resource: The web resource requested.
- User Agent: This is the user-agent identifier included within the HTTP request header. This allows us to differentiate mobile from desktop users.
- HTTP Referrer: This is the Referrer from the HTTP request header; it provides the URL that the client was redirected from.
- City ID: Using Maxmind, the anonymized IP addresses are mapped to their geolocation. Only requests for which the coordinates have an estimated accuracy of less than 20KM are tagged. This covers 75.91% of all requests. Each city is then associated with an anonymized numerical City ID.

Identifying Sessions. For the CDN traces, we take a simple but effective way of mapping the requests to sessions. For each log entry, we generate a session identifier by computing the following hash: SHA256(IP Address, Device, Browser). We then group requests into individual sessions using their identifiers. Overall, the data covers 62K unique user sessions. To remove incomplete sessions, we extract all sessions that contain requests within the first or last 5 min of the trace, and then filter them from the rest of the logs. This removes 15% of requests. Note that we also performed our analysis on the unfiltered data and only found slight differences.

3.2   Web Scrape Data

The CDN logs offer fine-grained insight into individual access patterns, but no metadata related to the content being accessed. Hence, we scrape metadata from the website front end for each video contained within the CDN dataset. The web scrape data, for each video, includes the category, the global view counter, the number of likes/dislikes and any associated hashtags. In total we gathered this metadata for 4.9 million videos, covering 91.1% of all videos in the CDN traces.

3.3 Ethical Considerations and Limitations

Limitations. We emphasize that the duration of our trace data limits our ability to make generalizable statements, particularly pertaining to longitudinal trends. Critically, this creates a clear bias towards shorter sessions that do not exceed an hour (we filter out longer sessions that do not entirely fall within the measurement period). Another limitation is that the data only covers a single portal from the vantage point of a single data center. Hence, we cannot quantify to what extent this applies to alternative deployments. We therefore temper our later analysis with these observations; despite this, we argue that the data offers a powerful first insight into traffic patterns within this domain.

Ethical Consideration. We took a number of steps to address ethical concerns. Before receiving the logs, they were first fully anonymized by the CDN, and there was no way to map logs back to specific users. Hence, all user identifiers were removed prior to access, including cookies and source IP addresses. We further anonymized sensitive data (such as content category tags) from the web data, instead generating a set of neutral tags. Although this restricted "semantic" analysis of the content, it reduced exposure to sensitive insight. Pre-processing was done by one author, who did not perform the subsequent analysis. Furthermore, all data was stored remotely in a secure silo with restricted access to just two authors. We obtained IRB approval.

4   Characterization of Corpus and Workload

We start by performing a basic characterization of the corpus served, as well as the overall site workloads observed at the CDN.

Resource Type. Typical sites consist of a wide range of media. To inspect this, we first look at the mix of content types encountered within the CDN logs. Figure 1a presents the fraction of requests to each resource type; this shows the distributions for both the number of requests and the number of bytes sent by the servers. The vast majority of requests are received for image content (mainly jpg), whereas the majority of bytes are attributed to the delivery of video content (mp4). In total, 63.4% of bytes transferred are attributable to video content, yet they constitute only 19.9% of requests. Closer inspection confirms that the dominance of images is driven by thumbnails, which makes the video portal image-heavy. We conjecture that these may be used heavily when browsing, due to the primarily visual nature of the content.

Video Duration. The above suggests that the majority of accesses are actually driven by non-video material. Despite this, due to its voluminous nature, the quantity of bytes transferred is dominated by video content. Hence, we next inspect the duration of video content available. We take this from the web scrape information, which includes the video duration. Figure 1b presents the duration of videos on the website, as reported by the video metadata. The majority of videos (80%) fall below 16 min, with a mean duration of 920 s. For completeness,

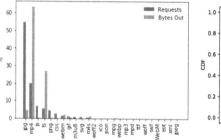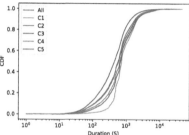

Fig. 1. (a) Percentage of requests to various file formats and the percentage of total bytes out; (b) CDF of consumed video duration based on category using all and top-5 categories. Note "All" refers to all content within any category.

we also plot the duration for videos within the top 5 most popular categories. Note for ethical reasons, we anonymize all categories. The shortest videos fall into the C3 category, with a mean of 657 s. This particular category of material focuses primarily all more homemade content. In contrast, the C1 category (which contains more professional material) has a longer mean duration (1086 s). That said, these categories show strong similarities in their distribution, showing a bias towards shorter content items.

View Counts. We next seek to explore the popularity distribution of the resources within our logs. Figure 2a presents the CDF of the number of requests we observe per-object, taken from the CDN logs. We observe a clear skew, where the majority of accesses are accumulated by a small number of videos: The top 10% of videos contribute 73.7% of all accesses.

This, however, can be deceptive as videos are quite diverse (*e.g.*, in terms of duration), and many of the objects downloaded are non-video. Hence, Fig. 2b complements these results by presenting the CDF of the number of chunks requested per *video*. Each chunk represents a subset of the overall video content. This provides insight into the number of sub-requests triggered by each video being consumed: By definition, longer videos will generate more chunk requests. Again, we separate chunks into their respective anonymized categories. We see that the *vast* majority of video fetches result in under 10 chunks being served. Initially, one might assume that this is simply because the videos are short. However, we find that the low fetch rates are also driven by user *skipping* and *cancellations*, leading to only subsets of a video's chunks be downloaded. We revisit this observation in Sect. 5.

Category Affinity. The above has shown that there are subtle differences between categories of content, *e.g.*, in terms of duration. A complicating factor is that many videos are tagged by multiple categories. On average, each video has 7 category tags. Hence, we next briefly test the coexistence between categories to identify commonly paired tags. To quantify this, we compute the fraction of the pair-wise coexistence of the top 6 categories and present the results as a heatmap in Fig. 3a. To compute this, we calculate the fraction of videos from

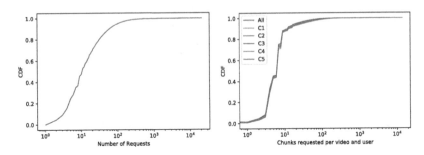

Fig. 2. (a) Number of requests per object; (b) Distribution of video chunk per video request

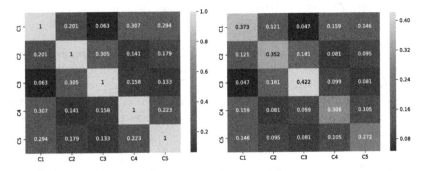

Fig. 3. (a) Heatmap showing the fraction of the pair-wise coexistence for the five most popular categories; (b) Heatmap normalised by the total number of videos (across all categories).

each category that *also* are tagged with another category. For completeness, Fig. 3b also normalizes the fraction based on the total number of videos. We confirm that there are varying levels of category co-location. In some cases, co-location is quite high, *e.g.*, 29.4% of videos tagged as C2 are also tagged a C3. In contrast, other categories are far less co-located, *e.g.*, less than 5% of C1 videos are co-located with C3. There are certain intuitive reasons for this, driven by the semantic nature of the categories. We posit that this may offer insight into how things like predictive caching could be introduced to such platforms.

5   Characterisation of Per-Session Journey

We have so far revealed a workload dominated by image and video content, as well as patterns which suggest that users rarely consume entire videos. Thus, we next proceed to focus on the behavior of individual sessions.

5.1   Intra-video Access Journeys

We first dive into the *intra*-video access patterns of sessions. Our focus is on understanding how users move between chunks within a single video.

Access Duration. We first explore the duration of time each user session dedicates to an individual video. Note that this is different to Fig. 1b, which is based on the video duration, rather than the access duration. To compute this, for each video access, we extract the *difference* between the first and last timestamp seen for chunks of the same video. For instance, if the first chunk of a video were requested at t^1, and the final chunk were requested as t^2, we estimate the duration as $t^2 - t^1$. This offers an approximation of access duration, although we highlight that the downloading of a chunk does *not* necessarily mean it is viewed.

Figure 4a presents the results as a CDF. This shows markedly different trends to that of Fig. 1b (which depicts the duration of the content). As expected, we find that access durations are far shorter than the underlying content duration that is being consumed. There are also subtle differences between the categories; for example, the average access duration for content within the C1 category is 1086 s *vs.* 657 s for C3 content. Around 80% of C1 videos are consumed for under 1000 s, whereas this is closer to 90% for C3 videos. To complement this, Fig. 4b presents a CDF of the number of bytes sent per [video, session] pair. Each data point represents the number of bytes downloaded for each request (note one session may generate multiple requests, even for the same resource). This shows a rather different trends, with the around 90% of fetches resulting in under 10^7 bytes being sent.

Overall, both plots reveal that the majority of videos only have only a subset of their content chunks fetched. It is worth noting that, even though videos rarely download all their chunks, we do find that requests for individual chunks are usually completed. 82% of individual chunk requests involve downloading in excess of 90% of bytes, whilst only 4% download under 10% of bytes.

Cancellations and Skip Rates. The fact that many videos are not downloaded in their entirety is driven by a combination of two factors: (i) viewers canceling video streams; and (ii) viewers skipping across video streams.

To get an idea of how many videos are watched sequentially, and then canceled towards the end, we compute the fraction of streams that request the first 90% of chunks, but lack the last 10%. We find that under 1% experience this, suggesting that early cancellations and skips are most prevalent. Figure 4c presents the skip rate of blocks. A skipped block is counted when the byte range is not directly adjacent to the previous block high range. For example, a contiguous block is: "100–200" and "201–300", whereas a skipped block is "100–200" and then "501–600". We observe that some videos have extremely high skip ratios (*i.e.,* above 0.8). This confirms that viewers skip extensively within videos, and rarely download all chunks contiguously. This has a dramatic impact on our earlier results. To quantify this, we subset all videos to leave those containing at least one skip (and remove any anomalous blocks as mentioned previously). This leaves all videos served that have *at least one skip*—this covers a 75.4% of the total requests, confirming that the majority of videos do include skips. This is likely to differ from long-play Video-on-Demand platforms (*e.g.,* Netflix) where users more likely view streams contiguously.

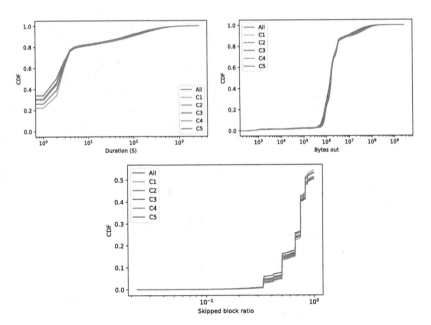

Fig. 4. (a) CDF of the approximate consumption for each individual video across sessions for all and top-5 categories; (b) CDF of the bytes out per User/Video combination for all and top-5 categories (c) Skipped blocks for each category.

5.2 Inter-video Access Journeys

The next aspect we inspect is how sessions move *between* videos.

Video Load Points. We first inspect which pages tend to drive the majority of video views. We conjecture that different viewers might have different patterns in this regard. To extract this information, we identify the HTTP Referrer in each request; from this, we take the previous page the resources was loaded from. We then map this to the page and type of object that has triggered the resource request. Figure 5a presents the overall distribution of videos watched from a page that users are visiting within the portal. Note that we anonymize category pages again. The majority of resources are watched from the Video Homepage (each video has its own page). This captures over 55% of unique videos accumulating 65.5% of bytes delivered on the site. That said, we also observe a notable quantity of material embedded within the Site Homepage and from the Search Page. For instance, around 45.5% of video visits come from Site Homepage. Interestingly 37% of the videos are referred from the Search Page but amassing just 5% of the traffic. The remaining referrals are from various sub-pages within the site, most notably several popular category pages.

Looking at this distribution in isolation, however, is insufficient to gain vantage into a sessions journey. This is because, as previously observed, videos are not always viewed in their entirety. To explore this further, Fig. 5b presents the

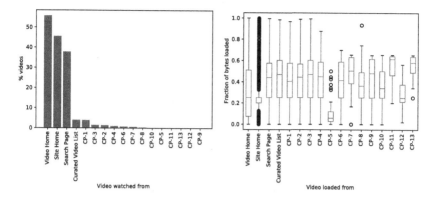

Fig. 5. (a) Where the videos are watched the most: 95.67% of videos are watched from either the main page of the video, the homepage of the site and the search page (b) Where the videos are loaded the most: Y-axis gives the ratio of bytes out and total file size (somewhat indicating what proportion of video has been watched) across users from various pages

fraction of bytes loaded across the various referrers previously discussed. For clarity, we list only the top pages observed. The median is relatively stable across most pages, however, there are key differences. For example, 45.69% of views from the homepage of the site result in under 25% of video bytes actually being loaded. This might indicate that content accessed from the front page is rarely done with great thought. Rather, users might informally click on videos on the chance that they might be of interest. Similarly, just 5% of video bytes are consumed when redirected from the search page, suggesting that users may load a large number of videos in the hope of finding a specific one (before canceling). We will seek to verify these conjectures in our future work.

Inter Video Navigation. Whereas the above inspects the number of videos loaded from a given page, it is also interesting to explore the transition of views between videos. To compute this, we sort each user session into its temporal order of access. This only covers video accesses. We then compute transition points as the move between one resource request to the next. Figure 6 presents a Sankey diagram to reveal the transition of accesses between videos. We find that the majority of sessions move between resources on the same page type. For example, 92.6% of accesses to the homepage of a video are followed by another video access from the homepage. This observation generalizes across most pages. For the top 5 accessed pages, we find at least 88.83% of videos are accessed from the same source as the previous video. We conjecture that this may be a powerful observation for performing predictive pre-fetching of content.

6 Discussion and Implications

There are a number of implications of our work. Here we briefly focus on potential work in relation to optimizing CDN delivery.

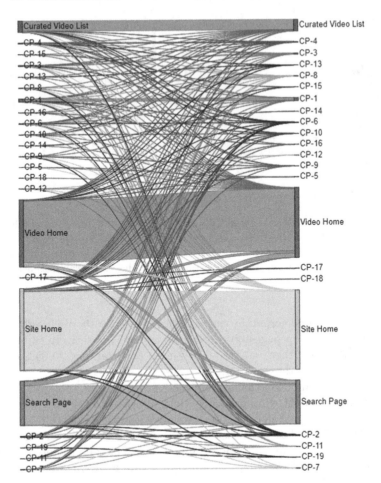

Fig. 6. Sankey diagram presenting the fraction of page transitions from locations (left) to destinations (right). This is computed by computing the time ordered list of resources and checking the previous resource request to determine the step-by-step journey.

Geo-Aware Caching. CDNs are primarily interested in improving their quality of provision, as well as overheads. This is typically measured via metrics such as cache hit rate *vs.* deployment costs. Our results confirm that, even though images constitute the bulk of requests, the majority of bytes delivered are video content. Furthermore, due to the presence of highly popular objects, we posit that there may be potential for edge caching of content. Although CDNs already deploy cache servers around the world, we next test the possibility of deploying a larger number of *geo-aware* caches.

As we do not have topological information about clients, we cluster users into a cache domain based on their city tags derived from Maxmind. Note that this creates a wider dispersal of cache servers compared to most CDNs [2]. We then

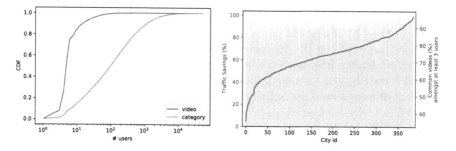

Fig. 7. (a) CDF of number of users who have watched the same video in their city (blue) or a video from the same category in their city (orange); (b) Percentage of traffic saved at back-haul by implementing city-wide cache (Y-1) and the percentage of users who would have benefit by the scheme (Y-2). (Color figure online)

sub-divide users into their cities, and filter any cities that have 10 or fewer sessions, leaving 385 cities. For simplicity, we assign all users in each city into a single caching domain, assuming that each region has its own dedicated geo-cache.

We first compute how many sessions in each city consume the same video. Figure 7(a) presents the results on a per-video basis. Unsurprisingly, we find that accessing the same video from a city is commonplace. In the most extreme case, one video is accessed by 98.9% of all sessions within a particular city. This leads us to hypothesize that such properties could be exploited for caching. Hence, Fig. 7(b) shows the percentage of traffic that could be saved (Y-1 axis) *if* a city-wide cache were to be deployed. Note, for simplicity, we assume the cache covers all users in the city and has unlimited storage for the one hour period of the dataset. For these high population locations, savings exceeding 90% are feasible. The Y-2 axis also presents the percentage of videos that have at least 3 user sessions within a city accessing them (*i.e.*, thereby resulting in a saving). We see that these are extremely high, with nearly all cities exceeding 50%.

Predictive Loading. The above confirms that caching is an effective tool in this domain. We also posit that a number of more innovative approaches could be taken for streamlining delivery. For instance, *predicting* popular chunks in the video and subsequently pushing them could improve Quality of Experience by reducing human-perceived delays. This would be particularly useful, as often videos are not viewed contiguously, making current buffering strategies ineffective. Predicting the next skip could therefore avoid wasted buffering. Furthermore, the heavy load created by thumbnails, suggest they could perhaps be pre-loaded in bulk for certain videos We have also confirmed that sessions have clear behavioral traits when moving *between* video pages. Again, we conjecture that these patterns could be predicted and exploited. For instance, the top video within a recommendation pane could be pre-loaded, much as we see done with Accelerated Mobile Pages [15]. In fact, due to the propensity for viewers to select such content, it might even be possible to dynamically select which videos to recommend based on what content is live in the most nearby cache. We posit that this may be able to satisfy user demand, whilst also reducing network costs for the CDN.

278 A. Grammenos et al.

7 Conclusion

This paper has explored the characteristics of a large adult video portal, with a focus on understanding in-session journeys. We first inspected the corpus and workload served by our vantage point. We found that, contrary to expectation, the bulk of objects served are actually image content, although video *does* make up the bulk of bytes delivered. In terms of videos, the majority of requests were for a small subset of the content, and we confirmed past observations related to the skewed distribution of adult content. This led us to focus on session-level behaviors, where we revealed distinct access patterns and briefly evaluated the potential of caching and pre-fetching to optimize delivery.

The work constitutes just the first step in our research agenda. We have so far studied the journey patterns within sessions, however, we wish to better understand *why* these patterns emerge. This generalizes beyond adult video to any type of website. Thus, we wish to do further comparative research with other portals. With these patterns, we also wish to develop optimized delivery systems that can learn behavior sufficiently well to predict and pre-load content per-user. Finally, we are keen to deep dive into the innovations discussed, and perform further experiments to understand how they can streamline delivery.

Acknowledgments. This work was supported by EPSRC grants EP/N510129/1 and EP/P025374/1. We would also like to thank the reviewers and our shepherd Oliver Hohlfeld.

References

1. Abrahamsson, H., Nordmark, M.: Program popularity and viewer behaviour in a large TV-on-demand system. In: Proceedings of IMC (2012)
2. Ager, B., Mühlbauer, W., Smaragdakis, G., Uhlig, S.: Web content cartography. In: Proceedings of the 2011 ACM SIGCOMM Conference on Internet Measurement Conference, pp. 585–600 (2011)
3. Ahmed, F., Shafiq, M.Z., Liu, A.X.: The internet is for porn: measurement and analysis of online adult traffic. In: 2016 IEEE 36th International Conference on Distributed Computing Systems (ICDCS), pp. 88–97. IEEE (2016)
4. Apostolopoulos, J.G., Tan, W., Wee, S.J.: Video streaming: concepts, algorithms, and systems. HP Laboratories, report HPL-2002-260 (2002)
5. Cha, M., Kwak, H., Rodriguez, P., Ahn, Y.Y., Moon, S.: Analyzing the video popularity characteristics of large-scale user generated content systems. IEEE/ACM Trans. Netw. **17**(5), 1357–1370 (2009)
6. Cha, M., Rodriguez, P., Crowcroft, J., Moon, S., Amatriain, X.: Watching television over an IP network. In: Proceedings of IMC, pp. 71–84. ACM (2008)
7. Gao, P., Liu, T., Chen, Y., Wu, X., Elkhatib, Y., Edwards, C.: The measurement and modeling of a P2P streaming video service. Netw. Grid Appl. **2**, 24–34 (2009)
8. Guo, L., Tan, E., Chen, S., Xiao, Z., Zhang, X.: The stretched exponential distribution of internet media access patterns. In: Proceedings of PODC, pp. 283–294. ACM (2008)

9. Hu, W., Wu, O., Chen, Z., Fu, Z., Maybank, S.: Recognition of pornographic web pages by classifying texts and images. IEEE Trans. Pattern Anal. Mach. Intell. **29**(6), 1019–1034 (2007)
10. Labovitz, C., Lekel-Johnson, S., McPherson, D., Oberheide, J., Jahanian, F.: Internet inter-domain traffic. In: Proceedings of SIGCOMM (2010)
11. Mehta, M.D., Plaza, D.: Content analysis of pornographic images available on the internet. Inf. Soc. **13**(2), 153–161 (1997)
12. Morichetta, A., Trevisan, M., Vassio, L.: Characterizing web pornography consumption from passive measurements. In: Choffnes, D., Barcellos, M. (eds.) PAM 2019. LNCS, vol. 11419, pp. 304–316. Springer, Cham (2019). https://doi.org/10.1007/978-3-030-15986-3_20
13. Nencioni, G., Sastry, N., Chandaria, J., Crowcroft, J.: Understanding and decreasing the network footprint of over-the-top on-demand delivery of TV content. In: Proceedings of World Wide Web Conference, May 2013
14. Ogas, O., Gaddam, S.: A Billion Wicked Thoughts: What the World's Largest Experiment Reveals About Human Desire. Dutton, New York (2011)
15. Phokeer, A., Chavula, J., et al.: On the potential of Google AMP to promote local content in developing regions. In: 2019 11th International Conference on Communication Systems & Networks (COMSNETS) (2019)
16. Raman, A., Tyson, G., Sastry, N.: Facebook (A) live? Are live social broadcasts really broad casts? In: Proceedings of the 2018 World Wide Web Conference, pp. 1491–1500 (2018)
17. Schuhmacher, M., Zirn, C., Völker, J.: Exploring youporn categories, tags, and nicknames for pleasant recommendations. In: Proceedings of Workshop on Search and Exploration of X-Rated Information (SEXI 2013), pp. 27–28, February 2013
18. Tyson, G., Elkhatib, Y., Sastry, N., Uhlig, S.: Demystifying porn 2.0: a look into a major adult video streaming website. In: Proceedings of the 2013 Conference on Internet Measurement Conference, pp. 417–426. ACM (2013)
19. Tyson, G., Elkhatib, Y., Sastry, N., Uhlig, S.: Are people really social in porn 2.0? In: Ninth International AAAI Conference on Web and Social Media (2015)
20. Tyson, G., Elkhatib, Y., Sastry, N., Uhlig, S.: Measurements and analysis of a major adult video portal. ACM Trans. Multimed. Comput. Commun. Appl. (TOMM) **12**(2), 35 (2016)
21. Vallina, P., Feal, Á., Gamba, J., Vallina-Rodriguez, N., Anta, A.F.: Tales from the porn: a comprehensive privacy analysis of the web porn ecosystem. In: Proceedings of the Internet Measurement Conference, pp. 245–258 (2019)
22. Wondracek, G., Holz, T., Platzer, C., Kirda, E., Kruegel, C.: Is the internet for porn? An insight into the online adult industry. In: Proceedings of Workshop on Economics of Information Security (2010)
23. Yu, H., Zheng, D., Zhao, B.Y., Zheng, W.: Understanding user behavior in large-scale video-on-demand systems. In: ACM SIGOPS Operating Systems Review, vol. 40, pp. 333–344. ACM (2006)
24. Yu, R., Christophersen, C., Song, Y.D., Mahanti, A.: Comparative analysis of adult video streaming services: characteristics and workload. In: 2019 Network Traffic Measurement and Analysis Conference (TMA), pp. 49–56. IEEE (2019)
25. Zhang, S., Zhang, H., Yang, J., Song, G., Wu, J.: Measurement and analysis of adult websites in IPv6 networks. In: 2019 20th Asia-Pacific Network Operations and Management Symposium (APNOMS), pp. 1–6. IEEE (2019)
26. Zink, M., Suh, K., Gu, Y., Kurose, J.: Characteristics of Youtube network traffic at a campus network-measurements, models, and implications. Comput. Netw. **53**(4), 501–514 (2009)

Untangling Header Bidding Lore
Some Myths, Some Truths, and Some Hope

Waqar Aqeel[1]([✉]), Debopam Bhattacherjee[4]([✉]),
Balakrishnan Chandrasekaran[3]([✉]), P. Brighten Godfrey[5],
Gregory Laughlin[6], Bruce Maggs[1,2], and Ankit Singla[4]

[1] Duke University, Durham, US
{waqeel,bmm}@cs.duke.edu
[2] Emerald Innovations, Cambridge, USA
[3] Max-Planck-Institut für Informatik, Saarbrücken, Germany
balac@mpi-inf.mpg.de
[4] ETH Zürich, Zürich, Switzerland
{debopam.bhattacherjee,ankit.singla}@inf.ethz.ch
[5] University of Illinois Urbana-Champaign, Champaign, US
pbg@illinois.edu
[6] Yale University, New Haven, US
greg.laughlin@yale.edu

Abstract. Header bidding (HB) is a relatively new online advertising technology that allows a content publisher to conduct a client-side (i.e., from within the end-user's browser), real-time auction for selling ad slots on a web page. We developed a new browser extension for Chrome and Firefox to observe this in-browser auction process from the user's perspective. We use real end-user measurements from 393,400 HB auctions to (a) quantify the ad revenue from HB auctions, (b) estimate latency overheads when integrating with ad exchanges and discuss their implications for ad revenue, and (c) break down the time spent in soliciting bids from ad exchanges into various factors and highlight areas for improvement. For the users in our study, we find that HB increases ad revenue for web sites by 28% compared to that in real-time bidding as reported in a prior work. We also find that the latency overheads in HB can be easily reduced or eliminated and outline a few solutions, and pitch the HB platform as an opportunity for privacy-preserving advertising.

1 Introduction

Online advertising is a multi-billion dollar industry, with estimated global revenues of more than 300 billion dollars (USD) in 2019 [19]. Revenues from advertising platforms exhibited a consistent positive growth rate over the last nine quarters [32], and are projected to reach 0.5 trillion USD within the next four years [19]. Programmatic advertising, which includes both real-time bidding (RTB) and header bidding (HB), dominates the online advertising space today: It accounts for 62% of the total advertising spend [32]. In this paper, we offer insights into the design and performance of HB auctions using *real* end-user measurements, which have not been available before.

© Springer Nature Switzerland AG 2020
A. Sperotto et al. (Eds.): PAM 2020, LNCS 12048, pp. 280–297, 2020.
https://doi.org/10.1007/978-3-030-44081-7_17

Header bidding, introduced around 2013[1] [9,50,57], is a nascent programmatic advertising technology that improves transparency and fairness in real-time bidding (RTB). In RTB, ad slots on a web page are offered to advertisers (or, more generally, buyers) following a *waterfall* model: one by one in a pre-determined order, where the first one to bid a high enough price wins the slot. The ordering is, moreover, not determined by the publisher (or web site owner), but by an *ad server*, a third party that facilitates the auctioning of slots to buyers. HB, in contrast, enables the publisher to solicit bids simultaneously from multiple *ad exchanges*, where each exchange is a marketplace for advertisers to bid on ad slots. Under HB, the publisher typically places some JavaScript code within the web page's HEAD tag that, when loaded in an end-users' browser, launches an in-browser auction for the ad slots on that page. This in-browser, publisher-controlled, real-time ad auction permits publishers, as we show later, to significantly increase their ad revenues. Perhaps as a consequence, HB has already gained significant adoption: 22% of the Alexa top 3k web sites use HB [1], and a more recent study reports 22–23% adoption among the top 5k sites [35]. If we remove sites that are ad-free (e.g., government and non-profit web sites) or which use an in-house ad platform (e.g., Google and Facebook), HB adoption among the top 1k sites is at 80.2% and growing fast [1].

Users might also benefit from HB: It could be leveraged to build a privacy-preserving and transparent advertising ecosystem, where the end users have control over their data. They could decide, on a per-web-site basis, for instance, what information (e.g., concerning their interests or preferences) to barter for helpful ads from advertisers. If properly designed, these auctions can also provide the necessary oversight into end-user tracking, and transparency that users often expect when seeing ads [55,56]. Any debate on such a novel advertising ecosystem is possible, however, only if the underlying HB platform is proven to work well.

Real-time auctions such as those in RTB and HB are latency-sensitive. Google AdX (one of the largest ad exchanges) requires, for instance, that all advertisers respond within 120 ms of the bid request being sent [22]. Setting aside a recommended room of 20 ms for unexpected delays, and 40 ms for bid computations and data fetches, leaves only 60ms for the round trip between an advertiser and Google AdX [36]. Given the state of latency in the Internet [10], it is not surprising that Google AdX recommends that advertisers peer directly or co-locate with AdX to minimize latency. Ensuring low latency for bid requests and responses is even more challenging in HB, since users' browsers cannot be co-located with exchanges. Publishers thus set very long deadlines (from 500 ms to 3000 ms) to ensure that all ad exchanges in an HB auction have a chance to bid. These long deadlines are consistent with the widespread belief that the in-browser auction held in HB imposes significant latency overhead [17,35]. The central theme of this paper is that these concerns may be overblown. In particular, we identify the sources of overhead and outline several avenues for lowering it. We summarize our contributions as follows:

---

[1] The lack of any formal specification or standardization process makes it difficult to nail down the exact time header bidding was introduced.

⋆ We developed a web browser extension, for both the Google Chrome and Mozilla Firefox browsers, to dissect in-browser HB auctions. We released the source code of the extension as open source software [6].

⋆ Prior work on header bidding [35] relied on regularly crawling websites from a single vantage point. Crawling is valid for some of the analyses they do, such as how many ads are on a web page, and which exchanges are involved, but it cannot provide any useful insights into networking timing for real users. Revenue measurements will also be inaccurate as advertisers bid only token amounts for synthetic user profiles. We gathered measurements of in-browser HB auctions from about 400 real users, who volunteered to install and use the extension for a period of 8 months. We also made the data set constituting these measurements publicly available [6]. We call this data set RUM.

⋆ Using the RUM data set, we demonstrate that ad revenue (estimated using the median of bids from ad exchanges) from HB is significantly higher (28%) than that reported for RTB in other studies. We also estimate the publishers' latency overheads when integrating with ad exchanges and discuss their implications for publishers' ad revenue.

⋆ We break down the time spent in soliciting bids from ad exchanges into its contributing factors and highlight areas for improvement. We do not find any *fundamental* problem with client-side HB (i.e., in-browser auctions) implementations. It is not necessary to move these in-browser auctions to ad servers or, more generally, away from end users to lower auction duration.

2   A Brief History of Programmatic Advertising

The introduction of real-time bidding fundamentally changed the way ads were bought and sold: RTB, by leveraging programmatic advertising, facilitated the sale and purchase of ads on a per impression or view basis [23]. Under RTB, publishers (e.g., www.nytimes.com) announce their ad slots in *real-time* (i.e., when serving content to end users) to ad servers (e.g., DoubleClick for Publishers). The ad servers then reach out to typically several *demand sources* (e.g., privately negotiated advertisers, Google AdSense, or an ad exchange), where advertisers either bid for a chance to place ads in the available slots, or have previously negotiated contracts to show a certain volume of ads for a price.[2] A bid, typically expressed in *cost per mille (CPM)*, represents the amount that an advertiser is willing to pay for one thousand impressions or views of the ad [61]. Advertisers estimate the worth of each ad slot using user-specific data from one or more *data brokers*, which track end users to compile a database of user profiles (e.g., comprising details such as a user's gender, age, and location).[3]

The Need for Header Bidding. In RTB, ad servers contact demand sources in a rank order (referred to as the *waterfall model*) determined *a priori* by the publisher and/or ad server. For a given ad slot, the process terminates as soon

---

[2] Ad exchanges and advertisers are also collectively referred to as *buyers*.

[3] For more details on data brokers, we refer the reader to [4,47].

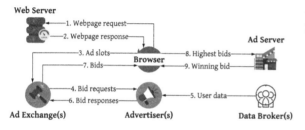

Fig. 1. Interactions between different elements in client-side header bidding

Table 1. A summary of the RUM data set

Attribute(s)	Value
Users	≈400
Duration	8 months
Cities; countries	356; 51
Web sites	5362
Ad exchanges	255
Page visits	103,821
Auctions	393,400
Bids	462,075

as the slot is filled by a source, even if those appearing later in the ordering might have offered a higher price. This static ordering, hence, treats the sources, and in turn advertisers, unfairly. Publishers suffer from lower ad revenues—due to lost opportunities—and a lack of transparency—they do not know of the demands across different sources, especially ad exchanges, to inform a better ordering.

Leveling the Playing Field. Header bidding was introduced sometime around 2013 or 2014 [9,39,50,57], to address RTB's shortcomings. HB allows the publisher to contact different advertisers and ad exchanges concurrently. Then, these bids are sent to the ad server so they can be compared to other demand sources. With this model, ad exchanges have a fair chance to bid for the slots, and publishers can monitor the demand across different exchanges. Over time, three different kinds of header bidding implementations have emerged: *client-side*, *server-side*, and *hybrid* (see [35]), although client-side is the original and still dominant implementation. For the rest of this paper, we focus our attention on client-side HB.

Client-Side HB. The publisher adds JavaScript in the web page's header, i.e., content enclosed by the HEAD HTML-tag that when processed by an end-user's browser, kick-starts an *in-browser* auction (illustrated in Fig. 1). The auction concurrently solicits bids from different exchanges for the ad slots on that page. The bids received until the end of the auction are then sent to the ad server to compare with those retrieved via the waterfall-model auctions in the ad server. Finally, the ad server chooses the highest bid, i.e., with the highest CPM, and returns the winning bid to the browser. The browser then contacts (not shown in the illustration) the winning bidder to retrieve the ad and display it.

3   Real User Measurements

Our objective is to passively observe the in-browser auctions of the client-side header bidding process. To this end, we developed a browser extension, released it to public, and, from real end users who used the extension for 8 months, obtained measurements pertaining to HB auctions.

The browser extension utilizes the Prebid library [40], for it is the most widely used HB JavaScript library, with 63.7% of the publishers using it as of

August 2019 [1]. The extension, *MyAdPrice*, is available on both the Google Chrome web store and Firefox Add-ons web site. It uses the JavaScript APIs for WebExtensions [31] to access the document-object-model (DOM) tree [30]. Via the DOM, it learns of (a) the ad slots on the Web page, (b) the name and IP addresses of the ad exchanges that were contacted to fill up those slots, (c) the bids received from different exchanges, and (d) which bids, if any, won the auctions and for which ad slots. The extension also uses the Web Performance Timing API (WPT) [59] to capture the time spent in each step of the request such as DNS resolution, performing TCP/TLS handshakes, soliciting bids from exchanges (i.e., transferring the data carrying the requests to the exchange's servers) for various ad slots, and receiving bids (i.e., retrieving the response data from the exchange's servers) from the exchanges. Outgoing ad server requests are also checked for query parameters.

In addition to releasing the source code for the extension as open source software, we announced it on university mailing lists and public forums to increase adoption. We recruited approximately 400 volunteers from diverse locations, with nearly 50% of the users from the US. The rest were mostly from European countries including Bulgaria, the United Kingdom, France, Norway, Germany, and the Netherlands, and a small, but significant fraction, also from Canada and India. Table 1 presents the high-level characteristics of the RUM data set, comprising real user measurements over a period of 8 months. The end users visited about 5k web sites, for a total of about 100k web page fetches. The users' browsing activity resulted in about 400k auctions involving about 500k bids from 255 ad exchanges. In total, we observed 916,447 requests issued by the users' browsers to ad exchanges and servers; 247,869 (27%) of these were to ad servers, while the remaining 668,578 were to ad exchanges. Our browser extension recorded the timestamp of each request using the browser's Navigation Timing API [58]. Using these timestamped requests, we estimated the duration of auctions and investigated the factors that affect an auction's duration.

3.1 Privacy and Ethics

Our extension, by *default*, sends *no data* from the user's browser. The extension uses the browser's local storage to store data pertaining to ad slots in different pages and the bids received for each. The extension uses this data to compute the "ad-worthiness" of the user—the money that advertisers intend to make off of the user, and allows the user to view this locally-stored information. Users may *opt in* to share data including domain names of web pages they visit, i.e., only those that use header bidding, ad slots on the pages, exchanges contacted for ads, bids received, timing information on various phases of the in-browser auction, and, lastly, their geographical location at city level. The data shared does *not* have any information to uniquely identify a user. This opt-in data from real end users constitutes the RUM data set. When we consulted our institutional review board, they declared that we do not require an approval since we do not gather any personally identifiable information.

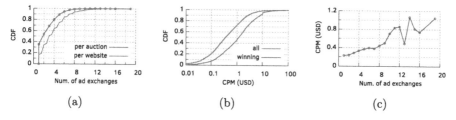

Fig. 2. (a) In the median, auctions involve only two ad exchanges and web sites (publishers) connect with only three ad exchanges. (b) Bid prices show significant variation, with approximately 30% of bids having at least $1 CPM. (c) The median CPM or ad revenue increases with number of ad exchanges contacted.

The strict privacy standards we set for ourselves also mean that our dataset has limitations. Since we don't upload any data by default, not all installations result in data collection. Also, since we don't identify users, we cannot tell how many unique users uploaded data to our servers. We also cannot track users across different websites, and cannot profile based on age, income etc.

We refrained from conducting any experiment that would harm end users or publishers or even the advertisers. The extension is merely a passive observer of the in-browser auctions. We did not crawl web sites, since that would generate synthetic ad impressions for which advertisers might have to pay the publishers. Crawling activities may also lead to exchanges flagging the publisher for suspicious activity. We did not craft synthetic user profiles for similar reasons.

4   Ad Exchanges, CPM, and Ad Revenue

The large number of ad exchanges observed in the RUM data set (in Table 1) suggests that publishers leverage HB to integrate with many buyers in order to maximize their ad revenue. To investigate further, we computed the number of ad exchanges contacted, derived from the count of distinct ad exchanges from which bids were received by the browser, per auction as well as per web site. The CDF of the number of ad exchanges contacted (Fig. 2a), across all auctions and web sites, reveals that most web sites (60%) use at most four ad exchanges, and 10% use at least twice as many. Per this figure more than a third (35%) of all auctions involve only one exchange and a fifth use at least four exchanges. Publishers seem conservative in connecting with many ad exchanges, even if HB libraries make it easy to establish such direct integrations. Prebid, the most widely used JavaScript HB library, for instance, offers more than 250 integration modules or "adapters" [43]; to integrate with an ad exchange, publishers simply have to enable or include the corresponding adapter.

The CDF of CPMs across all auctions, in Fig. 2b, shows a significant variation in bid values. While 20% of bids have at most $0.10 CPM, nearly 30% of the bids have at least $1 CPM. We also observed 2 bids with CPM between $500 − $1000 and 3 with more than $1000 CPM. We find that ad revenue in HB (for our volunteers) is not lower than that of RTB reported in other studies. For example, the median winning CPM that we observe ($1.15) is 28% higher than the RTB median of $0.90 reported in [37]. Furthermore, we grouped together ad slots based on the number of ad exchanges from which they solicited bids and computed the median value of bids in each group (Fig. 2c). The median value of bids increases significantly with the number of ad exchanges. It is indeed in the publishers' best interests to connect with many ad exchanges—at least more than the current number of ad exchanges (Fig. 2a) they are using.

Publishers could be contacting fewer exchanges for performance reasons. We investigate the implications of integrating with more ad exchanges for auction duration in the next section.

5   Auction Duration and Implications

The Prebid Javascript library does not provide explicit timestamps for auction start, and end. As an approximation, we use the first bid request from the browser to an ad exchange to signal an auction's start. A call to the ad server marks the end of an auction (step 8 in Fig. 1). Hence we approximate the auction duration as the time between the first bid request, and the ad server call. The CDF of these estimates, in blue in Fig. 3a, shows that auctions last for 600 ms in the median and some 10% of auctions last longer than 2 s. Despite the publishers integrating with a small number of ad exchanges, auction durations are fairly high.[4]

The CDF of the elapsed time between when the user arrives at a given web page and the end of the auction ("since visit" line in Fig. 3a) reveals that the browsers spend a large amount of time prior to launching HB auctions. Perhaps web browsers spend this time prioritizing content over ads. Web pages may also refresh ads based on user activity, e.g., scrolling down or reactivating an inactive tab, triggering some auctions much later than when the user arrived at the web page. These are separate auctions that are triggered in response to these events.

To ascertain the implications of auction duration for end users, we focus on the page-load time (PLT), and measure the time it takes for the browser to fire the onLoad event after the user navigates to the web page. We subtract the onLoad time of a web page from the bid-arrival times associated with the ad slots or auctions on that page, and plot the CDF of the resulting values in Fig. 3b. Only a small fraction of bids (18%) arrive before the page load is complete; 82% of the bids arrive after the onLoad event is fired. Although the shortcomings of the PLT metric in reflecting end-users' experiences is well-known, it is still the most widely used metric [26], and according to this metric auction duration does not significantly impact end-user experiences.

Longer ad auctions could, however, affect publishers and advertisers. The negative effect of latency on e-commerce sales is well-known [3], and [8] concludes that increased response latency decreases click-through rates for search results.

---

[4] Appendix C presents additional results on factors that may influence the number of exchanges contacted by a publisher.

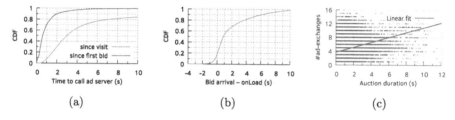

Fig. 3. (a) Auctions last for 600 ms in the median, and some 10% of auctions last more than 2 s. (b) Auctions, however, do not seem to affect the page load times: Most bids arrive much later than when the `onLoad` event fires. (c) Auction duration increases with the number of ad exchanges contacted.

Delay in showing ads likely has the same effect, since a longer duration implies a longer time to display the ad and engage the user. Furthermore, the display of an ad might alter the visual elements or rendering of the web page. Auction duration also increases with the number of ad exchanges contacted by the browser, as the linear fit in Fig. 3c shows. While publishers can limit the auction duration, a smaller timeout could lead to lost revenues, since a higher bid may arrive after the timeout is triggered. Clearly, publishers have to manage the trade-off between maximizing revenue and minimizing auction duration.

A simple approach to managing the trade-off is to cherry-pick ad exchanges that deliver high-value bids. We thus rank-order ad exchanges by *median CPM* of bids sent across all web sites and users. Figure 4a shows, however, no correlation between ad-exchange CPM and the median latency of its bid responses.

Rather than limit the number of exchanges, which is clearly not efficient, publishers could perhaps specify an early timeout. Figure 4b shows the CDF of bid-response arrivals with respect to auction start (i.e., the timestamp of the first bid request). 87% of the bids arrive within 1 s of the start of the auction. Also, the CDF of CPMs of bids as a function of the time they were received since auction start, in Fig. 4c, indicates that 90% of the total CPM is received within the same time span. This observation is in stark contrast with the estimates of auction duration in Fig. 3a ("since first bid" line). More concretely, per Fig. 3a, 30% of the auctions take longer than 1 s, suggesting that publishers are conservative in setting auction timeouts or deadlines: A lot of time is, hence, unnecessarily wasted on waiting for bids that will likely have no significant effect on the auction.

6   Sources of Latency in HB Auctions

In this section we delve into the factors that fundamentally determine the duration of the in-browser HB auctions. To this end, we dissect the latency of a bid request into its contributing factors and identify, wherever possible, avenues for mitigating the latency overheads.

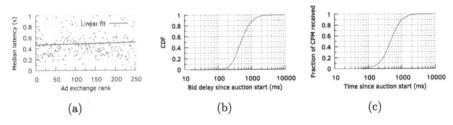

Fig. 4. (a) "High-CPM" ad exchanges are not any faster in responding with bids than "low-CPM" ad exchanges. (b) 87% of the bids and (c) 90% of the ad revenue, estimated through CPMs, arrive within 1 s of the start of the auction.

We define *bid duration* as the time between the start of the bid request being sent out and the end of the bid response being received. We can measure bid duration from two data sources—from within the Prebid JavaScript library (in-browser) and through the WPT API [59] (on-the-wire). in-browser measures the difference between the timestamps that Prebid records when it has prepared the bid request to be sent through the browser, and when it has finished parsing the bid response. on-the-wire is just the duration between the bid request and response as provided by the WPT API.

The CDF of bid durations calculated separately from these two sources, in Fig. 5a, shows, surprisingly, a difference of 174 ms in the median, which is fairly large. This difference is suggestive of poor implementation practices or bugs in HB libraries, specifically in the logic implemented in the adapters developed for integrating the publisher with an ad exchange or advertiser [41]; it could also be that publishers are using adapters incorrectly. Consider the scenario in which a publisher's web site contacts exchanges $\mathcal{A}$ and $\mathcal{B}$. Suppose that bid duration for exchanges $\mathcal{A}$ and $\mathcal{B}$ are 250 ms and 300 ms, respectively. In the ideal case, the adapters for $\mathcal{A}$ and $\mathcal{B}$ should be making concurrent, asynchronous requests. Suppose that $\mathcal{B}$ has a bug in its adapter: it makes a synchronous request. If the publisher integrated HB so that $\mathcal{B}$ is contacted before $\mathcal{A}$, given that $\mathcal{B}$ makes a synchronous call, the call to $\mathcal{A}$ will get delayed until the request to $\mathcal{B}$ completes. The auction now lasts for 550 ms instead of only 300 ms (in case of a correct implementation). Such pitfalls are detailed in [18] and [42].

The WPT API allows us to break down the bid duration into the various steps involved. We specifically gather the following measures: (a) the amount of time the bid request was waiting in the browser's queue ("Stall"), due to several factors such as preemption by requests with higher priority, exhaustion of the allowed number of simultaneous TCP connections (particularly with HTTP/1.0 and HTTP/1.1), and allocation of disk space for caching; (b) time spent in resolving the domain name ("DNS"); (c) time spent in TCP handshake; (d) time spent in TLS handshake; (d) time spent in waiting for the first byte of the response since start of request ("TTFB"); and (d) time spent in receiving the rest of the response ("Response"). We also marked an underlying TLS/TCP connection of a request as *persistent* if the time spent in TCP and TLS handshakes is zero.

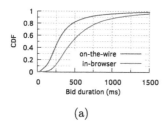

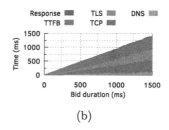

(a)   (b)

Fig. 5. (a) The gap between the "in-browser" and "on-the-wire" bid request durations suggests room for improving HB implementations. (b) Breakdown of time spent by requests over non-persistent connections into key contributing factors.

In breaking down the request latency to its contributing factors, we separate requests over persistent connections from those over non-persistent connections.

6.1 Persistent vs. Non-persistent Connections

Only 60% of the ad requests in the RUM data set were made with persistent connections. They were 34.7% shorter, with a median duration of 230 ms, than those using non-persistent connections. If we break down the latency of such requests into contributing factors, TTFB accounts for 93% and 79% of the total duration, in the median and 80th percentile, respectively. "Response" contributes 2.3% while "Stall" contributes the rest. "Stall" time continues to increase consistently for requests beyond the 80th percentile.

Figure 5b shows the latency breakdown for the remaining 40% of the ad requests made using non-persistent connections; we omitted steps with negligible contributions. The requests take 352 ms in the median and spend, on average, 38% of their time in TCP and TLS handshakes. The handshake times can be reduced to nearly zero if exchanges adopt newer protocols that support low-RTT session resumption such as TCP Fast Open (TFO) [46], TLS 1.3 [49], and QUIC [27]. We tested 228 ad exchanges and found only minimal support for such features: Only 11.4% of the ad exchanges tested support TLS 1.3 and 6.6% support QUIC. We found, however, that 75.9% of the observed IP addresses belonging to ad exchanges support TFO. However, this observation is misleading because even though clients support TFO, they rarely have it enabled (see Appendix A).

Response contributes, on average, 2.4% to the total duration, with a 5 KB median size response from the ad exchanges. TTFB also includes the time spent in conducting the auctions in the exchange and indicates room for improving the exchange-side auctions. Overall, per Fig. 5b, bid durations increase primarily because of increases in time spent across TCP, TLS and TTFB. That TCP, TLS, and TTFB times increase in lockstep suggests RTTs between users and ad exchanges as a key contributor to latency.

6.2   Ad Infrastructure Deployments

Using a commercial geolocation service, we calculated the *geodesic* [62] between the end users and the ad exchange servers.[5] Figure 6a plots the CDF of these distances for four of the eight most popular exchanges; we omitted the rest, which had similar results, for clarity. Index Exchange's servers (IND), deployed at 88 different locations are the closest to end users: in the median, the servers are about 180 km away from the users. The remaining exchanges each have servers in only 20 locations and are quite far away from end users—median distances for Rubicon Project (RUB), AOL, and Criteo (CRT) are approximately 520 km, 910 km, and 2410 km, respectively. Criteo seems to be directing almost all North American users to a single US West Coast location. (Appendix B presents other inferences derived from the locations of the users and ad exchanges.)

Index Exchange's geographically widespread deployments help in ensuring a low handshake time, as shown in Fig. 6b. The handshake times to servers of Criteo and AOL, despite the exchanges' comparatively poor deployment, are surprisingly low. We found that Criteo supports TLS 1.3, while Index Exchange does not. This can result in a drastic improvement in handshake latency as TLS 1.3 saves one complete round-trip in the handshake. Another reason that Index Exchange is not seeing even lower latency is that perhaps most of the latency is in the last mile. Since 60% of the bid requests use persistent connections, TTFB, and not handshake time, accounts for most of the request duration. Figure 6c shows that Criteo does an exceptionally good job, especially compared to Index Exchange, in keeping the TTFB low: The server-side auctions at Criteo are perhaps better optimized than those at Index Exchange.

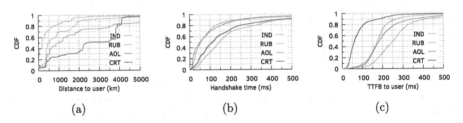

Fig. 6. (a) Ad exchanges typically are quite far from end users. (b) TCP/TLS handshakes account for a significant fraction of an ad request's duration. (c) Ad exchanges can quite effectively lower auction durations by optimizing the exchange-side auctions, and lowering the TTFB values.

7   Related Work

Header bidding, being a nascent technology, has received little attention in the literature. In [28], Jauvion et al. discuss how to optimize a buyer's bidding strategy in HB, while [45] presents a schotastic optimization model for optimizing

---

[5] We geolocate the end-user's IP address when the extension reports the opt-in data.

ad-exchange revenues. Cook et al. use machine learning models to identify relationships between data brokers and advertisers [16]. In [35], Pachilakis et al. present a measurement study of the HB platform. They focus on market aspects such as the most popular ad exchanges, number of ad slots found on web pages, and their sizes. They crawl web sites with blank user profiles from a single vantage point, so their revenue and network timing data does not reflect real users and network conditions. They also cannot identify the causes of HB latency. In contrast, our study uses real user measurements to study latency and its ad-revenue implications.

Orthogonal to header bidding, there is a rich body of work on online advertising, end-user tracking, and privacy that show how users attach monetary value to their personally identifiable information (e.g., [11,53]) and how to uncover advertising and tracking services by analyzing network traffic data (e.g., [48]). Venkatadri et al. propose a novel mechanism that enforces transparency on online advertising platforms [56]. Guha et al. and Toubiana et al. have presented designs for privacy preserving advertising that puts the client at the center [24,55]. These techniques, however, require sweeping changes for real-world deployments, and we argue that they can be ported over to the HB platform that is already enjoying widespread adoption.

8 Concluding Remarks

Within a span of roughly six years since its introduction, header bidding has gained a strong adoption: Among the top 1k web sites that use third-party ad platforms, 80% use HB. It decreases publishers' dependence on large advertising-market players, e.g., Google, and also improves publisher revenue [52]. Although there are widespread concerns that HB's in-browser auctions introduce significant latency overheads and affect end-users' browsing experiences [17] ([35] mentions high delays seen from one vantage point, and paints a gloomy picture without any analysis on what is causing the delay), our real-end-user measurements lessen these concerns. We showed that more than half of these overheads can be eliminated by adopting more modern protocols and also, perhaps, by fixing bugs in the JavaScript-based HB implementations. Since HB is widely adopted by publishers, shows promise in signficantly increasing the publishers' ad revenues (e.g., see Sect. 4), and has implementation overheads that are addressable with minimal engineering efforts, we propose that client-side HB be seen as an opportunity for privacy-preserving advertising.

The pervasive and commonplace tracking of users to improve targeted ads is unsustainable in the long term. Recent privacy violations and scandals [15,21,51] have raised users' awareness and lowered their tolerances: A recent study found 22% of surveyed users to be using *Adblock Plus*, the most popular ad-blocking browser extension [44], and, fueled by users' demands, Firefox ships bundled with a collection of privacy extensions (e.g., tracker and third-party cookie blocker) [33]. Such aggressive measures to block ads and trackers, nevertheless, is fundamentally at odds with the publishers' business model. Major news web sites have resorted to putting up paywalls [54], and asking for donations [60].

There is, unfortunately, an inherent flaw in today's approach to blocking ads and trackers: ads and trackers are treated equally. While users are sensitive about privacy, most do not mind seeing non-intrusive ads; users would be willing to share more if they had control over what is shared and with whom, and what kind of ads they would like to see [12]. Users also think that ad targeting based on tracking is often inaccurate: they see ads related to common stereotypes about their identity, or related to searches they made over a month ago [12].

The client-side HB platform gives us an opportunity to address these concerns: Since the browser has control over the in-browser auction, it can essentially control the entire ad-fetch process. Browsers must continue to block tracking mechanisms such as host fingerprinting [63] and third-party cookies [20], but could allow HB-based ad requests. They could even append such requests with user-profile data, obviating the exchanges' need for data brokers. The user-profile data could be based on a limited form of profiling or could consist of manually entered preferences as in Privad [24]. Regardless of the approach, the user has complete control and visibility into this data. Privacy-preserving designs for online advertising (e.g., [24,55]) are not novel, but they require sweeping changes for deployment in practice. Given HB's widespread adoption, porting over these techniques to work on top of the HB platform might mitigate the deployment issues.

When implemented correctly, these solutions will limit users' exposure to essentially IP-address-based tracking, which can be alleviated by tunneling the ad requests through a forward proxy operated by neutral or non-profit entities such as Mozilla or Brave; since these ad requests are encrypted, we do not need to trust the proxy operator. Such public proxies have been operated by Google [2] and Opera [34], albeit for other purposes. We could also incentivize such proxies by devising a revenue-sharing mechanism between the end user, publisher, and the proxy operator using an in-browser cryptocurrency wallet (e.g., MetaMask [29]).

A detailed investigation of such mechanisms will constitute future work. For now, we have shown that HB is already popular and generating higher revenues for publishers, and the perceived latency limitations are addressable, and not fundamental to the protocol. We hope that our insights will encourage both academia and the industry to take a deeper look into header bidding.

A   Client-Side TFO Adoption

In this appendix, we complement the observations on server-side TFO adoption (in Sect. 6.1) with some comments on adoption on the client side. Measuring TFO adoption on the client side is challenging. The Linux kernel disables TFO globally if it sees 3 consecutive TCP timeouts, before or after the handshake, for any destination [13]. The rationale is to avoid the extra cost of TFO failure or client blacklisting in case of middlebox interference [25]. macOS implements a similar backoff strategy and disables TFO [5], although it is a bit less conservative. Windows implements an even more conservative backoff strategy [7].

Even if the operating system has TFO enabled, the browser usually does not. The Chromium project, on which Google Chrome and some other browsers are based, has removed TFO from all platforms [14], while Firefox supports TFO, but keeps it disabled by default.

B   NA and EU Users: GDPR, Ad-Worthiness and Latencies

In this appendix, we examine the role that user location plays in HB. We coarsely divided our users into regions of North America (NA), Europe (EU), Asia (AS), and Oceania (OC), we observe that web sites contact more ad exchanges in North America: 13% of web sites, when visited by users in North America, contact 8 or more ad exchanges, but in case of EU users 99% web sites contact at most 7 (Fig. 7a). Perhaps this effect can be attributed to the strict privacy requirements of GDPR. The difference between European and North American users is even more pronounced when it comes to bid amounts (or CPMs). Web sites generate 4 times more CPM through a visit from a North American user than they do from a European user as shown in Fig. 7b. It is hard to conclusively determine the reason for this large difference as there are a multitude of factors that determine the "ad-worthiness" of a user.

The CDF of on-the-wire bid durations for users in different regions (Fig. 7c) shows that, in the 80th percentile, European (EU) users observe 12% higher bid durations than North American (NA) users. The auction durations for NA users are, however, 27% longer than that of their EU counterparts in the 80th percentile (Fig. 8a). These observations can perhaps be attributed to NA users contacting more exchanges, and that, as we have seen earlier in Fig. 3c, increases auction duration. Bid durations for Oceania (OC) users are alarmingly high: 23% of bids take longer than 1 s (Fig. 7c), which precipitates in long auctions for OC users (Fig. 8a). Only 7% auctions of OC users take, however, longer than 2.5 s compared to 10% of auctions in case of NA users. For a large fraction of OC users, even though bids arrive late, the JavaScript perhaps times out and terminates the auction, potentially introducing some loss of ad revenue for publishers.

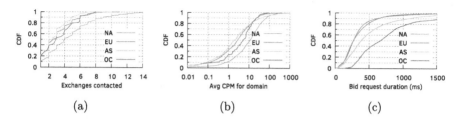

(a)   (b)   (c)

Fig. 7. Impact of a user's location on (a) the number of exchanges contacted, (b) the mean CPM obtained per web page, and (c) bid-request durations.

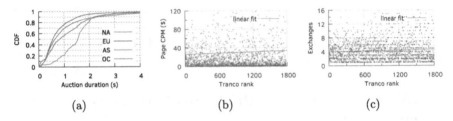

Fig. 8. (a) Impact of user's location on auction duration, and the impact of a web-site's ranking on (b) mean CPM and (c) number of exchanges contacted.

C Popularity Correlations

We investigate, in this appendix, how the popularity ranking of a web site affects its HB implementation and the CPM it receives on its ad slots. For popularity rankings, we used the Tranco list [38], a stable top list hardened against manipulation. We used the relative ranks of second-level domains observed in our measurements and filtered out web sites that have fewer than 10 data points.

Figure 8b shows the mean CPM per web-page visit, of a given web site, as a function of that site's relative Tranco rank. The linear fit, with a slope of 0.008, reveals a weak correlation, suggesting that web-site popularity is not a strong indicator of "high-value" audience for advertisers. For instance, `imgur.com` (rank 51), an image-sharing web site outranks `wsj.com` (rank 152), a major business-focused publication.

Increasing the number of ad exchanges contacted increases the auction duration, which may have implications for end-users' browsing experiences (refer Sect. 5). Figure 8c shows, however, no correlation between the rank of a web site (based on Tranco) and the number of ad exchanges it contacts: Popular web sites do not contact fewer exchanges than unpopular ones to improve user experience.

We also repeated these analyses with the Majestic Million top list[6] instead of Tranco. Majestic Million ranks web sites by the number of subnets linking to them, which is more of a quality measure than raw traffic. Regardless, we did not observe any significant change in the results and inferences presented above.

References

1. Adzerk: Ad Tech Insights - August 2019 Report, August 2019. https://adzerk.com/assets/reports/AdTechInsights_Aug2019.pdf
2. Agababov, V., et al.: Flywheel: Google's data compression proxy for the mobile web. In: NSDI (2015)
3. Akamai: Akamai "10For10", July 2015. https://www.akamai.com/us/en/multimedia/documents/brochure/akamai-10for10-brochure.pdf

---

[6] https://majestic.com/reports/majestic-million.

4. Anthes, G.: Data brokers are watching you. Commun. ACM **58**(1), 28–30 (2014)
5. Apple Open Source: tcp_cache.c, September 2017. https://github.com/opensource-apple/xnu/blob/master/bsd/netinet/tcp_cache.c
6. Aqeel, W.: MyAdPrice: an ad-tracking extension for Chrome and Firefox, January 2020. https://myadprice.github.io/
7. Balasubramanian, P.: Updates on Windows TCP, July 2017. https://datatracker.ietf.org/meeting/100/materials/slides-100-tcpm-updates-on-windows-tcp-00
8. Barreda-Ángeles, M., Arapakis, I., Bai, X., Cambazoglu, B.B., Pereda-Baños, A.: Unconscious physiological effects of search latency on users and their click behaviour. In: Proceedings of the 38th International ACM SIGIR Conference on Research and Development in Information Retrieval, SIGIR 2015 (2015)
9. Benes, R.: 'An ad tech urban legend': an oral history of how header bidding became digital advertising's hottest buzzword, June 2017. https://digiday.com/media/header-bidding-oral-history/
10. Bozkurt, I.N., et al.: Why is the Internet so slow?!. In: Kaafar, M.A., Uhlig, S., Amann, J. (eds.) PAM 2017. LNCS, vol. 10176, pp. 173–187. Springer, Cham (2017). https://doi.org/10.1007/978-3-319-54328-4_13
11. Carrascal, J.P., Riederer, C., Erramilli, V., Cherubini, M., de Oliveira, R.: Your browsing behavior for a big mac: economics of personal information online. In: WWW (2013)
12. Chanchary, F., Chiasson, S.: User perceptions of sharing, advertising, and tracking. In: Eleventh Symposium On Usable Privacy and Security (SOUPS), July 2015
13. Cheng, Y.: Pause fast open globally after third consecutive timeout. https://patchwork.ozlabs.org/patch/847640/. Accessed 16 Oct 2019
14. Chromium bugs: TCP fast open not supported on Windows 10 build 1607. https://bugs.chromium.org/p/chromium/issues/detail?id=635080. Accessed 16 Oct 2019
15. Confessore, N.: Cambridge Analytica and Facebook: The Scandal and the Fallout So Far. The New York Times, April 2018
16. Cook, J., Nithyanand, R., Shafiq, Z.: Inferring tracker-advertiser relationships in the online advertising ecosystem using header bidding. CoRR abs/1907.07275 (2019)
17. Davies, J.: Beware of page latency: the side effects to header bidding, September 2016. https://digiday.com/uk/beware-page-latency-side-effects-header-bidding/
18. DeWitt, G.: Improperly implemented header bidding tags cause page slowdown and decreased revenue for publishers, May 2017. https://www.indexexchange.com/improperly-implemented-header-bidding-tags-cause-page-slowdown-and-decreased-revenue-for-publishers/
19. Enberg, J.: Global Digital Ad Spending 2019, March 2019. https://www.emarketer.com/content/global-digital-ad-spending-2019
20. Englehardt, S., et al.: Cookies that give you away: the surveillance implications of web tracking. In: WWW (2015)
21. Gartenberg, C.: Seized documents reveal that Facebook knew about Russian data harvesting as early as 2014, The Verge, November 2018
22. Google: Latency Restrictions and Peering. https://developers.google.com/ad-exchange/rtb/peer-guide. Accessed 12 Oct 2019
23. Google: The arrival of real-time bidding, June 2011. https://www.rtbchina.com/wp-content/uploads/2012/03/Google-White-Paper-The-Arrival-of-Real-Time-Bidding-July-2011.pdf
24. Guha, S., Cheng, B., Francis, P.: Privad: practical privacy in online advertising. In: NSDI (2011)

25. Hesmans, B., Duchene, F., Paasch, C., Detal, G., Bonaventure, O.: Are TCP extensions Middlebox-proof? In: HotMiddlebox (2013)
26. da Hora, D.N., Asrese, A.S., Christophides, V., Teixeira, R., Rossi, D.: Narrowing the gap between QoS metrics and web QoE using above-the-fold metrics. In: PAM (2018)
27. Iyengar, J., Thomson, M.: QUIC: A UDP-Based Multiplexed and Secure Transport. Internet-draft, Internet Engineering Task Force, September 2019
28. Jauvion, G., Grislain, N., Dkengne Sielenou, P., Garivier, A., Gerchinovitz, S.: Optimization of a SSP's header bidding strategy using Thompson sampling. In: KDD (2018)
29. Lee, W.M.: Using the MetaMask Chrome extension, pp. 93–126. Apress (2019)
30. MDN web docs: Introduction to the DOM, May 2019. https://developer.mozilla.org/en-US/docs/Web/API/Document_Object_Model/Introduction
31. MDN web docs: JavaScript APIs for WebExtensions, March 2019. https://developer.mozilla.org/en-US/docs/Mozilla/Add-ons/WebExtensions/API
32. Meeker, M.: Internet Trends 2019, June 2019. https://www.bondcap.com/pdf/Internet_Trends_2019.pdf
33. Mozilla Firefox: Content blocking. https://support.mozilla.org/en-US/kb/content-blocking. Accessed 16 Oct 2019
34. Opera: Data savings and turbo mode. https://www.opera.com/turbo. Accessed 16 Oct 2019
35. Pachilakis, M., Papadopoulos, P., Markatos, E.P., Kourtellis, N.: No more chasing waterfalls: a measurement study of the header bidding ad-ecosystem. In: IMC (2019)
36. Pandey, P., Muthukumar, P.: Real-Time Ad Impression Bids Using DynamoDB, April 2013. https://aws.amazon.com/blogs/aws/real-time-ad-impression-bidsusing-dynamodb/
37. Papadopoulos, P., Kourtellis, N., Markatos, E.P.: The cost of digital advertisement: comparing user and advertiser views. In: WWW (2018)
38. Pochat, V.L., Goethem, T.V., Tajalizadehkhoob, S., Korczyński, M., Joosen, W.: Tranco: a research-oriented top sites ranking hardened against manipulation. NDSS (2019)
39. Prebid: A brief history of header bidding. http://prebid.org/overview/intro.html#a-brief-history-of-header-bidding. Accessed 9 Oct 2019
40. Prebid: Header Bidding Made Easy. http://prebid.org/index.html. Accessed 10 Oct 2019
41. Prebid: How to add a new bidder adapter, http://prebid.org/dev-docs/bidder-adaptor.html. Accessed 14 Oct 2019
42. Prebid: How to reduce the latency of header bidding with Prebid.js. http://prebid.org/overview/how-to-reduce-latency-of-header-bidding.html. Accessed 12 Oct 2019
43. Prebid: Prebid.org members . http://prebid.org/partners/partners.html. Accessed 15 Oct 2019
44. Pujol, E., Hohlfeld, O., Feldmann, A.: Annoyed users: ads and ad-block usage in the wild. In: IMC (2015)
45. Qin, R., Yuan, Y., Wang, F.: Optimizing the revenue for ad exchanges in header bidding advertising markets. In: 2017 IEEE International Conference on Systems, Man, and Cybernetics (SMC), October 2017
46. Radhakrishnan, S., Cheng, Y., Chu, J., Jain, A., Raghavan, B.: TCP fast open. In: CoNEXT, December 2011

47. Ramirez, E., Brill, J., Ohlhausen, M.K., Wright, J.D., Mcsweeney, T.: Data brokers: a call for transparency and accountability. Technical report, United States Federal Trade Commission, May 2014

48. Razaghpanah, A., et al.: Apps, trackers, privacy, and regulators: a global study of the mobile tracking ecosystem. In: NDSS (2018)

49. Rescorla, E.: The Transport Layer Security (TLS) Protocol Version 1.3. RFC 8446, August 2018

50. Sluis, S.: The rise of 'header bidding' and the end of the publisher waterfall, June 2015. https://adexchanger.com/publishers/the-rise-of-header-bidding-and-the-end-of-the-publisher-waterfall/

51. Snowden, E.J.: Permanent record. Metropolitan Books (2019)

52. Sovrn: The Past, Present, and Future of Header Bidding, February 2017. https://www.sovrn.com/blog/header-bidding-grows-up/

53. Staiano, J., Oliver, N., Lepri, B., de Oliveira, R., Caraviello, M., Sebe, N.: Money walks: a human-centric study on the economics of personal mobile data. In: Proceedings of the 2014 ACM International Joint Conference on Pervasive and Ubiquitous Computing, UbiComp 2014 (2014)

54. The Times Open Team: We Re-Launched The New York Times Paywall and No One Noticed, Times Open, August 2019

55. Toubiana, V., Narayanan, A., Boneh, D., Nissenbaum, H., Barocas, S.: Adnostic: privacy preserving targeted advertising. In: NDSS (2010)

56. Venkatadri, G., Mislove, A., Gummadi, K.P.: Treads: transparency-enhancing ads. In: HotNets (2018)

57. Videology Knowledge Lab: Header bidding: a byte-sized overview, October 2015. https://www.iab.com/wp-content/uploads/2015/10/VidLab-HeaderBidding-3.27.17V10.pdf

58. W3C: Navigation Timing, December 2012. https://www.w3.org/TR/navigation-timing/

59. W3C: A Primer for Web Performance Timing APIs, April 2019. https://w3c.github.io/perf-timing-primer/

60. Jim, W.: More than a million readers contribute financially to the Guardian. The Guardian, November 2018

61. Wikipedia: Cost per mille. https://en.wikipedia.org/wiki/Cost_per_mille. Accessed 9 Oct 2019

62. Wikipedia: Geodesic. https://en.wikipedia.org/wiki/Geodesic. Accessed 29 Oct 2019

63. Yen, T.F., Xie, Y., Yu, F., Yu, R.P., Abadi, M.: Host fingerprinting and tracking on the web: privacy and security implications. In: Proceedings of the Network and Distributed System Security Symposium (NDSS) 2012, February 2012

Understanding Video Streaming Algorithms in the Wild

Melissa Licciardello, Maximilian Grüner[(✉)], and Ankit Singla

Department of Computer Science, ETH Zürich, Zürich, Switzerland
{melissa.licciardello,mgruener,ankit.singla}inf.ethz.ch

Abstract. While video streaming algorithms are a hot research area, with interesting new approaches proposed every few months, little is known about the behavior of the streaming algorithms deployed across large online streaming platforms that account for a substantial fraction of Internet traffic. We thus study adaptive bitrate streaming algorithms in use at 10 such video platforms with diverse target audiences. We collect traces of each video player's response to controlled variations in network bandwidth, and examine the algorithmic behavior: how risk averse is an algorithm in terms of target buffer; how long does it takes to reach a stable state after startup; how reactive is it in attempting to match bandwidth versus operating stably; how efficiently does it use the available network bandwidth; etc. We find that deployed algorithms exhibit a wide spectrum of behaviors across these axes, indicating the lack of a consensus one-size-fits-all solution. We also find evidence that most deployed algorithms are tuned towards stable behavior rather than fast adaptation to bandwidth variations, some are tuned towards a visual perception metric rather than a bitrate-based metric, and many leave a surprisingly large amount of the available bandwidth unused.

1 Introduction

Video streaming now forms more than 60% of Internet downstream traffic [25]. Thus, methods of delivering video streams that provide the best user experience despite variability in network conditions are an area of great industry relevance and academic interest. At a coarse level, the problem is to provide a client with the highest possible video resolution, while minimizing pauses in the video stream. There are other factors to consider, of course, such as not switching video resolution often. These considerations are typically rolled into one quality-of-experience score. Streaming services then use adaptive bitrate algorithms, which attempt to maximize QoE by dynamically deciding what resolution to fetch video segments at, as network conditions fluctuate.

While high-quality academic work proposing novel ABR is plentiful, the literature is much more limited (Sect. 2) in its analysis of widely deployed ABRs, their target QoE metrics, and how they compare to recent research proposals.

M. Licciardello and M. Grüner—Equal contribution.

© Springer Nature Switzerland AG 2020
A. Sperotto et al. (Eds.): PAM 2020, LNCS 12048, pp. 298–313, 2020.
https://doi.org/10.1007/978-3-030-44081-7_18

The goal of this work is precisely to address this gap. Understanding how video platforms serving content to large user populations operate their ABR is crucial to framing future research on this important topic. For instance, we would like to know if there is a consensus across video platforms on how ABR should behave, or whether different target populations, content niches, and metrics of interest, lead to substantially different ABR behavior. We would also like to understand whether ABR research is optimizing for the same metrics as deployed platforms, which are presumably tuned based on operator experience with real users and their measured engagement.

Towards addressing these questions, we present a study of ABR behavior across 10 video streaming platforms (Table 1) chosen for coverage across their diverse target populations: some of the largest ones in terms of overall market share, some regional ones, and some specialized to particular applications like game streaming (not live, archived). Our methodology is simple: we throttle download bandwidth at the client in a time-variant fashion based on throughput traces used in ABR research, and monitor the behavior of streams from different streaming platforms by analyzing jointly their browser-generated HTTP Archive (HAR) files and properties exposed by the video players themselves. For robust measurements, we collect data for several videos on each platform, with our analysis herein being based on 6 days of continuous online streaming in total. Our main findings are as follows:

1. Deployed ABRs exhibit a wide spectrum of behaviors in terms of how much buffer they seek to maintain in their stable state, how closely they try to match changing bandwidth vs. operating more smoothly, how they approach stable behavior after stream initialization, and how well they use available network bandwidth. There is thus not a consensus one-size-fits-all approach in wide deployment.
2. Several deployed ABRs perform better on a QoE metric based on visual perception rather than just video bitrate. This lends support to the goals of recent work [22], indicating that at least some of the industry is already optimizing towards such metrics rather than the bitrate-focused formulations in most prior ABR research.
3. Most deployed ABRs eschew fast changes in response to bandwidth variations, exhibiting stable behavior. In contrast, research ABRs follow bandwidth changes more closely. It is unclear whether this is due to (a) a mismatch in target metrics used in research and industrial ABR; or (b) industrial ABR being sub-optimal.
4. Several deployed ABRs leave substantial available bandwidth unused. For instance YouTube uses less than 60% of the network's available bandwidth on average across our test traces. Similar to the above, it is unclear whether this is due to ABR sub-optimality, or a conscious effort to decrease bandwidth costs.

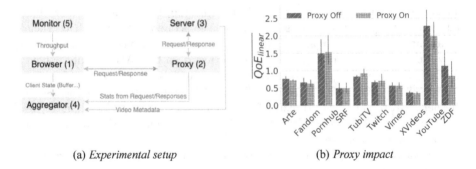

(a) *Experimental setup*   (b) *Proxy impact*

Fig. 1. (a) Player behaviour is influenced through bandwidth throttling, and is recorded from multiple sources. (b) The proxy has little impact on player behavior as measured in terms of average linear QoE ($\overline{QoE_{linear}}$); the whiskers are the 95% confidence interval.

2   Related Work

There is a flurry of academic ABR proposals [6,8,13,14,17,18,22,23,26,27,29, 32], but only limited study of the large number of deployed video streaming platforms catering to varied video types and audiences.

YouTube itself is relatively well studied, with several analyses of various aspects of its behavior [7,19,31], including video encoding, startup behavior, bandwidth variations at fixed quality, a test similar to our reactivity analysis, variation of segment lengths, and redownloads to replace already fetched segments. There is also an end-end analysis of Yahoo's video streaming platform using data from the provider [10].

Several comparisons and analysis of academic ABR algorithms [28,30,33] have also been published, including within each of the several new proposals mentioned above. In particular, [28] compares three reference ABR implementations, showing that the configuration of various parameters has a substantial impact on their performance.

Facebook recently published [16] their test of Pensieve [17] in their video platform, reporting small improvements (average video quality improvement of 1.6% and average reduction of 0.4% in rebuffers) compared to their deployed approach.

However, a broader comparative study that examines a large number of diverse, popular streaming platforms has thus far been missing. Note also that unlike ABR comparisons in academic work and head-to-head comparisons of methods in Facebook's study, QoE comparisons across platforms are not necessarily meaningful, given the differences in their content encoding, content type, and audiences. Thus, in contrast to prior work, we define a set of metrics that broadly characterize ABR behavior and compare the observed behavior of a large, diverse set of streaming providers on these metrics. Where relevant, we also contrast the behavior of these deployed ABRs with research proposals.

To the best of our knowledge this is the only work to compare a large set of deployed ABRs and discuss how their behavior differs from academic work in this direction.

3 Methodology

To understand a target platform's ABR, we must collect traces of its behavior, including the video player's state (in terms of selected video quality and buffer occupancy) across controlled network conditions and different videos.

3.1 Experimental Setup

Figure 1a shows our architecture for collecting traces about player behaviour. Our Python3 implementation (available at [11]) uses the Selenium browser automation framework [4] to interact with online services. For academic ABR algorithms, trace collection is simpler, and uses offline simulation, as suggested in [17].

While playing a video, we throttle the throughput at the client (1) using tc (Traffic control, a Linux tool).[1] The state of the client browser (e.g., current buffer occupancy) is captured by the Monitor (5) every a seconds. All requests sent from the client (1) to the server (3) are logged by a local proxy (2). Beyond the final browser state, the proxy allows us to log video player activity such as chunks that are requested but not played. We also obtain metadata about the video from the server (e.g., at what bitrate each video quality is encoded). Metadata is obtained through offline analysis by downloading the video at all different qualities. All information gathered from the three sources — the proxy, the browser and the server — is aggregated (4).

Certain players replace chunks previously downloaded at low quality with high quality ones ("redownloading") in case there is later more bandwidth and no immediate rebuffer risk. Using the proxy's view of requests and responses and the video metadata, we can map every chunk downloaded to a play-range within the video, and use this mapping to identify which chunks/how many bytes were redownloaded.

How Do We Add a Platform to Our Measurements? Most video platforms (all except YouTube, for which we use [5]) use chunk-based streaming. To evaluate such platforms, we use developer tools in Chrome to understand how the player obtains the download links for the chunks. Typically, a .m3u8 [21] file downloaded by the player contains the locations for all chunks at all qualities. This allows us to write code that fetches all chunks for the test videos at all qualities, such that we can use these videos in our offline simulation analysis of

---

[1] At the bandwidth levels seen in our traces, bottlenecks are at our client—our university's connectivity to large services is otherwise high-bandwidth, consistently resulting in the highest-quality playback available on each service.

the academic Robust MPC approach.[2] Having all chunks available also enables calculation of their visual perceived quality (VMAF [15]). We also need to map each chunk to its bitrate level and time in the video stream, by understanding how video content is named in the platform (*e.g.*, through "itags" in YouTube).

For online experiments through the browser, we need to instrument the platform's video player. We do this by automating the selection of the HTML5 video player element, and having our browser automation framework use this to start the video player and put it in full screen mode. We can then access the current buffer occupancy and current playback time using standard HTML5 attributes. We use a proxy to log the remaining statistics (*e.g.*, resolution played/fetched) because relying on the player alone would have required painstaking code injection specialized to each provider.

YouTube does not follow such chunked behavior (as past work has noted [19]). It can request arbitrary byte ranges of video from the server. We use an already available tool [5] to download the videos, and then learn the mapping from the byte ranges to play time from the downloaded videos.

3.2 The Proxy's Impact on Measurements

Some of our measurements (*e.g.*, redownloads) use an on-path proxy, so we verify that this does not have a meaningful impact by comparing metrics that can be evaluated without the proxy. For this, we use traces with constant bandwidth $b \in [0.5, 0.8, 1.2, 2.5]$ Mbps, repeating each experiment 5 times for the same video. For our comparison, we calculate QoE using the linear function from MPC [18] with and without the proxy. For every video-network trace combination, we calculate the mean QoE and show the mean across these, together with its 95% confidence interval with whiskers in Fig. 1b.

As the results show, for most platforms the proxy has a minimal impact: across providers, the average difference in QoE with and without the proxy is 7%. For YouTube and ZDF, the differences are larger, but still within the confidence bounds: for these providers, there are large variations across experiments even without the proxy, indicating differing behaviour in very similar conditions in general.

3.3 Metrics of Interest

Different video platforms serve very different types of content, and.target different geographies with varied client connectivity characteristics. It is thus not particularly informative to compare metrics like bitrate-based QoE across platforms. For instance, given the different bitrate encodings for different types of content, bitrate-QoE is not comparable across platforms. We thus focus on comparisons in terms of the following behavioral and algorithm design aspects.

---

[2] To avoid the unintended use of our scripts for downloading copyright-protected content, we refrain from publishing code for this part of our pipeline.

Initialization Behavior: We quantify how much *wait time* a video platform typically incurs for streams to start playback, and how much *buffer* (in seconds of playback) it builds before starting. We use traces with a fixed bandwidth of 3 Mbps until player's HTML5 interactions are available, thus always downloading items like the player itself at a fixed bandwidth. This is done to avoid failure at startup: some platforms cause errors if network conditions are harsh from the beginning. After this, we throttle using only the high-bandwidth traces from the Oboe [6] data set, which have a mean throughput of 2.7 Mbps. We start timing from when the first chunk starts downloading (per the HAR files; the player HTML5 interactions may become available earlier or later).

Table 1. We test a diverse set of large video platforms.

Provider	Description	Alexa rank	# Resolutions
Arte	French-German, cultural	270, France	4.0 ± 0.0
Fandom	Gaming, pop-culture	91, Global	5.0 ± 0.0
SRF	Swiss Public Service	45, Switzerland	5.7 ± 0.48
TubiTV	Movies and series of all genres	1330, USA	3.0 ± 0.0
Twitch	Live and VoD streaming service, gaming	39, Global	5.9 ± 0.32
Vimeo	Artistic content [20]	188, Global	4.2 ± 0.92
YouTube	Broad coverage	2, Global	6.5 ± 1.08
ZDF	German Public Service	47, Germany	5.3 ± 0.48
Pornhub	Pornographic video sharing website	46, Global	4.0 ± 0.0
XVideos	Pornographic video sharing website	67, Global	4.4 ± 0.52

Convergence: During startup, an ABR may have little information about the client's network conditions. How do different ABRs approach stable behavior starting from this lack of information? Stability in this sense refers to fewer bitrate switches. Thus, to assess convergence characteristics, we quantify the bitrate changes (in Mbps per second) across playback, *i.e.*, a single switch from 3 Mbps to 4 Mbps bitrate over a total playback of 5-s amounts to 0.2 Mbps/sec on this metric. We chose not to compare the raw *number* of switches/sec — one switch at YouTube is very different from one switch at TubiTV, due to the differing discreteness of their bitrate ladders.

Risk-Tolerance: ABRs can hedge against rebuffer events by building a larger buffer, thus insulating them from bandwidth drops. Thus, how much *buffer* (in seconds of video) an ABR builds during its stable operation is indicative of its risk tolerance.

Reactivity: ABRs must react to changes in network bandwidth. However, reacting too quickly to bandwidth changes can result in frequent switching of video quality, and cause unstable behavior when network capacity is highly variable.

To quantify reactivity of an ABR, we use synthetic traces with just one bandwidth change after convergence, and measure the evolution of *bitrate difference* in the video playback after the change over time (with the number of following chunk downloads used as a proxy for time).

Bandwidth Usage: ABR must necessarily make conservative decisions on video quality: future network bandwidth is uncertain, so fetching chunks at precisely the estimated network bandwidth would (a) not allow building up a playback buffer even if the estimate were accurate; and (b) cause rebuffers when bandwidth is overestimated. Thus, ABR can only use some fraction of the available bandwidth. We quantify this behavior in terms of the fraction of *bytes played to optimally downloadable*, with "optimally downloadable" reflecting the minimum of (*a posteriori* known) network capacity and the bytes needed for highest quality streaming.

For better bandwidth use and to improve QoE, some ABRs are known to redownload and replace already downloaded chunks in the buffer with higher quality chunks. We quantify this as the fraction of *bytes played to bytes downloaded*. Fractions <1 reflect some chunks not being played due to their replacement with higher quality chunks.

QoE Goal: Academic ABR work has largely used a QoE metric that linearly combines a reward for high bitrate with penalties for rebuffers and quality switches [17,18]. More recent work has suggested formulations of QoE that reward perceptual video quality rather than just bitrate [22]. One such metric of perceptual quality, VMAF [15], combines several traditional indicators of video quality. While it is difficult, if not impossible, to determine what precise metric each platform's ABR optimizes for, we can evaluate coarsely whether this optimization is geared towards bitrate or VMAF-like metrics by examining what video chunks an ABR tries to fetch at high quality: do chunks with higher VMAF get fetched at a higher quality level? To assess this, we sort chunks by VMAF (computed using [15]) and quantify for the top $n\%$ of chunks, their (average) playback quality level compared to the (average) quality level of all chunks, $\overline{Q_{top-n\%}} - \overline{Q_{all}}$. A large difference implies a preference for high-VMAF chunks.

3.4   Measurement Coverage

We evaluate multiple videos on each of 10 platforms across a large set of network traces.

Target Platforms: Table 1 lists the platforms we analyze (with their Alexa popularity rank, as of January 2020). While by no means exhaustive, these were chosen to cover a range of content types and a few different geographies. Note that Netflix, Amazon Prime Video, and Hulu were excluded because their terms of service prohibit automated experiments or/and reverse-engineering [1–3]. For Twitch, which offers both live streams and video-on-demand of archived live streams, we only study the latter, as live streaming is a substantially different problem, and a poor fit with the rest of our chosen platforms.

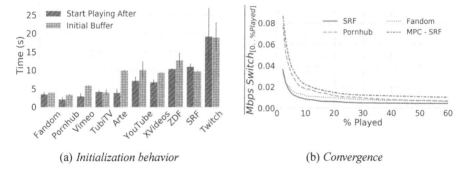

(a) *Initialization behavior*   (b) *Convergence*

Fig. 2. (a) Initialization: most providers start playback after one chunk is downloaded. (b) Convergence is measured in terms of changes in bitrate switching, *i.e.*, the (absolute) sum of bitrate differentials across all switches from the start, divided by the thus-far playback duration. As expected, switching is more frequent during startup, but the degree of switching varies across providers both in startup and later.

Different platforms encode content at varied resolutions and number of resolutions, ranging from just 3 quality levels for TubiTV to 6.5 on YouTube (on average across our test videos; YouTube has different numbers of resolutions on different videos.)

When comparing the behavior of deployed ABRs with academic ones, we test the latter in the offline environment made available by the Pensieve authors [17]. For each tested video on each platform, we pre-download all its chunks at all available qualities. We then simulate playback using the same network traces up until the same point offline for academic ABRs as we do for the deployed ones. We primarily rely on Robust MPC [18] (referred to throughout as MPC) as a stand-in for a recent, high-quality academic ABR approach. While even newer proposals are available, they either use data-dependent learning techniques [6, 17] that are unnecessary for our purpose of gaining intuition, or do not have available, easy-to-use code.

Videos: The type of content can have substantial bearing on streaming performance, *e.g.*, videos with highly variable encoding can be challenging for ABR. We thus used a set of 10 videos on each platform. Where a popularity measure was available, we used the most popular videos; otherwise, we handpicked a sample of different types of videos. Videos from each platform are encoded in broadly similar bitrate ranges, with most differences lying at higher qualities, *e.g.*, some content being available in 4K.

It would, of course, be attractive to upload the same video content to several platforms (at least ones that host user-generated content) to remove the impact of videos in the cross-platform comparisons. However, different platforms use their own encoding pipelines, making it unclear whether this approach has much advantage over ours, using just popular videos across platforms.

Network Traces: Our experiments use synthetic and real-world traces from 3 datasets in past work [6,9,24]. Unfortunately, a full cross-product of platform-video-trace would be prohibitively expensive—the FCC traces [9] alone would require 4 years of streaming time. To sidestep this, we rank traces by their throughput variability and pick traces with the highest and lowest variability together with some randomly sampled ones.

Our final network trace collection consists of the 5 least stable, 5 most stable, and 5 random traces from the Belgium trace collection [12], and 10 in each of those categories from the Norway [24], the Oboe [6] and the FCC datasets[3]. We also use 15 constant bandwidth traces covering the range from 0.3 to 15 Mbps uniformly. Lastly we add 10 step traces: after 60 s of streaming we suddenly increase/drop the bandwidth from/to 1 Mbps to/from 5 values covering the space from 1.5 to 10 Mbps uniformly.

In total, we use 130 traces with throughput (average over time for each trace) ranging from 0.09 to 41.43 Mbps, with an average of 6.13 Mbps across traces. Note that we make no claim of our set of traces being representative; rather our goal is to test a *variety* of traces to obtain insight into various ABR behaviors. If a trace does not cover the whole experiment we loop over it.

For quantifying reactivity, we only use the synthetic traces mentioned above, with a single upward step change in bandwidth. For quantifying startup delay, we use traces with a bandwidth of around 3 Mbps as noted in Sect. 3.3.

Ethics: We are careful to not generate excessive traffic or large bursts to any platform, measuring at any time, only one stream per service, typically at a low throttled rate.

4   Measurement Results

Overall, we see diverse behavior on each tested metric across platforms. We attempt to include results across all platforms where possible, but for certain plots, for sake of clarity, we choose a subset of platforms that exhibits a range of interesting behaviors.

Initialization Behavior, Fig. 2a: We find that most platforms' ABR simply waits for one chunk download to finish before beginning playback. This is reflected in the buffer occupancy at playback. Some players like ZDF and SRF use a larger chunk size (10 s), which is why they pre-load more seconds of buffer.

As one might expect, building a larger buffer before playback starts generally incurs a higher start time. Twitch stands out in this regard, as it downloads nearly 20 s of buffer before start. Some players, whilst downloading the same number of buffer seconds as others, do so at much higher resolution – *e.g.,* SRF downloads its first 10 s with 6× as many pixels as Arte. This is reflected in the disparity between their start times, despite both populating the buffer with 10 s of playback. More broadly, all such "discrepancies" are difficult to explain because startup is hard to untangle from other network activity, *e.g.,*

---

[3] Specifically, the stable collection from September 2017 [9].

some players already start downloading video chunks while the player itself is still downloading, thus complicating our notion of timing. (We start timing from the point the first chunk starts downloading. For most platforms, this provides a leveling standard that excludes variation from other downloads on their Web interface. It also helps reduce latency impacts that are mainly infrastructure driven, as well as effects of our browser automation framework.)

Convergence, Fig. 2b: As expected, during startup and early playback, every player attempts to find a stable streaming state. This results in many bitrate switches followed by much smoother behavior with more limited switching. Nevertheless, there are large differences across players, *e.g.*, Pornhub switches more than twice as much as Fandom and SRF in the beginning. In stable state, Fandom switches substantially more than SRF. We also evaluated the academic (Robust) MPC algorithm [18] on the same network traces and over the SRF videos. The MPC algorithm would use more than twice as much switching both in startup and later, compared to SRF's deployed ABR. Consequently, SRF scores lower than MPC on the default linear QoE model used in MPC. However, this does not necessarily imply that SRF's design is sub-optimal; it could also be optimizing for a different metric that values stability more.

For clarity, we only picked a few platforms as exemplars of behavior towards convergence instead of including all 10 tested platforms. The behavior is broadly similar with more switching early on, but the precise stabilization differs across platforms.

Risk-Tolerance, Fig. 3: We observe widely different buffering behavior across the players we tested. Of course, every player uses early playback to download lower quality chunks and accumulate buffer, but some, like YouTube, settle towards as much as 80 s of buffer, while others like Fandom operate with a much smaller buffer of around 20 s. Testing MPC's algorithm on the same traces across the YouTube videos reveals that it falls towards the lower end, stabilizing at 20 s of buffer.

Note that for approaches that allow redownloads (including YouTube), larger buffers are a reasonable choice: any chunks that were downloaded at low quality can later be replaced. This is likely to be a more robust strategy in the face of high bandwidth variability. However, for approaches that do not use redownloads, a larger buffer implies that all its content must be played out at whatever quality it was downloaded at, thus limiting the possibilities to benefit from opportunistic behavior if bandwidth later improves.

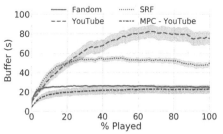

Fig. 3. Risk-tolerance: YouTube operates with nearly 4× the buffer for Fandom. The shaded regions show the 95% confidence interval around the mean.

Thus operating with a smaller buffer of higher-quality chunks may be preferable to filling it with lower-quality chunks. In the absence of redownloads, there is thus a tradeoff: a larger buffer provides greater insurance against bandwidth drops, but reduces playback quality. At the same time, redownloads are themselves a compromise: *if* better bitrate decisions could be made to begin with, redownloads amount to inefficient bandwidth use.

Reactivity, Fig. 4: We find that most deployed ABRs are cautious in reacting to bandwidth changes. This is best illustrated through comparisons between deployed and academic ABRs. Figure 4 (right) shows such a comparison between TubiTV and MPC evaluated on the same traces and videos. After the bandwidth increases (at x-axis $= 0$ in the plot), TubiTV waits for tens of chunk downloads before it substantially ramps up bitrate. In contrast, MPC starts switching to higher bitrates within a few chunk downloads. (The large variations around the average arise from the varied sizes of the step-increases in the used network traces and variations in the tested videos.)

While we have not yet evaluated a large number of mobile ABR implementations (see Sect. 5), we were able to experiment with Vimeo's mobile and desktop versions, shown in Fig. 4 (left). They exhibit similar ramp-up behavior in terms of how many downloads it takes before Vimeo reacts, but show very different degrees of bitrate change. The desktop version increases bitrate in several steps after the bandwidth increase, while the mobile one settles at a modest increase. This is along expected lines, as the mobile player, targeting the smaller screen, often does not use the higher-quality content at all.

A comparison between TubiTV and Vimeo (desktop) across the two plots is also interesting: Vimeo ramps up faster than TubiTV. (MPC ramps us even faster on the Vimeo videos.) One potential reason is the difference in encoding—TubiTV serves each video in only 3 resolutions, compared to Vimeo's 4–5. This implies that over the same network traces, TubiTV must necessarily see a larger change in bandwidth to be able to jump from one bitrate to the next, given its larger differential in bitrate levels.

Bandwidth Usage, Fig. 5a: Different platforms use bandwidth very differently. Arte discards a surprisingly large 23% of its downloaded bytes in its efforts to replace already downloaded low-quality chunks with high-quality ones. Some platforms, including YouTube, SRF, and Vimeo, show milder redownload behavior, while several others, including XVideos, Fanrom, Pornhub, and ZDF, do not use redownloads at all.

ZDF and TubiTV are able to use 80% of the network's available bytes for fetching (actually played) video chunks, while all others use the network much less effectively. While the uncertainty in future bandwidth and the desire to maintain stable streaming without many quality switches *necessitates* some bandwidth inefficiencies, we were surprised by how large these inefficiencies are. In particular, XVideos, YouTube, Twitch, and Fandom all use less than 60% of the network's available capacity on average across our trace-video pairs[4].

---

[4] Note that these inefficiencies cannot be blamed on transport/TCP alone, as on the same traces, other players are able to use 80% of the available capacity. We also carefully account for non-video data to ensure we are not simply ignoring non-chunk data in these calculations. For instance, audio data is separately delivered for Vimeo and YouTube, but is accounted for appropriately in our bandwidth use analysis.

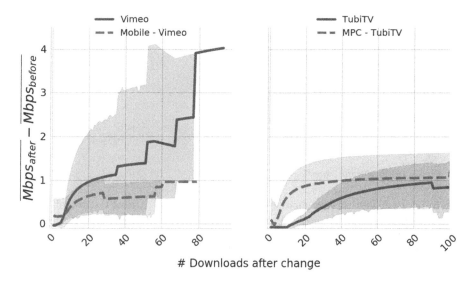

Fig. 4. We measure reactivity in terms of bitrate evolution after a bandwidth increase, *i.e.*, difference in average playback bitrate after and before the bandwidth change over time (in terms of chunk downloads). The plots show the reactivity differences between: (left) mobile and desktop versions of Vimeo; and (right) TubiTV and MPC.

This low usage is particularly surprising for YouTube, which uses several strategies—variable chunk lengths (as opposed to fixed-size chunks in other providers), larger number of available video resolutions, and redownloads—that allow finer-grained decision making, and thus should support more effective bandwidth use. Given these advanced features in their ABR design, it is more likely that their optimization goals differ from academic ABR work than their algorithm simply being poorly designed. While we cannot concretely ascertain their optimization objectives, one could speculate that given the large global demands YouTube faces while operating (largely) as a free, ad-based service, a profit maximizing strategy may comprise providing good-enough QoE with a limited expense on downstream bandwidth.

QoE goal, Fig. 5b: We find that some providers fetch high-VMAF chunks at higher quality than the average chunk. In particular, Twitch fetches the chunks in the top 20th percentile by VMAF at a mean quality level 0.79 higher than an average chunk. If instead of Twitch's ABR, we used a VMAF-unaware, simple, rate-based ABR[5] that uses an estimate of throughput to decide on video quality, this difference in quality level between high-VMAF and the average chunk would reduce to 0.46.

---

[5] This ABR estimates throughput, T, as the mean of the last 5 throughput measurements. For its next download, it then picks the highest quality level with a bitrate $\leq T$. It thus downloads the largest chunk for which the estimated download time does not exceed the playback time.

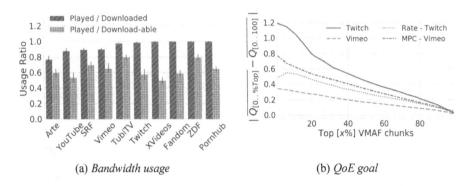

(a) *Bandwidth usage*   (b) *QoE goal*

Fig. 5. (a) Bandwidth usage: many players use surprisingly little of the available network bandwidth (Played/Download-able) despite the potential to improve quality with more bandwidth, *e.g.,* XVideos uses only 50% of it; and some players, like Arte, spend a large fraction of their used bandwidth on redownloads. (b) QoE goal: we measure how much a player prefers high-VMAF chunks by quantifying the average quality-level difference between all chunks and only the top-x% of chunks by VMAF (*i.e.,* $\overline{Q}_{[0...\%Top]}$). Some players, like Twitch, show a large preference for high-VMAF chunks.

Note that given the correlation between higher quality and higher VMAF, high-VMAF chunks are more likely to be fetched at high quality; what is interesting is the degree to which different players prefer them. Vimeo, for instance, shows a much smaller difference of 0.27 between the quality level of chunks in the top 20th percentile and an average chunk. If MPC's ABR were used to fetch chunks from Vimeo, this difference increases to 0.534, because MPC is willing to make more quality switches than Vimeo.

Our results thus indicate diversity in optimization objectives in terms of bandwidth use and QoE targets across deployed video platforms. It is at least plausible that academic ABRs produce different behavior over the same traces not because they are much more efficient, but rather the optimization considerations are different. While algorithms like MPC are flexible enough to be used for a variety of optimization objectives, it is unclear how performance would compare across a suitably modified MPC (or other state-of-the-art ABR) when evaluated on operator objectives.

5   Limitations and Future Work

Our first broad examination of a diverse set of widely deployed ABRs reveals several interesting insights about their behavior, but also raises several questions we have not yet addressed:

1. Does ABR behavior for the same platform vary by geography and client network? Such customization is plausible—there are likely large differences in network characteristics that a provider could use in heuristics, especially for startup behavior, where little else may be known about the client's network

bandwidth and its stability. However, addressing this question would require running bandwidth-expensive experiments from a large set of globally distributed vantage points.

2. How big are the differences between mobile and desktop versions of ABR across platforms? Unfortunately, while the browser provides several universal abstractions through which to perform monitoring on the desktop, most platforms use their own mobile apps, greatly increasing the per-platform effort for analysis.

3. If we assume that the largest providers like YouTube and Twitch are optimizing ABR well, based on their experience with large populations of users, can we infer what their optimization objective is? While there are hints in our work that these providers are not necessarily optimizing for the same objective as academic ABR, we are not yet able to make more concrete assertions of this type.

4. Does latency have a substantial impact on ABR? ABR is largely a bandwidth-dependent application, but startup behavior could potentially be tied to latency as well. We have thus far not evaluated latency-dependence.

6   Conclusion

We conduct a broad comparison of adaptive bitrate video streaming algorithms deployed in the wild across 10 large video platforms offering varied content targeted at different audiences. We find large differences in player behavior, with a wide spectrum of choices instantiated across virtually all metrics we examined. For instance, our results show that: (a) some deployed ABRs are conscious of perceptual quality metrics compared to others focused on bitrate; (b) no deployed ABRs follow available bandwidth as closely as research ABRs; and (c) several ABRs leave a large fraction of available network capacity unused. Whether this diversity of design choices and behaviors stems from careful tailoring towards different use cases and optimization objectives, or is merely a natural consequence of sub-optimal, independent design is at present unclear. But if large, otherwise extremely well-engineered platforms like YouTube differ so substantially from state-of-the-art research ABRs, then it is at least plausible that ABR research is more narrowly focused than desirable.

References

1. Amazon prime terms of use. https://www.amazon.co.uk/gp/help/customer/display.html?nodeId=201909000&pop-up=
2. Hulu terms of use. https://www.hulu.com/terms
3. Netflix terms of use. https://help.netflix.com/legal/termsofuse
4. Selenium webdriver. https://www.seleniumhq.org/projects/webdriver/
5. YouTube downloader. https://github.com/ytdl-org/youtube-dl/
6. Akhtar, Z., et al.: Oboe: auto-tuning video ABR algorithms to network conditions. In: ACM SIGCOMM (2018)

7. Añorga, J., Arrizabalaga, S., Sedano, B., Goya, J., Alonso-Arce, M., Mendizabal, J.: Analysis of YouTube's traffic adaptation to dynamic environments. Multimedia Tools Appl. **77**(7), 7977 (2018)
8. De Cicco, L., Caldaralo, V., Palmisano, V., Mascolo, S.: Elastic: a client-side controller for dynamic adaptive streaming over HTTP (DASH). In: IEEE Packet Video Workshop (PV) (2013)
9. Federal Communications Commission: Validated data September 2017 - measuring broadband America. https://www.fcc.gov/reports-research/reports/
10. Ghasemi, M., Kanuparthy, P., Mansy, A., Benson, T., Rexford, J.: Performance characterization of a commercial video streaming service. In: ACM IMC (2016)
11. Grüner, M., Licciardello, M.: Understanding video streaming algorithms in the wild - scripts. https://github.com/magruener/understanding-video-streaming-in-the-wild
12. van der Hooft, J., et al.: HTTP/2-based adaptive streaming of HEVC video over 4G/LTE networks. IEEE Commun. Lett. **20**(11), 2177–2180 (2016)
13. Jiang, J., Sekar, V., Zhang, H.: Improving fairness, efficiency, and stability in HTTP-based adaptive video streaming with festive. IEEE/ACM Trans. Netw. **22**(1), 326–340 (2014). https://doi.org/10.1109/TNET.2013.2291681
14. Li, Z., et al.: Probe and adapt: rate adaptation for HTTP video streaming at scale. IEEE J. Sel. Areas Commun. **32**(4), 719–733 (2014). https://doi.org/10.1109/JSAC.2014.140405
15. Li, Z., Aaron, A., Katsavounidis, I., Moorthy, A., Manohara, M.: Toward a practical perceptual video quality metric (2016). https://medium.com/netflix-techblog/toward-a-practical-perceptual-video-quality-metric-653f208b9652
16. Mao, H., et al.: Real-world video adaptation with reinforcement learning. In: Reinforcement Learning for Real Life (ICML workshop) (2019)
17. Mao, H., Netravali, R., Alizadeh, M.: Neural adaptive video streaming with pensieve. In: ACM SIGCOMM, pp. 197–210. ACM (2017)
18. Miller, K., Bethanabhotla, D., Caire, G., Wolisz, A.: A control-theoretic approach to adaptive video streaming in dense wireless networks. IEEE Trans. Multimedia **17**(8), 1309–1322 (2015)
19. Mondal, A., et al.: Candid with YouTube: adaptive streaming behavior and implications on data consumption. In: ACM NOSSDAV (2017)
20. Moreau, E.: What Is Vimeo? An Intro to the Video Sharing Platform. https://www.lifewire.com/what-is-vimeo-3486114
21. Pantos, R., May, W.: HTTP Live Streaming Draft. https://tools.ietf.org/html/draft-pantos-http-live-streaming-17.html
22. Qin, Y., et al.: ABR streaming of VBR-encoded videos: characterization, challenges, and solutions. In: ACM CoNEXT (2018)
23. Qin, Y., et al.: A control theoretic approach to ABR video streaming: a fresh look at PID-based rate adaptation. In: INFOCOM 2017-IEEE Conference on Computer Communications, IEEE, pp. 1–9. IEEE (2017)
24. Riiser, H., Vigmostad, P., Griwodz, C., Halvorsen, P.: Commute path bandwidth traces from 3G networks: analysis and applications. In: ACM MMSys (2013)
25. Sandvine: The global Internet phenomena report (2019).https://www.sandvine.com/press-releases/sandvine-releases-2019-global-internet-phenomena-report
26. Spiteri, K., Urgaonkar, R., Sitaraman, R.K.: BOLA: near-optimal bitrate adaptation for online videos. In: IEEE INFOCOM 2016 - The 35th Annual IEEE International Conference on Computer Communications, pp. 1–9, April 2016. https://doi.org/10.1109/INFOCOM.2016.7524428

27. Spiteri, K., Sitaraman, R., Sparacio, D.: From theory to practice: Improving bitrate adaptation in the DASH reference player. In: ACM MMsys (2018)
28. Stohr, D., Frömmgen, A., Rizk, A., Zink, M., Steinmetz, R., Effelsberg, W.: Where are the sweet spots?: a systematic approach to reproducible DASH player comparisons. In: ACM Multimedia (2017)
29. Sun, Y., et al.: CS2P: improving video bitrate selection and adaptation with data-driven throughput prediction. In: ACM SIGCOMM (2016)
30. Timmerer, C., Maiero, M., Rainer, B.: Which Adaptation Logic? An Objective and Subjective Performance Evaluation of HTTP-based Adaptive Media Streaming Systems. CoRR (2016)
31. Wamser, F., Casas, P., Seufert, M., Moldovan, C., Tran-Gia, P., Hossfeld, T.: Modeling the YouTube stack: from packets to quality of experience. Comput. Netw. **109**, 211–224 (2016)
32. Wang, C., Rizk, A., Zink, M.: SQUAD: a spectrum-based quality adaptation for dynamic adaptive streaming over HTTP. In: ACM MMsys (2016)
33. Yan, F.Y., et al.: Learning in situ: a randomized experiment in video streaming. In: USENIX NSDI (2019)

Exploring the Eastern Frontier: A First Look at Mobile App Tracking in China

Zhaohua Wang[1,2], Zhenyu Li[1,2,3(✉)], Minhui Xue[4], and Gareth Tyson[5]

[1] Institute of Computing Technology, Chinese Academy of Sciences, Beijing, China
zyli@ict.ac.cn
[2] University of Chinese Academy of Sciences, Beijing, China
[3] Purple Mountain Laboratories, Nanjing, China
[4] The University of Adelaide, Adelaide, Australia
[5] Queen Mary University of London, London, UK

Abstract. Many mobile apps are integrated with mobile advertising and tracking services running in the background to collect information for tracking users. Considering China currently tops mobile traffic growth globally, this paper aims to take a first look at China's mobile tracking patterns from a large 4G network. We observe the dominance of the top popular *domestic* trackers and the pervasive tracking on mobile apps. We also discover a very well-connected tracking community, where the non-popular trackers form many local communities with each community tracking a particular category of mobile apps. We further conclude that some trackers have a monopoly on specific groups of mobile users and 10% of users upload Personally Identifiable Information (PII) to trackers (with 90% of PII tracking flows local to China). Our results consistently show a distinctive mobile tracking market in China. We hope the results can inform users and stakeholders on the interplay between mobile tracking and potential security and privacy issues.

1 Introduction

Many mobile apps are bundled with mobile Advertising and Tracking Services (**ATSes**). These are used for various purposes, including monetization, app maintenance, and audience understanding [15,27,34]. This, however, can result in such apps exposing a wide variety of information to (third-party) services, often without a clear understanding of how it may be used. Due to the sensitive nature of data accumulated on mobile devices, their prevalence has therefore been a cause for concern [4,6,17,22,29,30]. This is particularly the case as tracking behavior often cannot be controlled by users, particularly after granting apps permissions [11,40].

Due to the importance of this topic, there has been a large body of recent research in this area, including studies that have used static app analysis [1, 2,11], dynamic device monitoring [12,25,26,28], and the inspection of network traffic [13,32]. They have revealed a number of insights, including the prominence of a small number of ATS platforms, the presence of privacy invasive leaks (*e.g.*

A. Sperotto et al. (Eds.): PAM 2020, LNCS 12048, pp. 314–328, 2020.
https://doi.org/10.1007/978-3-030-44081-7_19

phone numbers), and various attempts at cross-device tracking. Despite this range of insights, these studies have one common bias: they near exclusively focus on western countries, primarily in North America and Europe. Although these countries are both important and relevant, we posit that this bias introduces a deficiency into the mobile ATS research landscape. Specifically, we have little evidence related to how the above trends may generalize to the Chinese market. As one of the fastest growing countries in terms of mobile traffic [7], we argue that this deficiency must be addressed.

This paper performs the first characterization of mobile ATS traffic patterns in China. Using a dataset containing 28 billion anonymized access logs from mobile users, we explore the distinctive properties of the tracking market in China. Our analysis reveals a highly active ecosystem dominated by a set of (poorly understood) major players. Due to the presence of the Great Firewall of China (which blocks certain western services), a number of trackers are quite distinct from those observed in past works.

Our main findings are summarized as follows:

- We reveal a distinctive mobile tracking market in China that is dominated by several popular *domestic* trackers. A handful of trackers (35%) are present in 2 or more mobile apps, implying the prevalence of cross-tracking of users. Notably, the prominence of tracking in some types of apps (*e.g. InputMethod*) raises particular concerns for user privacy.
- Popular trackers regularly co-occur with non-popular ones. Non-popular trackers, however, tend to cluster into local communities; each community tends to track a particular relevant type of app.
- China's tracking services reach a majority of users, with some trackers showing a tendency to exclusively track specific groups of users. As many as 10% of users send PII data to trackers, implying the possibility of privacy leakage. Nevertheless, 90% of PII data is confined to China.

2 Dataset and Methodology

2.1 Data Description

Our dataset contains user access logs in a major 4G cellular ISP. The access logs are generated by combining the traces of Deep Packet Inspection (DPI) deployed at Serving Gateway (SGW) and the information provided by the Mobility Management Entity (MME). Each log corresponds to an HTTP request, and contains the following major fields: the anonymized unique ID of the user that initiates the request, destination IP Address, request URL, HTTP-Referrer, User-Agent, the data volume, and the timestamp of the request initiation. In addition, to identify the mobile apps which generate each HTTP request, the DPI appliances uses a rule-based approach introduced in SAMPLES [39]. To train the rule-set in SAMPLES, a crawl-download-execution pipeline is run across the major Chinese app markets The rule-set is then deployed on the DPI appliances for app identification, and is updated routinely to include new apps. In total, we identify 1,812 unique mobile apps.

Note that we naturally cannot extract URLs from HTTPS, accounting for around 20% of the mobile traffic observed. However, we note that many apps that use HTTPS *also* use HTTP. For instance, WeChat, the most popular mobile app among Chinese diaspora, relies on HTTPS for third-party APIs, but also issues requests to `imgcache.gtimg.cn` for cached images via HTTP. This means that, even though our vantage is constrained, we can still observe activities. Indeed, the Kendall correlation between the top-100 most popular apps in our dataset and that obtained from [8] is 0.85, suggesting that our app traffic is reflective of general usage. In total, the dataset contains 2,811,233,521 access logs of 3,516,828 users in a major city of China.

2.2 Identifying ATS Domains

Inspired by [18,27], we utilize four ATS-specific lists provided by: AdBlock-Plus [10] (the *easylist* and *easyprivacy* lists) and hpHosts [23] (the *ATS* list). We further incorporate the EasyList China list given that we target China's Internet. These contain a set of string matching rules, and are commonly used by ad blockers. We apply the rules to both the URL *and* HTTP-Referrer of each flow, such that we can also identify cases where a URL that is not classified as an ATS was requested by an ATS [16].

In total, we attribute 260M HTTP requests (9.2%) to ATS domains, in which 16.4% are unattributable flows labeled as *others* as mentioned above. These cover 24,985 unique fully-qualified domain names (FQDNs) and 8,773 unique second-level domains (SLDs). Note that our focus is not only on third-party tracking services like [3,15,33] where the first-party domains are considered to be trusted by users (even though they can still track users). Instead, we also inspect first-party trackers that collect personal data (contained within EasyPrivacy [24]).

2.3 Associating ATS Domains to Apps

Next, we identify the trackers that are used by individual mobile apps. Casual analysis [20,38] immediately reveals a highly skewed popularity distribution of mobile apps. The most popular app (WeChat) is accessed by 92% of users in a single day, whereas the majority of services (outside the top 500) are accessed by less than 0.1% of users per day. Hence, to simplify analysis, we focus on the top-500 mobile apps, which account for 86.7% of HTTP flows in our dataset.[1]

The easiest way to associate trackers with apps is to use the `HTTP-Referrer` and `User-Agent` in the ATS requests [13]. However, for the majority of ATS HTTP requests from unattributed apps, the HTTP-Referrers are empty and the User-Agents do not meet the specification required to identify apps. As such, we turn to an alternative heuristic approach inspired by [31]. The intuition is

---

[1] Among the top 500 apps, 29 mobile browsers are excluded in further analysis to avoid potential inflation or bias caused by web trackers bundled in web pages.

that if an ATS is associated with a mobile app, its requests should happen at a time close to the app's access. Hence, we can associate an ATS request to the closest app's request that precedes it. A problem here is that some apps may send background traffic, which may appear between the app's requests and the requests of the associated trackers. To mitigate this effect, we divide a user's requests into sessions [31], where a session corresponds to a set of user activities before an obvious pause. The session interval is set to 1 min, which is learned empirically as in [14].

Using the above approach, we obtain 193,527,553 sessions in total, and filter out the sessions that contain requests from more than one app. For the remaining sessions (4,238,015) containing only one identified app request, we can safely associate an ATS domain with the app. For each app, s, this results in a vector R_s, in which an element $<d_i, n_i>$ is an ATS domain and the number of users seeing their association. We further mitigate another possible effect that is relevant to the periodic requests issued by some trackers (*e.g.* statistic tracking services): One potential flaw in the above approach is that certain trackers may very rarely issue requests. Thus, these requests may appear in the sessions that contain only a single app's request (*i.e.* even when the ATS is not associated with the app). Given that this happens only occasionally, for an app s, we filter out those ATS domains T from R_s if $n_i < q$ $(i \in T)$, where q takes the mean of all $n_{j \in R_s}$. Finally, based on the inferred ATS domains of each app above, we process all access logs for each user to associate the ATS request with its host app (assuming the app's request precedes the ATS request less than 1 second). Importantly the filtered sessions include all of the top 500 apps, and are only used for ATS-to-app association. For other analysis (*cf.* Sect. 3.3), we use *all* access logs.

2.4 Limitations

It is important to highlight potential limitations in our data. The four ATS lists that we utilize for identifying ATS domains may not fully cover the current ATSes in mobile networks in China. But we have identified a number of prominent and recognized mobile tracker domains, which are in line with the Chinese mobile ecosystem. Additionally, the heuristic method for the ATS-to-app association may not fully capture the up-to-date ATSes of individual mobile apps. We utilize both the app Lumen [27] and the Lightbeam tool [21] to manually test existing ATS domains (SLDs) for the top 10 most popular apps. Our inspection revealed an association accuracy of F1-score 0.75 (precision: 0.7, recall: 0.82). Taking the popular video app Youku, for example, among 9 trackers inferred by our approach, 6 dominant ones can also be detected by Lumen or Lightbeam. One domain is not detected by our method but only monitored by Lumen; however, this domain has never been accessed in our dataset and is perhaps an additional tracker after our dataset was collected. Finally, although it has been shown in [39] that the rule-based approach for app identification can achieve a high accuracy, we are not aware of the exact accuracy because the DPI provider

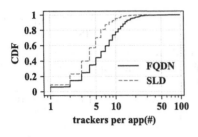
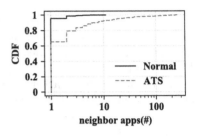

(a) CDF of #ATSes per app.   (b) CDF of #neighbors per ATS & other FQDN.

Fig. 1. The presence of ATSes among mobile apps

keeps its implementation details confidential. Thus, we cannot evaluate its accuracy, nor can we tell how false positives/negatives bias our results. Nevertheless, we find that 12% of the HTTP requests cannot be attributed to particular apps in our dataset and are labeled as *others*.

2.5 Ethical Considerations

The ISP routinely collects user access logs for the purpose of improving their service quality and security. When users subscribe to the ISP network, they are notified that the ISP may collect and analyze their personal and access information for the above purpose (including but not limited to tracking behavior), and may share the information with the research community for research purposes after anonymization. The dataset is kept in the ISP's data center with access being granted only to the authors' affiliation. Several precautions for protecting users' privacy have been taken by the ISP before access is granted. For instance, the unique user IDs are substituted with random numbers to delink the activities with specific users; all sensitive user data (*e.g.* IMEI) has been encrypted by hashing. We have obtained the approval from the ISP for accessing the request URL, HTTP-Referrer and User-Agent fields.

3 Results and Analysis

3.1 How Prevalent Are ATSes?

Presence of ATSes. Based on user request sessions produced in Sect. 2.3, we model the domains (FQDNs) accessed within an app as a bipartite graph $G = (U, V, E)$, where U denotes mobile apps, V represents the ATS domains and normal visited domains, and E is the set of edges connecting vertices in U to vertices in V. This 2-mode graph reveals connections between ATS domains and mobile apps. We first analyze the number of ATSes present in each app in graph G and present its CDF distribution in Fig. 1(a). Unsurprisingly, we

Table 1. Presence of the top 20 ATS domains (SLDs) on mobile apps.

ATS (SLDs)	#FQDNs	%App	ATS (SLDs)	#FQDNs	%App
qq.com	31	75	kuwo.cn	1	6
umeng.com	4	67	flurry.com	1	6
71.am	1	57	baidustatic.com	4	6
baidu.com	45	34	mmstat.com	3	6
uc.cn	3	28	hiido.com	2	4
360.cn	5	25	scorecardresearch.com	2	4
google-analytics.com	1	14	funshion.net	1	4
ksmobile.com	1	13	doubleclick.net	1	4
cnzz.com	33	9	ifeng.com	5	4
xiaomi.com	2	7	letv.com	3	3

confirm that ATSes are widely used by mobile apps. The median number of trackers observed per app is 6 for FQDNs, and 4 when classified by SLDs.

We also inspect the number of apps neighbored with each ATS domain in graph G in order to understand how well mobile trackers are connected with different apps. Figure 1(b) shows that ATS domains tend to appear on much more apps than normal ones: over 30% of trackers appear in at least two apps. To further get a handle on the "popularity" of ATSes among app developers, Table 1 presents the top 20 ATS domains (SLDs), as measured by the number of apps they are used by. The number of FQDNs associated with each SLD is also shown in Table 1. We see a skewed distribution, whereby the top 3 ATS domains are accessed by over half of all apps, while the bottom 12 ATS domains are used by under 10% of apps.

The ATS domains of qq.com are the most popular and accessed by over 70% of all mobile apps observed, showing its pervasive tracking. 31 FQDNs of qq.com are identified as mobile trackers and the top 5 are pingma.qq.com, zxcv.3g.qq.com, omgmta.qq.com, sngmta.qq.com and mi.gdt.qq.com, accounting for 70% of flows of SLDs. They provide services for link share, advertising aggregation and mobile analytics. Notably, unlike Europe which relies heavily on US trackers, China's tracking ecosystem is dominated by key *domestic* trackers: the top 6 most popular SLDs are all domestic (Chinese) ATS domains. Foreign trackers (*e.g.* google-analytics.com, flurry.com, scorecardresearch.com) make up the minority of ATS traffic: they are used by under 20% of apps. Many factors, including Internet censorship, language and unique local regulations, contribute to this unique ecosystem that differs greatly from the western countries.

App's ATS Usage. An obvious question is which apps are responsible for utilizing this wide range of ATSes within their code. To this end, we group the mobile apps into 23 categories collected from several Android app markets using [35]. The categorization is mostly based on the functionality of apps. Table 2 lists the

Table 2. App Categories, sorted by the user penetration percentage.

Category	App	User(%)	ATS(%)	Category	App	User(%)	ATS(%)
Commu.	15	98	23	Input.	5	37	5
Browsers	29	85	–	Security	12	36	8
Navigation	16	75	7	Photo.	4	31	2
Tools	45	64	12	Lifestyle	38	19	15
Shopping	27	63	13	Books	21	18	11
News	27	60	28	Business	8	15	8
AppMarket	25	59	11	Education	24	11	9
Video	42	57	23	Person.	5	6	2
Finance	46	57	12	Health	10	4	9
Social	16	53	14	Travel	13	4	6
Music	21	41	10	Other	14	5	7
Game	37	41	9				

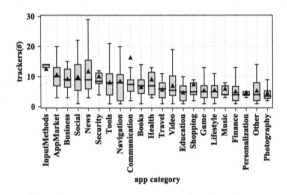

Fig. 2. The distribution of tracker domains (FQDNs) by different app categories.

number of apps, user popularity (measured by the share of users) as well as the percentage of ATS domains in each category.[2]

There is a strong propensity towards certain app categories, with *communication* apps (*e.g.* messaging services) being used by 98% of users. The percentage of trackers indeed is dependent on the number of apps of each category and also the apps' functionality. For instance, the communication category, which contains moderate number of apps, has over 23% trackers. This is probably because apps like WeChat are not only communication tools, but platforms for many third-party services (*e.g.* online payments). Trackers serving different purposes will thus likely be embedded in these apps. A closer look at the trackers of video apps shows the dominance of statistic services that collect QoE related metrics.

---

[2] As mentioned in Sect. 2.3, we do not show the number of trackers of the browser apps.

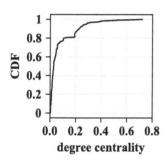

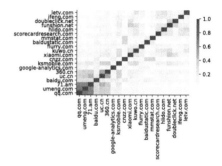

Fig. 3. The normalized degree centrality of ATS domains in projection graph G'.

Fig. 4. The co-occurrence prob. distr. of the top 20 ATSes (SLDs).The co-occurrence prob. distr. of the top 20 ATSes (SLDs).

To mitigate the effect of the number of apps in each category, we count the number of unique trackers of each app and present the box-plot distribution of ATSes (FQDNs) across app categories in Fig. 2. We rank each box in descending order by the median, which ranges from 4 to 13. It is notable that the number of trackers per app varies based on category (*i.e.* its functionality). *InputMethods* apps, which include five third-party keyboards, have the most trackers per app. This is particularly worrying, as they have incentives to log and collect user input to improve their services [5]. *Communication* apps hold the highest mean value of 16 ATSes per app; this is largely driven by certain extremely popular apps (*e.g.* WeChat and QQ). The category with the greatest diversity is *News*: although the median number is 9, the top 5% of news apps use over 26 ATSes. We note that this differs greatly from past western-oriented studies, where games and education apps are tracked by the highest number of third-party ATSes, and news and entertainment apps are exposed to a wide range of ATSes [27].

Takeaway. China's tracking market differs greatly from the western one. It is dominated by several popular domestic trackers. Over 30% of mobile trackers tend to be present in at least 2 apps, implying the prevalence of cross-app tracking of users. Tracking behavior varies across app categories mainly due to their functionality. The prominence of some types of apps (*e.g.* *InputMethods*) in tracking raises particular concerns for user privacy.

3.2   What Is the Community Structure of ATSes?

Co-location of ATSes. The mobile trackers usually appear on as many apps as possible to enable cross-tracking of users, which leads to implicit connections between trackers through mobile apps. Inspired by [19], we further focus on the co-location of ATS domains within mobile apps by inspecting the trackers' community structure. To this end, we create a 1-mode ATS-projection graph G' from the largest connected component in G. In G', the vertices only contain the

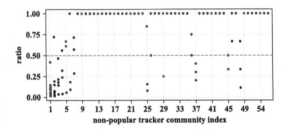

Fig. 5. Tracker Specialization Index distr. of non-popular tracker communities.

ATS domains in V and the edges are created if any two vertices share a common neighbor (app) in G. We find that trackers are very well-connected: nearly 99% of trackers appear in the largest connected component.

The ATS-projection graph G' captures the co-location of *multiple* tracking services used within individual apps. We first use the degree centrality (normalized by $N - 1$, where N is the number of vertices in G') to measure how likely a tracker tends to co-locate with others (see Fig. 3). We can clearly identify two types of trackers: the *popular ones* with the normalized degree centrality over 0.2, the rest are *non-popular* ones that sparsely connect with others in the graph. Indeed, the popular ones are present more pervasively among apps than the non-popular ones. We further utilize the global clustering coefficient to measure the degree to which nodes in the graph G' tend to cluster together [36]. The coefficient is as high as 0.52. We also calculate the clustering coefficients for individual nodes—the results reveal low coefficients for the popular trackers, but high coefficients for the non-popular ones. These results imply that G' a well connected graph, where the non-popular trackers form local communities,[3] while the popular trackers densely co-occur with the non-popular ones.

To verify the above conjecture on the structure of G', we remove the popular trackers from G' and obtain a graph G'' consisting of non-popular trackers. Approximately 62% of non-popular trackers appear in the largest connected component of G'' and the others consist of 46 isolated components in G''. We leverage the Clauset-Newman-Moore greedy method [9] for inferring community structure. We discover a total of 56 local communities, where 10 communities constitute the largest connected component. The global clustering coefficient of G'' is as high as 0.78. These results confirm the structure of G'. As we will show later, the trackers of each community tend to track one particular app category.

We next examine the popular trackers to see whether they are co-located in the same apps with each other. To this end, we compute the *Jaccard Similarity Coefficient* to quantify how likely two popular trackers, a and b, are to co-occur within the same target app. We calculate $\frac{|U(a) \bigcap U(b)|}{|U(a) \bigcup U(b)|}$, where $U(a)$ and $U(b)$ are the sets of apps tracked by a and b. Figure 4 presents the coefficients between each of the top 20 popular ATS SLDs. The lower left portion of the heatmap exhibits

---

[3] Communities are groups of vertices that are well-connected internally while sparsely connected with others.

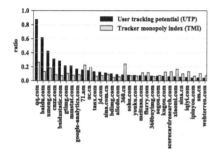
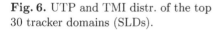

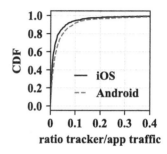

Fig. 6. UTP and TMI distr. of the top 30 tracker domains (SLDs).

Fig. 7. The distribution of the ratio of tracker/app traffic volume for each user.

high levels of co-location, primarily among tracking domains operated by qq.com, umeng.com, and 71.am, indicating that these popular trackers tend to co-occur with each other. Since their holding companies are Tencent, Alibaba, and Baidu, respectively, these three (Chinese) tech giants generally offer complementary, albeit competitive, services. In contrast, there are a number of trackers which show negligible correlation. Most prominently, international rival services, such as baidu.com and google-analytics.com, tend not to co-occur.

Specialization of ATSes. The above analysis leads us to explore the specialization of non-popular trackers, *i.e.* whether a local community of ATSes intends to occur in some specific app categories. To this end, we compute the *tracker specialization index* (TSI) to measure the extent to which an ATS local community is dedicated to a certain app category. The TSI is calculated as $\frac{|U(a) \bigcap U(b)|}{|U(a)|}$, where $U(a)$ and $U(b)$ are the sets of trackers in the ATS local community a and app category b.

We plot the distribution of the *tracker specialization index* for 56 non-popular tracker communities in Fig. 5. We observe that ATS local communities tend to be specialized in only one or two app categories with $TSI \geq 0.5$, *i.e.* they provide specialized tracking services relevant to particular apps. For instance, the *Education* apps are mostly tracked by some ATS local communities run by the companies providing educational related services. Specifically, the parenting app Yaolan is mostly tracked by the following ATS local communities: <yaolan.com, yaolanimage.cn> run by Yaolan itself and <pcbaby.com.cn, pconline.com.cn> run by the app PCbaby that also provides parenting or educational services.

Takeaway. Mobile trackers are interconnected because popular trackers are regularly co-occur (in the same apps) with non-popular ones. The non-popular trackers, however, form many local communities, and the trackers in each local community tend to track a special category of mobile apps. The very top ATSes are often co-located in the same app, implying pervasive tracking.

Table 3. Common UIDs host on mobile devices.

UID	Description	UID	Description
IMSI	SIM ID	MAC	Unique hardware ID
IMEI	Device ID	ADID/IDFA	Advertising ID
ICCID	SIM number		

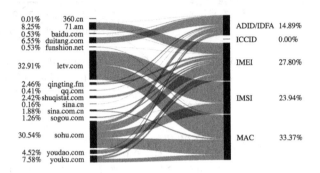

Fig. 8. Tracking domains (SLDs) that collect PII.

3.3 How Are Users Impacted by ATSes?

ATS Monopolies. The heavy-tailed distribution of ATS popularity leads us to conjecture that some may have a monopoly on certain user's data, *i.e.* a user may exclusively be tracked by a single ATS. To test this, we compute two metrics. First, *user tracking potential* (UTP) measures the number of users that can be potentially tracked by a mobile tracker. Given the set of all mobile users R, the tracker i's UTP is $UTP_i = \frac{|S_i|}{|R|}$, where $S_i \subset R$ is the set of users that the tracker i can reach. Second, *tracking monopoly index* (TMI) measures the extent to which a tracker reaches users that others do not have. Let m_j denote the number of mobile trackers that can reach the user $j \in S_i$. The TMI of the tracker i is $TMI_i = \frac{1}{|S_i|} \sum_{j \in S_i} \frac{1}{|m_j|}$. A high TMI indicates that some users are exclusively reached by the tracker and maybe due to trackers' high prevalence or specific coverage on mobile users.

Figure 6 shows the distribution of *user tracking potential* and *tracking monopoly index* of the top 30 ATS domains (SLDs). We rank the tracker domains in descending order by the UTP values. The result reveals a high penetration of the tech giants in China. For example, *qq.com* (owned by Tencent) holds a high UTP (over 0.8) and TMI (about 0.3) metrics, which reveals its high popularity and tracking monopoly. In addition, although under 20% of mobile users are tracked by *71.am* (owned by Baidu), *uc.cn* (owned by Alibaba) and *360.cn* (owned by 360 security), these trackers have relatively high TMIs. This indicates that there is a significant pooling of tracker data within this small elite, similar to that achieved by companies such as Google and Facebook in the western context.

ATS* vs. *App Traffic Volumes. Regardless of privacy implications, the data sent to trackers creates increased resource usage (on devices and within the network). We are next curious to see what volume of each user's traffic is generated by Atses. Thus, we compute the ratio of tracking traffic to app traffic for individual users, and plot the distribution in Fig. 7. The median ratio is around 1%. Nevertheless, 5% of users send over 10% of their traffic to trackers. That said, the tracking traffic ratio per user is actually lower than that observed in an equivalent European 3G ISP [32], possibly due to the pervasive availability of online videos (used by 57% of users) in the 4G network. Interestingly, the device OS also has an impact on this ratio: iOS users (median 0.9%) tend to send less data to trackers than Android users (median 1.5%). This observation is in accord with the 3G network [32].

PII Leakage in ATS and Regional Destination. We next proceed to explore if any personally identifiable information (PII) is uploaded to ATS domains. We process each URL from all user access logs in our dataset to test for the presence of any PII. We use regular expressions to detect the common UIDs on mobile devices, *e.g.* *\?imei=* or *&imei=*. Table 3 summarizes the things we check for, as inspired by [27,29]. In our analysis all the UIDs collected are anonymized to protect user privacy. To check whether the identified UIDs indeed contain PII, we leverage a small dataset of about 10K access logs collected at our lab's wireless access point for one day.[4] Each log in this dataset contains similar information to the ones used in this paper. We applied the UID detection to this dataset and found that 80% of identified IMEIs, 95% of IMSIs, 83% of MACs and 92% of ADIDs/IDFAs indeed contain PII. This lends evidence to the claim that inferred UID exposure detected from the DPI dataset is often correct.

Our analysis reveals a worrying volume of PII leakage: as many as 10% of users send their PII to trackers via their mobile apps. Figure 8 shows the distribution of how several popular tracker SLDs receive PII from apps. For each ATS domain, say sohu.com, the percentage on the left represents the number of flows that contain UIDs. For each type of PII, the percentage on the right represents the number of flows that belong to each of the SLDs. IMEI, IMSI, and MAC are equally likely to be collected by these trackers. The ATSes that upload the largest volume of PII are letv.com (ad online video service) and sohu.com (a mixture of services including ads and video): a remarkable 60% of PII relevant flows belong to them. Each ATS shows clear preferences towards certain PII (shown in Fig. 8). For instance, letv.com mainly collects IMSI and MAC information, while sohu.com shows balanced interests across four types of PII. In contrast, ICCID is only accessed by 360.cn (security service).

A particular concern is whether PII is sent across borders to other countries or regions [18]. We find that more than 90% of PII tracking flows are inside mainland China by mapping IP geo-locations in China [37]. This may be largely driven by the predominance of Chinese ATSes and the blocking of several key US trackers (*e.g.* Google, Facebook), as well as the extensive support for HTTPs in the majority of western countries (which is excluded from our analysis).

---

[4] Every member in the lab was notified about this experiment and consented.

Takeaway. Several tech giants in China track the majority of users. Some specialized trackers, while having relatively small user coverage, track specific groups of users that others do not track. For 5% of users, 10% of their traffic is attributable to ATS flows. 10% users are exposed to PII leakage. Nevertheless, 90% of the PII data is local to China.

4 Conclusion and Discussion

This paper provides insights into the distinctive mobile tracking behavior in China. We make several interesting observations with respect to ATS popularity and community structure, user monopoly patterns, and PII collection. This study not only validates many previous findings, but also facilitates fresh analysis of tracking behavior in China. We believe that our first look at China's mobile tracking patterns has significant implications for many stakeholders in the mobile tracking community (*e.g.* app vendor, tracker provider, adblocker). For instance, adblockers can leverage the community structure for new tracker detection and the prevalence of cross-app tracking raises serious privacy concerns. Many of the findings are indeed worth further exploration, such as the tracker detection, the PII collection, and the business relationships between mobile trackers.

Acknowledgments. We would like to thank David Choffnes for shepherding our paper and PAM reviewers for their useful feedback. This work was supported, in part, by National Key R&D Program of China under Grant No. 2018YFB1800201 and the Youth Innovation Promotion Association CAS.

References

1. Arzt, S., et al.: FlowDroid: precise context, flow, field, object-sensitive and lifecycle-aware taint analysis for android apps. ACM SIGPLAN Not. **49**(6), 259–269 (2014)
2. Backes, M., Bugiel, S., Derr, E.: Reliable third-party library detection in android and its security applications. In: Proceedings of the 2016 ACM SIGSAC Conference on Computer and Communications Security, pp. 356–367. ACM (2016)
3. Binns, R., Zhao, J., Kleek, M.V., Shadbolt, N.: Measuring third-party tracker power across web and mobile. ACM Trans. Internet Technol. (TOIT) **18**(4), 52 (2018)
4. Book, T., Wallach, D.S.: An empirical study of mobile ad targeting. arXiv preprint arXiv:1502.06577 (2015)
5. Chen, J., Chen, H., Bauman, E., Lin, Z., Zang, B., Guan, H.: You shouldn't collect my secrets: thwarting sensitive keystroke leakage in mobile {IME} apps. In: 24th {USENIX} Security Symposium, {USENIX} Security 2015, pp. 657–690 (2015)
6. Chen, T., Ullah, I., Kaafar, M.A., Boreli, R.: Information leakage through mobile analytics services. In: Proceedings of the 15th Workshop on Mobile Computing Systems and Applications, p. 15. ACM (2014)
7. Cisco: Visual networking index: global mobile data traffic forecast update, 2017–2022 white paper. Technical report. Cisco (2019)
8. CIW: ebook: top 200 mobile apps in China (2018). https://www.chinainternet watch.com/ebook/top-mobile-apps/

9. Clauset, A., Newman, M.E., Moore, C.: Finding community structure in very large networks. Phys. Rev. E **70**(6), 066111 (2004)
10. EasyList: The primary filter list that removes most adverts from international webpages (2016). https://easylist.to/
11. Egele, M., Kruegel, C., Kirda, E., Vigna, G.: PiOS: detecting privacy leaks in iOS applications. In: NDSS, pp. 177–183 (2011)
12. Enck, W., et al.: TaintDroid: an information-flow tracking system for realtime privacy monitoring on smartphones. ACM Trans. Comput. Syst. (TOCS) **32**(2), 5 (2014)
13. Gill, P., Erramilli, V., Chaintreau, A., Krishnamurthy, B., Papagiannaki, K., Rodriguez, P.: Follow the money: understanding economics of online aggregation and advertising. In: Proceedings of the 2013 Conference on Internet Measurement Conference, pp. 141–148. ACM (2013)
14. Halfaker, A., et al.: User session identification based on strong regularities in inter-activity time. In: Proceedings of the 24th International Conference on World Wide Web, pp. 410–418. International World Wide Web Conferences Steering Committee (2015)
15. Han, S., Jung, J., Wetherall, D.: A study of third-party tracking by mobile apps in the wild. University of Washington, Technical report UW-CSE-12-03-01 (2012)
16. Ikram, M., Masood, R., Tyson, G., Kaafar, M.A., Loizon, N., Ensafi, R.: The chain of implicit trust: an analysis of the web third-party resources loading. In: Web Conference (2019)
17. Ikram, M., Vallina-Rodriguez, N., Seneviratne, S., Kaafar, M.A., Paxson, V.: An analysis of the privacy and security risks of android VPN permission-enabled apps. In: Proceedings of the 2016 Internet Measurement Conference, pp. 349–364. ACM (2016)
18. Iordanou, C., Smaragdakis, G., Poese, I., Laoutaris, N.: Tracing cross border web tracking. In: Proceedings of the Internet Measurement Conference 2018, pp. 329–342. ACM (2018)
19. Kalavri, V., Blackburn, J., Varvello, M., Papagiannaki, K.: Like a pack of wolves: community structure of web trackers. In: Karagiannis, T., Dimitropoulos, X. (eds.) Passive and Active Measurement (2016)
20. Li, H., et al.: Characterizing smartphone usage patterns from millions of android users. In: Proceedings of the 2015 Internet Measurement Conference, pp. 459–472. ACM (2015)
21. Lightbeam: shine a light on who is watching you (2019). https://addons.mozilla.org/fr/firefox/addon/lightbeam-3-0/
22. Liu, M., Wang, H., Guo, Y., Hong, J.: Identifying and analyzing the privacy of apps for kids. In: Proceedings of the 17th International Workshop on Mobile Computing Systems and Applications, pp. 105–110. ACM (2016)
23. MalwareBytes: hpHosts (2019). http://hosts-file.net/
24. EasyList Policy: Filter evaluation (2011). https://easylist.to/2011/08/31/what-is-acceptable-first-party-tracking.html
25. Qiu, L., Zhang, Z., Shen, Z., Sun, G.: AppTrace: dynamic trace on android devices. In: 2015 IEEE International Conference on Communications (ICC), pp. 7145–7150. IEEE (2015)
26. Rao, A., Sherry, J., Legout, A., Krishnamurthy, A., Dabbous, W., Choffnes, D.: Meddle: middleboxes for increased transparency and control of mobile traffic. In: CoNEXT Student Workshop (2012)

27. Razaghpanah, A., Nithyanand, R., Vallina-Rodriguez, N., Sundaresan, S., Allman, M., Gill, C.K.P.: Apps, trackers, privacy, and regulators. In: 25th Annual Network and Distributed System Security Symposium, NDSS, vol. 2018 (2018)
28. Razaghpanah, A., et al.: Haystack: In situ mobile traffic analysis in user space, pp. 1–13. arXiv preprint arXiv:1510.01419 (2015)
29. Ren, J., Rao, A., Lindorfer, M., Legout, A., Choffnes, D.: ReCon: revealing and controlling PII leaks in mobile network traffic. In: Proceedings of the 14th Annual International Conference on Mobile Systems, Applications, and Services, pp. 361–374. ACM (2016)
30. Seneviratne, S., Seneviratne, A., Mohapatra, P., Mahanti, A.: Your installed apps reveal your gender and more!. ACM SIGMOBILE Mob. Comput. Commun. Rev. **18**(3), 55–61 (2015)
31. Su, J., Li, Z., Grumbach, S., Ikram, M., Salamatian, K., Xie, G.: A cartography of web tracking using DNS records. Comput. Commun. **134**, 83–95 (2019)
32. Vallina-Rodriguez, N., et al.: Breaking for commercials: characterizing mobile advertising. In: Proceedings of the 2012 Internet Measurement Conference, pp. 343–356. ACM (2012)
33. Vallina-Rodriguez, N., et al.: Tracking the trackers: towards understanding the mobile advertising and tracking ecosystem. arXiv preprint arXiv:1609.07190 (2016)
34. Wang, H., Guo, Y.: Understanding third-party libraries in mobile app analysis. In: 2017 IEEE/ACM 39th International Conference on Software Engineering Companion (ICSE-C), pp. 515–516. IEEE (2017)
35. Wang, H., et al.: Beyond google play: a large-scale comparative study of Chinese android app markets. In: Proceedings of the Internet Measurement Conference 2018, pp. 293–307. ACM (2018)
36. Watts, D.J., Strogatz, S.H.: Collective dynamics of 'small-world' networks. Nature **393**(6684), 440 (1998)
37. Xiang, C., et al.: No-jump-into-latency in China's internet!: toward last-mile hop count based IP geo-localization. In: Proceedings of the International Symposium on Quality of Service, IWQoS 2019, pp. 42:1–42:10. ACM (2019)
38. Xu, Q., Erman, J., Gerber, A., Mao, Z., Pang, J., Venkataraman, S.: Identifying diverse usage behaviors of smartphone apps. In: Proceedings of the 2011 ACM SIGCOMM Conference on Internet Measurement Conference, pp. 329–344. ACM (2011)
39. Yao, H., Ranjan, G., Tongaonkar, A., Liao, Y., Mao, Z.M.: Samples: self adaptive mining of persistent lexical snippets for classifying mobile application traffic. In: Proceedings of the 21st Annual International Conference on Mobile Computing and Networking, pp. 439–451. ACM (2015)
40. Zang, J., Dummit, K., Graves, J., Lisker, P., Sweeney, L.: Who knows what about me? A survey of behind the scenes personal data sharing to third parties by mobile apps. Technol. Sci. **30**, 1–53 (2015)

Author Index

Printed in the United States
By Bookmasters